AF328691

PLATO'S SECOND REPUBLIC

Plato's Second Republic

AN ESSAY ON THE *LAWS*

ANDRÉ LAKS

PRINCETON UNIVERSITY PRESS
PRINCETON & OXFORD

Published by Princeton University Press
41 William Street, Princeton, New Jersey 08540
99 Banbury Road, Oxford OX2 6JX

press.princeton.edu

All Rights Reserved

ISBN 978-0-691-23313-0
ISBN (e-book) 978-0-691-23606-3

British Library Cataloging-in-Publication Data is available

Editorial: Ben Tate and Josh Drake
Production Editorial: Jill Harris
Jacket Design: Chris Ferrante
Production: Lauren Reese
Publicity: Alyssa Sanford and Charlotte Coyne

Jacket image: Line engraving, 19th century, after an antique bust / Granger Historical Picture Archive

This book has been composed in Arno Pro

10 9 8 7 6 5 4 3 2 1

(Clinias:) [. . .] Acute is your sight, given your age.
(The Athenian Stranger:) As a matter of fact, every human being, when he is young, sees these matters in a way that is much hazier than he is capable of, whereas when he is old, his gaze is most acute.

PLATO, LAWS, 4.715D7–E1

Granted that it is easy to make better laws. It is impossible to make laws which men's passions do not abuse, as they have abused the earlier ones. To anticipate and to weigh all these future abuses is something which perhaps even the most consummate Statesman may find it impossible to do. Putting the law over man is a problem in politics that I liken to that of squaring the circle in geometry. Solve this problem satisfactorily, and the government based on this solution will be good and free from abuses. But until then, you may be sure that wherever you believe you have made the law rule, it will be men who will be ruling.

ROUSSEAU, CONSIDERATIONS ON THE GOVERNMENT OF
POLAND AND ITS PROJECTED REFORMATION,
CHAP. 1, TRANS. GOUREVITCH

CONTENTS

PLATO'S SECOND REPUBLIC

Introduction

I HAVE BEEN interested in Plato's *Laws* since the 1980s, a time when the work had not yet attracted much attention from students of ancient philosophy, or for that matter of philosophers in general. Things have changed, and the conditions for studying the *Laws* in a philosophical perspective, however one conceives of a philosophical perspective, are incomparably better. The level of discussion is today more refined, and above all more challenging than it was forty years ago. There is now a general consensus that the *Laws* does important conceptual work and that it may consequently be an important source of reflection on questions concerning, for example, psychological motivation, the rationality of emotions, and the function of choral performance, to mention three topics that feature prominently in the currently rather abundant scholarly production on the dialogue.

The motif around which my earlier studies revolved is not foreign to these preoccupations, far from it, but it did not address them directly. My interest went and still goes in the first place to the notion of 'law'/*nomos* and to the conceptual net Plato weaves around it, starting from the idea of a city that is "second to the best" because it is geared to 'human beings' rather than gods (or 'heroes' of yesteryear) and broadening to include the interrelated notions that structure this move away from the best paradigmatic city, such concepts as virtue and possibility,[1] persuasion and obedience, equality and freedom, excess and mean, which I will seek to articulate in my essay. Articulation, however, becomes a challenge, as well as an additional motif of interest, on account of a series of traits that are, to be sure, not alien to Plato's dialogues in general, but which have been less appreciated or even ignored in the case of the *Laws*, perhaps because of its dogmatic outlook. Among these are the complexity of its overall literary construction, its perplexing oscillation between terminological flexibility and the demand for precision, and above all the degree to which implicitness is at work in its argument (whether intentionally or not is a further question). All of these features must be taken into account if one is to get the crucial point in a number of key passages.

Plato's *Laws* (*Nomoi*) is radically novel in its project and of fundamental importance for the history of political thought, even more so, one could argue, than the *Republic* (*Politeia* lit. "constitution" or "political regime"). Its novelty lies, paradoxically at first glance but in fact quite understandably, in its very subordination to the *Republic*, for the gaze it casts on the political question is a distinctly anthropological one. Although it is undoubtedly different in its philosophical vision from Aristotle's attention to 'human affairs,' it looks in the same direction.

To be sure, the *Laws* builds, explicitly (sometimes) or implicitly (usually) on an already rich and complex lineage of legendary and historical lawgivers (Lycurgus, Solon); relevant poetic and dramatic works (Hesiod, Pindar, Aeschylus' *Eumenides*, the *Prometheus Bound*); historical and philosophical reflections of various kinds and scopes, such as Herodotus, Thucydides, Protagoras (possibly the author of a *Peri politeias*/*On Constitution*); Xenophon's *Education of Cyrus*; as well as, possibly, the anti-democratic pamphlet *The Constitution of the Athenians* and such utopian projects as those of Phaleas and Hippodamus of Miletus which Aristotle criticizes alongside Plato's *Republic* and *Laws* in the second book of his *Politics*. But as far as we can judge, the way in which the *Laws* brings together a systematic investigation into the foundations of legislation with a concrete examination of detailed laws is without precedent. The *Republic* is no exception; it is rather, an exceptional member of the older lineage.[2]

As for the *Laws'* influence, much of it has admittedly been indirect and channeled through works that had a more immediate impact and thus have contributed to obfuscate the source: Aristotle *Politics* in the first place, which, for all the criticisms it addresses to the *Laws* in Book 2.6 (after having dealt with the *Republic*), owes much to it (especially, but not exclusively, in Books 7 and 8); Polybius, who in Book 6 of his *History* analyzes Rome's constitution and gives it credit for the Empire's rise and eventual domination of the ancient world, in the light of a constitutional scheme advocated in the *Laws*; Cicero, who took the pair *Republic*/*Laws* as a model for his diptych *De re publica*/*De legibus*; and, perhaps less appreciated, the Church Fathers, who had a soft spot not only for the work's commanding theological agenda but also for its homiletic quality. The intrinsic power of the *Laws*, however, which explains its impact and its adaptations over the course of history, comes from the cluster of four basic principles at its core: that without accountability power corrupts, that law should rule, that a constitution that came to be somewhat mislead-ingly characterized as 'mixed' is the best human beings can achieve, and that laws require preambles. By "preambles" is meant not the kind that we are familiar with from modern constitutions or from other legal usages of the term; in the *Laws* their role is, rather, to persuade the citizen to comply with the law. This is not to suggest that there were no antecedents for most of these concepts, as is notably the case for the 'rule of law,' which was a traditional byword all through Athens' political history.[3] But the philosophical elaboration of these principles and their embeddedness in a global, powerful anthropology is unique, and this is what gave the *Laws* its remarkable momentum.[4]

Two lines of influence can be distinguished here, although they interacted to various degrees over the course of history. There is, first, the considerable influence that the *Laws* exercised over constitutional theory and constitutional practices, a sway much more profound than that of the *Republic*, which, for all its philosophical depth and literary brilliance, played more often the role of a utopian foil than of a conceptual resource for shaping cities and states—and this for sound reasons.[5]

A second factor responsible for the *Laws*' primacy in the subsequent history of political philosophy (and one with more diffuse but in a sense even more wide-ranging consequences) is that it develops a theological conception of law (i.e., of "true law"/*alêthês nomos*, 7.817b8). Its highest principle is the anti-Protagorean assumption that (a) god, and not (some) man, is the measure of political order. This theological anchoring of political laws, which Plato inherits from a remote past, is the counterpart of the anthropological turn that shapes the *Laws*' constitutional and legislative theory. It bestows on the *treatise* a seminal place in the debate over the proper relationship between theology and politics—the so-called theologico-political issue.

This compound phrase, which emerged at the beginning of the 17th century, some years before Spinoza's *Tractatus theologico-politicus* (1670) made it famous, is anachronistic when applied to the *Laws*, since its default frame of reference is the religions of the Book. The anachronism, however, also provides an appropriate entry into the work, for the theologico-political question initiated its fateful modern course centuries before it was named. Efforts to harmonize Plato's political theory with the Mosaic revelation of the law on the Sinai, for Jews like Philo of Alexandria or Christians Fathers who embraced this latter orientation, had sociopolitical dimensions from the start; it took a decisive turn with Constantine's promotion of Christianity, Eusebius' apologetic *Ecclesiastical History*, and Augustine's anti-Eusebian dissociation between the City of God and the worldly city. In the twentieth century, the expression has been most often linked to Carl Schmitt's thesis about modern political concepts being secular versions of theological antecedents, and to the ensuing discussion on his so-called political theology.[6] The way in which Leo Strauss involved the *Laws*, in the 1930s, in a discussion pursued under the sign of what he called "the theologico-political predicament," would require independent examination. It will be enough to say here that Strauss, in the wake of his criticism of Spinoza's enlightened rationalism and of his reading of Maimonides and al-Farabi, came to look at Plato's *Laws*, which he misleadingly considered "the most ironical of Plato's works," as a clue to the question of the relationship between philosophy, politics, and the revealed Law.[7] What is true is that the *Laws* engages with traditional accounts of gods 'revealing' their laws to the cities and pursues a philosophical project consisting in a rationalization of law, *in as much as that is possible* (a restrictive phrase that is crucial for the whole project), and, by way of consequence, the rationalization of god himself, which is its foundation. To clarify the way in which this works, with all the complexities—and obscurities—that go with this clarification, is the main objective of the present essay.

Although Plato does not spell out the distinction in those terms (here is one case of implicitness, of which there will be more), his argument makes clear that he takes the law to be both a certain content—a deontic proposition ultimately dictated by 'reason'/*nous*[8]—and a specific discursive form, an order or command usually followed by the threat of punishments in case of its infringement. To the extent that threat is a kind a violence (*bia*), it is an antipolitical element that should be eliminated as far as possible. Accordingly, Plato's project in the *Laws* is twofold. Besides fleshing out the content of a law as anchored in its ultimate principle, which bears different names at different junctures (*theos*/god, *nous*/reason, *metron*/'measure'), it aims at stripping the law of its threatening component through the introduction of persuasive 'preambles.' It is a remarkable fact that Plato emphasizes the novelty of this second, communicational objective, rather than the first, substantial one (the structuring of a second-best constitution and the related laws), which, for all its use of traditional views and institutions, is no less radically novel.

Two directions open here, which in the *Laws* receive a strikingly asymmetrical treatment. Command and threat can either yield to rhetoric, which looms large in the dialogue; or it can move toward philosophy, the rare and allusive but crucial appearance of which provides to the bulky environment something like a vanishing point (to use a pictorial metaphor): an alternate, quasi-Socratic way of educating the citizens. In between lies a scale of possibilities that reflect the notion, already at work in the *Republic*, that models are there to be approximated.[9] Discursive scalarity, which is grounded in Plato's paradigmatism, is the path that Plato explores the most insistently in the *Laws*, but the scheme evidently also applies to the constitutional and legislative contents themselves, which remain caught in an insuperable tension between the logical possibility of the paradigm and the conditions limiting its implementation and 'feasibility,' which are variable. Plato's second city itself serves as a paradigm for many others, which are fleetingly but unmistakably evoked in the course of the work.

An authentic political community, in Plato's *Laws*, requires the presence, on the rulers' side, of an 'expert wisdom' (signaled by three closely related words, *nous*/reason, *tekhnê*/expertise, and *phronêsis*/wisdom) and, on the side of rulers and citizens alike, of an unconditional though 'voluntary' (*hêkôn* and kindred words) obedience to the law in order to guarantee 'friendship' (*philia*) within the city—'friendship' being an awkward but hardly dispensable placeholder for the deep social bond and civic solidarity or 'fellowship' that guarantees civil peace.[10] The two demands clash, as the *Laws* shows, or rather as it stages, more than any other dialogue. In the *Republic*, political friendship and obedience to the philosopher-rulers is made possible by a discursive 'fiction' (*pseudos*)—the myth of the three human races, golden, silver and bronze, united by their common birth from Mother Earth—and a certain 'lie' (also *pseudos* in Greek) meant to preserve the high quality of offspring—Plato's infamous 'eugenics';[11] but the dialogue does not discuss persuasion in its own right.[12] Its visibility becomes greater in the *Statesman*, where the distinction between voluntary and constrained obedience plays a central, if ambivalent, role. But it is arguably only in the *Laws* that Plato faces *head-on* the question of persuasion's limits through an analysis of the term *nomos*/'law' for which there is no equivalent in the rest of the corpus. Aristotle regretted that "the greatest part of the *Laws* happened to be laws," wishing that Plato had said more about constitutions.[13] But the characterization is biased, for the *Laws*, which does talk also about "constitutional laws," is above all a metalegislative work that thematizes the tension between the normative character of law and the conditions of its acceptance.

Plato calls his second-best constitution—the best that human beings, in their present condition, can wish for—"the finest and truest tragedy." This is surely a provocation—not the only one in a work that also talks about voluntary obedience to the law in terms of "servitude." At a general level, the claim testifies to Plato's enduring hubris, voiced in his farewell to Homer, whom he means to replace as the father of the tragic genre (*Republic* 10.606e1–607b3), thus laying superior claim to the very foundations of Greek culture. But if we look for a tragic work that is particularly appropriate to serve as a rival as well as a foil to the *Laws*, then Aeschylus' *Eumenides*, staged in 458 BC, four years after the Areopagus was deprived of its ancient privileges by Ephialtes' reform, comes first to mind. This is not only or even principally because the constitution of *Laws* aims at holding a 'middle' ground that avoids the two extremes of despotic tyranny and democratic anarchy, thus fulfilling the wish expressed by the tragic chorus, although the reference is certainly not out of place.[14] What really makes of Plato's *Laws* his *Eumenides* is that, in both works, threat and fear retain in the end a secured place within human political institutions.

[Athena speaks:]

This is what I am doing in my kindness
towards these citizens [the Athenians], in settling firmly here
divinities [the Erinyes] that are great and hard to please,
For these are the ones that have been allotted to manage
    all human affairs.

AESCHYLUS, EUMENIDES, 927–930

The reasons and modalities of this integration are, to be sure, very different in the two works, and this is not the place to engage in a detailed comparison between them.[15] The relevant point is that divine retaliation and human threat, in Plato's *Laws*, mark the limit of a program that can be legitimately called 'eumenistic,' since the aim of Plato's legislative preambles is to be kind to the citizens and reduce the violence of the laws as much as possible in order that they be "of a good disposition" (*eumenôs*) toward the content of the law and that political friendship be achieved.[16]

Because the highly normative nature of its political proposals, the *Laws* inevitably raises the question of its actuality, of its actualization, and eventually of one's own political positioning, as may be seen, to take a particularly instructive example, in the role it played in ideological battles in Cosimo's fifteenth-century Florence, between aristocratic patricians and their republican opponents.[17] There is little doubt that the *Laws*, which in this respect does not differ from the *Republic*, can be read focusing not on the philosophical intricacies that it articulates, but rather on its political message which is also and inextricably part of its agenda.[18] The "second city" that is depicted in the *Laws*, for all its importance in the emergence of constitutionalism and republicanism, and in spite of the concessions it makes to 'human nature' and to the perceptible humanization of certain practices that were part of Plato's world,[19] accentuates rather than alleviates the most unpleasant tendencies of the *Republic*. Indeed, it shows a great number of traits that are at best, questionable, and at worst, to use another anachronistic term, 'totalitarian.' The word is of course inappropriate if one links it exclusively to the circumstances for which it was coined in the twentieth century; others have been proposed, in particular 'holism.'[20] Taken in an etymological sense, however, it captures a feature that is surely relevant in Plato's political thought and names a legitimate question.[21] The protest voiced by Schleiermacher in 1828 in his introduction to the *Republic* "from the standing point of Christianity," of which he was an eminent (Protestant) representative, has become the common property of Plato's liberal critics: the institutions advocated in the *Republic*, and above all the abolition of the family, are something "at which our more moral austerity is with justice shocked and dismayed."[22] Schleiermacher's indignation would not have abated had he instead applied himself to the *Laws* (which he did not have the time, or perhaps even the desire, to do[23]): for even if Plato's second best city now requires marriage and households—in keeping with the 'anthropological turn' taken in the *Laws*—everything yet remains subordinate to the well-being of the political community; the control of artistic production is as absolute as ever; an unredeemable atheism, the radical embodiment of 'free thinking' (in the modern sense of the term) is grounds for the death penalty. Cornford powerfully summarized the dark side of "Plato's Commonwealth" by drawing an intriguing parallel between the *Laws* and Dostoyevsky's Grand Inquisitor scene in *Brothers Karamazov*: if Socrates were to visit the city of the *Laws* and there promote the principle of free discussion, he would be arrested, expelled, and asked never to return, like Christ in Dostoyevsky's parable, or for that matter Homer, and the tragic poets should they approach Plato's second city.[24] The parallel is misleading, in particular because it is all but clear that Socrates, at least Plato's Socrates, has no role to play in Plato's second city, not only as an embodiment of virtue, but also a philosophical inquirer, even if philosophical activity is either restricted in the *Laws* to the highest political body (the Watch) or considered as an unrealizable ideal. But it is not as easy as one would wish—through contextualizing, historicizing, distancing, or transposing—to get around the challenge encapsulated by Popper's reading of Plato political projects in terms of a "closed society."[25] On the other hand, the discussion about the political principles that are put to work and articulated in Plato's second constitution—expertise, freedom, equality, friendship—can be detached, up to a certain point, from their embodiment in particular norms and practices that can be legitimately criticized, or for that matter defended, and evaluated in their own right.[26] I have tried to make of this possibility a methodological requirement, which does not mean that the dissociation is always an easy one.

I have not undertaken to write a commentary on the *Laws* (obviously not, given the modest dimensions of the present volume), nor for that matter on any of its sections (save a few minor ventures in this direction). Glenn Morrow's both synthetic and detailed exposition of Plato's 'Cretan City' and Klaus Schöpsdau's admirable commentary in three volumes discuss many more topics than I touch upon here.[27] Mine is a schematic essay of restricted scope. If I refer to this study as an essay, however, it is not only because of my deliberate selectiveness in the face of the daunting range of material that the *Laws* has to offer. It is also and above all because of its speculative nature. By 'speculative,' I am not only thinking about suggestions that come to mind when the text abandons us (which happens), but also and above all about a mode of reading that is sensitive to the promptings that emerge from the text itself in the absence of explicit statements or clarifications. Assuming implicitness is obviously moving onto slippery ground. But Plato's philosophical writing *is* slippery. This is why it is appropriate to signal here that several of my claims depend on two main assumptions: first, that in spite of a perceptible lack of final polishing, the *Laws* is an extremely refined literary construct, something that the reader must keep in mind in order to capture the scope and implications of some crucial episodes and sentences; and second, that my ultimate, all-things-considered interpretation relies on a small number of short, cryptic or sinuous passages, echoes, syntactical peculiarities, and stage directions. The slimness and fragility of these elusive passages stand in inverse proportion, so to speak, to the monumentality of the work they support.[28] The fact that these crucial passages most often coincide with what may well be conceptual blind spots in Plato's political thinking adds, it seems to me, to their philosophical interest. But they also provide rich material for anyone who is prone to conceive of philology as a springboard for philosophical reflection, and not only as the limiting frame that it also is.

———

The book is based on a series of previously published studies listed in the bibliography, and it contains several self-quotations of variable length. But all that I have taken up has been re-thought and re-written. Some objections raised against my former work on the subject, especially by Luc Brisson, Francisco Lisi, and Melissa Lane, concerning the function of legislative preambles, the issue of feasibility, and the question of freedom, have helped me reformulate a line of thought that has not, however, changed in its basics, which does not mean that I hope to convince, when disagreements depend not on matters of fact, which can in principle be settled, but on hermeneutics, which are quite another matter.[29] During my stay at Princeton in 2017–2019, where this project took shape, René de Nicolay and Owen Philipps translated from the French large sections of my 2005 book, *Médiation et coercition*, which I re-worked to fit the present essay. The conclusion is a shortened version of Christopher Rowe's translation of Laks 2010. Seminars taught by Melissa Lane and myself at Princeton in the spring semester of 2018, and the discussion group she organized during that academic year, which included Amanda Greene, Matthew Landauer, and René de Nicolay, furnished various impulses. So, too, in the course of the same year, did a short conversation with Rachel Barney about 'approximation.' Special thanks go to Carlotta Santini, who, among many other colleagues and friends too numerous to name, helped me find my way to many texts not available to me in Mexico, especially as Covid 19 imposed its laws on academic life; to Jeremy Reid, Melissa Lane, and the readers of Princeton University Press, who improved my English draft at different stages; to Amanda Greene, who spent much time revising with me my translations from the *Laws*; to David Lévystone, René de Nicolay, and Michael Vatter, for their reading of earlier versions of the manuscript and sharing with me their thoughts and works in progress, as well as to Pierre Judet de La Combe and Glenn W. Most for their observations on the draft of this introduction; to Eva Jaunzems, who did more to improve the text than copyediting it. A final word of gratitude goes to Ben Tate, who manifested his interest in the project during a conversation we had on the lawn of Princeton University in Spring 2018 and encouraged me to pursue it.

Editorial Note

Translations

Translating the *Laws* is not an easy task for anyone, let alone for a non-native speaker. I used to rely on Pangle's 1988 translation, which is more literal than Saunders' 1970 useful but colloquial version (reproduced in Cooper 1997). But a closer look at the passages I needed to quote gave me pause. Griffith's (2016) was too paraphrastic for my taste and often off the mark, I thought. So, I decided to take the risk and offer my own translations. I was helped in this by Schöpsdau's German version, in my view the most accurate in syntax and style,[1] and by Amanda Greene, who revised with me the language and the substance of my proposals. For Plato's other dialogues, I have as often as possible relied on the translations collected in Cooper (1997), revising or adapting them to the context when appropriate or needed. In these cases, I indicate the name of the translator after the passages quoted. The same principle applies to Aristotle's works, which are quoted on the basis of the *Oxford Revised Translation* edited by J. Barnes, and to the other ancient authors to whom I refer.

Transcriptions

For philosophically loaded or otherwise important words the connotations of which get lost in translation, I often add the Greek in transcription, on the model friendship/*philia*, *philia*/friendship, friendship (*philia*), or the like. Transcriptions of relevant expressions or sentences do not always reproduce the case, mood, or tense of the original Greek text.

Abbreviations

DK
: *Die Fragmente der Vorsokratiker,* ed. H. Diels, revised by W. Kranz, Berlin, 1951–52[6].

Kühner-Gerth
: R. Kühner and A. Gerth, *Ausführliche Grammatik der griechischen Sprache,* 2 vols., Hannover 1890–1904[3].

LM
: A. Laks and G. W. Most: *Early Greek Philosophy,* 9 vols., Cambridge MA: Harvard University Press (Loeb Classical Library), 2016.

Lobel-Page
: E. Lobel and D. Page, *Poetarum Lesbiorum Fragmenta,* Oxford: Clarendon Press, 1955.

Long-Sedley
: A. Long and D. Sedley, *The Hellenistic Philosophers,* 2 vols. Cambridge: Cambridge University Press, 2012.

LSJ
: H. G. Liddell and R. Scott, *A Greek-English Lexicon* (rev. H. S. Jones and R. McKenzie, rev. suppl. by P.G.W. Glare), Oxford: Oxford University Press, 1996.

PMGF
: *Poetarum Melicorum Graecorum Fragmenta,* vol. 1 (Alcman, Stesichorus, Ibycus), post D.L. Page ed. M. Davies, Oxford: Oxford University Press, 1991.

SVF
: *Stoicorum veterum fragmenta,* ed. H. von Arnim, Leipzig, 1905–24.

1

The Form of the *Laws*: An Overview

The maturity of the late works of significant artists does not resemble the kind one finds in fruit. They are, for the most part, not round, but furrowed, even ravaged. Devoid of sweetness, bitter and spiny, they do not surrender themselves to mere delectation. They lack all the harmony that the classicist aesthetic is in the habit of demanding from works of art, and they show more traces of history than of growth [. . .] it is the formal law of the work that must be discovered . . .

ADORNO[1]

Late Style

In spite of various family resemblances that allow grouping Plato's dialogues on the basis of some structural criteria (a trivial example of which would be the so-called Socratic dialogues), there is barely a single one of them that is not unique in its compositional pattern.[2] From a formal point of view, there is little in common between, say, the *Laches*, the *Protagoras*, the *Symposium*, the *Phaedrus*, and the *Statesman*: Plato's dialogues are, in this respect, not unlike Beethoven's piano sonatas, the quasi-totality of which invents a form of its own within the preexisting form.

The *Laws* is no exception. Quite apart from the length of the work, which exceeds even that of the *Republic*, the way in which the material is organized resembles nothing else in Plato's production. The topic itself imposes its rules and patterns, since beyond being a meta-legislative reflection on the nature of law, Plato's aim is to provide a full-fledged constitutional and legislative pro-posal. But the *Laws* also stands alone among Plato's dialogues in that it lacks some of their usual formal virtues. Schleiermacher, who praised highly the complex but clearly delineated architecture of the *Republic*,[3] would hardly have said the same of the *Laws*, had he dealt with it. The style is terse, and has been at times harshly criticized for this, although it has also been enthusiastically compared to Henry James' convoluted sentences—certainly an overreaction.[4] But the stylistic difficulties, which are undeniable, are not really the problem. A more serious obstacle is the sinuous construction of the work, which its ancient but not original division into twelve books reflects only partially. Within a given discussion, the sequence of thoughts can also be hard to follow at first.

The dialogue is certainly late. According to a plausible scenario, Plato may have started working with the bulky subject matter and complex issues it involves in the wake of the *Statesman* (usually dated *ca.* 358), which sets up the conceptual scene for the *Laws*;[5] but the traces of disorder and various inconsistences that the *Laws* present give credence to ancient reports according to which Plato died (in 348) before putting the final touches to the text. Philip of Opus, presumably the author of the *Epinomis* (a complement to the *Laws*, *Nomoi*, which is transmitted in Plato's corpus), is usually credited with having edited the book, whatever this 'editing' might have entailed.[6]

One should not be misled, however, either by the formal roughness of the work or by the circumstance of its not being fully polished. The construction is as firm and masterly as ever, even if the structure and the flow of the arguments are not as visible here as in other dialogues.[7] The fact that a portion of some argument may be characterized as an instance of "excessive wandering" (3.683a2–3) or, even more starkly, that the emerging legislation might at some point seem an accumulation of "disorderly" material (*khudên*, 9.858b4), draws attention *a contrario* to the solidness of the overall construction. In the rest of this chapter, I will try to sketch the general dynamic that drives this sinuous work, without yet entering into some crucial compositional subtleties that I will take up in due time.[8]

From Encounter to Synthesis

The *Laws* reports a conversation about legislation held in vicinity of Knossos, Crete's main city, between an anonymous visitor coming from Athens (the Athenian); a citizen of Knossos (Clinias), who plays an occasional role in the dialogue; and a third, rather self-effacing character, Megillus from Sparta. As Clinias will inform the Athenian at the end of Book 3 (702b4–d5), Knossos is about to set up a new Cretan settlement (a 'colony'), the name of which, Magnesia, is mentioned later in the course of the work.[9]

The three characters stand for their respective cities, which embody two different political cultures, with Athens on one side, Peloponnesian Sparta and Cretan Knossos on the other. Within this last pair, often characterized as 'Dorian' in the scholarly literature,[10] a certain prominence is given to the locality where the meeting takes place, that is Crete, which according to a tradition attested in Herodotus, was the source of Sparta's political institutions (and not the other way around).[11] The material encounter between the two parties anticipates the ambitious synthesis between Athens and Sparta, the two major Greek political forces of the fifth century, that the Athenian is about to undertake in the *Laws*. The asymmetry between the Athenian and his interlocutors is obvious and significant: he is the moving intellectual force behind the project, to which he seeks to draw his interlocutors. But his political proposal is in significant part (leaving aside its theological anchorage), based on the idea that the defects of each of the two cities can and should be compensated by features belonging to the other. This is a specific instance of the political principle of mediation based on a middle point (*to meson*) which is at work throughout the *Laws*.[12]

Both the exceptional value of Cretan-Spartan institutions and their fundamental shortcomings emerge from the discussion in the first three books, which form a block. Books 1 and 2 combine partial praise for a legislative model founded on an education that aims at a kind of 'excellence' (or 'virtue': *aretê*) with a devastating critique of its blindness to the complex nature of virtue and the irreducibility of the latter to courage alone. (Dorian education, the *agôgê*, known for its harshness, is geared towards war.[13]) Book 3, which begins with an account of how human beings came in the long run of history to live in cities politically organized by a constitution (*politeia*), leads to a eulogy of a political model, first represented by Sparta's 'mixed constitution,' which prevented the rise of tyranny, then by two regimes, ancient Persia under Cyrus and ancient (Solonian) Athens, which were able to find a balance between freedom and authoritarian rule. Education to virtue and an appropriate constitution, reshaped by Platonic principles and assumptions, will be the two pillars on which the political project elaborated in Books 4 through 12 relies. As its outline is progressively filled in, it takes on many features borrowed from or inspired by Spartan institutions and even more from Athenian institutions, without ever being reducible to either of the two.

The Walk

As the dialogue begins, the three old men are progressing along a path that, if pursued to its final destination, would eventually bring them to a sacred cave located on Mount Ida that bears Zeus' name (1.625b2). Their discussion is meant as a distraction to stave off the boredom and weariness of their long walk.[14] By the time the dialogue ends, however, we will have lost track of their destination.[15] The reason for this may be symbolic. Zeus' cave stands for Cretan legislation: according to a local tradition (reported at 1.624a7–b4), it is the place where Minos, the legendary king who first gave Crete its laws, received every nine years the pronouncements (*phêmas*) of his father, Zeus, who is to Minos in Crete what Apollo is to Lycurgus in Sparta (cf. 1.624a4), namely his divine warrant.[16] As for the conversation between the Athenian and his interlocutors, it bears on "the constitution and the laws" (*peri tês politeias* [. . .] *kai nomôn*, 1.625a6–7, cf. 641d9), a topic which the Athenian insists is appropriate to their age.[17] Thus, what the three old men are undertaking as they muse over "the constitution and the laws" is to arrive at the ultimate, divine source of (Cretan) legislation.[18] Since, under the Athenian's guidance, they will not only have achieved their original goal even before reaching the cave, but will in fact have turned it into a higher and more universal accomplishment, there is a sense in which it is appropriate that the cave vanish.

Practical decisions, on the other hand, lie beyond the purview of the dialogue. In spite of the practical orientation of the dialogue, its setting remains in the realm of theory, and none of the three participants bears responsibility for what will ultimately become the legislative program of the projected settlement. Clinias is only one of nine members belonging to the commission entrusted with the elaboration of the new constitution (3.702b4–d5); and we will never be told whether the Athenian, who has expounded his views all along as a simple if authoritative external adviser, will eventually accept Megillus' and Clinias' invitation, extended at the very end of the dialogue, to join the commission (12.969c4–d3); nor, for that matter, is it certain or even likely that the members of the commission will follow Clinias' advice or, should it come to that, the Athenian's recommendations.

Given these conditions, the political discussion remains an exercise undertaken at leisure, under no sort of pressure (cf. 6.781d9–e3; 9.857e8–858a6). In a sense, it remains a childish game (*paidia* 3.685a7) in spite of its seriousness. But the leisure and freedom that the interlocutors enjoy for the time being will play a fundamental role within the political scheme to be developed by the

Athenian in the course of the discussion: for these are not only the conditions required for a discussion of this sort to take place, but also the conditions towards which the Athenian's political proposals ultimately lead.

The First Focal Point: The Great Divide

The path the three old men follow is edged with trees, under whose shade they can rest. It is morning; we will learn much later that they have been walking since dawn (7.811c7); but in Book 4, it is already midday (*mesembria*, 722c8). Noon, the daily divide, marks a conceptual turning point, as the Athenian introduces the idea, which he emphatically presents as a major novelty of his legislation (722b4-c1and e1–7), that laws must be preceded by a "preamble"/ *prooimion*.[19] This I construe as the first of two focal points around which the entire dialogue revolves. The second, the importance of which is marked by different means, will occur in the next book, at 5.739a1–e5.[20]

The entire scene—the walk, the pause, the emphasis placed on the notion of a preamble as the sun reaches the zenith—is an obvious echo of the *Phaedrus*, the third most important hypotext in the *Laws* after the *Republic* and the *Statesman*. There, we saw Socrates and Phaedrus, who, like the three old men, have also left a city (in this case, Athens), resting at noon on the banks of the Ilissus and engaging in a discussion about rhetoric, as a follow-up to the three discourses on love that made up the first part of the dialogue.[21] This glance back at the *Phaedrus*, the dialogue on the art of speaking well, makes much sense: Plato's *Laws* is a work whose central concern is a certain type of rhetoric, namely the rhetoric of political obligation.[22]

The First Theologico-Political Treatise

It has frequently been noted, and it is indeed difficult to miss, that *theos*, 'god' or more accurately 'a god,' is the first word of the dialogue. It features in an interrogative sentence that emphasizes the polarity between gods and human beings: "Is it a god or some human being," asks the Athenian, "whom you take to be responsible for organizing your laws?" (1.624a1–2).

Clinias' answer is emphatic: "a god, stranger, a god" (1.624a3). As far as Knossos and Crete are concerned, Zeus is the god Clinias has in mind, and he mentions Apollo as relevant to Sparta (624a4).[23] In the course of the work, however, these Olympian gods linked to local traditions will yield, at least at the philosophical level, to a more generic kind of divinity whose identity, as

Plato will come to cautiously and periphrastically suggest, is captured by the term *nous*/reason. More generally, the idea that true law has a theological foundation recurs as a leitmotif throughout the work.[24] Indeed, the *Laws* constitutes a large-scale reversal, as far as politics is concerned, of Protagoras' statement about the "human being/*anthrôpos*" being "the measure of all things,"[25] an affirmation that Plato directly counters at 4.716c4–6: "The god, for us, would be most of all the measure of all things, and doubtless far more so than some human being, as they say."[26]

Plato's anti-Protagorean stance is encapsulated in an Orphic line that the Athenian alludes to in the opening sentence of the so-called general preamble to the laws—an opening that reshapes the very first words of the dialogue: in place of a question followed by a traditional, parochial response, we find a universal affirmation concerning an all-directing, definite if still anonymous god, while human beings now feature as the addressees of a speech rather than as a possibly alternative source of legislation: "The god (*ho theos*) [...], just as the ancient saying asserts, holds the beginning, end and middle of all things that are, completing his revolution in a straight line, according to nature [....]" (4.715e7–716a2).[27]

A bit earlier, the Athenian had asserted, echoing the passage of the *Republic* that introduces the philosophers-kings: ". . . there is no escape from evils and toils for those cities in which not a god, but some mortal rules" (713e4–6; compare *Republic* 5.473c11–e2).

In view of this statement, Plato could surely have coined the word *theocratia*/theocracy (as he most probably did for *theologia*/theology in *Republic* 2.379a5–6).[28] Its absence, or perhaps better its elision, from the *Laws* is as significant as the fact that the first occurrence of the word in Greek literature is found in Flavius Josephus in the first century CE. Josephus' God, the God of the Revelation, was clearly the one under whose authority the Jews stood *directly*: "Our lawgiver, however, did not look at any of these [i.e., forms of government: monarchy, oligarchy, democracy], but showed the constitution (*politeuma*) to be a 'theocracy,' as someone forcing the language might say, and attributed ruling (*arkhê*) and the power to decide (*kratos*) to God" (*Against Apion*, 2.165).[29]

The Athenian, in search of an appropriate name for his projected constitution—a constitution made for human beings and, for this very reason, one where it would not be human beings who would rule, but the law—has just observed that the so-called constitutions (*politeiai*) are not constitutions at all, but refer instead to mechanisms for the "administration (*oikêseis*) of cities that are despotically ruled and are enslaved to certain parts of themselves: each receives as a name the power (*kratos*) of the ruling despot" (4.712e9–713a2).

In the case of 'democracy,' political power is in the hands of the many; in an 'oligarchy' it is in the hands of a few people; in a 'monarchy,' in the hands of a single individual; and in an 'aristocracy,' in the hands of the best (see 712b2–5, where Clinias considers also 'kingship' and 'tyranny'). What name, then, should be given to the constitution the Athenian is advocating? His answer is convoluted: "If one had to give to our city the name of such a master (*despotês*), then it should be the name of the god who in truth rules as a master over those who possess reason (*nous*)" (4.713a2–4).

Is not the god in question *nous* itself, so that the proper name of the constitution should be 'noocracy'? Yes and no. Yes, because law/*nomos*, according to the famous Cratylean etymology that the Athenian offers, is the "(sur)name that we give to the distribution (operated) by reason" (*tên tou nou dianomên eponomazontas nomon*, 4.714a1–2).[30] But not quite, for according to the myth that the lawgiver is relating at that point (starting at 4.713a9), Kronos, himself an obvious placeholder for Intelligence/ *Nous*,[31] is said to have ruled the world *once upon a time*. Knowing that human beings would be unable to rule themselves, he placed divinities (*daimones*) at the heads of their cities to shepherd them, just as human beings presently shepherd their herds (713c8-d5). But Kronos' time, the argument goes, is not ours. At the present time, all that human beings can and must do is to imitate (*mimeisthai dei*, 713e6, cf. 713b3–4) the kind of life that they enjoyed under his rule (that is, under the rule of the relevant divinities); and this they achieve by living under the rule of law; i.e., another, more remote substitute for these divinities.[32] As a paradoxical consequence, the proper name of the constitution that is controlled by the appropriate divinity would not incorporate the name of this very divinity: it would be "nomocracy," rather than noocracy or for that matter Kronocracy. Perhaps, in place of a more straightforward designation, a complex expression such as 'theo-noo-nomocracy' would better capture what the Athenian is suggesting when he uses the periphrasis "the god who truly rules over those who possess reason."

Law between Form and Content

Whereas the walk towards Zeus' cave coincides with an intellectual progression towards divine *nous*/'reason' as the ultimate source of legislation, it is also emphatically presented as a moment of leisure and freedom, where the constraints of actual political action are temporarily suspended. This freedom echoes one central, apparently paradoxical motif of the dialogue, which is the Athenian's desire to postpone legislating as long as possible: whereas the source of legislation is divine reason, formulating the laws is unequivocally presented as an unwelcome 'constraint' or 'necessity' (for instance at 9.857e10–858c1, cf. 859b8–c2). At the heart of this paradox lies a tension between two aspects of the law, which depend on whether the word refers to legislative content or to legislative form (this distinction is one of those that are operative in Plato's argument without being terminologically captured). The tension is, more precisely, between the content of the law, in as much as it derives from reason (*nous*), and the irrationality of its form, in as much as it consists in an order (*taxis*) which, whether it is accompanied by the threat of penalties or not, is characterized as a certain kind of violence (*bia*, 4.722c2), and this to the point of deserving the strikingly strong qualification 'tyrannical' (cf. *tyrannikon epitagma*, 4.722e7–8).[33] Noon, when rhetoric comes in with the request that laws be preceded by preambles, marks the crucial moment of a philosophical and political decision: the true lawgiver is the one who navigates this tension. What the operation consists in and how successful he can be is the core question of the dialogue. It is tightly linked to the question of what human nature amounts to, which constitutes the second focal point of the work.

Two Critical Prologues (Books 1 to 3)

After the short introduction that places the legislative task under the banner of a god, Books 1 through 3 ask two general questions. In Books 1 and 2, which form a subunit within the broader unit of the first three books, the question is explicit. It has two complementary aspects: What is the goal of laws? And what does this goal exactly consist in? To the first question, there are two most general answers, namely that the goal of the law is to develop in the citizens all four virtues (wisdom/*phronêsis*, temperance, justice/*dikaiosunê* and courage/*andreia*, 1.631c5-d2, in this order)[34] and that these virtues and the unity they constitute result from a consonance (*sumphônia*) between reason on the one hand and feelings (pleasure and pain, love/*philia* and detestation/*misos*) on the other hand (2.653b2–6). As for the second question, which is not initially formulated as such,[35] it emerges in the course of an extended account about the origin and formation of constitutions, or rather about their rediscovery.[36] It consists in asking which kind of constitution (*politeia*) promotes the legislative goal as broadened and re-defined in Books 1 and 2.

There, the discussion had taken the form of a refutation of the false assumption on which the Cretan/Spartan institutions rely, in spite their divine origin: while rightly assuming that the goal of laws is excellence/virtue (*aretê*), they fail to take into account that virtue is a complex whole that includes four components or parts, of which 'courage' is only one.[37] At 1.631b3–632d1, the Athenian explains to Clinias what he would have wished him to be able to say in order to properly justify Cretan laws (cf. d1–3), and what also, as it happens, reflects the presupposition on which his own counterproposal will be based: namely, that wisdom is the only unconditional good and the one that makes real goods of all other (conditioned) goods, be they 'human' (health, beauty, physical strength and wealth) or 'divine' as wisdom itself is (temperance, justice, and courage). The critique progressively leads to a definition of education/ *paideia* (1.643c8–d3 and e4–6; 2.653b1–2 and 659c9–d4), specifically understood as education to virtue (as opposed to a technical skill). This definition builds on a comparison between human beings and puppets/*thaumata* (1.644b6–645c6): in Plato's revisionist understanding of the term, education is the process by which the nonrational motivations that move the human puppet are brought to converge and harmonize with its rational motivations, and this is what makes of the human puppet a wonder (*thauma*) of a sort. The argument is anything but straightforward; it is intertwined with an explanation, no less humorous than brilliant (whether humor is intended or not) of how drinking-parties (*symposia*) and the drinking of wine, when appropriately practiced, become a way to promote self-control and temperance (*sôphrosunê*). With this reference the Athenian manages to drag his interlocutors away from their exclusive attention to courage without yet involving the two other virtues.[38]

The Athenian shows that there are two closely related benefits that derive from the judicious drinking of wine—three in fact, for the first one is twofold: wine is a tool at the disposal of the lawgiver; by fostering fearlessness (*aphobia*) and an excess of confidence (*to lian tharrein*, 1.649a4–5) in the drinker, it provides an easy way to *test* the capabilities of an individual (1.648a9–b2);[39] by the same token, wine-drinking also serves the individual as an exercise in self-control and the cultivation of shame (1.648c7–e5; cf. 649d4–650b10). As a third benefit, wine-drinking also serves as a tool for the preservation (*sôtêria*, 2.653a3) of education in so far as, by loosening the minds and the bodies of elderly citizens, it frees them from the shame that might prevent their indispensable participation in the appropriate "choral dance" (*khoreia*), an institutionalized combination of dancing and singing that is the basis of the continued educative process of citizens from childhood (2.665d9–666c6).[40]

The relationship between virtue and political institutions takes a new turn in Book 3, which explains, by reference to past history, that only a certain kind of constitution, namely one that limits the power of the rulers, fosters the end of the lawgiver. This end, however, is now defined in a different and more complex way than in the first two books: not because wisdom and justice, the two virtues that were briefly mentioned alongside courage and temperance, would now be taken into consideration,[41] but because the goal of the lawgiver is now declared to include freedom/*eleutheria* next to wisdom and friendship (3.693b3–5 and 701d7–9). The reference to freedom is unexpected, not only given the silence of the first two books on the topic, but also and above all because of its immediate association with democracy. The question of what kind of freedom is meant remains implicit but is unavoidable.[42]

The Athenian's point is exemplified by the contrasting fate of three Dorian cities located in the Peloponnese—Sparta, Argos, and Messene. Sparta was able to avoid tyranny (and to this extent to preserve the freedom of its citizens) because it was lucky enough to possess from the very start an appropriate, 'mixed' constitution that relied on the limitation of political powers. This was not the case at Messene and Argos (3.682e8–693c5).

Though the Spartan constitution may well be 'mixed,' it nevertheless has shortcomings. To be sure, the Athenian does not engage in an explicit critique here as he did in the first two books; the praise is now without reservations; but it will become retroactively clear that, in the same way as Cretan institutions err in educating citizens to courage while ignoring the other components of virtue, the division of powers which Plato describes as the essential feature of Spartan constitution is deficient in that it lacks any reference to the only 'god' that ultimately counts, namely *nous*/reason. Divine providence may have contributed to securing civic friendship in the city and stability in its institutions (3.691d8-e1), but this falls far short of establishing Sparta as the 'theo-noo-nomocracy' that the city of the *Laws* intends to promote (cf. 4.713a2–4). The same is true, to a lesser degree, of the two other cases that Plato considers in Book 3 besides Sparta, namely Persia under Cyrus' reign and ancient Athens. Here the mixture is of a form related to, but importantly different from the one that characterizes Sparta: its ingredients are not different types of constitutions, but rather two constitutional principles, namely authority and freedom, which both Persia and Athens had in earlier centuries balanced in two opposite, but symmetrical ways.[43]

The present state of Athens and Persia, which, contrary to the partly virtuous Dorian cities, have given up mixture and yielded, in Persia, to extreme despotism, and in Athens to extreme democracy, is the upshot of the past. Past history, however, also points to the possibility of another future. Sparta, from the very beginning, Athens and Persia at a certain point, have shown each in its own way predispositions towards virtue and freedom: the political scheme which they share in different forms—an equilibrium stemming from some kind of mixture—could be reshaped in order to take into account the standard that they do not meet, which is education to full virtue under the guidance of wisdom and reason. The opportunity of doing so is given when Clinias, at the end of Book 3, discloses that he has been entrusted, with nine of his fellow-citizens from Knossos, with the task of establishing new laws for a group of citizens, a 'colony' (*apoikia*) drawn from the whole island (3.702c1–8). These laws may be "foreign," provided that they are "better," Clinias emphasizes at 702c7–8. It is as if the Dorian traditionalism he initially represents has, through him and his Knossian fellow-citizens, yielded to the superior principle of goodness.[44]

From Clinias' point of view, then, it is fortunate that the preceding discussion developed as it did (3.702b4–6; "a good omen," c2). The Athenian, for his part, should also have grounds for satisfaction. For responding favorably to Clinias' wish that the three of them now "construct a city in speech, founding it as it were from the very beginning" (702d1–2) enables him to fill in the outlines of the general principles that he has only sketched so far: Dorian cities cultivate virtue, albeit in a truncated form (Books 1 and 2), with Sparta continuing to do so, while Athens and Persia did in ancient times. This was possible because they benefitted from a mixed constitution or balanced political principles (Book 3). The proposed colony now offers a set of conditions that are favorable (as Book 4 will show) for bringing about new institutions appropriate to the goal of an authentic body of legislation.

One advantage of legislating for a colony is that the lawgiver in charge is in a position to address the colonists upon their arrival at the new site (cf. 4.715e3–5), thereby automatically complying with the requisite, which is about to be formulated, of having a 'preamble' (*prooimion*) preceding the laws. The speech that the Athenian begins at 4.715e7 (which goes, in a first step, down to 718a6, and then from 5.726a1 down to 734e2) is a preamble of this kind (cf. 4.718c3–6).[45] It constitutes one of the two most important preambles, in term of content as well as of length, among the nineteen instances or so of the genre that the *Laws* formally proposes. The other one is the foundational legislative preamble to the law on atheism in Book 10.[46]

Serendipity does not imply that the constitution and laws-with-preambles that the Athenian is about to present are meant for Magnesia in particular. This Cretan colony serves, rather, as an experimental field in which to work out the best possible institutions in general.[47] On the other hand, the proposals formulated by the Athenian are no more than that. It will be up to the nine members of the committee in charge of the refoundation to choose from among them and to adapt them to fit the local circumstances (3.702d1–5 and 5.739b3–7). Although the terms at play do not fully coincide, since the lawgiver of the *Laws* does not explicitly present himself as a philosopher, the dissociation between the exercise of political power and lawgiving, which runs throughout the *Laws* (see in particular 5.739a5–b7 and 746b5-d2), suggests that the idea of a coincidence between political power and philosophy, which is emphatically put forward in the *Republic* (5.473c11-e5) and will be later summoned up in the *Laws* (9.875c3-d2), is not considered as actually feasible. This situation is, rather, a special case of the necessity evoked in the *Statesman*: "it is necessary—so it seems—to come together and write things down, chasing after the traces of the truest constitution" (301e2–4, trans. Rowe).[48]

Slow Beginnings (Books 4 and 5)

Following the two introductory blocks, the critical block of Books 1and 2 on law and the historical block of Book 3 on constitutions, Books 4 to 12 are devoted to setting up institutions, both constitutional provisions and laws, that can and should guide future lawgivers. At a glance, it may look as if constitution is the subject of Book 6; laws ,the subject of Books 7 through 12; and that Books 4 and 5 have set out the preliminaries of this diptych. This is true in a broad sense and it may have been the rationale for the ancient division of the *Laws* into 12 books. A closer look, however, reveals a more complex picture.

Books 4 and 5 successively deal, in an order that is not entirely perspicuous (not the least because it switches from concrete issues specifically related to the Cretan colony to general considerations concerning legislative expertise), with the following points:

1. the location of the colony (including a discussion of the dangers caused by the proximity to the sea of a city that aims at cultivating virtue), 4.704a1–707d1;
2. the geographic and ethnic origin of the settlers, who must be sufficiently homogeneous, 4.707e1–708d9;
3. the definition of legislative activity as specific kind of expert knowledge, 4.708e1–709d9;
4. the nature of the power that would be needed to launch changes in existing institutions (with a paradoxical appeal to a temperate young tyrant), 4.709d10–712a8;[49]

5. the name of the constitution that would reflect its most essential nature, 4.712b4–715e2 (this is the passage on 'theo-noo-nomocracy');
6. the form of the law, with the first account of the nature of preambles 4.718b5–723d4. The passage includes by way of an example the prelude to a law here presented as the first of the legislative cycle (on marriage), 4.720e10–721d6.

This last section, which constitutes the first focal point of the work in terms of the order of appearance in the text, is itself sandwiched between the first and the second part of the so-called general preamble to the laws (4.715e3–718a6 + 5.726a1–734e2), a positioning that lends a distinctive weight to this general preamble, as well as to the general explanation of the notion of preamble.[50]

As previously indicated, the end of the general preamble officially marks the beginning of the legislation per se, according to a scheme that makes a law follow upon its preamble. But the term 'law' does not capture the situation with sufficient precision. This is for two reasons.

First, what will eventually follow upon the general preamble is not a law in the sense that has been put forward in the account about the nature of preambles, but a constitution, by which is meant the setting up of the components of a political system, deliberative bodies and offices, and the like. The terminology is deliberately hesitant. At 5.735a5–6, the Athenian treats "constitution" as a generic name covering on the one hand the establishment of offices and the officeholders responsible for the implementation of the laws that fall within their area of competence (*arkhôn katastasis*) and on the other hand the laws themselves that fall within the purview of the authorities in question (*nomoi tais arkhais apodothentes*).[51] But these "two kinds of constitution" (*duo politeias eidê*) are also what Plato, perhaps coining a phrase, has just called the *nomoi politeias* (5.734e5), "the laws of the constitution" or, as I shall say, "constitutional laws." Obviously, the term 'law' does not have the same extension or implications in the two cases. The laws that are to be enforced by the officeholders are not the constitutional laws that define these offices and the mode of selection of these officeholders. The latter is prior to the former.

Secondly, the constitutional laws that were supposed at 5.734e3–735a7 to follow the general preamble are themselves put off to later: "But before all these, we must reflect on the following" (5.735a7).

A first consideration, which is clearly still pre-legislative, concerns the human material on which the lawgiver will exercise his expertise: since the aim of legislation is virtue, the prospective settlers will first have to be selected and the group "purified" (*kathairein*, 735d7) from the elements that are inappropriate for this aim, just as a shepherd chooses the best animals for growing the herd in his care (5.735a7–736c4);[52] a second group of considerations concerns some already legislative but still extra-constitutional tenets (736c5–747e11). These bear on economic matters as well as on the ground plan and geographic situation of the city.

The Second Focal Point: The Retreat

The first of the economic measures, which consists in dividing the land into 5,040 lots (*klêroi*), corresponding to as many households, implies a departure from the scheme advocated in the *Republic*, where the guardians, at least, have nothing to do with either life in a household or agriculture.[53] The justification for this move constitutes the second focal point of the work in the order of their appearance in the text. It is in a sense the more important of the two, because of its broader impact: the whole legislative apparatus of the *Laws*, including the shape of its preambles, derives from it.

Whereas the novelty of Platonic legislation in the *Laws* lies in its contrast with traditional legislative practice, the division of land and the setting up of separate households are novel when contrasted with the organization of the just city in the *Republic*. "Human nature" is what it is, and the lawgiver has now to step back from his paradigm (*paradeigma*, 739e1) and allow citizens to be, if not owners, at least tenants of individual lots and to have families. This puts the city presently under discussion in second place; it is the "second in comparison to the best" (*deuterôs* [. . .] *pros to beltiston*, 5.739a4–5), as well as "closest to immortality and one in second" (*athanasias eggutata kai hê mia deuterôs*, 739e4).[54] The meaning of this ranking will be the topic of the two following chapters.

Specifying the Laws

At this point, we have entered legislation, as is indicated by Plato's use of the term *nomos* and its derivatives at 5.738a1 and b3 (cf. also 739a2 and 741e7) and also by the presence of a preamble (741a6–c6) to the law concerning the non-alienability of the tenured land (741b7–e3)—the third example of a preamble after the general preamble that straddles Book 4 (715e7–718a6) and 5 (726a1–734e2) and the first preamble on marriage in Book 4.721b6–c8. The fact that the official beginning of the (constitutional) laws announced at 5.734e3–6 does not happen until the beginning of Book 6 nevertheless suggests that the 'economic' laws formulated in the second part of Book 5, in spite of their crucial importance for the organization of Plato's city[55] are not on par with the 'political laws' (the topic of Book 6) and even less with the rest of the legislation.[56]

Book 6 begins by taking up the distinction between "two kinds, concerning the organization of a constitution" (*duo eidê* [. . .] *peri ton politeias kosmon*, 751a4) in approximately the same terms as 5.735a5–6: there is, on the one hand, the organization of the offices and the appointment of officeholders, and on the other, the formulation of the laws that are relevant to the business of each of these offices (6.751a4–b2). The rest of the book, down to 6.768e3, is devoted to the first kind of 'constitution.' This section is a counterpart to Book 3 in that it depicts the constitution that promotes virtue of a deeper and more complex description than anything Sparta, or even Athens and Cyrus' Persia, could ever achieve.

Officially, the 'postponements and hesitations,' as Plato calls them, end at 6.768d7–e3, once the constitution has been established: "We have presently reached the point where, the selection of the officeholders having taken place, it may be appropriate to move on from the previous issues and begin a laying down of laws, without need for any more postponements and hesitations (*anabolôn kai oknôn*)."

Thus, legislation 'proper' does not begin until as late as 6.771a5, once the organs of authority have been defined in the first part of Book 6 and various transitional matters discussed (6.768e4–771a4). But the situation, once more, turns out to be unstable. For it is not before the end of Book 7 and then Book 9 that the official pattern of legislation resumes, after an extended section devoted, first, to the organization of religious feasts (6.771a5–772d4, with an introductive, retrospective justification for picking 5,040 as the number of households at 5.737e1–2), and, second, to para-legislative and preamble-like considerations on marriage and procreation (from 6.772d5 onwards) that complete the indications given much earlier at 4.720e10–721e3 about the difference between law and preamble.[57]

The complexity of the picture, as far as Books 4–12 (and especially Books 4 through 6) are concerned, derives to a great extent from the various ways in which the term 'law' is used. These are quite clearly there to be seen, without however ever being formalized. As the work develops, the contrast between a law and its preamble comes more and more into focus. Expert legislation requires more than an artless conception of law that takes it to be 'simple' (*haplous*), i.e., no more than an order backed up by the threat of punishment in case of the order's infringement (4.721b1–3). The task of the lawgiver is a 'double' one (4.721b4–e3). Besides an order and the threat of punishment, there is also another form of legislative discourse, the function of which is to 'persuade' (*peithein*) the citizens to whom the law is directed: and this is the preamble. This broadening of the legislative task towards a form of discourse that conventional legislative practice, as Plato construes it, ignores, opens the road to the possibility, in spite of the distance that keeps them apart, of a discursive continuum not only between legislation and rhetoric, but between legislation and philosophy—a continuum which education/*paideia* actualizes as far as possible in both directions. In *this* sense, the first focal point of the work is no less broad in scope than the second one, and even has some claim to substantial priority over it.

The Centrality of the General Preamble

As already mentioned, the clarification of the notion of a preamble is sandwiched between the first part of a fictive exhortation to the colonists starting in Book 4 (715e7–718a6) and its continuation in Book 5 (726a1 down to 734e2). It consists in an extended, systematic homily on the range of practices that are "dear to god"; they deal in the first place with the gods themselves, followed by parents, friends, fellow-citizens, and, finally and crucially, one's own soul. This general preamble is not followed, as we also saw, by any law of the kind that preambles are meant to precede. The formal and conceptual consequences of this situation are remarkable: we are, literally speaking, at the center of a work entitled *Laws*, one major orientation of which results from a legislative innovation consisting in having laws preceded by preambles; but what we now get is a preamble without a law in the relevant sense, followed by a set of laws that are not punitive, but constitutional. This construction strongly suggests (though the thought is not spelled out) that a citizen living under the appropriate constitution who would follow the recommendations formulated in the general preamble would *ipso facto* abide by the content of the legislation, which amounts to saying that the law, at least as far as concerns its traditional, threatening form, is but an ultimate resource which could *in principle* be not only postponed but might in fact become superfluous. This utopian horizon of the *Laws* will come to the fore in Book 9, in the second version of an analogy between legislation and medical practice.[58]

Constitution and Laws (Books 6 to 12)

Lawgiving, now caught between the two poles of legislation understood on the one hand as nonviolent persuasion and on the other as punitive, officially begins in the second part of Book 6, after the 'constitutional laws.'[59] But only in a sense. For Book 7, which deals mostly with early education (thereby adhering to the implicit biographical scheme of the legislation by following directly after the law on marriage and procreation), considers laws of a specific kind, namely 'unwritten laws' (or 'unwritten customs,' *agrapha nomima*, 7.793a10). These, because they are oral and traditional in character, can act not only as equivalents, but even as desirable substitutes for the persuasive preamble. (Customs not only preclude legislative threats, but abolish the distance that still separates the city from the citizen when the latter has yet to be persuaded.) The praise of non-written laws confirms that the repeated postponements of legislation ultimately derive from a construal of law as fundamentally negative, in so far as it always implies a variable, but certain, degree of violence.

The laws that are eventually formulated follow an order that is not linked to the offices to which they are attached (cf. 6.751a3–b2). Instead they cleave in a more elaborate form to the program initially sketched at 1.631d2–632d1, just after the division of goods that makes wisdom the ground for all goodness. There, the Athenian mentioned the rules (*prostaxeis*: 'orders,' 631d3; laws, 632c4) that would be necessary to secure those goods in marriage, the education of the citizen from youth to old age, and in situations involving diseases, wars, poverty, and their contraries (632a5), wealth (632b2), appropriate and just treatment in social relationships (632b3-c1), and eventually burial and honors (632c2–4). Book 4 had begun to implement the program by using the law on marriage as an example to illustrate the notion of 'preamble.' Following upon the constitution in Book 6, the general framework of the legislation remains chronological: procreation, education, military service, civic activities, death. But there are also regulations that, while bearing on an important aspect of an adult life, do not lend themselves to a chronological sequence, such as those concerning the cultivation of land and the primary necessities of subsistence.[60] Finally, there is a typological classification of the most severe transgressions according to their degree of gravity, which is chronological only in the sense that young people are more likely to be offenders than older persons.

The treatment of the main phases of human existence extends from the second part of Book 6 through the end of Book 8 (including the "agricultural laws" from 842e6 onwards), with some extensions into Books 11 and 12. The laws that the Athenian, at the end of Book 9, says are directed to 'good and useful people' (*khrêstoi anthrôpoi*, 880d8) can be considered social regulations. By contrast with this first group, a second set of laws, which occupy most of Books 9, 10, and part of 11, concern the 'greatest' transgressions (9.853a5): public offences, homicides, violent aggressions, various kinds of hubristic behavior (including offences towards the gods), violations of laws relating to tenure, thefts, wrongdoings in regard to contracts, sales, and judicial procedure.[61] These laws are typical in the sense that they respond to a 'necessity' that is not linked to the means of subsistence (as is the case for agricultural laws, for example), but have their origins in deficient education. This is why this part of the legislative work is called 'shameful' (9.853b4). The last law to be formulated deals with funerals, the end of life (12.960b1–6), thus completing an impressive ring-composition that began with the discussion between the lawgiver and the poet in Book 4.719a7–e5.[62]

A Meta-Constitutional Law

The section that follows (12.960b5–969c2) reverts, before the short epilogue, to an issue which, though it would seem to belong to the section on constitutional laws in Book 6, is not discussed there. One can see why. On the one hand, the constitution is incomplete without an institution, the Watch, that takes care of the constitution itself and of its laws as a whole, but on the other hand, an institution of this description is more than a simple part of the constitution that it warrants.[63] Although the members of this leading board, half of it elderly people who have formerly exercised political functions, half young apprentices eligible for minor offices, are not characterized as philosophers, they certainly engage in philosophical reflection, since they discuss the question of the unity of virtue, which is likely to lead them to ultimate principles, such as the Good and the One. It is as if philosophy, which was the foundation of the exercise of political power in the *Republic*, had found its place of exercise, both at the center and at the margin of political life.[64]

A Last Complication

A last complication concerning the structure of the work comes from the flexible nature of the preambles. For while preambles are officially meant to precede laws (or sets of laws), in fact they sometimes turn into what seems to be a discussion, perhaps between the interlocutors of the dialogue, rather than an address aimed at the citizens who would be its natural audience. This has the effect of opening up a space, at the heart of legislation, for meta-legislative reflections of various kinds and scopes. Such are, to mention only a few passages, the encomium on a leisurely life (7.806d7–807d5), the re-description of the (second-) best constitution as the 'truest tragedy' (7.817a2-d8), or the analysis of responsibility (9.857b3–864c11).[65]

This freedom of composition encourages an anthological reading of the *Laws*—which does not mean that Plato thought that schoolteachers should extract appropriate passages from his book for pedagogical purposes, as the Greeks did with their poets.[66] Anthological passages are those, rather, where the legislative enterprise suddenly faces ultimate questions about what it is to be a human being and about the meaning of a human life. The fact that Aristotle, who complains in the *Politics* (2.6 1265a1–4) that the *Laws* is for the most part just that, namely laws (as distinguished from constitution, about which he wishes Plato had said more), was apparently not sensitive to this dimension of the work tells us more about Aristotle's disciplinary expectations than about the distinctively Platonic kind of depth which is no less characteristic of the *Laws* than of any other of Plato's dialogues.

The Bare Bones of the *Laws*

   I. Prologue. Book 1.624a1–625c5.

  II. The ultimate aim of legislation: virtue. Book 1.625c6 to the end of Book 2.

 III. Fundamental features of a constitution adapted to this aim (now extended to three targets): mixed and balanced models of the past. Announcement of the project of the foundation of a new Cretan colony. Book 3.

 IV. First set of preliminaries to the new legislation, including the law on marriage as a sample and the general preamble to the laws. Book 4 down to 5.734e.

  V. Second set of preliminaries to legislation, including economic laws. Book 5.734e4–747e11.

 VI. The projected 'middle' constitution (the 'constitutional laws'). Book 6.751a1–768e7.[67]

VII. The rest of the legislation. Book 6.769a1–12.960b5.

VII. The Watch. Book 12.960b5–969c2.

VIII. Epilogue: Invitation to the Athenian stranger to join the committee for the refoundation of Magnesia. Book 12.969c3–d3 (cf. 6.751d8–752a1).

2

Paradigms and Utopias

The *Republic* of Plato has become proverbial as a striking example of a supposedly visionary perfection, such as can exist only in the brain of an idle thinker, and Brucker has ridiculed the philosopher for asserting that a prince can rule well only insofar as he participates in the ideas. We should, however, be better advised to follow up his thought and, where the great philosopher leaves us without help, to place it, through fresh efforts, in a proper light, rather than to set it aside as useless on the very sorry and harmful pretext of impracticability.

KANT, *CRITIQUE OF PURE REASON* B372–3/A316,
TRANS. NORMAN KEMP SMITH

From the *Laws* to the *Republic*

In Book 5.739 of the *Laws*, the Athenian, referring to a city that borrows its main features (with one important exception, as will become clear) from the "just city" outlined in Book 5 of the *Republic*, calls it the *paradigm* (*paradeigma*) of the city that one must "hold on to" (*ekhomenous tautês*) while "seeking one that is to the highest degree like it as far as possible" (*tên hoti malista toiautên zêtein kata dunamin*) at the very moment when he declares that one must move away from it—must undertake a 'retreat' of sorts that constitutes the second (in order of appearance) focal center of the work, the first in terms of its scope and consequences. The retreat in question is likely, says the Athenian (5.739a1–3), to cause initial surprise (to interlocutors and readers alike), like an unexpected move by a player in a board game; and it might also be dismissed, he adds at 739a5–6, on the grounds that a lawgiver who is not exercising any political power (here represented by its most concentrated form, 'tyranny' (*nomothethêi mê turannounti*), has no reason to take a step of this kind.[1]

The term *paradeigma* comes from the *Republic,* which uses it, at the relevant juncture (5.472c4), in a pregnant way. We must get clear about what this use is in order to appreciate the articulation between the two dialogues. This in turn requires that we bear in mind the bare bones of the *Republic.* There should be nothing controversial in the outline I give in the next section. But things will get tougher in the ones that follow.

A *Republic* in Two Acts and an Epilogue

The *Republic,* more literally the *Constitution* (*Politeia*), is not introduced as a political dialogue bearing on the constitution in the way the *Laws* is from the start presented as an inquiry about (constitution and) laws. What the *Republic* asks in the first place is whether it is more beneficial for an individual to lead a just life, which is the position Socrates upholds, or an unjust life, which is what Thrasymachus claims.[2] The aporetic discussion of Book 1 ends with the observation that to answer this question one must first know what 'the just'/ *to dikaion* is (1.354b4–5). At Book 2.367e1–5, having set out the strongest possible argument for Thrasymachus' position (surely, if one could commit injustice without being *seen,* as Gyges' ring enabled him to do, one would go for injustice, which is beneficial), Glaucon requires from Socrates a counter-argument capable or showing, symmetrically, that the exercise of justice in itself confers benefits that have nothing to do with external awards or recognition, be they human or divine.[3] A long chain of preliminary arguments is necessary to respond to the challenge. The final answer will be provided in two stages, a first, general response which is reached at 4.445a5–b4, and a second, more precise, which will not be articulated until 9.591b8.

The first step consists in finding out, as required at the end of Book 1, what justice is. Since it is allegedly easier to spot in a city, where justice is written in capital letters, as the famous analogy goes, than in an individual (i.e., in his soul), Socrates undertakes to construct a city "in words" (2.369a6, *logôi*). This city turns out to be a functional whole made of three constitutive activities and the corresponding agents, the producers (farmers and craftsmen), the military (or "guardians" or "auxiliaries"), and the rulers (who preserve the city in a higher sense). Socrates then defines the three virtues attached, respectively, to these three functions, namely, in reverse order, wisdom/*sophia* (4.428a11–429a7), courage/*andreia* (429a8–430c7), and temperance/

sôphrosunê (430d6–432b1). In the process he discovers that justice/*dikaiosunê*, the fourth virtue that is still missing, is a sort of supervenient virtue that emerges when the three other ones are effective (4.432b2–434c3). Once this analysis of justice in the city is finished (at 4.434d1 or rather 435a4), Socrates turns to the individual, identifies his virtues by analogy to those of the city, and concludes that justice, which is to the soul what health is to the body, is indeed beneficial in its own right, whereas injustice, which is to justice what sickness is to health, is not (4.444d3–e3). At this point, the initial question has received an answer and Glaucon declares himself satisfied with it (4.445a5–b4). End of the first act.

Socrates, however, feels that this answer lacks precision (4.445b5–7). The second act of the *Republic*, from 4.445b5 to the end of Book 9, undertakes to fill in the missing details. It poses a further, extended set of preliminary questions that are functionally similar to those in the first act in that they, too, rely on the analogy between a city and a soul; but these now are more demanding, more complex, and they take longer to answer. Starting at 5.471c3, the question of the just city is tackled, at the request of Socrates' interlocutors. The approach is from a new angle, that of the *possibility (meaning 'feasibility')* of the construct elaborated so far. This issue is so wide-ranging that Socrates will characterize the ensuing argument, which extends to the beginning of Book 8, as a 'digression'[4]—which is somewhat misleading, since this particular digression would seem to be required, and this for two reasons. First, because the full picture of the just individual—that is, the philosopher—is still missing.[5] And also because this digression is the starting point for the analysis, in terms of a (paradigmatic) decadence, of unjust cities and correspondingly unjust souls, which was announced at 4.445c1–2. Books 8 and 9 (up to 591b8) can then follow with the account that was postponed because of the interlocutors' worries about the possibility of a just city. We now get all the precisions that Socrates was missing at the end of Book 4, including an assurance set in quantitative terms that the absolutely just, philosophical life is 729 times more pleasant than the absolutely unjust, tyrannical life praised by Thrasymachus in the first book (9.587d12–e4, echoing 1.344a4–b1). The question of the respective benefits attached to the just and the unjust life can now be definitively settled (9.588b1–591b8), and the narrative proceeds to a climatic appendix that describes how "an individual who possesses reason/*nous* (591c1) will behave in his own, present-day city (591c1–592b6). End of the second act.

At the end of Book 10, which, on this issue as on others, serves as a second closure, the myth of Er will add to the demonstration a discussion about a certain class of external benefits, namely the postmortem rewards or for that matter punishments souls can expect, depending upon whether they have led just or unjust lives.[6]

From Best to Possible

The political issue that triggers the discussion about the possibility of the just city and consequently about the nature of philosophy in Book 5 of the *Republic* is a law (*nomos*, 457c7, cf. 453d2) prohibiting guardians of the city from the "ownership of a spouse" (*tên tôn gunaikôn ktêsin*, 4.423e6–7) and of children. I shall refer to this law, which constitutes a hinge between the two main acts of the dialogue, as "the law of public ownership of women and children."[7]

This extraordinary proposal had been cautiously alluded to by Socrates in the course of Books 3 and 4, as a preparation for its full thematization in Book 5. Describing, at the end of Book 3, the conditions that should regulate the life of the guardians (only males are concerned for the time being; the female counterpart must wait until Book 5[8]), Socrates indicated, still in a most general and cautious way, that "[guardians] must have the kind of housing and other property that will neither prevent them from being the best guardians nor encourage them to do evil to other citizens" (3.416c5–d1, trans. Grube/Reeve) and that "none of them should possess any private property (*ousian . . . idian*) beyond what is wholly necessary" (3.416d4–6, trans. Grube/Reeve).

More precisely, guardians will be prohibited from "handling gold or silver" (417a3) and "acquiring private (*idios*) land, houses, and currency" (417a6). In Book 4, in the very sentence that proclaims the uselessness of immediately formulating laws that future well-educated guardians would easily discover for themselves, Socrates gets more specific and drops, as if it was a mere detail: ". . . as well as all the other things we are omitting, for example, that the possession of wives and the procreation of children, that all these must be made to the highest degree, in accordance to the proverb that says 'all that belong to friends is common'" (4.423e6–424a2).

Read in the light of the upcoming discussion about 'possibility' in the *Republic*, and even more of the fact that the first 'retreat' implemented by the *Laws* bears on this very issue, the phrase here translated with "to the highest degree" (*hoti malista*) acquires a weight that is likely to escape readers at first blush.[9] For the time being, it suffices to note that the preterition "all the other things we are omitting . . . ," followed by an explicit sample of some omitted issues, is an obvious provocation. Once completed the argument under consideration (which lists further issues that Socrates says he need *not* to tackle in the present context—and which will, as it happens, be dealt with in the

Laws), the three interlocutors understandably ask Socrates, at the beginning of Book 5, to clarify his views about barring guardians from having a family (5.449c2–450a2 and 450c1–5). Socrates begins with two precautionary remarks, the first of which introduces for the first time the distinction between what is best (*arista*) and what is possible (*dunata*), while the second warns about the incredulity that his views are bound to prompt (450c6–d2). He then turns in the first place to another law (*nomos*, 5.457b8), which states that women should be educated to guardianship in the same way as men are (5.451d4–457b6; this is the 'female' counterpart, 452c2, of male education to guardianship dealt with in Books 2.376e2–3.412b6). This plea for equal education, which represents the first and smallest (5.457c3–5) among the three "waves" of incredulity that Socrates will have to confront,[10] is in fact a necessary premise to the law on public ownership of women and children that will follow (5.457b7–471c2). This is presumably because the regulations concerning procreation under the guidance of the city require an appropriate type of woman if the right kind of progeny are to result (in other words, equal education is subordinated to eugenics).

The two laws about male and female guardians sharing the same education, on the one hand, and about public ownership of women and children, on the other hand, are meant to be the best (*arista, beltista*) and the most beneficial (*ôphelima, sumphorôtata*) for the city. But are such arrangements possible (*dunata*), or, to quote the fuller formula that will turn out to be crucial, "is it possible for them to come into being (*dunata gignesthai*)"?[11] The answers to these two questions, which, Socrates insists, must be treated separately, will require development through a quite lengthy argument (5.450c6–6.502c7). Socrates defeats these three "waves" one after the other, showing successively a) the *possibility* and then the *benefits* to be expected from the law on equal education, b) the *benefits* to be expected from the law of public ownership of women and children, and c) the *possibility* of this latter law as well as of his overall political program as developed since 2.369a5.[12] The last issue constitutes the most substantial of the three waves (5.457b7 and c4–5). The conclusion of the argument is eventually drawn in Book 6: "concerning legislation (*nomothesia*), it turns out that our proposals are the best, were they to come into being, but that it would be difficult for them to come into being (*khalepa genesthai*), though not altogether impossible" (6.502c5–7).

The double negation is unequivocal: difficult, yes; impossible, no. Hence, possible.

In the long history of the reception of Plato's *Republic* that begins with Aristotle's objections in Book 2.2–6 of his *Politics*, both claims, about the desirability of Plato's legislative scheme and about its possibility, have been passionately discussed and often harshly criticized.[13] Aristotle's objections were primarily directed at the issue of excellence rather than at the question of possibility, even if he mentions the latter as well.[14] It is easy to see why: a discussion about possibility loses much of its urgency if the proposals in question are not thought to be desirable in the first place. In effect, they have most of the time been considered either as damaging from Plato's own perspective (this is the path taken by Aristotle's internal critique of them in the *Politics*) or obnoxious from an ethical point of view (this characteristically modern approach is represented most notably by Schleiermacher in his Introduction to the *Republic*).[15] Here, by contrast, I shall focus on the notion of possibility: not primarily because this reflects Plato's own emphasis,[16] even though his emphasis is certainly relevant within the framework of the *Republic*, but because the question is crucial to an assessment of the relationship of the *Laws* to the *Republic*—and, more broadly, of Plato's place in the history of utopian thought.

The problem stems from some uncertainty about the exact scope of the term 'possible' as used by Plato at various junctures. Dealing with the first and smallest wave, Socrates had shown that equality of education for women is possible on the grounds that men and women share a common 'nature' (5.455d6–e2) in as far as they belong to the same species (*eidos*, 454c9), the idea being that the sexual differences between male and female are analogous to those between long-haired males and bald males within one and the same subspecies (454a4–9). When it comes to the second wave (and more generally to the whole "city in words"), however, the possibility of Socrates' proposals turns out not to be reducible to this naturalistic interpretation of possibility. The crucial passage begins at 5.473a5–b2. Having dealt with the (natural) possibility of treating women and men, with all their differences, on an equal footing, Socrates rapidly reviewed the benefits to be expected from this law at 5.456c4–457a2. Then, starting not with possibility, but with benefits, he laid out all the advantages (and here, the list gets longer and longer: 458b9–471c3) that would result from the public ownership of women and children.[17] Glaucon, having patiently listened to Socrates' eulogies, now, at 5.471c4 and e4, presses him to keep to the promise made back at 458b1–7 and to show "that" and "in what way" his proposals are not only beneficial, but possible (*to hôs dunatê gignesthai kai tina tropon pote dunatê*). Socrates' answer will extend from 5.472b3 to 6.502c8 (the conclusion quoted above). By far the largest section of this long development is devoted to the means by which what is possible can be realized (I take it that this is the "in what way" aspect of the question), namely through the coincidence of knowledge and power—an idea that implies a detailed thinking through of what the appropriate philosophy and philosophical education might look like.[18] The answer to the "that" part of the question is much shorter. It concerns the meaning of the term 'possibility' itself, which it crucially leaves indeterminate.

Approximating Approximation

Socrates' views on the question of the possibility of the just city is more nuanced, and hence more complex, than the unequivocally affirmative answer he gives to the question at the end of the whole argument (6.502c5–7) suggests at first sight. The complication comes from the fact that the implications of this conclusion, positive as it is, are co-determined by the way in which Socrates replies, back at 5.472a1–473b2, to Glaucon's impatient reminder about his promise to deal with the question of the possibility of the best city.

Socrates prefaces his answer to Glaucon with two remarks. First, he recalls (at 472b3) that the inquiry about "justice itself" and the "perfectly just individual" was undertaken "in order to have a model (*paradeigma*) [...] to discover both what justice itself is like (*hoion esti*) as well as the completely just man, if he should come into being (*ei genoito*), and what kind of man he'd be if he did, and likewise with regard to injustice and the most unjust man, in order to [...] be compelled to agree about ourselves as well (*kai peri hêmôn autôn*) that the one who was most like them (*homoiotatos*) would have a portion of happiness most like theirs, not in order to prove that it's possible for them to come into being" (472c4-d1, trans. Grube/Reeve modified).[19]

He then adds that this is also true of "the good city [...] we constructed in speech" (*logôi*)": this too was set up as a model/*paradeigma* (472d9–10).

Socrates' point, here, is only cautionary. He notes that the construction of a legislative model would still be valuable from a cognitive point of view, should it be impossible for it to come into being.[20] The portrait of a perfect human being, after all, does not lose its paradigmatical beauty if the artist is not able to also show that such a human being cannot come into existence (5.472d4–7). In sum, the paradigmatic model is no more, in this first part of Socrates' reply, than an *ideal-type* (to make a normative, non-Weberian use of the notion).

Of course, the fact that the good city was not intended to be more than an ideal-type does not mean that the latter *cannot* "come into being," since a lawgiver, provided that he collaborates with an appropriate political power, possesses a (certain degree of) transformative capacity that is not within the range of a painter's possibilities (human beings are not as malleable as colors). This explains why Socrates, now prepared to engage in the demonstration Glaucon has requested (if only "in order to please" him, as he somewhat misleading insists), affirms at 5.472e7 that yes, the just city is possible—though with one important qualification: "Don't compel me to show that what we've described in words (*en logois*) can also come into being entirely as we have described it. Rather, if we're able to discover how a city could come to be governed (*oikêseien*) in a way that most closely approximates our description, let's say that we've found that the things that you have ordered us to show are possible" (5.473a5–b1).

This is, obviously, a revisionist usage of the term 'possible' ("let's say that x is so . . ."), whereas something is normally considered to be possible if reality matches the corresponding concept (the content articulated in speech).[21] Socrates does, however, allow for a certain difference, provided that what comes into being is "closest" (*eggutata*) to the conception in question.

What "closest" amounts to, however, is open to interpretation. The degree of proximity that can be reached will depend on the knowledge of the lawgiver (who will soon turn out to be the philosopher), and also on the material he has at his disposal as he begins to mold it (that is how his model comes into being). Two options for interpretation open up here, one carrying less weight than the other. According to the weaker interpretation, the just city will be declared 'possible' if the realization differs from the model only in matters of details, such as can be due, for example, to local specificities and customs, to the place and time in which the model is to be realized, and so on.[22] According to the stronger interpretation, the material on which the lawgiver operates is of such a nature that the closest he can possibly get to the model turns out to be significantly distant from it. A clear and most relevant illustration of this conceptual constellation is found in the *Statesman*, where the best way to imitate the ideal political expert, whom no law should bound, is to do the exact contrary of what he does, namely strict stick to the laws.[23]

The *Republic* does not provide a clear-cut answer as to how 'closeness' should be construed, and it is certainly possible, on a first reading, to take it in the weak sense.[24] But the strong interpretation gains ground as the argument develops and the paradigmatic city-in-words progressively ceases to be a simple heuristic tool and becomes a normative model for action, as *paradeigma*, too, shifts its meaning. As a matter of fact, the word *paradeigma* may refer (1) to a 'sample' or an 'example,' without any epistemological or axiological value attached to it, as it often does in Plato (and more generally in Greek); or (2) to a 'model' that aids in understanding or deciphering a similar but more complex item, here with an epistemological dimension, but still without any specific axiological charge, as happens in the *Sophist* (218d8–9) and to a certain extent in the *Statesman* (277d1–2, 278b4–5, c4 and e9);[25] or (3), finally, to an axiologically loaded model, which one should imitate (as far as possible).[26] The *Republic* illustrates the transition from (2) to (3). The city-in-speech first introduced at 2.369a5–6 (*gignomenê polis* [. . .] *logôi*) as a device that aids in deciphering more easily what justice is in an individual soul, is surely a *paradeigma* in sense (2). It acquires sense (3) in two steps. The first occurs at 5.472d4–9, when the model of the city is itself compared with an idealized picture of a human being; the second when the model is first located "in the soul" (*en têi psukhêi*) at 6.484c7–8 and then applied to the Forms at 6.500e3 (*tôi theiôi paradeigmati khrômenoi*) and even more conspicuously at 7.540a9, where the Good itself (*to agathon auto*) is said to serve as a paradigm for the philosophers-rulers (*paradeigmati khrômenous autôi*) as they "put the city, its ordinary citizen and themselves in order (*kosmein*)." I take it that the famous reference at 9.592b2 to the paradigmatic city-in-words as located "in the sky" incorporates this additional axiological value, which may (and should) be read back (on a second reading) into 5.472c, to which the passage in Book 9 explicitly refers: "But perhaps, I said, it is a model (*paradeigma*) lying in the heaven for anyone who wants to look at it and to make himself its citizen on the strength of what he sees" (9.592b2–3; Grube/Reeve modified).[27]

This has important implications for the way in which we look at the political program of the *Laws* as it "draws back" from the most conspicuous proposals of the *Republic* (the law on public possession of women and children, to begin with). The retreat is to be understood as a consequence of the paradigmatic status of these proposals and does not signify that Plato is recanting them, quite the contrary.[28] What the construction of the *Republic* implies on this reading, even though Plato never says it this way, is that what is logically possible may in fact not be feasible.

From *lexis* to *praxis*

Socrates justifies the request he addresses to Glaucon ("don't compel me . . .") by pointing to the difference between what one says in speech (*lexis*) and action (*praxis*): "Is it possible that anything be put into practice [lit.: 'acted'] as it is spoken (*prakhthênai hôs legetai*)? Or is it in the nature of things that action (*praxis*) does not grasp truth (*alêtheias ephaptesthai*) as readily as speech (*lexis*) does, even if somebody should think otherwise?" (5.473a1–3).

The sentence is cryptic, and one wishes Plato had said more about the relationship between its three key terms, *lexis*, *praxis*, and *alêtheia* (in addition to revealing the identity of his contradictor), for the question of how to construe 'closeness' in Socrates' next remark depends on this relation. Still, the mention of *alêtheia*, "truth," definitely supports the strong, rather than the weak interpretation of the term, as the two are distinguished above. To be sure, the just city is not a Form—quite apart from the fact that Platonic Forms have not yet been introduced at this stage of the argument (they are part of the long section about philosophers and philosophy that is about to begin[29]). But it is no less obvious that Plato is already building on an analogy between, on the one hand, the one perfect, fully true city conceived in speech and its practical implementation, and, on the other, a Form and its sensible instantiation. Seen in this way, the difference between language (*lexis*) and action (*praxis*) is of an ontological nature. As such, it is unbridgeable.[30] "Truth" (*alêtheia*) must refer to an objective reality that possesses a normative dimension.[31]

A confirmation that Plato is operating with a strong version of closeness lies in the mention of the 'possible' in the sentence that speaks, at the next step of the argumentation, about the coming to be of "the constitution we have been describing": "it [i.e., this constitution] will never be born *to the extent of the possible*(*eis to dunaton*) or see the light of the sun [unless political power and philosophical knowledge fall together]" (5.473e1–2, trans. Grube-Reeve, slightly modified).[32]

The question now will be to define what are the limiting conditions on which the realization of a model depends; that is, to state the measure or the criterion of the possible. This, however, is not a topic that gets discussed in the *Republic*.

The Philosopher as Craftsman

What 'comes next' (*to de meta touto*, 5.473b4) in the discussion about the possibility of the just city does not specify what a city "closest to what has been said" (*eggutata tôn eirêmenôn*, 473a8) nor for that matter its genesis would look like, which would have led to the question about the material (that is, ultimately, human beings) at the disposal of the lawgiver hypothetically endowed with political power. Instead the text shifts to an explanation of why the coincidence of philosophy and political power would be enough to make possible (in an indefinite sense) the coming into being of the just city (that is, a city as close as possible to the paradigm). This does not mean that the inquiry that follows does not relate to the first question in an important way—of course it does, since it, too, deals with 'possibility' (cf. *dunatou de*, 5.473c4). But the 'possibility' at issue is not so much that of the institutions of the just city, as rather the feasibility of a the best *condition* of its approximation (on the reading suggested above, it is an answer to the question "in which way" or "how" it is possible, rather than an affirmation "that" it is possible). To be sure, the condition of the whole process of approximation must itself be possible. In this sense, there is no discontinuity between the section devoted to the philosopher-king (5.473b4–6.502c7, which then develops and takes the discourse up to the end of Book 7) and the preceding one. But the hypothetical coincidence of power and knowledge is not by itself an approximation of the paradigmatic city, only a trigger that sets the process of approximation going. This is reflected in the very sentence that specifies the one single change in currently (*nun*, "now") existing cities that would initiate such an approximation to the paradigm—a change that is certainly not easy, although it is "possible," too (473c4):[33] "Until [. . .] political power and philosophy entirely coincide [. . .], the constitution we've been describing in speech will never be born to the extent of the possible [. . .]" (473c11–e2).

The restriction "to the extent of the possible" can only refer here to the distinction between (theoretical) speech and (practical) action, as formulated in 473a1–3, when the coincidence of political power and philosophical wisdom (which the long argument that follows claims to be itself 'possible') will launch the process of approximation. 'Practice' is thought of as a specific case of 'production'; namely, the re-production of the paradigmatic model articulated in speech in a certain material, the nature and quality of which affect the degree of closeness to the model that a craftsman can reach. *Mutatis mutandis*, the philosopher-king is in the same position *vis-à-vis* his material as the Demiurge in the *Timaeus vis-à-vis* the disordered, primitive, elementary stuff that he has to cope with (52a8–53a8), and which he brings *as far as possible* to the likeness of the paradigmatic Forms at which he is looking.[34]

As a consequence, we need to distinguish between two cases in which the term 'possible' applies. The first refers to a prerequisite, the legislative craftsman, who is the condition of possibility of the city that will stand at the least possible distance from the paradigm; the second refers to this city itself, as a product of the craft. The argument of the *Republic* exclusively tackles the first issue, i.e., the possibility of the prerequisite (the philosopher-king) becoming a reality, which is eventually asserted at 6.502c7. Of course, we can (and should) ask, in the light of Socrates' cautionary observations about possibility voiced at 5.472b3–473b3, *to what extent* the philosopher-king, i.e., the coincidence between political power and philosophy is itself possible.[35] By the same token, the question about how close to the model the hypothetical philosophical ruler might succeed in bringing the just city (as far as possible) is left blank. The only thing that we learn, at the end of Book 7, about the practical genesis of the just city is that the philosopher-ruler of a given city will relocate to the countryside (i.e., the section of the lot that is situated outside the city) all the population aged over ten so as to be left with malleable young children to educate (540e5–541a7). And this preliminary step may arguably be counted as another paradigmatic prescription, even if the general scheme on which it relies is less unrealistic that we might think.[36]

Contradictory Signals

The long argument that follows Socrates' two qualifications about the possibility of the just city and the corresponding individual soul proceeds in two steps. First, Socrates defines at length what a true philosopher is (he is in the first place one who knows the Forms, and above all the Form of the Good, the ultimate piece of knowledge), and has arrived at the understanding that he is suited by nature (*phusei*, 5.474c1) both to philosophize and to rule the city, and this despite the discrediting of philosophy and its degeneration into sophistry that has taken place in actual cities. The second step shows that, although it is likely that a philosophical nature will be corrupted in the context of a corrupt city, no argument can establish that this kind of corruption is inevitable, so that, once one considers the immensity of time and of space available on earth, the real possibility of a coincidence of philosophy and power cannot be ruled out. Shortly before drawing the conclusion ("it is possible"), Socrates omits the restrictive "as far as possible" as he reaffirms, more forcefully, the thesis previously stated at 5.473c11–e2:

> [...] we were compelled by the truth to say that no city, constitution, or even individual man will ever become perfect until either some necessity invests by chance those few philosophers who aren't vicious (the ones who are now called useless) to take charge of a city, whether they want to or not, and the city obeys them, or until a god inspires the present rulers and kings or their offspring with a true erotic love for true philosophy. Now, I affirm

that there is no argument to the effect that one of these situations or both is impossible. For if this were the case, we'd be justly ridiculed for indulging in wishful thinking (*eukhais homoia legontes*). Isn't that so?—It is.—Then, if in the limitless past, those who were foremost in philosophy were forced to take charge of a city or if this is happening now in some foreign place far beyond our ken or if it will happen in the future, we are prepared to maintain our argument that, at whatever time the Muse [i.e., philosophy] controls a city, the constitution we've described will also exist at that time, whether it is past, present, or future. Since it is not impossible for this to happen, we are not speaking of impossibilities. That it is difficult for it to happen, however, we agree ourselves. (6.499b1–d5, trans. Grube/Reeve, with modifications)

The first part of the summary, concerning the definition of a philosophical nature, ensures that a philosopher-king is possible in the straightforward sense that was previously applied, at a different level, in the (naturalistic) argument about the identical nature of men and women. The second step also treats the possibility of the philosopher-king as a *de facto* possibility that can even be projected in time (to the past, present, or future) and into space (maybe not in Greece). As a matter of fact, at the end of the long 'digression' that has led to the description of the best regime (*aristocratia*, 8.545b9, cf. 4.445d6), the just city is supposed to have come into existence. Its decline is at last about to begin, in conformity with Socrates' initial intention, voiced at the beginning of Book 5, to explain how each of the five constitutions (the single just one, and the four unjust ones) "pass from one to another" (*ex allêlôn metabainein*, 5.449b1). The cause of the initial decline from aristocracy to 'timocracy' (basically, a certain version of the Spartan regime) follows from an ontological principle, according to which everything that comes into existence is doomed to perish (8.546a1–3).[37] But, clearly, positing the existence of the paradigmatic city is itself an aspect of the paradigm, given that ontological principles do not apply less to the coming into existence of the just city than to its decline—this is the scope of the restrictive clause "as far as possible" at various junctures.

As will have become clear, the textual data concerning the question of possibility in the *Republic* are delicate to handle. While *Republic* 5 requires that we distinguish between a sense of the term 'possibility' (the first to come to mind) according to which the realization of the model matches the model exactly, and a looser one which counts "closeness" to the model as a sufficient criterion for declaring the model 'possible,' we get no clue about what counts as 'closeness,' either in the case of the just city, which is clearly liable to some restrictions deriving from the difference between theoretical construct and practical realization, or (and even less) in the case of the would-be philosopher-king. Should we read the cautionary passage about 'closeness' in Book 5 in the light of the later straightforward assertion of possibility at 6.499a11–d5, or on the contrary read the strong conclusion in the light of the former passage? The answer is left to the reader. What is sure is that the second option, which relies on a strong, ontological notion of paradigmatism and is the one I embrace, allows for the kind of conceptual continuity between the *Republic* and the *Laws* that the *Laws* itself asserts—a continuity which is not only compatible with, but in fact requires the series of changes that occur between the former and the later work, including the relationship between the ruler and the law. It is to this one crucial change that the Athenian refers in the lines that constitute the first epigraph of my essay, according to which one's gaze is more acute in old age than in youth (4.715d7–e1). What the aging Athenian stranger now says and what was not said in the *Republic* by the younger Socrates, nor for that matter by Plato, is that law should be the master (*despotês*) of the rulers (the officeholders), and the rulers its slaves (4.715d3–6). As for the question of possibility, the views put forward in the *Laws* is compatible with that of the *Republic* on the condition that both complexities, that of the relevant argument put forward in the *Republic* and that of the *Laws* itself be taken into account. What is true is that the emphasis is now on impossibility rather than on possibility. This only to be expected, since potential possibility and actual impossibility are two complementary faces of one and the same paradigmatism.

The Possibility of the Wise Ruler

The hypothesis of a coincidence between knowledge and power is evoked in two passages of the *Laws* that are no less delicate to handle than the corresponding sections in the *Republic*. The first one bears on the desirability, from the point of view of a true lawgiver, of an encounter, that is a collaboration, with a temperate tyrant (4.709d10–712a7), the other on the corrupting effect of power, and more specifically of absolute power (9.874e8–875d5). The two passages look in opposite directions, too. But they are no less compatible than the seemingly contradictory signals in the *Republic*, if one keeps in view the distinction between the two kinds of possibility—the logical and the real—that we find there.

I begin with Book 9.874e8–875d5, which, in the reading that I shall defend, differs from the related passages in the *Republic* in that it brings up the issue of duration in dealing with the question of the possibility of a wise ruler. The passage is made of three blocks, which I call A (with subdivisions a, b, and c), B, and C in the quotation that follows. The crucial sentence consists in the ensemble B + C, and in particular C.

[Aa] [. . .] it is necessary for human beings to have laws established and to live according to laws, or not to differ in any way from the beasts that are the most savage in all respects. The cause of this is that there is no nature (*phusis*) of any human beings that is capable (*hikanê*) both of knowing what is useful to human beings as far as a constitution is concerned and, knowing this, of being able and willing to always to do what is best.

[Ab] For, to begin with, it is difficult to know (*gnônai*) that the true political art necessarily cares not for the private (*to idion*) but for the common (*to koinon*)—for the common binds cities together, while the private tears them apart—and that it is useful for the common and the private, both of them, if the common, rather than the private [875b], is fashioned well (*kalôs tithêtai*).

[Ac] Secondly, even if someone should ever acquire adequately, with expertise (*en tekhnêi*), the knowledge (*to gnônai*) that this is the way things are by nature, but after this should rule the city without being accountable (*anupeuthunos*) and having alone the power of decision (*autokratôr*), he would never be able (*ouk an pote dunaito*) to persist (*emmeinai*) in this belief and keep throughout his life (*diabiônai*) consolidating (*trephôn*: lit. nourishing) in the city what he considers to be common, with the private following behind the common; rather, his mortal nature (*hê thnêtê phusis*) will always (*aei*) urge him toward having more (*pleonexia*) and acting as a private person (*idiopragia*), irrationally fleeing pain and pursuing pleasure, putting both of these [sc. two feelings] before [875c] what is more just and better, and producing darkness within itself [i.e., within the mortal nature], it will in the end fill both itself and the whole city with all the evils.

[B] For, if ever some human being who was born adequate in nature by a divine dispensation, were able (*ei pote* [. . .] *dunatos eiê*) to obtain these things (*tauta paralabein*, i.e., both the relevant knowledge and the power to endure),[38] he would not need any laws ruling him. For no law or order is stronger than knowledge (*epistêmê*), nor is it right for reason (*nous*) to be subordinate or a slave to anything [875d], but it should rule all things, if indeed it is really true (*alêthinos*) and free (*eleutheros*) according to its nature.

[C] But in fact (*nun de*), it is so nowhere or in any way, except to a small degree [or, I shall specify, 'for a short period': *all' ê kata brakhu*]. That is why one must choose what comes second: order and law—which see and look to most things but are incapable of seeing every thing. (trans. based on Pangle, with modifications)

What block [A] denies is not the possibility that knowledge and power might be united at some point in one and the same individual, but that this conjunction would persist over time (*ouk an pote dunaito emmeinai toutôi tôi dogmati kai diabiônai* [...], 875b4–5).[39] Note that the reason why it is difficult to acquire expert political knowledge in the first place, which is not explicitly mentioned, is also what makes it impossible for anyone to stick with it in a situation of absolute power (that is, when one is irresponsible in the political sense of not having to account to anyone): namely, mistaken self-interest which, if unchecked, always gets the upper hand in a human soul.

Block [B] introduces a counterfactual perspective: "For, if ever some human being who was born adequate in nature by a divine dispensation, were able to obtain these things, he would not need any laws ruling over him."[40]

The notion that this counterfactual sentence contradicts the impossibility (in the real sense of the term 'possibility') of a wise, virtuous autocrat responsible to no one (875b3–4) or, for that matter, of the philosopher-king declared 'possible' in the *Republic* seems at first sight to be supported by the fact that the emphatic double negation signaling an absolute denial (*oudamêi oudamôs*, picking up the *ouk an pote dunaito* at 875b4) gets limited by a qualification ("except," *all' ê*) in the clause "In fact (*nun de*), however, it is so nowhere or in any way, except *kata brakhu*" at the end of [C].[41] Does not exceptionality imply (real) possibility?

The decision depends on two related determinations. The first concerns the scope of the impossibility in question, the second the meaning that we assign to the (fairly common) quantitative expression *kata brakhu*, which can take different values depending on the kind of quantity or quantifiable term to which it applies. In Plato, we find it in the sense of "briefly," for pronouncements; "gradually," for progression; "rarely," for events; and "in small pieces," for breakable entities.[42] In my 2005 book, I suggested that in the present case the expression does not mean either "in a small amount"[43] or "rarely" (which is admittedly the first meaning that comes to mind when the question at stake is possibility), but "for a short time," which sits well with the fact that the denial of possibility in section [A] specifically and emphatically bears on maintaining a certain conviction (*emmeinai toutôi tôi dogmati*, 875b4) and living accordingly through one's whole life (*diabiônai*, b5), specifically by giving priority to the common political good over the private (alleged) interest. On this reading, *kata brakhu* takes into account a momentary possibility which cannot count as the more robust possibility that is required in the case of a monarch.[44] So what is possible in a sense turns out to be actually impossible.

The complementary passage in Book 4.709d10–712a7, to which I now turn, is equally slippery.[45] It is part of the technical preliminaries to legislation that aim to identify "the easiest and quickest way" (711a2–3, cf. 710d8) to bring about a political change (*metabolê*).[46] A "true lawgiver," meaning one who would, hypothetically, possess true political expertise, is unable to implement his project if he does not have at his disposal a force (*rhômê*) capable of mastering "the mightiest persons in the city" (who would presumably mount the strongest resistance to changes that are not in their interest, as they see it). What is needed is a force that is simultaneously the smallest numerically and the strongest possible. The most efficient regime from this point of view is a tyranny (709e6, 710d8, 711a2), whether it resorts to persuasion (for tyrants too know to persuade) or to violence (711b8–c4). The other regimes can then be ranked according to their degree of efficiency: after tyranny comes monarchy, then "a certain (i.e., moderate) form of democracy," and oligarchy takes the last place.[47]

The tyrant whom the lawgiver conjures as the fulfillment of his fondest wish (*euksasthai*, 709d2, *eukhê*, d5; compare *Republic* 6.499c4–5 for the implication of impossibility) is not a tyrant in the ordinary sense of the term; his name is a placeholder for a neutral political power that could, circumstances permitting, foster virtue rather than vice (cf. 711b7–9). This tyrant, an unusual figure in the writings of Plato, who rarely bestows a positive evaluation on the word 'tyrant,' is closer in a sense to real historical situations than his own philosopher-king.[48] The wished for tyrant will possess qualities which make of him, if not a full-fledged philosopher, at least a man with a philosophical "nature," according to the passage of the *Republic* that is almost literally quoted at this juncture: he will be young, endowed with a good memory, quick to learn, courageous, generous, and temperate.[49] If "chance" (*tukhê*, 710c8, cf. *eutukhês*, c7) causes him to cross the path of an expert lawgiver (the situation could in principle have been, but in fact was not, that of Dionysus II of Syracuse receiving Plato at his court[50]), the god will then have done all that is possible for the happiness of his city.

In what follows, a shift is noticeable. The complementary figures of absolute power and full legislative expertise, distributed at first between two different individuals, come gradually together, until the conclusion, at 711d6–712a3, re-introduces the model of the individual in whom power and wisdom coexist. The condition that results from the best constitution and the best laws (712a2) is described in terms that are again practically identical to those of the *Republic*: "when the greatest power coincides (*hotan . . . sumpesêi*) in a human being with wisdom (*phronein*) and temperance (*sôphronein*), then the genesis of the best regime develops (*phuetai* [. . .] *genesis*), and laws of the same kind; other-wise, there is no way that this would occur" (711e8–712a3).[51]

The word "tyrant" does not appear here; it has been replaced by its func-tion, that is the highest degree of political power. As for "wisdom," it may here refer to the political expertise that figures prominently in the *Statesman*, rather than (or as well as) to the philosophical knowledge of the *Republic*. To this extent, it may not be entirely accurate to identify the powerful and wise person with the *philosopher*-king; but the relevant point is that the passage clearly asserts that given "the immensity of time" (*en tôi pollôi khronôi*, 711d2–3), a coincidence of this kind may arguably have happened. *A fortiori*, it is 'possible,' in some sense of the term.

And yet Plato makes clear in the very same breath that the affirmation of the possibility of a wise ruler as a *real* possibility depends on an assumption about the nature of 'time' that in effect suppresses the difference between gods and heroes on the one hand and human beings on the other hand—a differ-ence on which the entire legislative project of the *Laws* relies. Having evoked "the nature of Nestor" as a possible embodiment of a virtuous political ruler, "[. . .] Nestor, who is said to have surpassed all human beings in temperance (*tôi sôphronein*) even more than he surpassed them in the power of speaking (*têi tou legein rhômei*)" (711e1–3),[52] the Athenian immediately adds a qualifica-tion that amounts to a denial of its real possibility as far as human beings are concerned. The point is that time is not homogeneous. "The time of Troy" (*epi Troias*) to which Nestor belongs is distinct from "our time" (*eph'hêmôn*, 711e4). Thus, the initial assertion, at the beginning of section [A], according to which "There is no nature of any human beings that is capable both of knowing [. . .] and, knowing this, to be able and willing always to [. . .]," which could *in princi-ple* register an empirical fact[53] rather than an impossibility *de jure* ("in the immensity of time"), turns out actually to be an impossibility *de jure* in a pe-riod of time when human beings are, as they are in the present day, quite other than "gods and children of gods" (5.739d6). This clear-cut distinction recurs in Book 9: "But we are not legislating, as did the ancient lawgivers, for children of gods, the heroes, as the present account has it; they themselves sprang from gods and legislated for others who were born from those; we are human beings legislating now for the seeds of human beings" (9.853c3–7).[54]

The story of Nestor at Troy (which is called a *muthos*) may be true, and to this extent, may serve as an "oracle" for a future that is left undetermined (712a4–5) and can be only hoped for. This is the reason why it is the matter of a "wish" or a "prayer" (*eukhê, eukhesthai*).[55] In the epic traditions, as they were interpreted by and reflected among others in the *Iliad*, the Trojan War brought heroic times to their end.[56] Ours is a time of human beings, and human beings are necessarily corrupted, in Plato's perspective, by the actual exercise of power.[57] Once again, 'possible,' in Plato's both odd and deep construal of possibility, turns out to be compatible with the 'impossible.'

The Moot Question of Utopia

At this point, we might ask whether it is legitimate, or for that matter helpful, to think of Plato's just city (as well as the first city of the *Laws*, which, as I have already hinted at, does not coincide with the former) as a utopia. The situation is as elusive as the concept of utopia itself.[58]

Given that in some sense of the term 'possible,' the just city of the *Republic* is possible in Plato's view, it is perfectly understandable that he uses the language of 'wish' (*eukhê*, the object of one's prayer and aspiration) and 'dream' (*onar*) to refer to what his just city is *not*.[59] To this extent, the modern word 'utopia,' in as much as it implies 'wishful thinking' or a 'pure dream,' cannot appropriately be applied to Plato's just city. But when Cicero in his *De re publica* presents Plato's just city as "an object of wish rather than of expectation,"[60] the implication is that it in fact *is* a dream. As for opponents of Plato's political program, they use these very terms and other deprecatory ones to characterize what Plato's 'beautiful city' (*Kallipolis*)[61] is from their critical point of view, namely, to quote Jacob Brucker's famous formula, "a fiction that could exist only in Plato's brain."[62] If 'utopia' is taken in this negative sense, then Plato's critics are perfectly entitled to call Plato's proposal a 'utopia,' or for that matter a dystopia. What the term conveys in this case is a negative judgement which does not claim to reflect Plato's views on the subject.

The true complication, however, lies elsewhere. It consists in the fact that in virtue of Plato's paradigmatism, there is a sense of the word 'possible' that is compatible with an impossibility of a sort (the impossibility, namely, of reproducing the model in practice exactly as it is in speech). To this extent, there is no reason after all why 'impossible' could not be used to characterize

Plato's just city in the *Republic*, and hence no reason not to refer to it as a utopia (implying unrealizability).

Two objections have been raised against this characterization. The first is that the word *utopia* is anachronistic, since the neologism was introduced by Thomas More in 1512 in his *De optimo rei publicæ statu, deque nova insula Utopia* ("On the Best State of a Republic and on the New Island of Utopia"). The second objection is that the just city of the *Republic* does not share the characteristic traits of the literary genre spawned by Thomas More's work (nor for that matter does the *Republic* considered as a whole). It is not framed as the discovery of a certain island at the end of a sea voyage where, by definition, an ideal state is presented as realized.[63] This last objection is superficial, because it rests on a specialized, restricted definition of "utopia" which may be useful to define the literary corpus, but which appears as an implausible purism if it is meant to bar further application of a notion that would turn out to be extremely powerful in later intellectual history and in history *tout court*. For it is certainly not illegitimate to extend the meaning of the word 'utopia' beyond the specific use that Thomas More made of it, provided that the extended meaning retains some essential features that are felicitously captured in the word.

As for the first objection, one can argue, positively, that the word *utopia*, late as it is, no less felicitously captures the *question* that is articulated in the *Republic*, or for that matter in a number of other ancient works describing ideal states.[64] This is true whether the prefixed *u-* of *utopia* represents a negation (*ou* in Greek) so that More's title is taken to mean a *nonexisting place*, a notion that was on More's mind before the publication of the book (he calls it *Nusquama* in his correspondence with Erasmus) or rather, as More finally decided, it represents the adverb *eu*, taking *utopia* to mean *a good place*.[65] Aristophanes' *Birds* (v. 9) refers to the city of birds as being "nowhere on earth" (*oude pou gês*)—a line that Plato must have had in mind when, at the end of *Republic* 9, he has Socrates countering Glaucon's observation that Socrates' "city in words" is "nowhere on earth" (*gês* [...] *oudamou*), with the suggestion that it may be "lying in heaven as a model (*paradeigma*)."[66]

Thus, what is at stake in Plato's *Republic* cannot be reduced to either an unproblematized reading of Plato's final statement ("it is possible") or to the verdict of his anti-utopian critics ("it is impossible"). To this extent, Kant was right when, reacting against Brucker, he construed Plato's just city as an Ideal of reason and a regulative principle.[67]

Of course, Plato and Kant work with two very different conceptions of 'possibility': for Kant, 'to exist' amounts to "to be posited."[68] By contrast, in

Plato's construal 'to come into being' is not 'to be' in the strong, proper sense of the term. Between Being and Becoming, *lexis* and *praxis*, there is an ontological loss. But this is precisely what makes it possible to treat the model not only as a regulative Idea, but as a utopia. For, in spite of additional complexities that will be addressed in the next chapter, it does capture the distinction, in the language of Plato's *Laws*, between a "first city," which, desirable as it may be, is a city conceived "for gods and sons of gods" and a "second city," which is meant for human beings (e.g., 5.739d6-e1). In this sense, Plato himself can be seen as fathering the long and enduring tradition of his anti-utopian critics—a fascinating situation in its own right.

3

Paradigm and Retreats

A central line was called "the holy line," since the loser resorted to it last of all;
whence the proverb, "to move from the holy line," used of people in despair
needing to turn to their last resource. [. . .] Alcaeus gives the saying in full:
"and now he is master, having moved the stone from the holy line."

EUSTATHIUS, *COMMENTARY ON ILIAD* 6.169,
TRANS. D. CAMPBELL

The Duplication of the Paradigm

"But let us try first to found (*katoikizein*) the city in speech (*logôi*)," says Clinias at the end of Book 3 of the *Laws* (702e2–3). This will be Plato's second city, no less a city "in speech" than the just city of the *Republic* (*logôi*, 2.369a6). And yet, contrary to the *Republic*, the *Laws* receives its main momentum from a 'practical' question. It is important to get clear about what 'practical' means here. To begin with, the characterization of the *Laws* as practically oriented may seem to be problematic if one looks at it from the point of view of the distinction between *lexis* and *praxis* as drawn in the *Republic*, since the notion of a 'practical realization in speech' rings distinctly oxymoronic. This apparent snag in logic, however, aptly captures a double-sidedness that is essential to the *Laws*. For what the *Laws* aims at is simultaneously (a) to provide a 'practical' version, though still at a theoretical level, of the paradigm set up principally in the *Republic* and in so doing sketch the guidelines for a constitution to be realized, and (b) to provide guidance for implementations at a further 'practical' level—his example is Magnesia, in the circumstances described in the dialogue.[1] The simultaneity of these two aims does not entail their identity.

53

They must on the contrary be kept distinct, the more so as they do to some extent converge. The practical project of a new Cretan settlement mentioned at the end of Book 3 is subordinated to the general aim, of which it constitutes the pretext.

The general scope of the practical project, which is the Athenian's primary concern, comes to the fore in Book 5, with the evocation of the paradigm from which the *Laws* "draws back," or, to use a metaphor that he employs a bit later (5.746c2) in a related context, "deviates from" (*ekklinein*):[2] "This is why one should not look elsewhere [i.e., than to the *Laws*' 'first city'[3]] for a paradigm (*paradeigma*), at any rate, of a constitution (*politeia*), but should hold on to this one and seek the constitution which is most like it as far as possible (*tên hoti malista toiautên zêtein kata dunamin*" (5.739e1–3).[4]

A few pages later, however, the term *paradeigma* turns out to apply not only, as in its first occurrence at 5.739e1, to the first city, but also to the second city, the economic characteristics of which have in the meantime been disclosed (*ta nun eirêmena panta*, 5.745e8–9, referring to 741e7–746e6). Anticipating a possible objection as to the realizability of his proposals, which are 'true' in a certain, perhaps weaker sense of the term (*alêthê* [. . .] *tina tropon*, 746b5), the Athenian observes:

> [. . .] that for each future action considered, the most just thing to do is this: he who shows the paradigm (*paradeigma*) for how the thing that is attempted ought to be must not in any way abandon (*apoleipein*) its finest and [746c] and truest features; but in the event that it is impossible (*adunaton*) for someone that some of it come about, he should deviate from this very feature (*touto* [. . .] *auto ekklinein*) and not act on it; instead, whatever among the rest is the closest (*eggutata*) to it and is the most akin (*suggenestaton*) to what is appropriate to do, he must contrive that this comes about, and let the lawgiver fulfill his wish (*telos epitheinai têi boulêsei*);[5] once this has occurred, he should then investigate in common with him which of his proposals are useful and what in the proposed legislation is too arduous (*prosantes*). For even a craftsman (*dêmiourgos*) of the meanest [746d] object, if he is going to be worth mentioning, must produce something that is consistent with itself, I suppose (5.746b5–d2).[6]

The relationship that was taken to hold between the first and the second city at 739a1–3 is now said to hold between the second city and its realization in certain circumstances and conditions (cf. 745e7–746a1). The expression "most beautiful and most true" now applies not to the first paradigmatic city, but to the second, in virtue of its, too, being a paradigm.[7]

The paradigm of a second city that would approach the first city in the closest possible way turns out to be, in some crucial respects, quite different from it, as we shall see shortly, to the point that it requires in certain cases just the contrary of what the (first) paradigm demands.[8] This should cause no surprise, since the conditions of realization in question are very different indeed in the *Republic* and the *Laws*. The point here is not that the political project of the *Laws* has been developed with a view to a concrete case, that of the new settlement in a proximate future announced at the end of Book 3, by contrast with the *Republic* which at the end of Book 7 fleetingly evokes what would be the best condition for initiating a political change.[9] For whereas the shaping of a new constitution for Magnesia (a city which happens to be located in Crete) helps to focus on the idea of a realization *hic et nunc*, it is definitely neither the only nor the main consideration that guides the institutions worked out in the *Laws*. Next to and above the 'now' of the Cretan colony, there is the 'now' of our actual humanity (*eph'hêmôn*), as opposed to the heroic 'time of Troy' (4.711e4).[10] The possibility of coming closer to the paradigm of the first city than the second city would ever be able to come rests on the quite remote chance that heroic times might someday return.

Completion and Revision

The centrality given in the *Laws* to the question of realization, with its complexities, has wide-ranging consequences. The first of these is quantitative rather than substantial: whereas the legislation laid out in the *Republic* was reduced, beyond the provocative, to the indispensable minimum and remained there at the level of general principles and broad orientations (to be fleshed out by the future rulers),[11] it is highly detailed in the *Laws*, even if quite a few regulations are omitted and some (limited) room is left for later refinements and revisions.[12] This might suggest, as it did in a sense suggest to Aristotle and seems to have suggested to Cicero, too, that Plato's *Laws* is only engaging in a *completion* of the legislative program of the *Republic*.[13] Whereas there is *some* truth in this construal, since a number of legislative regulations stated in the *Laws* can be seen as unpacking principles formulated in the *Republic* (for example and most conspicuously all that concerns children's education in Book 7), it is also and more importantly the case that the completion derives from a fundamental *revision* of the original paradigm that the *Laws* now cashes out in a systematic way. This is to be seen in all the laws, most of them central to the new scheme, that represent a weakening—which may be stronger or lighter—of the regulations advocated in the *Republic*, such as the attribution of tenured allotments to the 5,040 households which serve as an illustration for the second, more general focal center of the work:

> First, have them distribute the land and the households and have them not farm in common, since this has been said to be too much for the present generation, upbringing, and education (*meizon è kata tên nun genesin kai trophên kai paideusin*). And so have them manage the distribution bearing in mind a thought of the following kind, namely that each who receives a portion must think of it as the common property of the whole city and take care of it more than a mother her children since the land belongs to his fatherland and also is a goddess who is the mistress of us mortal beings [. . .]. (5.739e8–740a7)[14]

This revision, which is presented as a "retreat from the sacred line" at 5.739a1, far from calling into question the unity of Plato's political thought, is its clearest expression. One can even say that Plato's overall project as a political thinker precisely *consists in* the articulation of a fundamental tension, the purest and most radical form of which is to be found in the polarity (irreducible in the end, though resistible to a certain extent) between the human and the divine.[15] The centrality of the question of possibility, in the perspective of implementing the paradigm, derives from this polarity.

A Parallel with the *Timaeus*

The lawgiver of the *Laws*, no less than the philosopher of the *Republic*, is a craftsman, potentially at least (should he become associated with political power). But whereas the genesis of the real, non-paradigmatical city is passed over in the *Republic* (since only its condition of possibility is dealt with), the *Laws* accomplishes for the city, *mutatis mutandis*, the equivalent of what the *Timaeus* does in the domain of cosmo-physiology.[16] Both the *Laws* and the *Timaeus* include a detailed (though not exhaustive) account of the whole (the world, the city) they respectively consider, as well as of its most important parts and components. The relevant section of the *Timaeus* begins with the totality of the world (*to pan*, 29d7) and moves downward to the world-soul and the heavens, moves on to the different kinds of living beings, and finally looks at human psychology and physiology; the *Laws*, the progression of which is much more sinuous, elaborates an encompassing system of legislation and explores the details of constitutional mechanisms and everyday life's regulations.

The parallel holds when it comes to the highest explanatory principles. Corresponding to the 'paradigm' (*paradeigma*, *Timaeus* 28a6–7, 31a3–4, 48e4–49a1) to which the Demiurge is looking as he orders the world; i.e., the living being that encompasses all other intelligible living beings (30c3–d1), we have the paradigm of the 'first city': in place of the material receptacle (*khôra*) from which the elementary triangles and the four elements first emerge in the *Timaeus* (49a1–55c6, developing 30a3–6), we get the human material, out of which the lawgiver (also a human being) generates a political body. Even more striking—and deep in its implications—is the fact that the Demiurge, who has to face the constraints of the "necessity" that the material receptacle imposes upon him, just as the lawgiver of the *Laws* does, is able to "persuade" (*peithein*) this necessity, in virtue of a disposition of the *khôra* itself to be shaped by the Forms of which it contains "traces," in the same way as newborns take spontaneous pleasure from orderly movements and music, which makes possible their further education.[17]

The *Laws*, however, incorporates a dimension that is not relevant in the case of the cosmo-physiological account of the *Timaeus*. The difference is between the history of a world that can be called 'natural,' one that ends up with the formation of human living beings, and a human history which is not reducible to this natural history although it is part of it. What is at stake is the existence of two different temporalities: at the end of the *Timaeus*, the world, with the human beings that are one of its components and are now ready to actuate, will have been generated forever, whereas the city of the *Laws* is still to be realized.[18] Hence the importance given in the *Laws*, upstream, to the lessons of past history (in Book 3) and, downstream, to the indeterminacy of the future, with the recurrent evocation of different options and of choices that actual lawgivers will have to make in due time. The material which these human lawgivers deal with, far from having the prime indeterminacy of the *khôra*/'material receptacle' of the *Timaeus*, results from previous trajectories, both individual and collective, that the filtering of would-be citizens of the new colony cannot alter, even if the lawgivers may also hope to be able to match past achievements (illustrated by cases such as Sparta, Ancient Athens and Cyrus' Persia in Book 3). As for the lawgivers, they are, unlike the divine craftsman of the *Timaeus*, human beings, whose relationship to 'the good' may not be as immediate as that of the Demiurge, who *is* essentially good (cf. *Timaeus*, 29e1), and whose human action depends on other human beings. It is in this context that the mention at *Laws* 5.739a7 and e5, of a "third" city in addition to the first two cities (the best and the second-best), makes sense. Whereas this third city has *something* to do with the city that will eventually come into existence, outside the scope of the dialogue, on the territory of the Cretan Magnesia, it represents above all the entire series of possible cities that could be founded under conditions that Plato does not specify, but which will be different from those that the Cretan colony offers.[19]

Types of Distancing

The necessary steering away from the 'first city' is already at work in the *Laws* in Books 3 and 4, with the formulation of the "axiom of corrupting power" (as I call it), according to which excessive political power is bound to be abused to serve selfish interests.[20] But it is not thematized as such before what I have identified as the second focal center of the work, which occurs in Book 5.739a1–e7 and regards the issue of land distribution, which it introduces (739e8–741a5), before, that is, the setting up in Book 6 of the constitutional framework for the main legislative body of the *Laws*. This positioning is significant as it places the legislation to come (both constitution and laws) in the light of its guiding principle: the requirement to take into account what is ineradicably "proper" (*idion*) to human nature. This is because the allotment of land, which is not only an infringement of the strict application of the principle of non-ownership of goods in the *Republic*'s just city, but a renunciation of the principle of the public ownership of women and children (since households host families). There could scarcely be a more vivid illustration of why the institutions of the first city must be trimmed to the measure of human beings.

The *Laws* is in effect dominated by the figure of a 'retreat,' which Plato compares at 5.739a1 with the retreat of a pebble, in a board game, from a line called "the sacred line." The proverbial phrase "to move the pebble from the sacred line," first attested in Alcaeus,[21] was put to a variety of uses and interpretations in Antiquity, but in the context of the *Laws*, it is best taken to illustrate inescapable necessity.[22] The move from "the sacred line" on the board (with a feminine substantive, *grammê*, understood in the Greek) becomes in the *Laws* a move away from something "sacred" in general (*phora* [. . .] *aph' hierou*, in the neuter, 739a1), i.e., from the divine.[23]

The coordinates of this "retreat from the sacred," when it comes to politics rather than board games, are spelled out by way of two related pairs of opposites. Generally speaking, the city of the *Laws* is said to occupy the 'second rank' in contrast to the 'best.'[24] More specifically, its institutions are directed to human beings (*anthrôpoi*), as opposed to gods, "children of gods" or heroes, all of whom represent different versions (and gradations) of the "sacred."[25] The two pairs of opposites are functionally equivalent (cf. 739d5–e3). This implies that the 'first' (the best) and the 'second' (i.e., the 'second-best') are not to be conceived as two degrees on a continuous scale, but rather as two orders, separated by a gap that is by definition insuperable—even if the issue is complicated by the fact that the relationship between 'human' and 'divine' is not reducible to a mere opposition, given the divine side of human beings (more on this in the next chapter).

The retreat considered in Book 5, which concerns the allotment of land to the 5,040 households, and not to a specific class of citizens (as in the just city of the *Republic*), is one among others, but it is representative of the rest.[26] In each case, the point is to take into account the inborn human drive that seeks pleasure and avoids pain, either as a concession to human nature or in order to prevent its unfortunate consequences. There are different levels of application. The rule of law, understood as an alternative to the rule of human beings, and the 'middle/mixed' character of the constitution are institutional in nature. [27] But there is also the necessity for the lawgiver to resort to purely human arguments (related to pleasure), next to divine ones (related to virtue) in shaping his preambles (in this case, the general preamble to the laws), given that the quest of pleasure and the avoidance of pain constitute the potentially strongest motivations for human beings.[28] And the very setting of the *Laws* as a whole can be counted as a global retreat. For, although the best way to initiate a constitutional change would be to begin from scratch with a population of children under ten years of age (as suggested at the end of Book 7 of *Republic*), or (according to a formulation that is found only in the *Laws*) under the authority of a (temperate) tyrant (arguably in an actual city with grown up citizens),[29] nevertheless the lawgiver must consider other configurations, among which the setting up of a colony like Magnesia in the circumstances described in the dialogue is arguably the most favorable.[30] Next to these first-order retreats (as one might call them), which touch the relationship between first and a second cities, there are further retreats that respond to the particular circumstances that may and arguably will impede the full adoption of the best human paradigm (i.e., the second city).[31]

There is no systematical treatment of these different retreats in the *Laws*. The relevant passages occur in different books and in different contexts, and no explicit connection is established between them. But all the retreats are unmistakably consonant with the basic anthropological view, first exposed in the puppet analogy in Book 1, according to which human nature (*anthrôpinê phusis*) is under the compulsion of pleasure and pain, feelings that are human nature's most intimate 'property.' To what extent these two forces can be mastered will be the subject of the next chapter.

What Is the Second City Second To?

Although "the sacred line" from which the second city draws back has much to do with the just city of the *Republic*, it cannot be straightforwardly identified with it. As a matter of fact, the *Laws* generates to a certain extent a 'first city' of its own, based in various measures on considerations that come in part from the *Republic*, but also from the *Statesman*, as well as some that originate in the *Laws* itself.

That the "first city" described in the key passage of *Laws* 5.739b8–d5 for the most part adopts traits characteristic of the just city of the *Republic* is beyond doubt, since it refers in a detailed and emphatic way to the public ownership of women, children, and goods, and champions the unanimity of feelings, emotions, and opinions among its citizens (what they praise and blame):[32]

> The first city and constitution and the best laws [739c1] are where the old saying holds as much as possible throughout the whole city: what it says is that really the things that belong to friends are in common. If this is the case somewhere now, or if it should ever exist someday—if women are in common, children are in common, and all possessions are in common—and if what is called 'one's own' (*idion*) has been everywhere completely removed from one's life by all device; if it has been contrived insofar as possible to make somehow common the things that are by nature one's own (*idia*), such as making the eyes, the ears and the hands seem to see and hear and act in common; [739d] if, again, everybody praises and blames at best with one single voice, delighting and feeling pain at the same things, and if laws, whatever they are, produce a city that is unified (*mia*) as far as possible— then no one will ever set down a more correct or better standard (*horos*) of what constitutes absolute perfection as regards virtue than all this. (5.739b8–d5)

There is, however, one formulation in the passage that makes the "first city" of the *Laws* different from the just city of the *Republic*: for whereas the law of public ownership is restricted, in the *Republic*, to the guardians, the *Laws* presents it as on a par with the unanimity of feelings and opinions and the old proverb ("the things that belong to friends are in common") and foresees it "holding as much as possible *throughout the whole city*" (739c1–3). One might observe that this formulation is not necessarily at odds with the restrictive application of the law of public ownership as pertaining to the guardians alone in the *Republic,* since the phrase "holding as much as possible" states a general principle that could be cashed out in just the way that the *Republic* does—in other words, restricting the principle to the guardians would be "just what was possible." But this reading is unlikely in the present case. The *Republic* does not present the scope of the law as a necessary limitation imposed upon a potentially universal principle (whatever the necessity may be), but as a consequence of the function of guardianship itself (the guardians' attention must be entirely geared towards the community, secure from the distraction that a family represents). If that is so, we are led to take at face value the expression "as much as possible throughout the whole city" and to assume that Plato, for the sake of the *Laws,* is modulating the scheme of the *Republic* at the very moment when he emphatically echoes one of its most prominent features. We should, it would seem, distinguish between the *Republic,* referring to the work written by Plato, and the '*Republic*' that he refers to in the *Laws.*[33]

The situation is clearer when it comes to some other prominent features of the second city; namely the rule of law, the 'middle' constitution, and the place given to persuasion (the legislative rhetoric), a set of issues that constitute the core of the political views discussed in the *Statesman,* but which are either conspicuously absent (the institutional framework) or left unproblematized (the scalarity of persuasive discourse) in the *Republic.* A simple enumeration speaks for itself. What we learn in the *Statesman* is: (a) that the king's reason (*nous*) is superior to law in that he can, on the one hand, adapt to individual cases and changing situations and on the other, furnish answers to questions, which is a first reason to rank the law as second best; (b) that there is a difference between a king and a tyrant from the formal point of view of the exercise of power (persuasion vs violence); (c) that an authentic king may never arise; (d) that weaving and mixture are the fundamental categories that must guide the true statesman's action; (e) that the norm is given by the 'right measure' (*metron*), which counts the 'right moment' (*kairos*) as one of its specifications; and, last but not least, (f) that there can be only one true monarch (or at least very few)—all issues that make of the *Statesman* a Janus-like dialogue, looking backwards to the *Republic* and forward to *Laws.* One major difference between the *Statesman* and the *Laws* is that the former rests at the general level of principles, expounded in a discussion that is subordinate to an exploration of the dialectical method, whereas the *Laws* unpacks a political project that brings to light the tensions that remain unresolved or marginalized in the *Statesman*.[34]

There is, moreover, one paradigmatic feature from which the *Laws* draws back that does not feature in the *Republic* and goes beyond what is found in the *Statesman*. This is related to the notion that the law is tyrannical not only in the sense that it is mute, but in the sense that it is formally violent (threatening). A crucial passage in Book 9, to which I shall return in due time, suggests that the preambles introduced at the end of Book 4 as a major legislative novelty may *in principle* be more than exhortations based on praise and blame and may take the form, in ideal circumstances, of a philosophical dialogue based on rational arguments.[35] This ideal of a rational discussion between a lawgiver and a citizen (a properly *legislative* utopia, to be distinguished from a *constitutional* utopia), in comparison to which the rhetorical persuasion that characterizes most of the preambles to the laws appears as yet another 'second-best,' has no counterpart either in the *Republic* or in the *Statesman*. The latter, in spite of its insistence on distinguishing between the king and the tyrant at a relatively early stage of the discussion, also puts forward a view, in a later passage, which runs against the neatness of that distinction. The manner in which the *Laws* tackles the problem confirms that its first city, for all it owes to the *Republic* and the *Statesman*, also rests also on an ideal of its own making. Significantly, this ideal relates hyperbolically to the first of its two focal points, the one whose novelty Plato particularly emphasizes.

A Note on the Titles *Republic* and *Laws*

A systematic approach of the relationship between the *Republic* and the *Laws* in terms of paradigm and approximation leads to reflection on their respective titles. The Greek word that *Republic* translates is *politeia*, a more usual and better, if not perfect, rendering of which would be (the) "constitution." (Not perfect, because a *politeia* is not reducible to its constitutional framework, but includes the way in which the citizens behave and live their lives within that framework.)[36] Although the title *Republic*, which derives from Cicero's *De re publica*, captures an essential dimension of Plato's political project—the public thing, or interest, is what is common to all the citizens—something gets lost in the translation: namely, the fact that *politeia* (constitution) and *nomoi* (laws) are interconnected concepts. The relation in question is a flexible one, but on one construal of the pair, which is attested in the *Laws* itself, a *politeia*/constitution primarily defines the structure of political bodies (councils, assemblies, offices and the procedure for the selection of officeholders), whereas the laws lay down the norms that political authorities are to implement in the exercise of their functions.[37] That Cicero was aware of this complementary relationship is shown by an observation he puts in Marcus' mouth in his own *Laws* (*De legibus*): "Plato, who is the first to have written on the *res publica*, and also in a separate work about its (*eius*) laws. . . ."[38]

This construction is problematic in two complementary respects: on the one hand, the *Republic/Constitution* formulates laws that are laws of its own; and on the other hand, the *Laws* also includes a constitution which differs in important ways from that of the *Republic*—in spite of the similarities that unite the two projects.[39] Moreover, the constitution in question is also construed by Plato as a piece of legislation when he refers to the constitution as "the laws of the constitution" (5.734e5).[40]

Is there a way, then, to account for the two titles? One could of course say that *Politeia* being already taken, *Laws* would recommend itself as a handy substitute, given that the two notions are tightly associated. A stronger hypothesis is possible, however, if we accept that Plato's analysis of the law in the *Laws* (which is unique to this dialogue) is ultimately taken between the two poles of its noetic content, which is 'normative,' and its form, which is violent.[41] For this tension suggests that, from the point of view that takes agreement and friendship as a constitutive element of a political community, the question of law is in a sense more fundamental than the question of the constitution, even though, in another sense, the latter remains prior to the former (a double perspective that the composition of the *Laws* reflects, with the developments of Book 4 through 5 on the law and the preamble preceding the constitution of Book 6, which is then followed by the laws in the remaining books). In this perspective, focusing on the laws is itself a consequence of the global retreat the *Laws* instantiates: one could say that Plato's *Constitution* is now explicitly read for what it is, namely "*The Constitution*" (meaning: the constitution *par excellence*).[42]

4

What Is Human?

Grace appears most purely in that human form which has either no consciousness or an infinite consciousness. That is, in the puppet or in the god.

KLEIST, "ON THE MARIONETTE THEATER"

A City for Human Beings

If the *Laws* sketches civic institutions that are in second place, and if their being 'second' derives from the fact that they are designed not for "gods or children of gods," but for human beings, then it makes sense to say that, in the light of 'possibility,' namely human or real possibility, these institutions are the best ones possible. The importance of this point is obvious, for it means that it is in the *Laws*, not in the *Republic*, that we find Plato's picture of the *really* (if not truly, according to Plato's strongest construal of truth) best city.[1]

The next question is, then, what kind of being is a human being or, what boils down to the same thing, what kind of a thing is his soul.[2] To put it in comparative terms: in what respect does a human being differ from a god, given that the "gods and children of gods" that Plato is appealing to in the relevant contexts very much resemble, immortality apart, human beings? Indeed, gods and heroes would seem to be much like the human beings who might be able to live in the first city (a remarkable anthropomorphic view of the gods that is pretty much in keeping with the traditional representations of the gods): "whether gods or the children of gods inhabit (*oikousi*) such a city, they administer (*katoikousi*) it in this way, with more than one passing their whole life in happiness" (5.739d6–8).[3]

64

The point of putting the question in comparative terms is that, whereas human beings are not gods, they cannot be said to be human *simpliciter*, either: human beings need to be educated in the proper way in order to become the kind of tame animal they are, namely a tame animal that, in spite of *being* tame, needs all the same to *be tamed*, which means educated. In fact, this process makes them as tame and divine as animals can be. The notion gets its clearest formulation in a passage in Book 6 where the Athenian, discussing the best constitution, makes the office of curator of education (*ho tês paideias epimelêtês*, 6.765d4–5) "by far the greatest of the highest offices in the city" (*tôn en têi polei akrotatôn arkhôn polu megistên*, 765e2):

> The human being, we assert, is gentle (*hêmeron*); still, if this being benefits from a correct education and a fortunate nature, it is wont to become the most divine and the most gentle animal, but if its upbringing is insufficient or not of the right kind, it is the most savage of all that earth makes grow. (6.766a1–4)[4]

Plato's Anthropology

Plato's fullest exposition in the *Laws* of what a human being is and is capable of features early in the work (1.644c1–645c1) as part of the section dedicated to the seemingly subordinate question of how drinking wine can be made into a useful educational tool in the framework of regulated wine parties (*symposia*), which Spartan institutions prohibit, as they do other opportunities for getting drunk (1.636e8–637b6).[5] Its deeper function, however, is to serve as a first step towards a general definition of education (*paideia*, see 1.645c1–6) which will eventually make of "choral dance" (*khoreia*) the basis of an educative process that occupies not only the early years, but, alongside other more advanced types of learning, the entirety of a human life (2.653b1–c4).

The starting point of the exposition is a clarification of the current expression "to be superior (*kreittôn*) [or inferior (*hêttôn*)] than oneself," which makes sense both to the Athenian (at 1.626d1–2 and e7–8) and to Clinias (at 626e2–5), although arguably not on the same grounds.[6] This is the same issue as the one raised in the *Republic* in an account of self-control/*enkrateia* at 4.430e6–431a1. What the phrase means is difficult to fathom if the "one" in question is taken to be a homogeneous entity. In the case of a city, one sees how to cash out the claim: "to be better than itself" will be a way of saying that within one and the same city, a group of citizens (which is immediately identified with the minority of better and just citizens) defeats the majority (which by the same token is composed of worse and unjust individuals); and the other way round for "to be worse than *itself.*" But how does the expression apply to a single individual? The issue requires clarification (1.644b6-c1). In the *Republic*, a first step towards the upcoming argument about the tripartition of the soul (4.435c4–441c8) consists in the admission that there is, within one and the same individual, a better and a worse component (4.431a4–5). In the *Laws*, the description of the psychological make-up and dynamic that constitutes a human being, not being bound by the tri-functional model of the city that is distinctive of the *Republic* (producers-warriors-philosophers), focuses on the primary divide between "better" and "worse." The description takes the form of a comparison between a human being and a certain kind of puppet, *thauma* in Greek. The initial triad, which in spite of obvious points of contact and overlap differs from the one that the *Republic* makes correspond to the political tripartition (appetite/*to epithumêtikon*—spirit/*to thumoeidês*—reasoning component/*logistikon*[7]), is rapidly absorbed in the more fundamental dyadic scheme.

Each of us, while being an individual 'one' (*hena*), shelters in himself a triad of "states" (*pathê*, 1.644e1):[8] pleasure and pain (which I shall call 'feelings'); "beliefs about the future" (*doxas mellontôn*) which are types of "expectation" (*elpis*); namely, confidence (*tharros*) and fear (*phobos*);[9] and, in the third place, "reasoning (*logismos*) as to which among them [i.e., of feelings and expectations] is better or worse."[10] This is the reasoning that is said, succinctly and somewhat parenthetically, but emphatically, to "receive the name of law when it becomes the belief (*dogma*) of a city" (644d2–3, repeated at 644e6–645a2 with slight variations; the belief is arguably the end result of the reasoning). These three states that occur in a single self are motives for action. Pleasure and pain, the most rudimentary of feelings and the ultimate sources of expectations, are united, beyond their contrariety (*enantiô*, 644c6), by their inability to reflect (they are 'deprived of sense,' *aphrone, ibid.*). If they play the role of 'counselors' (*sumboulô, ibid.*) it is not because they reason and communicate reasons, but because of the power of attraction or repulsion they exert on the soul. Their blind "advice" is reflected both in inappropriate attitudes toward the future and in our reasoning, when it goes wrong and thus ceases to be 'fine' (*logismos kalos*, 645a5).[11]

The three states/*pathê* are compared to "tendons or strings inside us that are drawing us and pulling one another in opposite directions" (1.644e2–3), like the strings of a puppet (*thauma*).[12] Fine reasoning is like a golden cord, precious but solitary and fragile, which is also called "sacred" (*hiera*, 645a1). The rest, both primary feelings and derivative psychic states, are multifarious and, taken collectively, as hard as iron. What comes about when rational pulling is victorious (*nikâi*, 645a7) over nonrational is excellence/virtue (*aretê*); wickedness (*kakia*) results when the pulling of nonrational motivations defeats beautiful, correct reasoning.[13]

The Athenian suggests that with this account of the human puppets' make-up and the two options it offers, "the story of virtue may well have been saved" (645b1–2),[14] and the meaning of the expression "to be superior [or inferior] to oneself" has become "in a certain way more obvious" (645b1–3). Both the restriction 'in certain way' (*tropon tina*) and the (correlated) comparative ('more obvious') are noteworthy. For even if the clarification yielded by the image (*eikôn*, 644c1) will serve as a basis for explaining, in the section that follows and extends almost to the end of Book 2, what education (*paideia*) in general consists in (and why wine can be put to good use in the educative process), it leaves unanswered three interconnected questions (no one of which is explicit in the text): First, in what does the assistance that (fine) reasoning as well as the law, which is its political expression, *consist*? Second, where does this assistance *come from* (it can't be from the rational motivation itself, since it is the cord that is requesting assistance in the first place)? Finally, what *kind of victory* of the golden kind over the other ones is contemplated (1.645a7–8), given that the aim of the struggle is peace? An answer to these three questions ultimately depends on an analysis of the concept of 'law' that goes much beyond its quasi-parenthetic characterization, in the description of the puppet's make-up, as "the common belief (*dogma ... koinon*) of a city" (1.644d2-3, cf. 644e6–645e2). I shall return to them in the course of this essay.[15] But the issue of 'victory' can at least be anticipated on the basis of a closer consideration of what being a puppet (*thauma*) exactly entails.[16]

A Wonderful Puppet

Human beings are compared to puppets (*thauma*) that are said to be "divine" (*theion*, 1.644d6–7). Fundamental features of Plato's anthropology depend on how we construe not only the qualification, but the substantive itself.

The word *thauma* originally means 'wonder,' 'object of admiration.' It is in this sense that Plato and Aristotle use the term, when they make *thauma* the origin of philosophy.[17] It is also used, usually in the plural, for puppets and, when appropriate, for self-moving mechanisms (*automata*), as well as for other tricks (including magic).[18] The reason is, obviously, that puppets (and *automata* even more) are astonishing objects: by means of strings (called, among other things, *neura*, lit. "tendons") manipulated by external or mechanical tractions, they artificially produce movements that by nature belong to living beings. There is no doubt that it is in this derived sense that the word *thauma* must be taken in the passage of the *Laws* under consideration, where puppets appropriately illustrate the dynamics of human motivation as pulls exerted by different strings in opposite directions. It would be a mistake, however, to disregard the connotation conveyed by the first meaning of the word: for there is a sense in which the human puppet *is* a wonder—a connotation that is also reflected in Aristotle's sentence about *thauma* being the origins of philosophy, where he refers to "those of the puppets that are self-moving [i.e., the *automata*]."[19] This aspect of Plato's human puppet has been ignored by most commentators. As far as I can see, this is due to an inadequate understanding of the word "divine" in the phrase "divine puppet"/*thauma theion*.

This formula has generally been read in the light of the later passage in Book 7, which, referring explicitly to Book 1, describes the human puppet as "devised [namely, by the god himself] as a certain play-thing of god [in the singular]" (*theou ti paignion memêkhanemenon*, 7.803c4–5).[20] According to this reading, "divine" in the "divine puppet" of Book 1 would be a way of saying "belonging to the god," and the condition of being a play-thing (*paignion*) a consequence of this belonging. This easily leads to a bleak, pessimistic view of the human condition as that of puppets in the hands of the gods. Megillus' reaction goes in this direction ("Stranger, you are thoroughly vilifying our human race!" 7.804b5–6).

But it's a bit more complicated. It is true that Plato here provides some support for a pessimistic reading of the comparison of human beings with puppets. For, while the alternatives posed by the Athenian at 1.644d8–9— whether the human puppet must be seen as an entertainment for the gods (*paignion ekeinôn*) or might serve some serious purpose—is left open in Book 1 on the grounds that human knowledge is limited,[21] he definitely opts, in Book 7, for the first hypothesis, which is certainly open to a disparaging interpretation of the kind Megillus puts forward. On the other hand, the fact that human beings are conceived as puppets for the entertainment of the gods does not mean that they are worthless, and this is the sense of the Athenian's reply. To be sure, the worth that human beings possess is low, compared to that represented by the gods, but it is far from nonexistent: for not only must games played by the gods arguably be as serious as games can be, but, more importantly, human beings are animals of a kind capable of becoming, as noted above, "the most [. . .] divine animal," provided that they are appropriately educated with the aim that their best rational motivations overcome the nonrational ones. So, whereas the epithet "divine"/*theion* applied to the puppet is compatible with the idea that human beings "belong to the god(s)" (a thought that returns in the *Laws* and is attested elsewhere in Plato[22]), it is also the case that the gods do not arbitrarily "play" with them, as the expression "play-thing of the gods" might mistakenly suggest. The gods are not pulling the strings of human beings; they might even take pleasure in the spectacle virtuous human beings have to offer.[23] In sum, the adjective "divine" in Book 1, while presupposing the idea that human beings are "possessions of the gods," points in the first place to the possibility that they may become what they are (tame animals) by engaging in a process of divinization.[24]

The Fragility of Choral Dance

The wonder that puppets present when harmoniously moved has an analogy, and in fact its first manifestation, in the human attraction to music and dancing, provided that dancing is construed (as Plato construes it) as a pleasurable sequence of ordered, harmoniously coordinated movements: dance of this kind provides a paradigmatic, low-level but for this very reason crucial case of a human convergence between pleasure and reason.

The argument at 2.653d7–654a7 distinguishes human beings from other animals in that the latter are not sensitive, as the former are, to the difference between disordered movements and sounds and ordered ones, which are rhythmic and harmonious (and to this extent rational): this is to be seen in newborn children, who take pleasure, beyond agitation and yelling, in regular rocking and appropriate singing. This is wonder in its primitive stage. The association of pleasure with virtue would not be possible without this foundational convergence, which is a potentiality out of which other forms of wonder can emerge. Education builds on it.

The pleasure provided by dance, which is present from early childhood, perpetuates itself in the delight (*khara*) felt by adult citizens, whether participating in or enjoying the spectacle of the chorus (*khoros*) during religious feasts, which are an essential part of the life of the citizen in Plato's city, as was the case in Athens.[25] This is the reason why choral dance is at the center of the program of education that Plato sketches in Book 2, in the wake of the comparison between human beings and puppets, and in the more detailed discussion of Book 7.[26] Dancing and singing, provided that they are performed in the appropriate way, are a first step to the divinization of the human puppets as they progress on their way to meeting the gods' and god's expectation.[27]

The path to divinization, however, is long and arduous, as is the path to virtue itself (cf. 4.718e1–719a3, with the quote from Hesiod[28]). The difficulty, which makes the wonder what it is, is rooted in the fact that pleasure, while it is spontaneously (as the result of a divine gift) associated with order and harmony, knows of other sources as well, which are distinctively human: for every human being delights in (and consequently praises, *khairein te kai epainein*, 2.655e2) the representation of a character that is identical to his own, which can be good, but will often be bad.[29] This means that pleasure, considered apart from order, is always at risk of conflicting with the pleasure initially taken in orderly movement and music. The problem finds its theoretical expression in the "intolerable and impious (*oute anekton oute hosion*)" assumption by the majority according to which "what defines the correctness of music is the power to provide pleasure to souls" (2.655c8–d2)—a view whose danger shows, more clearly than in any other poetic production, in theater, the arch-competitor of true law.[30] The correctness of music is not warranted by the pleasure it procures, but rather by the correctness of the pleasure in question, which has its own criterion. The following passage, which should be read in conjunction with the (more famous) radical criticism of Athenian democracy as a "theatrocracy" in Book 3,[31] illustrates with shibboleth-like clarity what is at stake in the quarrel between legislation and poetry—a special case of the "quarrel between philosophy and poetry" that Plato registers in Book 10 of the *Republic*: [32]

> I, too, agree with the many at least to the extent that music must be judged by pleasure—not by anybody's pleasure whatsoever, however, but the finest Muse, isn't it, is the one who delights the best and the adequately educated persons, most of all the one who is superior in virtue and education. [659a] The reason why we assert that the judges of these matters need virtue is that they must partake of wisdom generally speaking (*tês allês phronêseôs*) and especially of courage. For neither should the true judge learn from the audience (lit.: from the theatre, *para theatrou*) and be driven out of his sense by the tumult of the many and his own lack of education as he judges, nor should he, while he knows, because of a lack of manliness and cowardice, lie and pronounce an easy-going judgment [659b] issued from the very same lips that invoked the gods as he was about the judge. For, at least as

justice goes, the judge does not sit as a learner taught by the spectators but rather as their teacher, and he will oppose himself to those who bring pleasure to the spectators in a way that is not appropriate nor correct. For this was possible under the ancient, Hellenic usage (*nomos*); by the same token the present Sicilian, Italic usage, which leaves it to the multitude of spectators, and decides the winner by a show of hands,[33] has corrupted the poets themselves (for they compose in function of the pleasure of the judges, which is base, so that the spectators themselves [659c] educate them), and it has corrupted the pleasures of the audience itself: for while they should always be hearing about characters better than their own, and hence getting a better pleasure, what is now happening to them is that they make entirely the opposite. (2.658e6–659c5)

Whereas the *khoreia* includes a non-discursive side, which makes the representation and imitation of characters (*mimêmata tropôn*, 2.655d5) easier, the criterion for its correct use (*orthotês*, 655d1) is ultimately based in a discursive, propositional dimension. Words (*ta legomena*, 2.660e1), which are sung, are in principle separable from the music (and dancing) into which they are woven. They become the focus of attention as the analysis of the educative program unfolds. While the link between nondiscursive and discursive items is a given, it is also fragile. Book 2 gives a sense of the difficulties that await the program of translating the in-born pleasure for order to the extra-kinetic and extra-melodic sphere of linguistic statements and opinions, as the heterogeneity of pleasure and rational order progressively take precedence over the primitive hints at their association.[34]

Musical education consists less in the imitation of characters through movements and sound than in imparting opinions founded in reason. *Khoreia*, in other terms, is an inchoate form of rhetoric (in the broad sense of the term which Plato gestures at in Book 4 [4.722d3–6]), which in exceptional cases can develop into philosophy itself.[35]

Aspects of the Human Wonder

There are different ways, not only in the course of individual lives, but also in the long run of human history, in which human beings can manifest behavior that is worthy, to various degrees of the wonderful puppets they are. To begin with, there is 'shame' (*aidôs*), a rational emotion[36] which is an expression of acquired spontaneity just as much as dance is; but there also is the capacity to be persuaded by praise and blame (which are the dominant discursive mode of preambles);[37] to hold sound opinions in important matters (above all when it comes to the existence of gods); and to adopt appropriate customs and political mechanisms such as those employed in Sparta, ancient Athens, and ancient Persia.[38] From this point of view, the 'middle' constitution described in Book 6 looks to a great extent like a particular instantiation of the human prodigy—an 'institutional prodigy,' one might say. All these are manifestations, at various levels, of a potentiality inherent in human beings that can be construed as an analogue of the elementary "traces" (*ikhnê*) which, in the *Timaeus*, are already present in the disordered *khôra*, before any imposition of the Forms.[39] And this is of course grounds for hope—a hope that is present and thematized throughout the *Laws*, even though it remains dependent on and thus mitigated—quite radically, indeed—by a global framework which, without ever forgetting the divine aspect of humanity, puts the emphasis on human weakness. Retreats and constraints of all sorts certainly weigh more in the *Laws* than manifestations of a prevailing harmony and domestic calm that remains, like the first city itself, on a paradigmatic horizon.

Indeed, the ways in which the prodigy can be realized are confined within limits set by the humanity of human beings, which limits are the remnants of a bestiality that is no less primordial than its drive to orderliness. In fact, the irrationality of primary feelings and expectations is tenacious, and in the end ineradicable. One of the strongest declarations found in the *Laws* runs "Pleasures, pains and appetites most of all (*malista*) belong by nature to human beings (*estin* [. . .] *anthrôpeion*), just as though the whole mortal animal by necessity hangs from them, while being suspended from them by means of the greatest impulses" (5.732e4–7).[40]

Were this not the case, there would be no need to conceive of a second, distinctively human city. By the same token, education, in spite of its name, which refers to childhood (*paideia*), is not restricted to childhood but extends through the whole of human life; though one could also say, inversely, that it is because of human beings' ineradicable dependence on pleasure and pain that they never cease to be children.

The lawgiver copes with this constitutive irrationality of the human puppet by means of education, which takes two opposite forms: persuasion or constraint, adding in compromise, when the constitutive irrationality of human beings is granted something that can satisfy and thus placate it. The *Laws* can and should be read as an extended exploration of the variegated configurations generated by this constellation, which allows even for wonder, when rationality and irrationality happen to converge at one level or another. Reading the *Laws* in this way means taking note of the different kinds of mediation and gauging, at the same time, what each may achieve and its inevitable limitations without sacrificing one perspective for the other. There is thus a constant oscillation between optimism and pessimism, which accounts for what I call the 'scalarity' of the *Laws*. And at the core of this oscillation lies the notion of possibility. It is never as perceptible or as delicate to handle as in the *Laws'* requirement that political knowledge coincide with political power, an echo of the famous declaration in the *Republic* according to which a city will never see the end of its miseries until either philosophers rule as kings or kings philosophize.[41]

5

The Multiplication of Goals

So is it with the Lacedaemonians [...]. Free they are, yet not wholly free; for law is their master, whom they fear much more than your men fear you. This is my proof—what their law bids them, that they do; and its bidding is ever the same, that they must never flee from the battle before whatsoever odds, but abide at their post and there conquer or die.

HERODOTUS, 7.104, TRANS. GODLEY

Aims and Targets

The ultimate goal of legislation, according to the *Laws* (and for Plato more generally), is *aretê*, excellence or 'virtue,' understood as 'the totality of virtue.' The Athenian says this early on, first in *Laws* 1.630d9–e4; and he insistingly repeats it, in different wordings, at 3.688a6-b4 and 4.705d2–706a4 (cf. also 6.770c7–e1); Clinias mentions it once more at 12.963a1–4 as an assertion that has been recurring all along. And the leading principle of the Watch which, being the highest organ of preservation of the city, should itself "possess the whole of virtue" (12.962d2–3) is, "not to roam about by aiming at many things, but to look at a single goal and always shoot everything toward it, like arrows" (962d3–5).

And yet, there is a sense in which the lawgiver knows of more than one goal. There is, to begin with, the happiness of the citizens of whom he is the would-be lawgiver; then come, both at the individual and at the collective level, the different virtues that make up virtue in the singular—of which there are four, as in the *Republic*—wisdom, temperance, justice, and courage (in the order in which they first appear at 1.631c5-d2[1]); but friendship and freedom, too, are

74

declared in Book 3 to be legislative goals that the lawgiver must 'look at' or 'consider' (*blepein pros*, 3.693b5). They rank next to wisdom, as we shall see shortly; equality will later be *de facto* added to the triad in Book 6. 3.693b5.

What is the relationship between these different goals? I shall henceforth call the lawgiver's ultimate goal the 'aim,' which is virtue, and 'targets,' the goals that are in some way linked to this ultimate aim, while using 'goal' as a neutral term for either or both of them.

In the case of happiness, the link between aim and target is easy to see: given Plato's assumption that happiness is the necessary outcome of virtue, it can in fact substitute for it in appropriate contexts.[2] The relationship between virtue in the singular with the virtues in the plural is more difficult to capture. This is a consequence of their inherent complexity, as well as of a certain and arguably related instability in the description of their nature and mutual relationships, which contrasts with the systematic, clear-cut presentation in Book 4 of the *Republic* (427e6–444e6). In the programmatic division of goods (*agatha*) that includes an enumeration of the four virtues (1.631b6-d2), temperance is referred to, at least on the most probable reading of the text, by the periphrastic "a temperate state of the soul accompanied with reason [i.e., the first virtue]" (*meta nou sôphrôn psukhês hexis*, 1.631c7);[3] justice is then said to result "from the mixture of those two [i.e., wisdom, which has been previously named the leading good, and this temperate state] with courage" (*ek toutôn de met'andreias krathentôn*). The fact that 'courage' (*andreia*), which features in the mix that is constitutive of justice appears to be independent of wisdom arguably reflects an inversion of the Spartan/Cretan view that the Athenian is criticizing at this juncture, for the Athenian's considered view is that courage is directed against pleasure no less than against pain at 1.633c8–634c4, and is indissociable from temperance.[4] At 3.696b6–697c4, temperance is said to be present in the three other virtues (courage [b6-c1], justice [c2–7], and wisdom c8–11]), which gives it a prominent place among the psychic goods (697b2–4). Last but not least, the leading virtue itself can be analyzed into its constitutive elements, of which wisdom, which was said at 1.631c5–6 to be the leading virtue, is only one: the lawgiver has "to look to the whole of virtue, and especially at the first virtue, which is the leader of the whole of it, which would be wisdom (*phronêsis*), reason (*nous*), and opinion (*doxa*), accompanied by love (*erôs*) and a desire (*epithumia*) that follows those (3.688b1–3)," a sentence that both makes a distinction between *phronêsis* and *nous* that does not figure in other passages, and which in turn opens the way to the mention of further aspects of the leading virtue—a certain 'opinion' on the one hand, 'love' and 'desire' on the other.[5]

Some have found Plato's flexibility "irritating,"[6] and the fact that the unity of virtue, which is presupposed all the way through, reappears at the end of the dialogue in the discussion about the Watch (12.963a1–965e7) as a difficult (*ouk eupetes*, 963d6–7) and still open question, has been taken as signaling the 'aporetic' character of the passage.[7] Are the virtues four in number, or one (12.963c5–d7)? Should we look to virtue as one (*hen*), or as a whole made of parts (*holon*), or as both, or whatever (965d6–7)? But there are three related reasons not to read the evidence is this way. To begin with, the apparent wavering could be part of a conceptual and linguistic strategy that Plato is using at various important junctures in the *Laws* (as we shall see); secondly, the question of the relationship between *the one virtue*, which is their general form (*mia idea*, 965c2), and *the virtues* is one that the members of the Watch must be capable of answering "adequately"/*hikanôs* (964c7) and "precisely"/*akribôs* (965c10); finally, the subordination of the other virtues or parts of virtues to wisdom (*phronêsis* or *noûs*), which is the leading good that makes all the other goods real goods, is certainly a unifying factor.[8] More specifically, what the unity of virtue fundamentally consists in can be deduced from the emphatic conclusion of the comparison between human beings and puppet-like wonders at 1.644b9–645c1. If the image is said to have "saved the talk (*muthos*) of virtue" (645b1–2), it is because virtue consists in the internal condition of a person whose rational motivation (his correct reasoning about what feelings and expectations are better or worse) is stronger than the nonrational tractions that pull in other directions, and thus gets the upper hand (*nikâi*, 1.645a7). This what the expression "to be superior to oneself" means. For, as was made explicit at 1.626d1–e5, there certainly is, for Plato, a war-like state that is internal to the individual (1.626e4–5).

Victory, however, is not properly the end of a war, only peace (*eirênê*) is. This we learn very early in the dialogue from the following passage refuting the Cretan/Spartan exclusive focalization on external war:

> Is it not for the sake of the best that every [sc. lawgiver] would establish all his regulations (*nomima*)? [...] The best, however, is neither war nor civil war (*stasis*)—indeed, that these are required is something to be deprecated— rather, the best is peace and at the same time goodwill towards one another; and in particular, a city's being victorious over itself, as it seems, does not belong to what is best but to what is necessary. (1.628c6-d1)[9]

If so, psychic victory can only be a step towards a condition that will be soon described as a state of inner agreement or consonance (*sumphônia*) between feelings and affections on the one hand and reason (*logos*) on the other hand. And this consonance is "the whole of virtue":

> When pleasure and love, pain and hatred come about in the right way in the souls of those who can't yet use reason (*logos*) for understanding, and then when they acquire reason, are consonant with reason by having been habituated in the correct way by the appropriate habits, this consonance is the whole of virtue. (2.653b2–6)[10]

Plato goes so far as to call this state *sophia*—a term for which there is no better translation, unfortunately, than the very same 'wisdom,' although the striking definition that the Athenian gives of "the greatest *sophia*" at 3.689d6–7 ("the most beautiful and greatest of harmonies") indicates clearly that it is different from the partial, although leading virtue called *phronêsis* or *nous* (see also 3.696c8–10). Complementarily, the name given at 3.689a7–9 to the "dissonance between pleasure and pain on the one hand, and the opinion that is according to reason on the other" is ignorance/*amathia*.

What corresponds at the level of a city to this psychic consonance is political friendship (*philia*, 1.628a3), which is also a certain form of agreement. So it is not difficult to see why wisdom and friendship can be picked out, as well as peace and happiness, as two items that stand for the rest, i.e., for the three virtues of temperance, justice, and courage, and why they can be regarded as legislative goals in their own right. Wisdom is the virtue from which all other virtues depend (they have *nous*/reason as their ultimate source), and friendship, which guarantees peace within the city, has been clearly pointed to as an essential feature of a political community.[11] In Book 3, they feature as two prominent legislative targets out of three.

Freedom Comes In

But in Book 3, 'freedom' is mentioned alongside wisdom and friendship as a third target as a result of a political argument that does not concern virtue in the first place (which is the focus of Books 1–2), but constitution, which is the new topic broached in this book.

The issue emerges when a discussion about the origins of human political organization that opens the book reaches a point where the positive question about what an appropriate constitution should look like can be raised.[12] The Athenian, turning to the example of the Persian Wars, argues that the reason why Sparta lent support to Athens in its defense of Greece's freedom is that its constitution did not allow a single individual to exercise absolute, undivided power, but was, rather, what would soon be called (arguably from Aristotle onwards) a "mixed constitution" (the phrase is not found in Plato's work in this precise form[13]). According to Plato's version of Sparta's history, Lycurgus, the legendary lawgiver whose human nature was itself "mixed" (*memeigmenê*, 3.691e2) with a divine power, devised a constitutional scheme that combined (*meignusi*, 691e3) kingship, which was bifurcated from the start due to the fortunate birth of twins within the royal family (691d8-e1), with two other sources of power—a council of twenty-eight elderly members (a gerontocratic body which Aristotle considered representative of oligarchy at *Politics* 2.6 1265b37–38, but which could also be taken as embodying 'aristocratic' wisdom) and five representatives of the people (the 'ephors'[14]). Thus, the kingship, being "mixed" (*summeiktos*), was preserved from despotism and acquired 'measure' (*metron*) (692a7–8).

Sparta's willingness to fight for Greece's freedom, the Athenian goes on, must be thought (cf. *dianoêthentas*) as due to a constitution where powers are both limited ("not great") and "not unmixed" (*ou . . . megalas . . . oud'au ameiktous*, 693b2–3), a condition that makes "a city [. . .] free and wise and friendly within itself." This is why "the lawgiver should lay down his laws with a view (*blepein pros . . .*) to these [goals]" (3.693b3–5).

Thus, not only wisdom and friendship are legislative goals, but freedom is also. This will be repeated in the conclusion of the long discussion about freedom that follows, using slightly different terminology and with the three items in a slightly different order (with freedom in the first place in both cases, however): the lawgiver, when legislating, must ensure that the city he is legislating for be free, in a state of internal friendship, and possess reason (at 3.701d7–9, with *nous* in place of *phronêsis*).

There is certainly nothing strange about an Athenian invoking national freedom (independence) by citing the Persian wars. Their victory over Persia was felt by the Greeks as marking (and arguably did mark) a new historical era. Herodotus, in the famous passage reproduced in the epigraph to this chapter, has the deposed Spartan king Demaratus mention Spartan freedom as he extolls Spartans' obedience to the law as the source of their courage.[15] But in the context of Plato's argument, freedom comes rather unexpectedly. This is for two related reasons. The first, merely negative and so possibly weaker reason is that freedom was not mentioned or even anticipated in the course of the first two books, even though their subject was defining the aim of legislation. The second reason, which is positive and much stronger, is that the inclusion of freedom among the lawgiver's targets raises a question about the relationship that freedom entertains with virtue, and for that matter with the leading virtue among the four, namely wisdom.

By contrast with the sonorous motif of national independence, the issue of civic (and, more remotely, individual) freedom enters the scene, somewhat discreetly, and by implication rather than thematically. Freedom here arises as a logical outgrowth of measures taken to curb despotism, which, by definition, treats citizens as if they are slaves. In other words, Spartan political freedom, which is implicitly advanced as the motivation for Sparta's fight for national independence, is a derivative of the division of powers in Sparta's mixed constitution.[16] To be free, in the latter perspective, is to be free from political oppression.

This, however, is not Plato's last word about freedom. For the next argument, and even more the following books of the *Laws*, point to a notion of freedom that goes beyond both the reference to the Spartan mixed constitution and Herodotus' blunt opposition between law and freedom ("Free they are, yet not wholly free; for law is their master"), in particular through a new construal of the relationship between law and 'voluntariness.'

In the meantime, the Athenian expects his interlocutors (and Plato his readers) to be surprised. He would not otherwise have had the Athenian anticipate their reaction by asking them *not* to be surprised (*mê thaumasômen*, 693b5–6):[17]

> Let's not be surprised if, having already often put forward some goals (*pro-themenoi atta*), we said that the lawgiver should look at them when he legislates, while those don't appear to us to be the same each time; rather, we must reckon that when we say that one should look towards being temperate (*to sôphronein*), or towards wisdom, or friendship, the aim (*ho skopos*) is not different but the same. And if many other words of this sort come about, it should not disturb us. (3.693b5–c5)[18]

This declaration, to which I attach more importance than other interpreters, in fact adds to the surprise it is meant to dispel. As Clinias' immediate reaction shows, the term 'freedom' is omitted in the very sentence that is supposed to provide an explanation for its inclusion among the legislative targets. The surprise is compounded, moreover, by the fact that the place of the missing freedom is taken by temperance (*to sôphronein*). The triad is still there, but not with its original constituents. To be sure, the inclusion of temperance among legislative targets does not by itself constitute a problem, since it is one of the four virtues featuring in Book 1;[19] but its mention at *this* juncture, combined with the disappearance of freedom, is striking: it is as if 'temperance' could be substituted for 'freedom,' while 'freedom' was just one of many words that could be used to refer to one and the same thing, and so can be rather casually interchanged. Maybe the Athenian is suggesting that 'temperance' is an appropriate designation for 'freedom,' or even an *equivalent* that could replace it without harm, perhaps even advantageously?[20]

This line of thought was certainly open to Plato, and it captures a central aspect of his construal of freedom, which will ultimately take an even more radical turn.[21] But it is not in that direction that he has the Athenian now direct the argument. Clinias, who is unsatisfied (understandably so) with an answer that may be interpreted as an attempt to get around the question of freedom, asks his interlocutor to clarify his views. In reformulating the question, he leaves out 'temperance' and reintroduces the term the Athenian omitted: "[...] But presently, concerning friendship, wisdom and freedom, tell us what you wanted and were about to say concerning the goal that the lawgiver should aim at" (3.693c7–d1).

Sparta, Ancient Persia, Ancient Athens

The Athenian complies and now proceeds to an explanation of why not only freedom, but also friendship feature next to wisdom among legislative targets, for it turns out that the two terms are interdependent.

> Listen, then. Constitutions have, as it were, two mothers of a sort, and someone saying that the other ones derive from them would speak correctly; and it is correct to call one monarchy and the other democracy, and to say that the Persian people have reached the highest grade of the former [i.e., despotism], and we [sc. the Athenians] that of the latter [i.e., an extreme form of democracy]. Almost all other regimes, as I have said, are variations derived from these. Thus, it is appropriate and necessary that they partake in both of them if there is to be freedom and friendship together with wisdom: this is what the argument wants to prescribe to us when it says that no city can ever be governed well if it does not have a share of those [i.e., monarchy and democracy]. (3.693d2–e3)

One important aspect in this declaration is that it settles a point left unclear in the first formulation of the triadic legislative target—and this is the first motive for surprise mentioned above. At first blush, one could understand Sparta's willingness to join Athens in its fight for Greek independence as the uncomplicated result of the desire to preserve its freedom as an independent city (cf. 3.687a7). But while this is certainly part of the story, it cannot be the entire story. For, seen in this way, freedom as a legislative target would have meant only that the lawgiver must care for the defense of the territory. This is not, however, what is implied by the genealogical scheme that the Athenian is now putting forward. Freedom is here considered as an internal constitutional feature that precedes the need to engage, when necessary, in a war of independence.

Now the description of Sparta's mixed constitution at 3.691d8–692b1 as a combination of a double kingship with an oligarchic and a democratic constituent (the council of the elders and the ephorate) does not explicitly refer to freedom as one of its benefits. An explicit integration of freedom in a constitution occurs for the first time in the *Laws* in relation *not* to Sparta but with the complementary pair formed by ancient Athens (basically represented by Solon's laws) and ancient Persia (under Cyrus' reign).[22] These two regimes provide two remarkable, symmetrical instances of political organizations that assign a suitable share to freedom (the democratic principle) without endangering authority (the monarchic principle). The way in which each of them achieves this from an institutional point of view (which prevailed, for all its schematism, in the presentation Sparta's constitution) remains admittedly vague. But the important point is that the triadic scheme that was at work in Sparta's mixed constitution has now yielded to a dyadic one.

This is first illustrated in the case of ancient Persia:

The Persians, at a time when, under Cyrus, they still better maintained a due measure (*to metrion*) between slavery and freedom, first became free and then masters (*despotai*) of many others. For, because the rulers gave a share of freedom to the ruled and led them toward equality, the soldiers were more friends [694b] with their generals and gave themselves over to danger with eagerness. On the other hand, if someone among them was wise and capable of deliberating, he would share publicly his capacity for wisdom to make it common, since the king was not envious but allowed freedom of speech (*parrhêsia*) and honored those capable of giving counsel; as a consequence, everything improved for them at that time because of freedom and friendship and the sharing of reason (*nou koinônia*). (3.694a3b6)

Freedom appears here under two aspects. One concerns the relationship between the rulers, especially in their military capacity, with the ruled, here represented by the soldiers, while the second one concerns the relationship between the king and his advisers. As far as the military is concerned, we are not told how freedom materializes—no more than we know exactly what is implied by the formula 'leading toward equality' (nor, for that matter, do we learn anything about the freedom of the many, the *dêmos*, which is not reducible to the army).[23] We can see, however, from the description of how the regime later declined, that this freedom essentially resulted, negatively, from an absence of oppression and exploitation, and, positively, from adequate attention being paid to their interests (primarily those of an economic nature, one might suspect).[24]

> We say that the cause [sc. of Persia's decadence] is that by excessively depriving the people (*dêmos*) of freedom, and by introducing more despotism than is appropriate, they destroyed the friendship and what is common (*to koinon*) in the city. Once this is corrupted, the plans (*boulê*) of the rulers are no longer made for the sake of the ruled and the people, but rather for the sake of their own rule [. . .]. (3.697c7–d3)

The second aspect (*au*/"on the other hand" at 694b2) is more precise. Freedom appears as "freedom of speech" (*parrhêsia, b3*), a distinctive feature of the (Athenian) democratic regime here adapted to Persia's situation, where it becomes a commendable measure rather than a marker of potential excess (freedom has conditions; it is limited by the capacity of giving good advice). The implication is that it is restricted to a small group of 'counselors,' and not the business of the many. [25]

As for ancient Athens, there are no positive indications about how freedom is constitutionally embodied. An extended, preexisting freedom seems, rather, to be presupposed—Athens being primarily associated with freedom, just as Persia was with kingship—only to be then contained, negatively, by a counterbalancing factor which draws from the opposed, monarchical principle. At 3.700a3–5, the Athenian refers to the *dêmos* (the people) as the part of the city that is concerned by this limitation:

> Under the ancient laws, my friends, the people in our city was not sovereign (*kurios*) on certain matters but rather voluntarily enslaved, in a certain sense, to the laws.[26]

The range of questions about which the people (*dêmos*) *was not* (or for that matter *was*) sovereign is not specified in this elliptical sentence, which relies on an implicit contrast between the ancient state of affairs and a later one, when the members of the democratic assembly would decide on many issues that, according to the Athenian, should not have been their concern. But it is obvious that the issues in question are of importance. This focusing on the *dêmos* may reflect Plato's distrust in the judgment of poorly educated people, but it should be clear from an earlier remark that the limitation applies to the four (economic) classes of citizens, here collectively referred to as "we, Athenians":

> For at that time [...], there was an ancient constitution and officeholders coming from four classes, and a certain despotic mistress—shame (*aidôs*)—because of whom we were willing to live as slaves of the laws of that time. (3.698b2–6)[27]

What the Athenian insists on in his depiction of ancient Athens, then, is the limiting effect of an authoritative element, namely the laws, which now represent the monarchical principle. In what follows, we get, in sharp contrast with Athens' ancient constitution, the famous description of an "excessive growth of the free way of life (*tên tou eleutherou lian epidosin tou biou*)" in the course of Athens' subsequent evolution, beginning with the neglect of musical rules, which are also laws of a certain kind (they are binding), followed by unchecked democracy, and ending in an apocalyptic regress to man's 'ancient Titanic nature' (701c2) in the form of a democratic 'theatrocracy' that lies at the opposite pole from Plato's wished for 'theo-noo-nomocracy':[28]

[Clinias:] Which laws are you speaking of?

[the Athenian:] First those concerning the music of that time, so that we may go through the excessive growth of the free way of life from the start. At that time our music was divided into certain genres and the types that belong to each, [700b] and one genre of song was the prayers to the gods, which were called 'hymns'; opposite to it, there was another genre of song which one would best dub 'laments.' 'Paeans' were another, and another, on the birth of Dionysus I think, was called the 'dithyramb.' And they gave the very name *nomoi* ['nomes,' lit. 'laws'] to another sort of song, which they called 'citharoedic.' Once these genres had been thoroughly ordered, as well as some others, it was not permitted to use one genre for a different genre of song (*melos*). [700c] The authority that was knowledgeable about these matters and knowingly passed judgment about them and penalized anyone who disobeyed, was not the whistle, nor the unmusical [i.e., untrained] cries of the multitude (*plêthos*), as is the case nowadays, nor, inversely, the applause that bestows praise. Instead, the resolution (*to dedogmenon*) of those who had gone through education was to listen in silence until the end, while for the children, their attendants, and the greatest part of the crowd (*okhlos*), admonition came about through the cane that keeps order. [700d] Thus, the majority of the citizens were willing to be ruled in an ordered way and did not dare to render their judgement through uproar. Later, however, as time passed, poets who were by nature creative (*poiêt-ikoi*), but ignored what is just and lawful as far as the Muse is concerned, initiated an unmusical disrespect of the law (*paranomia*):[29] in Bacchic frenzy, more in the grip of pleasure than they should have been, they mixed lamentations with hymns and paeans with dithyrambs, imitated the sound of the flute by using kitharas and jumbled together every genre with all others, [700e] and, because of their folly, they involuntarily spread the lie that there is no correctness whatsoever in music, and that it is absolutely correct to judge by the pleasure of the person who enjoys it, whether the person be good of bad.[30] By producing poems of this kind and using words of this kind, they instilled in the many lawlessness as regard music and audacity as if they were capable of passing judgment. The result is that audiences became vociferous [701a] instead of voiceless, claiming to know what is fine in the domain of the Muses and what is not; and instead of an aristocracy in musical matters, what came about was a worthless theatrocracy of sort.

For if a democracy of free men had only come about in the field of music, what occurred would not be *that* terrible. But in reality, music in our place was the starting point for the pretense of wisdom of all with regard to everything and disrespect of the law, and freedom followed suit. They became fearless, pretending to know, and fearlessness generated shamelessness. For [701b] not to fear the opinion of someone who is better out of boldness, this is exactly what worthless shamelessness would be, it seems, as the result of some sort of freedom that is excessively audacious. (3.700a6–701b3)[31]

Plato's discussion in Book 3 on the place of freedom, an official legislative target, in a mixed and balanced constitution, yields an incomplete picture of the function and nature of freedom. As far as Sparta is concerned, what freedom connotes is clear at the national level: it means the independence of the city as a whole from Persia's domination. What it means at the civic level, within the city and for the citizen, is not specified; one can see, by analogy, that the citizens' freedom derives not from the total removal of domination, as occurs at the national level, but from its automatic, quantifiable reduction, which results from the division of political powers; whether it is also more positively represented by the democratic ephorate issued from the people and, if so, what the relation of this freedom to the negative one might be, is difficult to assess. In ancient Persia, with no democratic assembly or division of power mentioned, freedom takes the form of a freedom of speech that bears the name, but not the characteristics of democratic *parrhêsia*, since it consists in the possibility for a restricted group of counselors to advise the king. In ancient Athens, the institutional localization of freedom, derived from the division of power, as in Sparta, is represented by an Assembly with limited competence (it does not decide on all issues) but composed of 'educated' citizens disposed to obey (to be slaves to) the law voluntarily (on the basis of an internal motivation).

The next step will be to ask where freedom is to be found in the constitution of Plato's second city as described in Book 6. For it is striking that, by contrast with Book 3, which explicitly revolves around freedom even if much of what is said about it remains under-determinate, the few occurrences of free/ *eleutheros* and kindred words in Book 6 are marginal (they refer only to the social, statutory meaning of the term, which distinguishes the free master from the slave).[32] The absence is the more remarkable as a later passage in Book 8 characterizes the citizens living under "the constitution we are legislating for" as "free from one another" (832c9–d2), by contrast with all other constitutions that the Athenian qualifies at this point as "non-constitutions." Can we make sense of the nominal disappearance of freedom between Books 3 and 6? We will be in a better condition to answer this question after reviewing an essential feature of Plato's second constitution.

6

Mixtures, Blends, and Other Metamorphoses

Do not praise
either a life without rule
or a life under despotism:
in everything god has given pre-eminence to the mean (*meson*),
though he governs different spheres in different ways.

AESCHYLUS, *EUMENIDES*, 526–31, TRANS.
SOMMERSTEIN SLIGHTLY MODIFIED

Middle and Mean

As indicated in the previous chapter, the entrenched formula 'mixed constitution' adequately characterizes Sparta's constitution, given that Plato makes it result from a certain mixture. But the formula lacks precision if we apply it without further ado to the two other constitutions considered in Book 3 (ancient Persia and ancient Athens), and the shortfall is even greater when it comes to the 'official' constitution of the second city set up in Book 6. It is true that this constitution displays a series of features that bears some resemblance to the Spartan mix in the sense that power is divided across a variety of political institutions, most of them, the Watch apart, of distinctively Athenian provenience or inspiration—namely, an Assembly, a Council, judicial courts, and various boards of officeholders. But whereas the Spartan political power division can be described, even in Plato's presentation of the case, in terms of checks-and-balances, this is definitely not the case of Plato's second-best constitution, which is pyramidal, with the all-important Watch, a

Platonic creation, at its human summit.[1] As a matter of fact, the language that Plato uses in the crucial passage where he points to the highest formal principle in this constitution, is not that of 'mixture.' The critical factor is, rather, a certain 'middle point' or 'mean' (*meson*). The crucial sentence follows a description of how the members of the Council are chosen (selected) by the Assembly:

> A selection (*hairesis*) occurring in this way would hold the middle (*meson ekhoi*) between a monarchic and a democratic constitution, which the constitution should always maintain (*meseuein*). (6.756e9–10)

In this sentence, the term 'middle'/*meson* (whose weight is reinforced by its grammatical function as an internal complement of the verb *meseuein*) applies in the first place to a specific aspect of Plato's constitution, namely the procedure that he sees as optimal for making selections that hit the "mean"; but it also extends, as the last clause of the sentence just quoted indicates, to the constitution taken as a whole—not only as regards this or that selection, but in terms of the overall structure and functioning of the different political organs and social institutions that the term *politeia* covers.[2] The two levels need to be considered separately.

The possible scope of the term *meson* itself must be discussed first. For given Plato's views and his wonted terminological flexibility, it cannot be excluded *a priori* that 'middle' and 'mixture' boil down to the same thing. As a matter of fact, Plato's second constitution is often referred to in the scholarly literature as a 'mixed constitution.' There are reasons to think, however, that the terms convey two different, though surely related meanings. 'Mixture' primarily applies to a mix in which the constituents stay, paratactically so to speak, next to one another—which is the case of Sparta's constitution as described in Book 3 and of Plato's own distribution of powers in Book 6. The notion of a 'middle' or a 'mean' suggests, rather, an appropriately proportionate blend in which the constituents lose their distinctive identity, merging into a third, synthetic something,[3] like water and wine blending in a crater, to take up the comparison used by the Athenian when he talks later in the same book about the appropriate choice of one's spouse:

> ... it is not easy to comprehend the fact that a city must be blended (*kekramenên*) in the same way as wine in a bowl in which it seethes when it is poured in but once it is chastened by a different and sober god, it forms a fine partnership and generates a drink that is good and measured. (6.773c8-d4)

The thought, which has arguably something to do with Aristotle's construal of virtue as a mean between two extremes (*Nicomachean Ethics* 2.5 1106a26–2.7 1108b10), is grounded in a central passage of the *Statesman* (283c3–285c2) that divides the "art of measurement" (*metrêtikê*) into two "very different" species (284e9–10). The first provides measures that are relative to one another (*pros allêla*); they admit a 'more' and a 'less,' and so can be excessive or deficient ('long' and 'short' is the example given at 283a11). We are dealing here with things that can be counted, such as "number, lengths, depths, breadths and the speeds of things in relation to what is opposed to them" (284e4–5). The second kind of measurement determines "the due measure (*to metrion*), what is fitting (*to prepon*), the right moment (*ton kairon*), what ought to be (*to deon*)"; that is, to quote the general formula that illumines all references to a "middle" in the *Laws*, "everything that removes itself from the extremes (*panta hoposa* [...] *apôikisthê tôn eskhatôn*) to the middle (*eis to meson*)" (284e6–8) (trans. Rowe modified).

Legislative 'measure' clearly falls under the second category.[4] But the way in which the principle is implemented in the selection of Plato's Council is not obvious, because the borders between 'mixture' and 'middle-point' are implied rather than clearly drawn. Whether this fuzziness is contingent or not is a further question, but an all-things-considered characterization of the constitution presented in Book 6, above all in the passage about the two equalities that I will discuss in a moment, leads us to see it as neither a mix nor a middle, but as a mixture (*sit venia verbo*) of a 'mix' and a 'middle.'[5]

Balance

The *Laws* prepares us for the distinction between 'mix' and 'middle' in the section of Book 3 that discusses the balance between (democratic) freedom and (monarchical) servitude in ancient Persia and ancient Athens (693d2–e3 with the ensuing development). There, Plato does not talk of 'mixing,' the term he used earlier in the same book to characterize Sparta's constitution (which mixes the two kings, the council of the elderly, and the ephorate), but of constitutions "having a share" (*metalabein*, 3.693d8) in the two "mother-constitutions," namely monarchy and democracy.[6] To be sure, to say that a constitution 'has a share' in another constitution is compatible with saying that it is a 'mixed constitution' (a mixture of different items, considered as a whole, may be said to have a share in all the items that are part of it); nevertheless, the notion of 'sharing' is more appropriate when the leading question is not that of the distribution of political power over different political bodies, as is the case in Sparta, but the way in which citizens (in ancient Athens) and subjects (in ancient Persia) relate to political power and political power to them. This is again the question of their freedom, now explicitly treated from a general dyadic perspective (monarchy/democracy), rather than indirectly on the basis of a triadic institutional scheme (kinship/council of elders/ephorate).[7] Accordingly, the terms 'monarchy' and 'democracy' in this context name something different from the traditional regimes called by those terms, which does not mean that they do not *also* refer to those. The substitution of the abstract neuters *to monarkhikon* and *to eleutheron* (at 3.693e5) for the feminine substantives *monarkhia* and *dêmokratia* a few lines earlier (at 693d4–5) is in this respect significant. Plato is implicitly distinguishing the current denominations of regimes, which are based on the quantity of rulers (one for monarchy, numerous for democracy) from the principles on which they respectively rely, but which can be considered independently of them: whereas democracy stands for the principle of freedom (*to eleutheron*), monarchy stands for a principle that one might dub, for lack of a better denomination, the 'principle of domination.'[8] When the Athenian speaks of "holding the middle between a monarchic and a democratic constitution" at 6.756e9–10 (the lines are quoted at the beginning of the present chapter), he has in mind their principles, not only obedience and freedom, but also two conceptions of equality.

Clearly, this kind of balance between principles is something different from, and more refined than the paratactical mixture of political powers representing various regimes—monarchic, gerontocratic, democratic—that is at work in Sparta; but it is not yet a blend or a mean. It is so to speak on its way to becoming one, a potentiality on the way to (and, in the present case, in search of) its actualization. What if ancient Persia and ancient Athens, instead of evolving in opposite directions toward the two excesses in the implementation of the principle they respectively represent, were to converge towards a still deeper synthesis than those that prevailed in the past in Athens and Persian—in other terms, what if past history led to an open, hopefully better future rather than to an actual, distressing present, culminating in despotism in Persia and Titanic license in Athens?

As noted in Chap. 5, the equilibrium symmetrically reached in ancient Persia and ancient Athens between the monarchic principle of domination and the democratic principle of freedom is not reflected in the structure of institutionalized power, which was left rather vague.[9] By the same token, the notion of a middle point is not illustrated, in the constitution of Book 6, in relation to the distribution of power between different bodies (which are no less divided and 'mixed,' in a specific way, than those of the Spartan constitution). It must be reconstructed, rather, on the basis of the implications embedded in the selection procedure that serves as a hinge to the statement of the general principle.

Two Equalities

The elaborated procedure by which the Assembly selects the 360 members of the Council—four groups of 90 issued from each of the property classes Plato distinguishes (6.756b7–e8)—is summarized by Jeremy Reid as follows:

> Over four days, councilors are nominated from each of the four property classes; on the first two days, everybody must vote on a penalty of fine; on the third day, the lowest class is not subject to a fine if they don't vote; on the fourth day, the third and fourth classes are not subject to a fine if they don't vote, but those from the second class receive three times the fine and those from the first class receive four times the fine if they don't vote; on the fifth day, the names of the nominees are published and the top 180 candidates from each class are selected, then, of these 720, half are selected by lot to be councilors.[10]

How does this procedure satisfy the claim that it holds to a middle point or mean between a monarchic and a democratic constitution (that is, between their respective principles)? The fact is that the gist of the explanation that follows (introduced by "for"/*gar*) does not bear on the manner in which both monarchic and democratic principles, that is authority and freedom, are implemented in the procedure in question, even if it eventually provides a justification for its ultimate step (the selection by lot of half of the already selected body), nor does it specify the respect in which it holds to the 'middle' that is its goal. Most of the section is devoted, rather, to explaining why a middle/mean should always be considered as the goal (in other words, the explanation bears primarily on the second part of the sentence, which is of a general nature, and not on the first, which concerns the case at hand). Political friendship is the pivot of the argument. I quote the famous passage in full.

> A selection occurring in this way would hold the middle between a monarchic and a democratic constitution, a middle which the constitution should always maintain. For slaves and masters would [757a] never become friends, nor would unworthy and honest persons, if both were declared equal when it comes to honors [*timai*, here referring to offices]—equal shares for unequal individuals would become unequal, if they did not strike the [due] measure (*ei mê tungkanoi tou metrou*[11]). For these are the two causes why constitutions are filled with internal dissension (*stasis*). In effect, an ancient saying that is true, namely that 'equality produces friendship,' is on the one

hand perfectly correct and in tune. But the fact that it is not absolutely (*sphodra*) clear what the equality may be that has the power to do just this, has an absolutely (*sphodra*) confusing effect on us. For there are two equalities which bear the same name (*homonuma*) but are in effect (*ergôi*) [757b] opposed in many respects, one would say (*skhedon*); every city and every lawgiver is able to bring forward one of the two when it comes to honors [i.e., offices]—namely, the equality that consists in measure and weight and number—regulating distributions by means of the lot. But to perceive the truest and best equality is no longer easy for everyone. For that is Zeus's judgement (*krisis*), and it never assists men to any but the smallest extent, yet every bit of assistance that it does provide to cities or even to private individuals produces all that is good. For it distributes (*nemei*) [757c] more to the greater, less to the smaller by assigning duly measured shares (*metria*) to each according to their nature; and in particular when it comes to honors [i.e., offices], it distributes (*aponemei*) in each case (*aei*) greater ones to those who are greater as regards virtue, and to those in the contrary state regarding virtue and education, what is fitting (*prepon*) according to proportion (*kata logon*). For the political principle (*to politikon*), too, is in fact always for us precisely this, that which is just (*to dikaion*); and it is also for this that we should now strive, and to this equality that we should now look, too, Clinias, as we found the city [757d] that is now growing. And if someone founds another one sometime, he should legislate with the very same aim in view, and not by reference to a few tyrants, or to a single individual, or else to the sort of decisional power that belongs by the many (*kratos dêmou ti*), but always to what is just (*to dikaion*). And the latter is, as has been said—that equal [i.e., the proportional] share which conforms with nature, and which is in each case given to individuals who are not equal.

Nonetheless, it is necessary for every city sometimes to use these two as similar expressions (*parônumia*), if it is going to avoid [757e] partaking of internal dissension (*stasis*) in some part of itself; for adjustment (*to epieikes . . .*) and indulgence (*. . . kai suggnomon*), when they occur, are always infringements of right justice, that is of its perfection and exactness. This is why necessity compels us to make use of the equality of the lot, because of the discontent of the many (*hoi polloi*), and to pray both to the god and to good fortune in this case too that they direct the lot toward what is most just. Thus, we must of necessity [758a] use both equalities, but the one that depends on fortune should be used as rarely as possible. (6.756e9–758a2)

The explanation makes clear that the middle point that the constitution aims at would in principle be the best way for securing friendship, i.e., political peace, within the city—the second of the legislative targets according to the triad presented in Book 3 (wisdom, friendship, and freedom). For this friendship cannot come about, we are now told (this was not explicit in Book 3), under either of the two 'mother-constitutions' (or, by way of consequence, in any constitution where a certain balance between the respective constitutional principles is not respected): not in a despotic monarchy, "for slaves and masters would never become friends" (6.757a1),[12] and not in an Athenian-like democracy, because it is equally impossible for friendship to exist between individuals who are given the same amount of political authority independent of their merits (the best would feel wronged): "equal shares for unequal individuals would become unequal, if they do not strike the [due] measure (*to metron*)" (757a2–3).

The master/slave relationship can be read (and is usually taken) as a specific, extreme instance of inequality, in contrast to the extreme form of equality represented by arithmetic equality, which would presumably leave us with geometric equality as a virtuous middle between equality and inequality.[13] But it can also function as a reminder that freedom, of which the slave is by definition deprived of and which the master statutorily enjoys, is a necessary condition of friendship, as shown in Book 3—a reading that would give a broader scope and a more systematic turn to the argument.[14] Whichever way we prefer to take it, however, it now turns out that equality, or rather an equality of a certain kind, is a legislative 'target' that the lawgiver has to "look to, too" (*kai pros tautên tên isotêta apoblepontas* at 6.757c7–8) besides the three that feature in the Book 3's triad. It is not announced with fanfare, as occurred in Book 3 with freedom, but its status as a fourth target is no less certain.

The asymmetrical treatment of equality and freedom raises an interesting compositional question: why does freedom appear to be more of a target (as far as visibility is concerned) than equality? This is the more surprising since 'true' equality is related to virtue (since proportionality is based on its recognition), whereas political freedom is little more, at least for the time being, than a necessary counterpart of the limitation of power. Might it be that, despite appearances, freedom is the more important member of the pair, because, contrary to equality, which is a comparative relation between two terms, freedom primarily concerns an individual, and so touches the question of its relationship to virtue in a more substantial (albeit problematic) way than equality? I shall later suggest that, although Plato never calls it 'freedom,' there is, in fact, a kind of freedom, or rather a freedom of sort, which satisfies the demands of virtue as defined in the first two books of the *Laws*, because it derives from one's submission to. the law. Before coming to the thorny issue of freedom in Plato, I shall now consider the case of equality.

Equality, the additional legislative target, raises a difficulty which is not exclusive to it (for it affects 'freedom' as well, in a different way) but which Plato treats explicitly only in its case. It stems from the fact that two related, but distinct notions bear the same name (they are 'homonymous'/*homonumoin*, 757b2), which is a source of a 'deep unclarity' ("not absolutely clear," *mê sphodra saphês*, 757a7–b1, is best taken as a euphemistic expression). In a mathematical terminology that goes back to Plato's contemporary Archytas of Tarentum,[15] and which was to become traditional (though Plato does not use it in the *Laws*), there is an equality that is "arithmetic" and one that is "geometric."[16] The first kind of equality, "the equality that consists in measure [sc. counting units][17] and weight and number," assigns indiscriminately the same amount to every individual, on the ground that each individual is no less a unit than any other individual unit. Selection by lot as practiced in Athens is the political expression of this equality, to the point that Plato can speak of "the lot-related equal," as one might render the dense expression *to tou klêrou ison* at 757e3. The second kind of equality, which defines what is "political," namely justice (757c7), is the one that relies on proportionality and "distributes more to the greater, less to the smaller" (757c1–6).[18]

This equality is the "truest" and "best" one (757b6)—the truest, because it is in conformity with the nature of equality in as much as the latter bears on two terms of unequal worth, and the best, because it would in principle provide the greatest goods (in particular, friendship and peace) to a city that took it as the basis for distributing powers and honors. But what most people ordinarily understand by 'equality' is not this kind of equality, but the numerical equality, which in many respects brings about "the opposite" of true equality (757b2–3), that is discord and bad government. Apparently, even the mathematical education imparted to children in Plato's educational program (which is described at 7.817e5–822d3[19]), will not adequately prepare every citizen to see the point and override a personal drive for arithmetical equality that must ultimately stem (although Plato does not say so explicitly) from an overestimation of one's own self.[20] It is to cope with this situation that the lawgiver concedes to this kind of equality a certain place in the constitution, namely to allowing selection by lot in certain circumstances. In the case under consideration, the "equality of the lot" constitutes the last step in the choice of the members of the Council, whereby the one hundred eighty citizens who have been elected (*eklexantas*, 756e5–6) in each property class are reduced to ninety. This appeal to the lot is described as a "infringement" or "chipping away" of strict justice (*paratethrausmenon*, 757e2), an 'indulgence' (*to suggnômon*) and a kind of 'adjustment' (*to epieikes*).[21] There are a few other instances of selection by lot in Plato's constitutional scheme, all of them relatively unimportant, as one might expect, given Plato's misgivings about selection by lot.[22]

Does the "middle" the selection under consideration is said to hold result from this *in extremis* integration of the lot as a part of the procedure, which is a concession to a common cognitive limitation? (The question of course applies to other similar selections as well.) Or is not the middle point aimed, rather, at the proportional equality that would be located between extreme inequality and arithmetical inequality?[23] As a matter of fact, one can see that the gist of the procedure that is described, before the concession made eventually to the worse of the two equalities (resulting in a paratactical mix), can be read as an expression of a deeper middle course, one that settles on a point where the opposition between numerical and proportional equality loses its relevance.[24]

It should be noted, to begin with, that numerical equality, the Athenian translation of which is selection by lot, is also institutionally at work in Plato's *Laws*, given that the Assembly there is, in principle, a general gathering of all the citizens.[25] Various indications featured in the context of Book 6 and elsewhere in the work show that most offices in the city, including and perhaps most surprisingly, the all-important Guardians of the laws, are selected by this Assembly.[26] To be sure, specific regulations suggest that the (relatively) wealthier citizens will at the end of the day be better represented than the (relatively) poorer ones: whereas participation is compulsory for the two higher property classes, this is not the case for the two lowest ones. Still, the principle of all-inclusiveness is beyond doubt honored.[27] It is also true, of course, that Plato's Assembly, does not have, any more than the Assembly in (Plato's) ancient Athens did, a say on a range of questions that were in its hands in later Athens—far from it; but it has the power to empower, and this indirect power is decisive, since it determines to different degrees who will serve as officeholders in the city.[28] According to this scheme, some officeholders would be chosen, and thus empowered, in a two-tied procedure, by some already existing, and more select board (the minister of education, for one, is appointed by the Guardians of the law within their own body). The arrangement is not undemocratic on some conceptions of democracy (the one, for example, that is now called 'representative'), and it should not obfuscate the fact that Plato's Assembly is, at the end of the day, at the origin of the chain of selections. This certainly represents one of the most salient traits of the 'democratic' component of Plato's constitution in the *Laws*.[29]

More importantly, there is no point, once constitutions are considered as embodying principles, in keeping the two sides apart from one another as typically occurs in a mix—equality goes with freedom on the democratic side, 'power' with competence (authority) on the monarchic side: the whole point is the mediating synthesis that permeates each and all constitutional bodies and procedures. The 'monarchic' (i.e., authoritative) element is democratic insofar as it is selected by the citizens themselves; conversely, there is a 'monarchic' dimension to the democratic institution of the Assembly, since it is in charge of electing competent officeholders. Insofar as the middle constitution manages to bring about concord and 'friendship' at the cost of a few additional concessions to the 'democratic' lot, it can claim to be the only regime that is truly constitutional. As a matter of fact, Plato declares in a later passage (8.832b10–c3) that all the so-called constitutions listed at 4.710e3–5 (tyranny, monarchy, democracy, oligarchy, cf. 712c2–5, 714a2–4) are in reality 'non-constitutions.' This is not incompatible with the fact that both rulers and ruled, who are human beings, stay under the despotism of the law (which, ultimately, means of reason/*nous* and of god), provided that the corresponding servitude is 'voluntary' (more on this below).

Seen in this way, the middle that should always be aimed at by the lawgiver is a privileged middle point where two extremes, (monarchical) despotism at one end and (democratic) freedom at the other, are such that both *disappear* as such in virtue of the reciprocal compensation effected by their respective characteristics. If this middle point could be implemented, it would be a perfect blend rather than a simple mix, amounting to a political and conceptual transformation of the two extremes into a third, independent term. That this metamorphosis is not total in Plato's best human constitution does not strip it from being a metamorphosis all the same.

The reading just suggested is, admittedly, speculative. The metamorphosis is never identified as such by Plato, nor is of course 'metamorphosis' his term. But this does not mean that "it lacks," as a current objection goes, "any textual basis." For one is led to it by thinking about the text as a whole, which yields something different from what explicit statements can convey.[30]

On this scheme, selection in the *Laws* supposes the exercise of an educated, informed and in this sense 'aristocratic' judgment in the choice of the Councilors and other officeholders, while all citizens have in principle the possibility to be empowered in the course of their life and to serve as an aristocratic member of the Council or as an official. No wonder, then, that the official responsible for education is said to be "by far the greatest of the highest offices in the city" (6.765e2).

Thus, Rousseau's famous statement about the *Republic* in the first pages of his of his *Emile* ("It is not at all a political work, as think those who judge books by their titles; it is the most beautiful educational treatise ever written," trans. Allan Bloom[31]) applies even more to the *Laws*, with the difference that Plato, far from separating the two domains of 'education' and 'politics,' makes the first the foundation of the other. To this extent, Plato's constitution is circular in its actual functioning: without an appropriate education, an appropriate government is impossible; without an appropriate government, there won't be any appropriate education. This circularity, which equally affects the *Republic*, raises, of course, the question of where it all begins. When it comes to introducing new laws or selecting the first officeholders, who will be in charge? The difficulty is paradigmatically illustrated by the crucial and primary need to select the Guardians of the laws.[32] This is not the only enigmatic circle in the *Laws*, and it is perhaps not the most intractable. That distinction goes to the demand that law rule, rather than human beings—Rousseau's "squaring of the circle" quoted in the general epigraph of the present essay. For whereas human despotism must yield to legitimate political authority, human authority itself is required to subordinate itself to the higher despotism of a law ultimately grounded in divine reason.

Kinds of Freedom

What becomes of human freedom, then, on this scheme? I have suggested that whereas freedom and equality have the same political function, which is to preserve civic friendship, they differ in their structure and in their grammar: whereas equality is a two-party relation, freedom, even construed as relative term (to be free is to be free from something or somebody), also stands on its own as a personal quality. On the other hand, the word 'freedom' is used in the *Laws* in different contexts, in relation to different entities and with different implications, without ever being the object of an *ex professo* discussion (such as we do get for equality) that would explain the difference between its various uses and how they are related. A reconstruction of these relationships leads to the thorny question of the nature of 'freedom' in the *Laws*, and more generally in Plato.

What the qualification 'free' (*eleutheros*) refers to and what is at the base of all its uses in the *Laws* is an absence of submission to a master (*despotês*), a negative trait commonly taken to reflect the primitive, proper sense of 'freedom' (although this is far from certain from an etymological point of view).[33] Masters, however, are variegated. A free man is one who is not a slave, the implication being that he himself can be, and in context of a Greek city usually is the master of his domestic slaves. This statutory meaning is extremely frequent in the *Laws*, where slaves are self-evidently part of the landscape.[34] By analogy, a city or a nation, for example Greek cities and Greece in general, are free when they are not under submission to a foreign master, such as Persia and its Persian king. By the same token, the citizens of a given city are free when they are not ruled by a despot, and an individual is also free in a way which differs from his statutory freedom when he is not the prey of a passion, and especially not of the tyranny of *Erôs*, which can be conceived either as an external master (divinities attack from the outside), but also as an irresistible drive coming from within one's soul.

In one way or another, all human beings, including statutory free men, are or are likely to be, to some degree or another, psychological slaves. By contrast, reason/*nous*, being 'really' (*ontôs*) free according to its nature, cannot be obedient or the slave of anything else, in particular not a slave of law:

> For no law or order is stronger than knowledge, nor is it right for reason (*nous*) to be subordinate or a slave to anything, but it should be ruling all things, that is to say if it is really true (*alêthinos*) and free (*eleutheros*) according to its nature.[35] (9.875c6–d2)

The addressees of the laws, in Plato's *Laws*, are free citizens in the first sense of the term. But the freedom that defines their status is not, and cannot be, the freedom which the lawgiver makes one of his targets. It provides him, at best, with a starting point.

One might think of two reasons why the lawgiver makes of freedom one of his targets, one rather specific, the other more general (they are not formally distinguished by Plato). The specific reason, which is the one that visibly guides the lawgiver in Book 3, concerns the exercise of political power. The assumption here is that no despotic power, even on the unlikely hypothesis that it could fall into the hands of a competent and wise man, can escape corruption and avoid eventually driving the city to its ruin, an assumption that is historically illustrated by the case of the two Dorian cities of Messene and Argos.[36] On this scheme, freedom is the result, not of the defeat of a foreign despot, but of preventive measures taken to limit internal power and distribute it between different political bodies or for that matter offices. The freedom resulting from this reduction and division of powers is a quantifiable entity that will vary, depending on the type and modalities of the measures from which it derives, as in a system of communicating vessels. The other, more general reason is that any kind of subordination that is not recognized as legitimate is detrimental to civic friendship, that is to the second of the three official legislative targets. In this perspective, freedom is not the automatic counterpart of the division of power. It is, rather, a tool in the hand of the lawgiver to guarantee concord within the city. But whether freedom is viewed as a consequence or as a tool, it is never considered as possessing an intrinsic value on the same footing as 'virtue.' In other terms, there is an asymmetry between the legislative targets, and this asymmetry is a source of tension. Does the freedom that comes to the fore in Book 3 eventually fare well alongside virtue?

In order to sketch a possible answer to this question, one might ask what happens when reason or wisdom, which is the first of the legislative targets and the leading virtue that conditions the goodness of all the other virtues, rules a city and its citizens by means of a law that is on the one hand and by definition binding, but which is also what makes them 'virtuous,' according to the picture of virtue as virtue was defined in the first two books.

The question can be considered from two different perspectives. On the one hand, Plato is prepared to say without any further precision that human beings, whether ordinary citizens or officeholders, should be 'slaves to the laws.' He says as much on two occasions, first in Book 4:

> [...] in a city where law is subordinate [lit. 'ruled,' *arkhomenos*] and lacks authority, I see ready destruction for such a city; but when the law is master over the officeholders (*despotês tôn arkhontôn*), and *the officeholders are slaves to the laws* (*douloi tou nomou*), there I behold salvation [...]. (4.715d3–6)

And then in Book 6:

> Every man must reflect about all human beings that he who is not a slave cannot come to be a master (*despotês*) worthy of praise either, and that one should pride oneself on being a good *slave* rather than a good ruler, in the first place *to the laws*, in the thought that *this is a servitude to the gods* [...]. (6.762e1–5)

That servitude to the law is servitude to the gods is also implied at 4.713a3–4, in the passage where, looking for an appropriate name for a constitution worthy of the name, such as Sparta's is (to a certain extent), the Athenian refers to "... the name of the god *that is the true master* (*alêthôs ... despozontos*) *of those who possess reason* (*tôn ton noun ekhontôn*)."

The reference to god(s) as the ultimate master reduces in a certain sense the provocation implied by placing slavery above freedom, which represents a radical inversion of the social values commonly attached to the two terms. This slavery is not a slavery in the ordinary, negative sense of the word.[37] In as much as this slavery is not only to the law, which represents reason, but to the gods themselves (who are certainly not alien to reason), it is a component of virtue, which, paradoxically, makes human puppets 'free' to the extent that they are not slaves to the psychic tyranny of irrational desires.[38]

To be sure, Plato never talks, either in the *Laws* or elsewhere, of a 'true freedom' to be distinguished from another kind or other kinds of freedom, as he does in the case of "the truest and best equality" (6.757b5–6), or for that matter of "true pleasures" in the *Philebus* (36c6–e13). On the other hand, there is no doubt that he knows of a most positive notion of freedom. The clearest evidence of this comes at the conclusion of *Phaedo*'s final myth, where freedom, next to 'truth' (in the sense of 'truthfulness'), is tightly associated with the virtues. Here Socrates assures his interlocutors that if one lives "[...] regulating one's own soul to no alien adornment, but to its own: with temperance, justice, courage, freedom (*eleutheria*), and truth (*alêtheia*)" (*Phaedo*, 114e4–115a1, trans. Emlyn-Jones & Preddy), he can be confident about his future destiny.[39] A passage like this, taken with the affirmation, in the *Laws*, that *nous*/reason is really free, suggests that Plato, while still operating with a traditional conception of freedom, is opening the way to a view according to which to be virtuous, i.e., obedient to reason, *is* to be free in a nonconcessive sense. Rousseau would later formalize this as the difference between independence and liberty.[40]

Voluntary Servitude to the Law

The fact remains that in the *Laws*, the emphasis falls on the obedience that is required by the law, and hence on human heteronomy, rather than on (the kind of) freedom that Plato's own construal of virtue arguably authorizes. Still, it is crucial that the phrase 'servitude to the laws,' which is used absolutely in the two passages quoted above, appears on two other occasions accompanied by a qualification that, no less paradoxically, goes against the very notion of an indiscriminate servitude. Speaking of ancient Athens, the servitude required by the lawgiver is said to be 'voluntary' in the sense of 'accepted.'

> For at that time [. . .], there was [sc. in Athens] an ancient constitution and officeholders coming from four classes, and a certain despotic mistress—shame (*aidôs*)—because of whom *we were willing* (*ethelein*) to live as *slaves of the laws* of that time. (3.698b1–6)

> Under the ancient laws, my friends, the people (*ho dêmos*) in our city did not decide (*ouk ên . . . kurios*) on certain matters *but was in a certain way* (*tropon tina*) *voluntarily enslaved to the laws*. (3.700a3–5)

The scope of these passages is not restricted by the fact that they concern ancient Athens. For the Athenian, speaking at the level of general principles in a passage located between the two previous quotes, characterizes law as ruling over consenting people, in quite stark opposition to the tradition (attached to Pindar's name) that sees it as constraining and 'violent':[41]

> [. . .] the ruling of the law that takes place over those who are voluntarily ruled (*tên tou nomou hêkontôn arkhên*) and not by constraint is not against nature, but in agreement with nature. (3.690c1–3)

Thus, the point is not mere servitude to the laws, but 'voluntary servitude.' Although the oxymoron that Plato signals by adding "in a certain way" seems to introduce a new difficulty, it is in fact an element of the solution to the question of the relationship between obedience and freedom.

The formula should be read in the light of the passage from the *Symposium* (184b5–c7) that shows the paradox of a 'voluntary servitude' at home in no less familiar a setting than the field of erotic relationships.

> [Pausanias, giving an account of Athenian views on love:] Then according to our custom, if one intends to grant favors nobly to a lover, there is only one way left. For our custom (*nomos*) is that, for lovers, even as any kind of willing servitude to the beloved (*douleuein ethelonta hêntinan douleian*) by means of favors is neither flattery nor reprehensible, by the same token also there is only one other voluntary servitude (*douleia hekousios*) remaining [i.e., for the beloved] that is not reprehensible, which is the servitude relative to excellence (*hê peri tên aretên*). For we think that if somebody is willing to serve (*therapeuein*) somebody else while thinking that he will become better thanks to him, either in some kind of wisdom or in some

other part of excellence, this voluntary servitude (*ethelodouleia*, probably a neologism) is, again, not shameful nor a flattery.

One can see why the oxymoron comes easily to mind in the context of love relationships. Servitude is the direct and natural counterpart of representing *Erôs* as a tyrannical master, according to the entrenched representation that Cephalus, for example, echoes at the beginning of the *Republic*.[42] Both lover and beloved yields to the other's demands. This slavish obedience has a ground, namely love. This feeling is what makes an obedience that amounts to servitude 'voluntary,' to the extent that it is conceived of as having its source in the individual who stays under its spell (as opposed to being caused by the actions of an external divinity). Plato's further transposition in the *Laws* of the scheme of *voluntary* servitude from erotics to politics points to a structural similarity, which does not imply that love and politics as similar (although *Laws* 3.688b2–4 makes of a certain 'love'/*erôs* and 'desire'/*epithumia* a component of the leading virtue).[43] But there are more common 'voluntary' motives than rational love that can trigger obedience to the laws, in particular 'shame' (another such internal despot, cf. 3.698b5–6); 'persuasion' (*peithô*), referring to the state induced by a persuasive discourse, could also be mentioned.[44]

This is the work done, I submit, by the term *hekôn*, an eminently flexible word for which there exists no better translation than 'voluntarily' in spite of its misleading reference to the will in various modern languages. To qualify an action as voluntary/*hekôn* is only to say that the action in question comes "from within the agent himself."[45] As we shall see in the next chapter, there is a place in Plato's construal of 'voluntary' obedience for a situation attested as early as Homer. When in the fourth book of the *Iliad* Zeus yields to Hera's desire to destroy Troy, he does so "willingly with an unwilling heart (*hekôn aekonti thumôi*)" (*Iliad* 4.43); and Aristotle discusses similar cases, including voluntary obedience to tyrants, in *Nicomachean Ethics* (3.1 1110a4–b9). 'Willingly' would also cover the situation where the irrational component of the soul is in accord (*sumphônia*), as a result of an appropriate early education, with the prescriptions of law and reason. "Shame," which appears to be the internalized form of law's 'despotism' in Plato's ancient Athens, reflects this circumstance. By the same token, nothing prevents an action performed for reasons that are rational and, in this sense, 'free,' from being called 'voluntary/*hekôn*.'[46] Seen from this perspective, to act freely in the relevant sense (i.e., in accord with reason) would constitute *either* a special case of action done 'voluntarily' (so that the scope of *hekôn* would simply be broader than that of *eleutherôs*) *or* a species, next to 'voluntarily' but of a higher genus never mentioned as such by Plato, which might be dubbed 'self-determination.' This last suggestion is likely to be the more interesting philosophically. It raises a question related to that posed by the puzzling expression "to be superior to oneself": Is there is room in Plato for an ultimate self beyond the 'parts' that make up a soul and apart from the motivations that we host—the Platonic placeholder, so to speak, for a new concept of freedom or, for that matter, of the will. It also leads to the question of how a law can be persuasive and willingly accepted without duress—and the observance of that law still count as a servitude, even though it is of another kind.[47]

Statutory Freedom and Its Obligations

As mentioned above, the statutory notion of freedom is met with frequently in the *Laws*, where the term *eleutheros* ('free') and its antonym *doulos* ('slave') refer, in a legislative or educational context, to the legal status of an individual, for example in formulas such as "if a slave kills or inflicts injuries on a free man. . . ."[48]

But whereas statutory freedom is a given (one is either born or made a slave, or is a free person), it also carries obligations. Social status, in other words, must be distinguished from the set of normative qualities and behaviors that are or should be attached to it. The distinction has, thus, a critical potential, because if social status entails norms that have a qualitative dimension, then it is conceivable that one's social status could be de-legitimized if one does possess the relevant qualities.[49] In the *Laws*, Plato plants this critical potential in describing what it is to be free for a truly free man in a way that goes beyond the fundamentally negative, derivative, or instrumental conception of freedom that dominates the understanding of freedom in Book 3. This is a metamorphosis, too, albeit of another kind and at another level than the constitutional metamorphosis considered above. The trajectory leads eventually to the notion of the persuasive legislative preamble which will be discussed in the next chapters, as well as to the picture of Plato's accomplished free man as occupied full-time with the cultivation of virtue.

The revisionist process that leads to this re-conceptualization and re-definition of freedom (what it takes for a human being to be fully free) takes the form of an argument designed to deepen and broaden what is meant by a series of normative characteristics that are usually attached to the status. One can draw a rough scale going from arguably more traditional qualities and behaviors—most of which range, seen from a modern perspective, from deeply prejudiced to unacceptable—to more refined and in some cases properly philosophical ones. One can further distinguish, along this scale, between a still relatively moderate reshaping of the qualities expected in usual social circumstances and more radical and innovative re-definitions that are crucial for the establishment of a relationship between law, rationality, and freedom. The most relevant texts, which I have numbered from [T1] to [T15], are scattered throughout the twelve books of the *Laws*. The following quotes, in which I have italicized the significant sentences, are disposed not in their order of appearance in the text, but as steps progressively leading to Plato's considered views on 'true' freedom.

A free citizen is in the first place characterized by his shunning of vulgar behavior—he moves his body in a certain way, in appropriate rhythms and to appropriate tunes. This excludes his participation in the performance of comedies:

[T1] The latter [i.e., the Muses] would never make a mistake such as composing words fitted for men and then attaching them to the coloring and tunes of women, or putting together *the tunes and postures of free men* and then joining them *to rhythms fitted for slaves and men who are not free,* or, again, having laid down *rhythms and a free (eleutherion) posture* provide a tune or speech opposite to those rhythms. (2.669c3–8)

[T2] Regarding what we said choral dances should be, our discussion about beautiful bodies and noble souls is now completed. But it is necessary to consider and to know about ugly bodies and thoughts, as well as about those who turn to the objects of comic laughter, whether in speech and song, dance, and the comic representations of all these. [. . .] *We must order slaves and hired strangers to represent such matters.* There should never be any seriousness whatsoever about those, *nor should any free person, woman or man, be openly seen learning these things.* (7.816d3–9 and e5–10)

He practices certain kinds of hunting, not others:

[T3] O friends, may a desire or love for hunting on the sea never seize you, nor for angling, or in general for the hunting of aquatic animals with weels that do all the work of a lazy hunt, whether you are awake or asleep! [. . .] May an enticing and far from liberal (*eleutherios*) love of bird-hunting never come upon any of the young! What is left for our athletes is only the hunting and catching of land-animals [. . .]. (7.823d7–e2 and 823e5–824a2)

He does not engage in trade (money-making) and manual work:

> [T4] For the activity of money-making is not really present in such an [sc. economic] organization, and it follows from it that it is not necessary, nor is it permitted, that anyone make money *by using any of the illiberal (aneleutherôn) ways of money-making,* given that the blameworthy so-called 'base work' (*banausia*) deters a free character. (5.741e1–6)

He knows what a true praise is and praises appropriately:

> [T5] [Clinias] Praising you in speech, stranger, would be something rather burdensome, but it is in actuality that we shall express our strong praise: we shall eagerly follow your words, *which is the way in which someone, at least a free man, clearly shows that he is praising or not.* (3.688d6–9)

He is knowledgeable in a certain number of scientific matters, but only in a certain way:[50]

> [T6] Let these be the customs ordained by laws about each choral dance and the relevant learning, that those concerning the slaves be kept apart from those concerning the masters [. . .] *Furthermore, for the free persons there are three things to be learned.* One is calculation and what pertains to numbers; the second is measurement of length, surface, and volume, taken as a single matter; and the third [is an understanding] of the revolution of the stars in relation to one another as they follow their path. But the majority should not labor at all at such exacting matters, but only a restricted few [. . .]. (7.817e1–818a2)

> [T7] So one should say *that free men must learn, in each of these subjects, as much as* does the great mass of children in Egypt, along with reading letters. (7.819a8–b2)

Conversely, free citizens must also be *treated* in a specific way:

> [T8] Of course, one must punish slaves in a just way, *and not make them indolent by exhorting them, as if they were free persons.* And every address to a servant should be as it were a command, without ever joking with servants in any way [. . .]. (6.777e4–778a2)[51]

> [T9] Let them [the *euthunoi,* officeholders in charge of checking the conduct of other officeholders] divide all the officeholders into twelve parts *and examine them by means of every test appropriate to freedom.* (12.946c5–7)

The overall picture that emerges thus far from this set of passages is clear enough. A free man, in a statutory perspective, is free not only because he is no one's slave, but also because he does not work with his hands (that is what slaves are for), nor, for that matter, does he engage in trade (this is for foreign residents, *metoikoi*[52]). Furthermore, all that is associated with shameful, 'banausic' behaviors and activities (*banausia*), such as comedy, is alien to him. Not being constrained by manual work, he enjoys free time, that is, 'leisure'/*skholê*.

How does a free man occupy his leisure time? In the classical tradition mainly linked to Aristotle's name, free time is dedicated to education and the cultivation of knowledge, to be systematized later under the telling expression "liberal arts." We can, in fact, describe the qualities, dispositions, and modes of behaving that characterize or should characterize a free man as possessing 'liberality' (taken in a broader sense than Aristotle gives it[53]). It is a certain spirit, a way of life that Plato describes at one point (9.865d–e) as a life "lived in a liberal state of mind" (*en eleutheroi phronêmati*), something that is not altogether easy to pin down:

[T10] It is not easy to legislate with any precision on the grounds that one or another thing is liberal (*eleutherikon*, i.e., appropriate for a free man) vs. another that is not (*aneleutheron*), but let this judgement rest instead with those who have obtained the first prize in their hate of the latter and approbation of the former. (11.919e2–5)

The kind of decent person that Plato alludes to here is, in a sense, beyond legislative rules (which does not mean that he is above them), because he knows, without recourse to rules, how to behave in every circumstance in the appropriate way.[54]

There are two specific characteristics of Plato's free man, however, that go much beyond his natural adherence to socially recognized norms and ideals. These two features derive from a crucial and bold move that conjoins the notion of freedom and the free time that makes freedom possible: first, with the exercise of rationality [T11–T12], and then with the possession of virtue [T13].

By contrast with the activities mentioned in T1–T9 (money-making, physical movements, hunting, etc.) and the state of mind evoked in T10, texts T11–T12 bear on the specific relationship between a doctor and a patient, which serves, not only in the *Laws* but throughout Plato's corpus (most prominently in the *Gorgias* and the *Statesman*), as a model for *political* relationships.[55]

The two passages, which I shall quote when I return to them in more detail in the next chapter, deal with the relationships between two kinds of doctors and two kinds of patients, which rest on whether they are (statutorily) free or slaves. The main point of this parallel is that just as a free doctor cures free men and exercises persuasion in a way that implies explanations and arguments than can be, in the strongest version of the comparison, "close to philosophy" (9.857b2), slave doctors resort, as tyrants do, to bald commands.[56]

On the other hand, a free life devoted to cultivating excellence (virtue) is also a rigorously regulated life, as is most clearly brought out in the following, no less bold passage:

> [T13] We say that the work (*ergon*) that is left for those who live in this way [i.e., free of any material needs and spared the necessity to work][57] is neither the smallest nor the basest one, but the greatest of all that is ordered by a just law. For the life which we have most correctly said is devoted to the care of the body in general and to the virtue of the soul *suffers a lack of leisure that is double and much more* [sc. than double] *compared to the life that implies a total lack of leisure for all other tasks*, the one that aims at victory in the Pythian or Olympian games. [807d] For no side-activity coming from other activities should be an obstacle to furnishing the body with appropriate exercises and food and, on another hand, the soul with appropriate pieces of knowledge (*mathêmata*) and habits (*ethê*); *the whole night and day so to speak are sufficient time for someone who is acting precisely in this way, to obtain those things completely and adequately.* Since this is the nature of things, *there should for all free persons be a schedule regulating how they spend all their time, beginning so to speak at dawn until the very next dawn to follow and rising of the sun.* (7.807c1–e2)

Not unlike the substitution of 'freedom' for 'temperance' which I pointed to earlier[58] and to which it is substantially related, this significant and disturbing passage opens the way to a conception of freedom where the word 'freedom' in its common usage is not appropriate any longer. Freedom manifests itself here concretely in the strict obedience to a severe schedule regulating the everyday life of the citizens. We are on the threshold of the transformation of freedom into a kind of servitude. How much time can be devoted, in this schedule, to the lengthy argument that are required by a free legislative discussion is a question that is not considered by Plato at this juncture. It will re-emerge in relationship with the discussion of preambles.[59]

7

Construing the Preambles

Only the philosophers voluntarily do what the rest of humankind does against their will, because of law.

XENOCRATES, FRAG. 3 HEINZE, QUOTED BY
PLUTARCH, *ON MORAL VIRTUE*, 7.446D

The Violence of the Law

The diverse meanings and connotations of the word *nomos*/law in Greek are the legacy of a complex socio-political history. Plato's dialogues, not least the *Laws*, reflect this diversity.[1] But the way in which *Laws* organizes and structures the lexical field, in its own unsystematic albeit systematic style, around two complementary poles that I call the legislative 'form' and the legislative 'content,' is unique. This distinction, as in the case of 'aim' and 'target,' is not one that Plato explicitly draws, even though, on his way towards the notion of a 'preamble,' he uses the expression "the form of the law" (*en skhêmati nomou*, 4.718b6) to contrast the traditional formulation of the law with the elusive kind of discourse he is trying to capture at that point. But the relationship between law and preambles, which is at the core of Plato's legislative project, is best understood as resulting from a tension between these two poles. For whereas the content of the law is rational (noetic) to the extent that it encapsulates, in the terms of the comparison of human beings to puppets in Book 1 (644d–645c1), the pull of appropriate reasoning (an intimate relationship that is reflected in the alleged derivation of the word *nomos*/law, among others, from *nous*/reason),[2] its form is both irrational and apolitical to the extent that it makes use of constraint and 'violence' (*bia*).

107

The association of law with constraint, which comes to the fore in Book 4, is familiar from the formula, which Plato explicitly attributes to the sophist Hippias in the *Protagoras*, according to which "*nomos*, which is a tyrant over human beings, commits violence upon many things against nature," and also from Antiphon's argument which, without reference to tyranny, considers laws as working most of the time against nature ("most of the things that are just according to the law are established in a way that is hostile to nature").[3] The thought can be traced back, not without some interpretive tweaking, to a famous fragment of Pindar quoted in the *Gorgias*, according to which, in Plato's or for that matter Callicles' reading of it, the law of nature is the domination of the stronger, who exercises violence (*bia*).[4]

The endorsement by the Athenian at this juncture of a line of thought that associates law with violence has something surprising about it. The surprise, not registered on this occasion as it is on others,[5] comes not only from the convergence between the Athenian's characterization of law and a criticism characteristic of certain 'sophists,' but also and above all from its apparent conflict with two of his own statements in previous books concerning the nature of law. For in Book 3, the Athenian had asserted, against the (Calliclean-) Pindaric views that force or violence is the supreme 'law,' that law rules over *willing* individuals:

> [. . .] I would not say, cleverest Pindar, that the ruling of the law over *those who are voluntarily ruled* (*tên tou nomou hekontôn arkhên*) and not by constraint is against nature, but in agreement with nature. (3.690c1–3)[6]

Moreover, we know from the puppet analogy in Book 1 that the "reasoning (*logismos*) [. . .] which, having become the common belief of the city, receives the name of law" (1.644d2–3), is fragile when it is "fine" (*logismou kalou ontos*, 645a5–6)—this is why it needs assistance—so that there is a sense in which the law, far from being violent, shares reason's fragility. The contrast between the two descriptions, however, is precisely the point: what the characterization of law as 'tyrannical' and exercising 'violence' in Book 4 reveals is that, given the 'fragility' of the noetic content that the true law expresses, its 'voluntarily acceptance' in Book 3 is part of a normative program. The 'violence' of the law that the Athenian is now talking about belongs to a law that has already received some sort of 'assistance' and reinforcement.[7]

Law can be said to be violent in two senses, one of which is less visible than the other, but no less important. Typically, a law is constituted of two elements, an order (explicit or implicit) and a threat that will come into play if the order is not respected. Plato illustrates this dynamic, which was already well attested and would remain classical, [8] with an example that, given the biographical structuration of his own legislation, constitutes the first law to be formulated:[9]

> One [scil. a man] must marry when he reaches the age of thirty and before the age of thirty-five. If not, he must be punished with fines and disgrace, fines of such and such amount, and disgrace of such and such kind. (4.721b1–3)

Violence takes here the form of a threat appended to the legislative command (*epapeilêsas tên zêmian*, 4.719e9). It is, I submit, one among the possible assists that a law, insofar as it is weak, needs to gain strength.[10] But there is a sense in which a law is violent at a more primitive, deeper level, that is present in the command/*epitaxis* itself, of which Plato says at 4.723a5, as if in passing but in a sensitive context,[11] that it is "what the law precisely is" (*tên epitaxin, ho dê estin ho nomos*). As a matter of fact, a simple command could be viewed as even more violent than the penal threat that accompanies it, because a threat, which has a dissuasive force, can still count as a form of persuasion, and consequently as being able to trigger voluntary obedience (on a weak construal of the term 'voluntary'/*hekôn*);[12] a command, on the other hand, does not provide any reason at all, not even of a dissuasive kind. Whether law is considered as including threat or as a bare order, however, the violence of the law is the reason why Plato calls an 'unmixed' (*akratos*) law, that is, a law which is not preceded by a persuasive preamble, a "tyrannical command" (*tyrannikon epitagma*, 4.722e7–723a4), in a clear allusion to Hippias' formula.[13]

The problem that arises at this point is obvious: the reinforcement contradicts what the law is normatively supposed to be, namely a rule that triggers voluntary obedience in a more obvious and also more generous sense of the term 'voluntary.' The *Laws* is to a large extent a reflection about whether this contradiction can be, if not removed, at least minimized, and if so, how so? That is, can the content of the law can be strengthened without betraying its own nature? Hence the centrality of persuasive preambles, which Plato presents, understandably, as a major novelty of his legislation.[14] Whether preambles succeed in making law adequate to the requirements of its true concept is of course a further question. As we shall see, Plato's answer, which is staged rather than stated, falls on the negative side, since the notion of a preamble that would fulfill the persuasive function without the help of the form of the law only appears at the level of what I call a 'legislative utopia.' What preambles can at best achieve is to reduce the constraint and increase the voluntariness with which the citizens will obey a law, even though punishment remains the ultimate resource of the lawgiver—the divine one no less than his human representative. Human nature permits this much, but no more.

Correcting the Past

Laws that have been set up in the past, observes the Athenian as the sun reaches its peak and the company is taking a rest, have exclusively relied on (a certain kind of) violence (*bia*), which makes of lawgiving (if we accept the reading of the manuscripts) a "fight (*makhê*)":

> It seems that none of the lawgivers has ever reflected on the fact that whereas it is possible to use two means in order to legislate, persuasion and violence, to the extent that this is possible with an uneducated crowd,[15] they use only the latter; for they legislate without mixing fight with persuasion but use only unmixed violence. (4.722b4–c1)[16]

The claim is taken up in Book 9.857c1–3: "You have woken me up [...]" says the Athenian to Clinias, "and reminded me of what I was already thinking about earlier—namely, that the establishing of laws has never been accomplished in anything like the correct way."

The contrast between this correct way and the traditional one is more fully developed by reference to two medical practices, which are the object of two similar though not entirely overlapping sections in Books 4 and 9. The analogy between legislation and medicine introduced in Book 4.719e7–720e6 aims at clarifying the notion of a preamble. In order to fully appreciate its implications, it must be situated in the broader context of a four-step argument (from 719a7 to 723d4) that takes the form of a dialogue between the lawgiver and a poet that covers (1) the nature of the norm on which legislative prescriptions are founded, that is the content of the law; (2), the comparison between two kinds of lawgivers and doctors; (3), an example of the new model of legislation; and (4), and the definitive demarcation between preamble and law. The comparison (2) is then taken up in Book 9 in a shorter passage (5) that deepens and radicalizes the comparison between legislation and medicine. In what follows, I consider the substance of these five steps in turn.

Poet and Lawgiver on 'Measure'

The Athenian, projecting himself in a possible future, imagines that the colonists "have arrived and are present [sc. on the site of the colony]" (4.715e3–4). He addresses them with a fictive speech that will, as it turns out, inaugurate an entirely new legislative genre, the preamble (*prooimion*), still unnamed at this stage. This address, the first part of a whole that will be considered in more detail in the next chapter, consists in a series of prescriptions that state what "a man in his sense (*ton emphrona*) should and should not do and think" (4.716b6, cf. 719b1–2) about god and his parents, the two most important objects of his care.[17] They belong to the parainetic tradition of which Hesiod's *Works and Days* is the classical representative (cf. *parainein*, 718d3),[18] and they depend on one foundational assumption, namely that:

> The god (*ho theos*) [...], just as the ancient saying asserts, holds the beginning, end, and middle of all things that are, completing his revolution in a straight line, according to nature [...]. (4.715e7–716a2)

The ancient saying alluded to is this famous Orphic line:

> Zeus was born first, Zeus with bright lightning, last / Zeus is the head, Zeus the middle, and by Zeus all things are made.[19]

Plato's remarkable exegesis, which combines, oxymoronically, the linear inevitability of the accomplishment (the "straight course") with the circularity of the noetic and cosmic revolution, is directed to the reader, rather than to the colonists, who would not have grasped that the traditional exhortation relies on doctrinal views that would be fleshed out, much later, in the first preamble to the law on impiety in Book 10—the most philosophically demanding of all preambles.[20] The same is true of the transparently anti-Protagorean formula that the Athenian uses a few lines later to present the god in question as "the measure of all things":

> The god, for us, would be most of all the measure of all things, and doubtless far more so than some human being, as they say. (4.716c4–6)[21]

'Measure' (*metron*) is here taken in the specific sense of a measure calculated to be appropriate and not disproportionate, and to this extent are 'measured' (*metrios*, 716c3). It follows that the moderate or temperate person (*ho sôphrôn*, 716d1) and his actions, which are also measured, are dear (*philon*) to the god, since to be measured, i.e., temperate, is to be like him (*homoios gar*, 716d2).[22] This understanding of measure as referring to what is 'measured' in the appropriate sense of 'moderate' is not congenial to the poet, who has all the more reason now to reject the lawgiver's views since the latter has previously denied him the freedom to compose as he deems appropriate (4.719b4–7, referring to Book 2.656c1–d2, cf. 660a3–8). He is now given a chance to argue against these restraints. His claim is that he, the poet, and not the lawgiver, is the one who knows the measure of things and hence possesses the authority concerning "what we should do and say" (719b1–2).[23] His argument targets the last example of 'measured' ('moderate') behavior mentioned by the lawgiver at the end of his address to the colonists, which regards the burial of one's parents. The lawgiver had located 'moderation' between a shortcoming and an excess:

> when parents die, the beautiful funeral is the most moderate (*sôphrones-tatê*) one, which neither surpasses the customary dimensions nor falls short of those which the forefathers posited for their parents. (4.717d7–e1)

In his reply to the lawgiver, the poet presents this 'in-between' as a "middle":

> a funeral can be either excessive, or insufficient, or measured (*metrias*); you chose one of these, the middle one (*tên mesên*): you recommended the latter and praised it without any qualification. (4.719d4–7)

The poet sees in this recommendation a clear indication of the lawgiver's ignorance about what 'measure' really consists in ("if you knew what we should do and say, isn't it obvious that you would also declare it?" 719b1–2). The praise of moderate burial neglects, according to the poet, cases in which moderation is *not* fitting, for example when the dead is either rich or poor, i.e., not himself of a modest condition (719d7–e3). Unlike the lawgiver, the poet knows that a moderate burial is appropriate only when the family is of modest means, and he knows also how to determine the correct measure in other cases. The dispute turns on what measure/*metron* means. The Athenian construes measure as being always one and the same, since what is moderate, *metrion*, is ultimately determined by a single middle point, *meson*, between an excess and a shortfall.[24] By contrast, the poet adapts measure to social circumstances that are variable by definition.

"For the lawgiver, however, it is not possible to say two things about one topic, for when it comes to law one must always make a single declaration about each subject" (4.719d1–2), the poet rightly observes.[25]

Important as it is in terms of its anti-Protagorean stance, however, the passage is not primarily geared towards the content of the lawgiver's theological assumption. In fact and most ironically, the lawgiver is more than ready to subscribe to the poet's view according to which his recommendations, as exposed in his address to the colonists, are 'not yet' a law (*mêpô* [...] *nomon*, 719e5), provided that 'not yet' be referred to the form of the utterance rather than to its content and be understood in its primary, temporal sense, as qualifying a discourse which *precedes* the law.

Whereas the recommendations in question are not laws, they are nevertheless prescriptive, since, like the laws, they state what should be done and what should not (for instance, whether burial expenditures should be moderate in an absolute sense or proportionate to the wealth of the family concerned). The difference is that they are not backed (for the time being) by any threat of punishment should they not be respected, as a law typically would be, but rely on exhortation and persuasion (*paramuthias kai peithous*, 720a1).[26] The Athenian presents them as a supplement to the law (cf. *prosdidôi*, 720a2) but places this supplement "at the beginning of the laws" (719e8) and not afterward, in the position that legislative threats would normally occupy ('do such and such; if not, the penalty will be . . .').[27] Such are the general characteristics of the legislative discourse that will eventually come to be called a 'preamble'—a persuasive discourse that precedes the law.

At this point, one might ask, given that a preamble is no less prescriptive than a law, could it *replace* a law, at least in principle?[28] The Athenian suggests as much in the important 'preliminary' (*prorrêthentôn*, 7.823d3) to the preamble about hunting. There, reflecting on the relationship between praise and law, he characterizes "the perfect [lit. 'highest'] citizen" (*ton akron politên*, 823a5) as one who is bound by the statements of "what the lawgiver thinks is fine and not fine no less than by the things prohibited by legal penalties" (823a4–6), which means, in the specific matter of hunting, to "honor more, and carry out more fully, the orders uttered in praise (*ta met'epainou rhêthenta* [. . .] *kai prostakhthenta*) than the threats accompanied by penalties and what has been set down by law (*nomothetêthenton*)" (823c7–d2).[29] This is also the issue at stake, at a higher level of abstraction and idealization, in the double treatment of the medical analogy in Books 4 and 9, to which I now turn.

The Medical Analogy, First Version

The first version of the analogy between medicine and politics occurs in the *Laws* at 4.719e7–721e6.[30]

Is the one who is in charge of the laws [. . .] just going to state straightaway what must and must not be done, add the threat of a penalty, and turn to another law [720a], without adding any single piece of exhortation or persuasion to the laws he has formulated? The same happens when one doctor is accustomed to cure us in one way, another one in another way—but let's recall what each of the two modes is, in order that we beg the lawgiver, in the same way as children would beg the doctor to cure them as gently as possible. But what am I exactly saying? I am saying that there are, aren't there, certain doctors and certain assistants, whom we also call doctors [...] [720b8]. Are you also aware that, given that among the sick people in the cities there are both slaves and free persons [720c], it is for the most part slave doctors who, whether running through the city or working out of a surgery, treat the slaves, and that none of these doctors gives or receives any account (*logon didôsi kai apodekhetai*) of the illnesses afflicting the servants? Instead, as if he had an exact knowledge, he gives his orders on the basis of beliefs that come from experience (*ex empeirias*), with arrogance, like a tyrant, before hurrying off to another sick servant, thus providing relief to his master by caring for their patients. [720d]. *The free* doctor, on the other hand, most often *cures and looks after the diseases of free persons.* He investigates the onset of the sickness from the beginning (*exetazôn ex arkhês*) and takes note of its nature. Sharing what he notices with the patient himself and his friends, he both learns something himself from the affected relatives and, as much as he is able (*kath'hoson hoios te estin*), teaches (*didaskei*) the sick person, puts off giving orders until he has in some way persuaded her; at this point, still using persuasion (*meta peithous*) in order to secure the docility of the sick person, he attempts to bring her to full health (4.719e7–720a6 and 720b8–e2).

This passage must be read alongside the second version, which will be quoted below, and in the light of other treatments of the parallel between medical and political expertise.[31] The general framework is provided by the *Gorgias*. There, the basic analogy according to which there is an expertise concerning the soul and a corresponding expertise concerning the body (464b2–c3) is expanded into a complex eight-term scheme that breaks down the two kinds of expertise, the one that concerns the soul and the one that deals with the body, into two branches, one preventive, the other curative, and then also makes a second analogical subdivision of as many counterfeits of these four genuine fields of expertise, four counterfeits that aim at producing pleasure rather than the good. In the *Gorgias*, this systematic construct is meant expose rhetoric as being no more than "the counterpart (*antistrophon*) in the soul to what [pleasurable] cooking is in the body" (465d6–e1), or, in more abstract terms, as "an image (*eidolon*) of a part of politics" (463d2). We get the following chart (based on 464b2–465e2):

1. Expertise concerning the soul = politics, subdivided into legislation/ *nomothetikê* (preventive) and judicial practice/*dikastikê* (curative).

2. Expertise concerning the body (unnamed), subdivided into gymnastics/*gumnastikê* (preventive measures) and medicine/*iatrikê* (curative measures).

3. Counterfeit of the expertise concerning the soul (unnamed), subdivided into sophistics/*sophistikê* and rhetoric/*rhetorikê*.

4. Counterfeit of the expertise concerning the body (unnamed), subdivided into cosmetics/*kommôtikê* and the art of cooking/*opsopoiêtikê*.

In the argument that follows, which introduces a distinction between ends and means in order to refute Polus' contention that tyrants, since they do whatever they want, are therefore the most powerful men in their cities, Socrates brings in (among others) the medical analogy:

> Do you think that when people do something, they want the thing they're doing at the time, or do they want the thing for the sake of which they do what they're doing? Do you think that people who drink medicines prescribed by their doctors, for instance, want to do what they are doing, the act of drinking the medicine and suffering,[32] or do they want to be healthy, the thing for the sake of which they're drinking it? (467c5–10, trans. Zeyl slightly modified)

The *Gorgias*, however, does not dwell on the means that are at the disposal of the doctor, which are simply assumed to be painful and imposed by him, whether the patient wants them or not. The conceptual setting of the argument precludes valuing rhetoric as a resource at the disposal of the political expert, since it falls, by virtue of the analogy, among the counterfeits of the genuine craft. This is in line with the passage of the *Statesman* that dismisses persuasion as incumbent upon the expert ruler on the grounds that the only criterion that he need consider is the end, not the means:

> [The Eleatic Stranger] Yes, but these people [sc. the few existing experts in politics], whether they rule over willing or unwilling subjects, whether according to written laws or without them, and whether they rule as rich men or poor, we must suppose—as is now our view—to be carrying out whatever sort of rule they do on the basis of expertise. Doctors provide the clearest parallel. We believe in them whether they cure us with our consent or without it, by cutting or burning or applying some other painful treatment, and whether they do so according to written rules or apart from written rules, and whether as poor men or rich. In all these circumstances we do not at all scruple to say they are doctors, so long as they exercise

expertise in caring for us, by purging or otherwise reducing us, or else building us up—it is no matter, if only each and every one of those who care for our bodies acts for our bodies' good, making them better than they were, and so preserves what is in their care. It's in this way, as I think, and in no other that we'll lay down the criterion of medicine and of any other sort of rule whatsoever; it is the only correct criterion. (*Statesman*, 293a6–c3, trans. Rowe)

This passage is clearly an elaboration of the comparison that Socrates, towards the end of his discussion with Callicles, makes between himself, claiming that he is one of the few and indeed the only true Athenian expert in politics (521d6–8), and a doctor accused by a cook before a jury of children on the grounds that "he destroys the youngest among you [children] by cutting and burning them, and by slimming them down and choking them he confuses them. He gives them the most bitter potions to drink and forces hunger and thirst on them. He doesn't feast you on a great variety of pleasurable dishes the way I do!" (521e8–522a2, trans. Zeyl slightly modified).[33]

The function of the corresponding statement in the *Statesman* requires interpretation, given that the overall thrust of that dialogue is to establish a clear distinction between a tyrant and a king and that it allows scope for rhetoric (*rhetoreia*) as one of the king's most important resources (it is one of the king's three "auxiliaries," alongside military skill and justice, 303e10–304a2)—in line, this time, with the brief evocation of "the expert and good orator" who rather unexpectedly pops up at the end of the *Gorgias* (506d5–6).[34] My present point, however, is that the *Gorgias* and the *Statesman* develop the analogy between politics and medicine only in reference to the goal of each of the two practices, i.e., the health of the body and that of the soul, without taking notice in their definitions of the two crafts of the issues of command and compliance. The dismissal of persuasion as a criterion necessary to medical and legislative experts alike stands in stark contrast to the *Laws*, which focuses, in the development of the analogy, on the relationship between patient and doctor on the one hand, and lawgiver and citizen on the other. Viewed from this perspective, it is no longer appropriate to say that medicine has to do with the body only: since, in order to heal his patient, the doctor must also *address* him, and this he cannot do unless his expertise includes a 'rhetorical' component. Thus, whereas the *Gorgias* distinguishes between authentic medicine and legislation and their counterfeits (cooking and sophistry), on the basis of their *aims*: "pleasure" in the case of cooking and sophistry, "the good" in the case of medicine and legislation, the demarcation in the *Laws* turns instead on a distinction between two *means* that have the same aim, namely persuasion and coercion.

To be sure, the comparison of the citizens with "children who beg the doctor to cure them as gently as possible" (4.720a4–6) seems at first to suggest that an expert lawgiver would be as successful without persuasion as with it, which is the conclusion that emerges in the *Gorgias* and is still lingers in the *Statesman*, in spite of its vindication of kingship over tyranny.[35] What distinguishes the *Laws*, however, is that the children's request is recognized as legitimate. The therapy, as efficient as it may be, would be in a certain way, namely politically, a failure if the patient were healed at the cost of slavish and despotic treatment. Friendship and freedom are at stake. Persuasion safeguards the patients' freedom in the quasi-political relationship implied by medical practice.

Consequently, the Athenian develops the analogy from a different angle. He assumes that medical assistants (*hupêretai*, 720a7)—whose existence is attested in the Hippocratic corpus—were called 'doctors,' just as the doctor they were assisting.[36] The difference between the two categories of doctors lies first in the fact that the assistants' practice is not grounded in a knowledge of the nature of things (*kata phusin*, 720b4) but rather on a familiarity with medical procedure gained through experience (*kat'empeirian*, b3). Since they execute the orders they receive without any teaching (in contrast to the free doctor's pupils), these 'assistants' can be called 'slave-doctors' (this would be true even if their social status were to be that of free men). The nature of their practice is, furthermore, reflected in the status of their patients. For the collaboration of the assistant, in the Platonic reconstruction, is less about taking care of certain parts of medical procedures (as was probably the case in reality) than about relieving the master of a certain number of patients in order to permit a 'free' treatment of others: the assistant, who is a slave, is supposed to take care of slave patients, just as the master, who is free, cures patients who are equally free.[37]

If the medical relationship can serve as a *comparans* for the political relationship, it is because both practices deliver prescriptions that are commands of a kind (*prostaxis, epitaxis*). Seen from a political perspective, however, an assistant who, by virtue of his status as well as his training, is a slave, treats his patients like a tyrant (720c6–7). The despotic character of his treatment comes from the fact that he does not accompany his prescriptive 'orders' with any type of explanation to his patient (*oute tina logon* [...] *didôsi* ...); nor for that matter does he receive any (... *oute apodekhetai*) from his patient. The phrase "to give and receive an account" (720c3–5) is in this context a clear echo of the famous Socratic-Platonic formula.[38] The expression thus prefigures what the reformulation of the analogy in Book 9 will show to be ultimately at stake, namely the relationship between legislation and philosophical discussion.

In contrast to the slave-doctor who acts despotically with his numerous patients, the free doctor provides an example of what a non-despotic, properly political legislative practice would be. The free doctor takes time to inform himself about individual cases, not only by talking with the patient, but also with his family (720d3–4). He thereby enriches his own knowledge while "teaching (*didaskei*) the sick person in so far as possible (*kath' hoson hoios te estin*)" (720d5–6).[39]

The way in which the free doctor proceeds, however, does not simply substitute for the slave's practice: rather, it includes it. For the prescription, even preceded by dialogue and explanation, remains a constituent part of the therapeutic act. That is why the relevant contrast is not between a slavish-tyrannical and a free persuasive method, but, as stated in the conclusion (720e2–5), between a "one-sided" or "exclusive" method (*monakhêi*), which issues its prescriptions only in the form of commands, and one that is "twofold" (*diplêi*), with persuasion preceding prescription. The latter is to be preferred to the former, not because it is more efficient and leads to better results, but because the exclusive method is "more savage" (*agrioteron*, 720e4). The fact that the Athenian attributes the same efficiency to both (*tên mian apotelôn dunamin*, 720e3) is striking: one would have thought that a craft based on the knowledge of the 'nature' of things would be in a better position to cure than a practice relying on empirical acquaintance. On the other hand, considering that both methods as equally efficient highlights the fact that the only criterion relevant in the context is relational: the focus on the formal conditions for procuring health, rather than on health itself, is meant to show that the formal structure of lawgiving is an integral, and indeed essential part of *political* expertise.

An Example: Marriage (4.720e7–721d6)

The duality of medical practices has a counterpart in the field of legislation. The law on marriage can here serve as an appropriate example because, as already noted, the order in which Plato presents the laws is determined "according to nature" (720e11), that is, following the sequence of events in a human life. But this perspective remains implicit. What claims our attention instead is the two possible forms that the law in question can assume.

The 'simple' form would command men to marry between the ages of 30 and 35, and would then state the penalties for noncompliance (a fine and a political sanction)—the passage has been quoted above.[40] The alternate "double" form also begins with an order; but instead of immediately listing the consequences of disobedience, it puts forward a *reason* in support the legislative prescription. The reason, which is meant to be persuasive (this is an example of a legislative preamble) is, in this case, a version of Diotima's argument in the *Symposium* (206c1–207a4): the goal of marriage is procreation, which is required by the eternity of the world and consequently for the eternal preservation of humankind, and is at the same time an ersatz for impossibility of personal immortality. The citizen is invited to 'reflect' (*dianoêthenta*, 721b7) on this argument.[41] Only if he remains unpersuaded will he become subject to the law, that is to the penalties it includes.[42]

Preamble vs. Law (4.721d7–723)

A twofold legislative statement, in contrast to a simple one, is not "double" in the sense that it is twice as long (721d8–e3): this would be, according to the pun at 722e6, "a rather simple(- minded) duality," for "it is pretty naive to discuss whether writings should be plentiful or sparse; for what must be honored [. . .] are the best writings, not the shortest or the long ones" (722a7–b1). It will in fact turn out that a preamble can be long if that is what is needed to reach its aim.[43]

The relevant point is that there are dual means at the disposal of the lawgiver—namely persuasion and violence (*duoin* [. . .] *peithôi kai biai*, 722b6), one of which, besides being only twice as good in terms of the excellence of the (legislative) practice, also confirms the relevance of the medical analogy (722b3–4). Giving persuasion its proper place means that the lawgiver does not view his law-giving as a kind of fight against an adversary, but instead opts for a certain blend (*kerannuntes*, ibid.) that includes persuasion.

What does this exactly look like? Should force be blended with persuasion as wine with water, so that the separate identity of both constituents disappears in the mix, as the participle *kerannuntes* could suggest? The mix that the Athenian has in mind at this juncture is, rather, that of a 'compound' in which each of the two ingredients retain their specificity (the model is paratactical, as in the case of the 'mixed constitution.'[44]) The free doctor, insofar as he prefaces a prescription with persuasion, provides a good example of appropriate juxtaposition. So does the succession of prelude and song, in the field of musical performance. The technical name *prooimion*, to be translated with 'prelude' rather than 'preamble' in this context, offers the advantage, from the point of view of a lawgiver, that the song that follows the prelude in the case of kitharoedic poetry (722d6–7) bears the same name as the law, namely *nomos* (which in this case gets translated by 'nome').[45] The duality can be transposed to political laws:

> Yet when it comes to real 'laws,' those we say are political, no one has ever spoken of a prelude [= a preamble] nor has there come to be a composer that brought one forth into the light—as if it did not exist by nature. (722e1–4)[46]

Legislative rhetoric as recommended by the *Laws*, like the political rhetoric (the *rhetoreia* mentioned in the *Statesman* [304a1] as one of the three auxiliaries of the true monarch), perfectly fits the spacious definition that the *Phaedrus* gives of the art:

> Isn't the rhetorical art (*hê rhêtorikê*), taken as a whole, a way of directing the soul (*psukhagôgia*) by means of speech, not only in the lawcourts and on other public occasions but also in private? Isn't it one and the same art whether its subject is great or small, and no more to be held in esteem—if it is followed correctly–when its questions are serious than when they are trivial? Or what have you heard about all this? (261a7–b2,trans. Nehamas and Woodruff)

The *Laws* broadens the perspective even more by observing that preambles, which by Plato's time had acquired a firm place in rhetoric, do not belong to articulated speech only, but to any kind of vocal emission:

> For all speeches and whatever voice partakes of, there are 'preludes'— something like introductory movements—that offer a kind of useful initiating of what is going to be achieved. (4.722d3–6, cf. 723a3–4)

The general reference to 'voice' points to an overarching genus of which rhetorical speech and singing would constitute two species.[47]

The Medical Analogy, Second Version

The second version of the medical analogy occurs in Book 9.857b9–e7.[48]

> We did not make a bad comparison, when we represented all those who are now living under laws as slaves being cured by slaves. There is no doubt that

if one of those doctors who practices medicine on the basis of experiences (*emperiai*) that lack justification (*aneu logou*) should ever come across *a free doctor* [857d] *carrying on a dialogue (dialegomenos) with a free person who is sick* and using arguments that come close to philosophizing (*tou philosophein eggus*), grasping the disease from its origin (*ex arkhês*) and going back up to the nature of bodies as a whole, he would quickly burst out laughing and say nothing other than the words that most of the so-called doctors always have ready at hand about these matters. For he would declare: 'You stupid fellow! You are not curing the sick patient, instead you are almost educating him, as if what he needed were to become a doctor, rather than healthy.' (9.857c4–e1)

The Athenian, who is speaking in this passage, has just legislated on theft without spelling out the various kinds of infractions and their gravity. Clinias manifests his surprise at the omission (9.857b4–8). In response, the Athenian goes out of his way to confirm the relevance of the comparison between the relationship of existing legislative codes to the citizens and that of slave-doctors to their slave-patients: "We did not make a bad comparison . . . ," he says at 857c4–5, harking back (somewhat euphemistically, but for this reason even more strongly) to the analogy set out in Book 4 (the appropriateness of which was already noted at 722b3–4). But the way in which the analogy is now developed includes a remarkable inflexion. In the previous passage, the medical analogy, kept within the limits of an attested medical practice (even if it was located in a somewhat idealized sociological framework), only served to capture the general form of a legislative preamble as a persuasive introduction capable of making the citizen more disposed to obey the ensuing law. The passage in Book 9, while moving on the same ground, gives the comparison an unexpected twist by endowing both the medical analogue and its legislative counterpart with features that are this time idealized in a much stronger way. For whereas the 'free' medical practice depicted at 4.720d1–e2 consisted first in "receiving and giving an account" in the weak sense of collecting the information relevant for the medical diagnosis, it is now presented as a discussion that, having started with questions that concern the ailment that affects the patient, ascends to the entire nature of bodies (857d3–4: *peri phuseôs pasês epanionta tês tôn sômatôn*). We are not informed any further about the precise course of the conversation, but the terms used (*epaniôn*, for ascending to higher principles; *phusis*, for the nature of a given item; *pasa*, to mark generality and inclusiveness) sound as if the two parties were now engaging in an inquiry belonging to natural philosophy. Indeed, the Athenian, in a remarkable move, characterizes the discussion as "close to philosophizing" (*tou philosophein eggus*, 857d2), one of the two mentions of philosophy that appear in the entire work.[49] The reason why the medical discussion remains 'close' to philosophizing without turning properly philosophical is not stated, but we can see clearly that a discussion between a doctor and his patient, idealized as it may be, remains here subordinate to the medical practice under consideration, whose aim is to cure bodies. In Book 10, the lawgiver will engage, in the first preamble to the law against atheists, in an inquiry about the origin of bodily movements which the lawgiver would arguably not hesitate to characterize as straightforwardly philosophical, rather than quasi-philosophical. The link between the two situations remains subtle, but it is inescapable. It raises a crucial compositional problem to which I shall return in the next chapter.

In the present context it will be enough to emphasize that the quasi-philosophical medical discussion depicted in Book 9 is close enough to philosophy to hypothetically trigger mockery in a slave-doctor attending the scene (857c7–e1).[50] The practice of the free doctor, he observes, goes far beyond the requirements of his craft in a therapeutic context, as the free doctor seems to be training a disciple rather than curing a patient.

The reaction of the slave-doctor is understandable. What the Athenian has just provided is a hyperbolic interpretation of the teaching (*didaskei*) that the free doctor gives his patient "as far as he is able" according to the version of Book 4.720d5–6 (cf. *didaskousi* at 720b5). For, although the terminology of teaching and learning is already in place in Book 4, there is no reason to think that the teaching in question at that point consists in anything more than giving to a layman the necessary clarifications so that he accepts the prescription the doctor is about to deliver.[51] Hence Clinias' question, which suggests that the slave-doctor has a point: "Would not he be right in saying that [namely, that the free doctor is not curing but teaching his patient]?" (9.857e2).

However, whereas the reaction of the slave doctor is not unfounded with respect to the practice of medicine (it points to the limited function of communication in a therapeutic situation), things look quite different when it comes to the second member of the analogy, namely lawgiving, for legislative expertise aims at *eliminating* the formal violence of the law (its "tyrannical" side, according to Book 4). More precisely, it "educates" (*paideuei*) the citizens rather than legislates (9.857e4–5). The slave's criticism can thus be interpreted positively as pointing to a crucial difference between an ordinary therapeutic situation and a pedagogical legislative process which, if successfully pursued to its term, would eventually make the form of the law superfluous. In a further move, the whole discussion about the constitution, which distinguishes between what is best and what is imposed by necessity, is presented by the Athenian as the prototypic example of a free, ideal discussion that teaches the citizens, as a lawgiver should do before formulating the law. This teaching, by a new turn of the screw, consists in the very inquiry (*en skêpsei*) about political matters that the *Laws* itself reports.[52]

On this reading, the lawgiver's ideal would be not only to have a legislative preamble precede the law, but—in accordance with the suggestion I made earlier concerning the preamble on hunting—even to dispense with the law altogether, insofar as it is a command, in favor of a didactic discourse that would not only be "close to philosophy," nor, by the same token, a preamble *to the law*, but philosophy *tout court.* [53] The elasticity of the form of the preamble opens to the lawgiver, whose speech is prescriptive by definition, the possibility of such a perspective. According to the *Laws*, no statement can be made without a preamble; but a preamble, the primary function of which is to strip the command from its tyrannical character, can now always be viewed as leading to a statement the force of which is no longer based on the coercive dimension of the law.[54] The fact that Plato recurrently makes a strict distinction between (scientific) instruction (*didakhê*) and (doxastic or rhetorical) persuasion (*peithô*) is no argument against this idealizing trajectory, given that it *is* an idealization.[55]

Legislating, in the *Laws*, always operates in a realm that extends beyond legislation. The preambles are the first prominent expression of this extension of law's empire. At the end of the day, however, preambles are not the only way in which law formally transcends itself in order to be conform to its 'nature': what is implied is an educative process that extends throughout one's life. Preambles, which implement locally, so to speak, the project of limiting the violence of the law, which means reducing as much as possible the gap between the rationality of its content and the irrationality of its form, have as their vanishing point (as in a perspectivist painting) a 'teaching' (*didakhê*) to which persuasion (*peithô*) hyperbollicaly tends. Their ultimate horizon is that of a 'legislative utopia,' meaning the ideal of a legislative discourse that would be nothing other than a philosophical dialogue—the discursive counterpart of the paradigm of the first city evoked in Book 5.739b8-c2.[56] The horizon is not only remote, but also fragile. It is the more important to spot its presence since it stands in a work that focuses on retreats.

8

A Rhetoric in the Making

The universe of laws is infinitely larger than the body of legal norms.

ALAIN SUPIOT, *HOMO JURIDICUS*, P. 42

Three Scales

We saw in last chapter how the radicalized version of Book 9 foresees the possibility of a more philosophy-like discussion between a doctor and his patient, one that deepens the subject to look beyond an ailment at "the nature of bodies." But how close to philosophy should this discussion come? And does the 'proximity' clause, which applies to the medical *comparans*, also apply, and if so to what extent, to the legislative *comparandum*? Is the Athenian suggesting that a free legislative dialogue would be a philosophical dialogue in its own right, or only "close to philosophy," as is the medical dialogue? The answer cannot be straightforward, because it all depends on the aspect of the law that is under consideration. If we look at the law only from the vantage point of its content, we are led to say that the lawgiver, in an ideal situation, would indeed engage with the citizen(s) in a truly philosophical dialogue, as the Athenian certainly does, even though within limits that are explicitly mentioned, in the (meta-legislative) conversation reported in the *Laws* itself. On the other hand, if we admit that legislating is by definition different from philosophizing, then the best a lawgiver can achieve in his political function of lawgiving and educating the citizens will remain, as in the case of the doctor, "close to philosophy," having 'something to do' with it, sometimes more, sometimes less. It will not be philosophy proper. This does not mean, of course, that the content and terms of the legislative dialogue will be identical to those of the medical dialogue, although Plato does in fact suggest that they are closely related. *Mutatis mutandis*, when it comes to persuading, the situation recalls the passage of the *Republic* that declares 'possible' the paradigm of the just city, provided that its realization in practice be "closest" to it (5. 473a5–b1), and to the related passage in *Laws* 5.739e1–3 that makes the second city as close as possible to the first, paradigmatic one, to which one must always "hold on."[1] There is a scale in this case, too.

Legislative preambles, in the *Laws*, reveal this scalarity no less than the rest of the political program of which they are part; but they show it more insistently and more vividly, because the number of preambles and their diversity present us with a concrete range of possibilities, whereas possible constitutions and institutions are only evoked occasionally, through the mention of other cities to come—among which is a "third" one—and more generally of open-ended processes involving local decisions. The fact that scalarity comes to the fore in the discussion of legislative discourse is not contingent. For what is ultimately at stake in the *Laws*, from a philosophical point of view, is the status of philosophy as a kind of discourse, one among others. The present chapter considers this scale on the basis of a representative selection of preambles, which is the only way to respond to the rather confused debate about whether Plato's preambles are 'rational' or 'irrational.'[2]

Two Typologies

Some twenty preambles can be identified in the *Laws*.[3]

Table 1

	Preamble	Law	Topic
1 (General preamble)	4.715e7–718a7, 5.726a–737d5	[None in particular, cf. above, Chap. 1, p. 28]	Respect to be paid to the gods, to one's soul, to others, and how should one live his life
2	4.721b6–d1	721d1–d6 (cf. 721b1–3)	Age for marriage
3	5.741a6–e6	741e7–744a7	Non-alienability of the tenured land
4	6.772e7–774a1	774a3–c2	Spouse and progeny
5	7.823b1–824a10	824a11–19	Hunting
6	9.853d5–c8	854d1–856a8	Temple robbery

Continued on next page

Table 1 (*continued*)

	Preamble	Law	Topic
7	9.870a1–871a1 (7a) and 872d5–873a4 (7b)	871a1–872c6 873a4–c1	Murder and patricide
8	9.879b5–880a8	880b1–880d7	Violence against elderly people
9	9.880d8–881b3	881b3–882c4	Violence against parents, patricide
10	10.885b-907d3	907d3–910e4	Impiety
11	11.916d4–917b7	917b7–918a6	Frauds
12	11.918a6–919d2	919d2–920c	Retailing
13	11.923e5–923c2	924e4–925d6	Will
14	11.925d7–926a3	926b6–d7	Forced marriage
15	11.926e10–927e8	928a1–d4	Orphans
16	11.930e5–932a8	932a8–d8	Respect due to parents
17	11.937d6–938a7	938a7–c5	Courts
18	12.941b2–c3	941c3–942a4	Money stealing
19	12.942a5–943a	943a1–d4 (+943d5–944c4)	Military service
20	12.959a4–d2	959d3–6	Burial

As mentioned earlier, the sequence in which these preambles-with-laws appear in the course of the work reflects, globally speaking, the main stages of human life: after the death of one's parents has been skillfully introduced as a topic in the discussion between the lawgiver and the poet about the correctness of the lawgiver's discourse to the colonists in Book 4, we get preambles and laws about marriage, birth, education (hunting), old age, and then again, death.[4] To be sure, we also find, inserted within this biographical trajectory, three sets of laws (with or without preambles) that are 'thematic': laws regulating the economy, the structure and the religious life of the city (the end of Book 5, starting from 5.741e6), land cultivation (the end of Book 8, starting from 842e6), criminal laws, which are classified according to the gravity of the crime committed (9.853a1–10.910c4), and rules of contractual relationships (*sumbolaia*, 11.913a1–932d8). These different topics, however, can be to a large extent integrated into the biographical pattern—perpetrators of crimes are likely to be young,[5] and rules of good conduct fit into the ordinary course of an adult life in Plato's agricultural city. The only preamble that does not fit this chronological perspective is the general preamble in Books 4–5, which is unsurprising, since its portrait of the best and happiest life as a whole cannot be accommodated in a chronological continuum.

But preambles can also be ranked according to their modes and degree of persuasiveness, that is, from a rhetorical point of view. This classification is independent of the order of their appearance in the text, and hence much less visible than the already somewhat sinuous biographical scheme. Still, lurking beyond the various instances of persuasive discourse, there is something like a treatise on rhetoric in the making.

The preambles are described using a number of terms that were already technical in the field of rhetoric before Plato and would remain standard after him. Pertaining to the speaker are the terms for 'praise' (*epainos*) and 'blame' (*psoggos, oneidos*), which two are certainly the most important categories of Platonic rhetoric; 'admonishment' (*nouthetêsis*), 'advice' (*parainesis*), 'exhortation' (*paraggelma, protropê*), and 'dissuasion' (*apotropê*). On the recipient's side are the adjectives for being 'well-disposed' (*eumenês*) and 'learning easily' (*eumathês*).[6]

Despite some overlapping with Aristotle's *Rhetoric*, Plato's unwritten rhetoric takes, not unexpectedly, a very different line from the Aristotelian. Aristotle divides the art of speech into three kinds (deliberative, epideictic, and judiciary) and assigns different topics, aims, and modes of persuasion to these different kinds—advice (positive, *protropê*, or negative, *apotropê*) belongs to the so-called deliberative speech (*sumbouleutikos*); praise/ *epainos* and blame/ *psoggos* to the epideictic speech (*epideiktikos*), accusation/*katêgoria* and defense/*apologia* to the judiciary speech.[7] Plato's rhetoric is, by contrast, monolithic. Given that its main categories are 'praise' and 'blame' and even more that all of it is geared towards virtue (in agreement with the ultimate legislative goal), it matches in very significant ways Aristotle's description of 'epideictic' rhetoric. (As a matter of fact, a good way to make sense of Aristotle's strikingly narrow and somewhat idiosyncratic characterization of epideictic rhetoric is to hypothesize that he has the *Laws* as one of his main models.[8]) On the other hand, Plato's legislative protreptic to virtue is as flexible in its realizations as it is unified by its aim. The manner in which Aristotle occasionally points to some commonalities and possible transpositions between 'praise' and 'advice' and to some hybrid genres [9] is a far cry from Plato's exploration of the rhetorical modalities of a genre that is for him one and indivisible and which—consequently—extends its empire to modes such as incantation (*epôidê*), 'mythical narrative' (*muthos*), and 'threat' on one side of the scale, reflection and didactic argumentation and on the other—modes that fall outside the scope of classical rhetoric or at best remain at its margins.[10] The preambles extend over a continuum that oscillates between the two equally crucial requirements of Platonic legislation, namely ensuring obedience and providing reasons. Here is a sample of the possibilities that are embodied to various degree in the preambles of the *Laws*.

Appealing to Reflection (On Marrying)

Two laws on marriage open the biographical cycle of legislation. The first bears on marriage in general (2a), the second on the choice of a particular spouse (2b). The preamble attached to the first of these laws is one of the relatively few preambles that straightforwardly illustrate the Athenian's initial account of the status of his address to the colonists, which is not surprising, since it is meant to exemplify a pattern. Most of the other preambles (including the general preamble, the beginning of which triggers the question of the nature of the speech previously given[11]) will not fully correspond, if at all, to the kind of persuasion the first preamble on marriage mobilizes. Indeed, an important number of preambles contrast with this model, either (and most of the time) in the sense of a progressive reintroduction of threat within a form of discourse that was supposed to eliminate it, or on the contrary (and exceptionally), by the introduction of an argumentation possessing a demonstrative character. The two most important preambles of the *Laws* in terms of both content and form (including length), the general preamble that straddles Books 4 and 5 and the preamble of the law against the atheists in Book 10, are especially interesting in this respect (I consider them in Chapter 9).

What the first law on marriage illustrates is the fundamental distinction between a "simple" and a "twofold" or "mixed" law, a dichotomy that sets up the formal framework of all the laws to come. As we have seen in the last chapter, a 'simple' law is a law devoid of any persuasive introduction. It plainly states what should be done (in the present case, a man should marry between 30 and 35) before naming the penalties that the contravener will incur (4.721b1–3). The "twofold" law, on the other hand, spells out reasons that justify the command by way of an argument (721b6–c8) inserted before the mention of penalties (721c8–d6). In the latter case, the argumentative moment is integrated into the command itself through an appeal to reflection which anticipates, at the very point when they are distinguished, the possibility that the content of the law be reflected in the preamble:

> One must marry when he reaches the age of thirty and before the age of thirty-five, reflecting (*dianoêthenta*) that . . . (4.721b6–7)[12]

The argument in question bears only on the general question of the appropriateness of marrying itself in order to beget children, not on the appropriate age for begetting them. It includes three steps: 1. Everyone desires an immortality which can only be attained at the level of the species. 2. Procreation is the only way human beings can perpetuate the species. 3. The 'sacred' character of humankind's immortality makes it an obligation for each of its members to contribute to this perpetuation.

The argument recasts Diotima's explanation in the *Symposium* (206c1–207a4) of the meaning of sexual desire, but it does this in a properly legislative setting.[13] Diotima explains and thus legitimates erotic desire by interpreting it as a desire for immortality, in order to show that other types of procreation and immortalization have love (*erôs*) as their source. The reason why "reproduction and birth in beauty" is wanted is—

> because reproduction goes on forever; it is what mortals have in place of immortality. But it is necessary to desire immortality along with the good, if what we agreed earlier was right, since love wants to possess the good forever. It is thus necessary, according to our argument, that love also desires immortality. (206e7–207a4; trans. Nehamas/Woodruff with modifications)

Diotima is here explaining a fact, the desire for reproduction, by a desire for immortality. In the *Laws*, by contrast, the desire for immortality, the most common manifestation of which is procreation, is itself presented as part of the world's order that is "sacred" (*hosion*, 4.721c7) and with which one is exhorted to collaborate. This view, in turn, is ultimately founded in the idea that "the species of human beings is something that is naturally bound up with the entirety of time (*sumphues tou pantos khronou*)," which is mentioned at 721c2–3 (and is recalled in the second law on marriage).[14] In this case, too, the argument might motivate those among the colonists who would have read the *Timaeus* and perceived its implications (that the species of mortal living beings, once created, is bound to be as indestructible as the world itself)[15] but can hardly be the primary source of its persuasiveness in the framework of a legislative preamble.[16] What makes the relevant preamble persuasive for the interlocutor in the first place is its appeal to belief in the existence of a world order, or, more precisely and interestingly, to a convergence between the fact that human beings are sexually differentiated[17] and this rational because divine order. The argument thus builds on a premise which is taken to be widely accepted (an *endoxon*, in Aristotle's terminology). Obviously, the argument has its limits, but, as far as it goes, it is a good one, given that the common belief to which it appeals can be philosophically founded in a full-fledged argument that is available elsewhere—not only in the *Timaeus*, but also in the first section of the preamble of the law against the atheists in Book 10 of the *Laws*.

Praise and Blame (On Hunting)

Book 7, which sets up a full-fledged educational program responding to the concept of education elaborated in Books 1 and 2,[18] ends with a series of prescriptions regarding hunting (822d3–824a19). This follows a development dedicated to the basic theoretical knowledge to be acquired during one's youth, and thus hunting appears as a foremost example of an activity that shapes one's character.[19] It can be the object of either praise or blame (824a10), depending on criteria that are set up in a preliminary classification of various kinds of hunting (823b1–c1). This classification recalls the divisions of the genre "hunting of living beings (*zoôtherikê*)" in the *Sophist* (220a7–223b7, in an attempt to define sophistic as a "hunting of rich and famous young men," 223b4–5), but its aim is this time axiological: it is to show that not all kinds of hunting are equally conducive to courage and endurance. In particular, practices that, in one way or another foster sloth are to be forbidden: this is the case of fishing (in its various species) as well as of piracy (*lêsteia*), construed as a form of water-hunting (823e2–4). Bird hunting is not categorically condemned, but, given that it requires cunning and that the latter is not worthy of a free man, we are left with only the hunting of quadrupeds as worthy of the lawgiver's praise (on the condition that it does not itself use unworthy practices such as taking turns for sleeping[20] or using nets and other forms of traps). What mainly garners praise is the cultivation of a kind of courage that is called 'divine' (824a9), and which applies only to the hunting of quadrupeds using horses, dogs, or one's own body.[21]

Compared to this preliminary praise, the law that follows (824a11–19) presents the drawback of being unable, due to the flat generality of its command, to handle ethical considerations. Although it adopts the same tripartition as the preamble (between terrestrial hunting of living beings, bird hunting in the air, and water-based hunting), it neither clarifies what it is about these different activities that determines their worth or lack of worth, nor does it define the nature of their respective relationships to virtue. This deficiency appears clearly in the case of fishing. On the sole basis of the prescriptive part of the law, it would appear that fishing is allowed with certain restrictions:

> As for the hunter who hunts in waters, let's permit him to hunt in some waters, but not in harbors, sacred rivers, marshes, and ponds. (824a16–17)

But only the praise and blame in the preamble warn of the danger of being caught by an appetite or love of fishing in all its forms (823d7–e2). Moreover, praise can go into more detail than is appropriate for a law: it tells us, for instance, that catching the prey with one's own hands is more praiseworthy than killing it from a distance (824a8–9). In this sense, the preamble fulfils the function of a law better than the law itself. It is like a law stripped of its specific form and limitations.

As expected on the basis of the account given in Book 4, praise and blame regarding hunting precede the corresponding law (824a11–19). But it is significant that in the preliminary, general explanation that in this case precedes the preamble itself (as a kind of methodological meta-preamble), the Athenian recommends that the lawgiver write not only the laws, but, "interwoven" with them (*nomois empeplêgmena*), "all that seems fine and not fine to him" (823a3–5). Although succession can be considered as a particular form of 'interweaving' (as juxtaposition was taken to be a form of mixing at 4.722c1), the word calls to mind a more complex kind of composition, like a discursive web in which the law and the preamble tend to lose their pre-assigned functions. As already noted earlier, the preamble is no less prescriptive than the corresponding law; as a matter of fact, the word *ta* [. . .] *prostakhtenta*, "commands," occurs at this juncture (823d1).

From Argument to Incantation
(On the Choice of a Spouse)

The second law and preamble on marriage featuring in Book 6 (772e7–774a1) bears specifically on the choice of a spouse, but also provides two important refinements to the first, general law on the obligation to marry and the corresponding argument (4.721b6–d6). First, the eternity of humankind, which was given as the justification for the obligation to marry, is now explicitly referred to a theological principle, according to which gods need servants

(6.773e6–774c1), a function that only human beings can fulfil (a justification for the existence of the human race that differs from the one that features in the *Timaeus*). This explains why procreation was said in 4.721c7 to be a 'sacred' (*hosion*) duty. Ultimately, marriage is nothing but the expression of man's subordination to the god.[22]

The specific issue of the choice of a spouse exemplifies the difficulty involved in persuading not only through rational argumentation, but also through praise, which always relies on a background agreement. The lawgiver must make sure that preferences in the choice of a spouse are in line with one crucial target of legislation, which is that the city as a whole display the appropriate homogeneity (*homalon*) and equilibrium (*summetron*, 6.773a6)—no doubt because these contribute to "friendship" between the citizens, although the word does not appear in this context. What is aimed at is—in agreement both with the program set up at the end of the *Statesman* (310a7–311a2) and the general principle of mixing and blending here represented by the comparison of the city to a krater (*polin dikên kraterous kekramenên*, 773d1)—a union where the differences existing between the two parties will complement each other, both in matters of wealth and character traits such as irascibility and apathy (773a7-b4). This implements the principle stated at the beginning of the general preamble, according to which the measure of all things must be the precisely appropriate measure (*mêtriotês*). It is from this principle that the "talk (*muthos*) about marriage (*gamou*)" (773b4–5) draws its authority.[23]

Human beings, however, are not by nature political animals, at least not in the sense required by the lawgiver. They are naturally driven, instead, towards what most resembles them, which, as a consequence, they find most pleasant (773b6–7).[24] Egoism claims independence from legislative authority in the domain of the 'private' decisions where marriage falls, being by itself, like land-tenure, a concession to human nature.[25] When the decision concerned marriage in general, exhortation could count on a natural aspiration, whether reflective or unconscious, to immortality. Persuasion came easily, and could rely on more rational grounds. The choice of a specific spouse is quite a different matter, as personal inclinations tend to get the upper hand. As in the case of funeral expenses discussed in the fictive exchange between poet and lawgiver in Book 2, social status carries a lot of weight.

The means at the disposal of the lawgiver who wishes to avoid resorting to law, the coercive force of which (*anagkazein*, 773c6, *biazomenon*, e4) is emphasized by the fact that it is "written" (773e3), will need to be less argumentative and more oblique here than in the preceding cases. The task of persuading candidates to marriage is entrusted to a group of wise men (773a1–2) whose "exhortations"/*paramuthia* (773e5) consist of "incantations" (*epaidonta*, 773d6) and "blame"/*oneidos* (773e2). To fathom the content of these exhortations is, in this case, left to the reader. As the Athenian notes in his general conclusion on the issue of marriage,

> One could say all this and yet more about marriage to the effect that one should marry, by formulating a preamble in a correct way. (774a1–3)

Clearly, the preamble is an open form.

The Reintroduction of Threat

As an introduction to the law on patricide, Book 9 distinguishes two kinds of laws:

> It seems that some laws exist for the sake of honest men, in order to teach them (*didakhês kharin*) the way in which they should deal with one another in order to live in friendship, while others are for those who reject education and whose naturally tough natures have not been softened enough to stop them turning to absolute wickedness. (9.880d8–e3)

Whereas the laws of the first kind amount to preventive recommendations to avoid everyday conflicts,[26] the gravity of the crimes considered by the second kind is such that they should not occur, in principle, in a city that is organized so as to generate virtue. This is why it is "in a certain way shameful" to have to legislate about such matters (9.853b4–d4, cf. 872c7–d7). The reason why the Athenian must nevertheless consider them is that some individuals remain "unmelted by laws, as hard as they may be" (853d3). The model set up by the analogy between lawgiving and free medicine cannot accommodate crimes that are difficult to cure or incurable (854a3). "Temple robberies" and similar offences are not to be expected from citizen who "have been correctly brought up." Still, there can be such persons, especially if they are young and have not received the proper education:[27] the worst crimes in fact actualize an "illness" inherent in "human nature" (853d10–854a1). Their meaning, therefore, extends beyond a particular case, as is shown by the mention, at this juncture, of the general principle that presides to the writing of the *Laws*: for the present lawgivers (the interlocutors of the dialogue) are not like those "ancient lawgivers, who [. . .] legislated for children of gods, the heroes" and who, "being themselves sprung from gods, legislated for others of similar origin." They are, rather "human beings legislating now for the seeds of human beings" (853c3–7, cf. 5.735e3–7 and 739d6–7).

To fight against the greatest crimes, the lawgiver must use forms of persuasion that, by the lawgiver's own characterization, are violent—very far from the program of a free legislative teaching set out in the relevant passages of Books 4 and 9 discussed in the previous chapter.

The reintroduction of the law within the preamble was foreshadowed at the very beginning of the general preamble of the *Laws* (4.715e7–716b7) by its preliminary appeal to "the order of things" (cf. *tauta oun houtô diatetagmena*, 716b5–6) and divine retaliation (*timôria*, 716b4), which is both undifferentiated and (paradoxically) out of proportion with the crime committed:[28] for, after a deceptive delay during which injustice seems to have the upper hand, the curse provokes the ruin not only of the culprit, but also the asymmetrical misfortune of his family and of his city (716b4–5).[29]

This is the "order of things," and it is here used to explain why one should act in a way "dear to the gods" (716c1)—in harmony, that is, with the specifications of divine law, which the rest of the preamble spells out by listing the "honors" (*timai*) due to them. Obviously, the threat of divine retaliation has a different status from the 'violence' of human punishments (which are available in the here and now and take into account personal responsibility). But it reintroduces within the persuasive preamble, and at a very prominent place indeed, a divine, and for this reason incomparably harsher equivalent to the legislative violence which the preamble was supposed to eliminate. "Should we call it a tale (*muthos*) or an argument (*logos*)?" asks the Athenian at 9. 872d7–e1—only to answer his own question by observing, significantly, that the name does not really matter (". . . or whatever it ought to be called").[30]

The kind of threat with which the general preamble opens features in several passages which, in Book 9 in particular, refer to some version of a myth of retaliation. According to 9.870d5–e3 (= preamble 7a), the murderer will pay (*tisis*) in Hades, before suffering in a new life, in agreement with a "justice in accordance with nature" (870e1–2), the fate of his victim. The belief in this myth will be spread by the "initiated" and fill the hearers with fear, which in this context is closely associated with persuasion (*peithomenôi* [. . .] *kai pantôs phoboumenôi*, 870e4). From this point on, the law, which is sung (*humnein*) just as an incantation would be, simply takes over from the preamble: it repeats the threats, but at the level of human legislation.[31]

The same logic explains why the *muthos* (or the *logos*) told by the "old priests" at 872e1–2 (in the preamble to the law on patricide) is described as a 'law' (872e3). According to the account in question, anyone who kills his father will, in a future life, be killed by his children. The implementation of this law will be supervised by "avenging Justice" (872e2–3). It may be significant that the terms 'preamble' and 'persuasion' do not occur here—though certainly abstaining from crime under the pressure of fear (873a3–4) could still qualify as acting 'voluntarily' (*hekôn*, 872d6).[32] The lawgiver, however, has no illusions about the deterrent power of divine threats on criminals: his last resort will be to suggest that since otherworldly punishment won't be enough to dissuade souls capable of, for example, laying hands on their parents, "punishments inflicted here on these men during their life for those acts" must "not be inferior to those in Hades, as far as possible" (881a8–b2).

This reintroduction of threat and fear within the persuasive preamble blurs the border between law and preamble no less than the fact that the preamble is by itself prescriptive and, therefore, law-like. However, there still are ways to maintain a distinction of sorts. For instance, the preamble to the law about temple robbery (= preamble 6) is concise (9.854a4–5) because the crime is so great that it is best read as the manifestation of an inherited curse, in which case the potential criminal is more a victim than a culprit. The compulsion to rob temples comes from an evil that is "neither human nor divine," but "a certain madness (*oistros*) that is implanted and grows within human beings because of ancient and unpurged injustices" (854b1–4).

The idea of projecting the "evil desire" (854a6) in the archaic form of an 'avenger' (cf. *alitêriôdês*, 854b4) is that the alleged victim will be all the more disposed to cooperate and "avert" the crime with all his strength (*eulabeisthai* [...] *panti sthenei*, 854b5) seeing as he is not personally responsible for the ancient curse. The potential temple-robber is invited to undergo purification rites, to pray in sanctuaries, to practice self-exhortation, and even to anticipate his punishment by taking his own life.[33] He is thus in a position to meet, at the lowest possible level, the requirement of a "dialogue" (cf. "both dialoguing and exhorting," *dialogemenos te kai paramuthoumenos*, 854a5–6, cf. 888a6)—a dialogue that, once more, has little in common with the discussion "close to philosophy" that features at a prominent place just a few pages later (857d2–4).

The tension between extreme forms of persuasive discourse is obvious. It takes another form in the case of the two exceptional preambles to which I now turn.

9

Two Exceptional Preambles

THE *LAWS* INCLUDE two preambles which, each in its own, very different way, go beyond the dynamic that characterizes the polar relationship between law and preamble. The first of these is the address to the colonists that begins at 4.715e7 and constitutes the general preamble to the laws. The second is the preamble to the law on impiety that is the foundation of Plato's legislation in Book 10.

Socrates Implemented

The first striking fact about the general preamble is that it does not quite fit the official pattern of a preamble as construed in Book 4.[1] To begin with, the development starts, as noted in the previous chapter, with a law-like threat about the inevitability of divine retribution based on the existence of an ultimate cosmic order. The rest of the preamble consists in an invitation to follow a set of prescriptions:

> Now, given that things are ordered in this way, what should and should not the wise man (*emphrona*) do and think with regard to these things? (716b5–7)

Analogously and no less remarkably, the detailed set of prescriptions is followed not by any law in particular, but by the whole legislative body (preambles included) that occupies the rest of the work, from 5.734e3 through 12.969c3. Given that the laws in question are said to encompass two "kinds of constitution" (*duo politeias eidê*, 5.735a5), namely "the laws pertaining to the constitution" or "constitutional laws" (*nomous politeias* 5.734e5), and the laws to be applied by the officeholders (735a6), the general preamble can be compared, with all due differences noted, to the preambles that give their general orientation to modern constitutions: they formulate a set of guidelines derived from ultimate principled assumptions. To argue in favor of these ultimate assumptions, which in the case of Plato's *Laws*, are of a theological nature, will be the role assigned to the preamble against impiety, the second exceptional preamble that features in Book 10.

The prescriptions in question are not meant to be persuasive in the same sense as regular preambles to laws. Rather, they list and describe in a systematic way the topics that a legislative rhetoric must address. It is in this sense that the general preamble can be said to function like any other preamble: it prepares the citizens to comply with the entire set of laws that follows. Once more, however, it is not clear that a citizen who was fully persuaded by this meta-persuasive development would have need of these laws any longer, except perhaps as specifications of the ultimate "measure" that god provides—i.e., the laws that are meant to teach "good, [*or* useful] human beings."[2] In this sense, the general preamble of the *Laws* is a self-contained piece, setting goals—targets, more exactly—directed to the citizen rather than introducing specific laws.[3]

The encompassing description of the virtuous life is inescapably reminiscent of Socrates. To be sure, few if any of the citizens in Plato's best human city are likely to have the inquiring mind of a Socrates, even if members of the Watch will still need to reflect on the unity of virtue—but aren't these citizens supposed to be implementing Socratic principles? Doesn't the second city of which they are citizens embody in a compact way the Socratic values that are dispersed throughout the *Laws* and the rest of Plato's dialogues?[4]

The development, starting at 4.716c1, follows a systematic plan based on a distinction between relationships (*homilêmata*, A) and ethical qualities and character (*poios autos ôn*, B):

A. Relationships
   A1. With gods and parents 4.716d4–718a6 (cf. 5.726a1–6)
   A2. With oneself: soul, body, and possessions 5.726a6–729a2
   A3. With others: children and members of the family, friends, the city
        and its fellow-citizens, and foreigners 5.729a2–730a9 (announced
        at 4.718a5–b5)
B. Personal character: virtues and affections, 5.730b1–734e2
   B1. The divine perspective, independent of pleasure: 5.730b1–732d7
   B2. The human perspective, taking pleasure into account:
        5.732d8–733d6
   B3. The different modes of human life, 5.733d7–734e2

Sections A and B fall under the headings "honor" and "praise/blame," respectively, as distinct from law. The distinction echoes the one that Aristotle draws in the *Nichomachean Ethics* between two categories of goods: those that deserve be honored (*timia*) and those that are worthy of praise (*epaineta*).[5] Gods and the soul, which are the first and most important items in the first part of the preamble, are given by Aristotle as two prime examples of *timia*, while virtues belong to the goods worthy of praise. The list of items in Plato's list (A) is more fully furnished, since it includes, in addition to god, "relations with parents, with oneself, and with one's possessions, with the city as well as friends and relatives, those that concern strangers as well as natives" (5.730b1–3) but the distinction it makes between the two kinds of goods is clearly the same as Aristotle's, as is the requirement that they be treated differently from a rhetorical point of view.

The sentence at 5.730b1 marks a thematic break that cuts across the distribution of the general preamble between Books 4 and Book 5. As we shall learn in retrospect at 730b3, the section formed of 4.715e7–718a6 + 5.726a1–730a9 is devoted to the various kinds of "relationships" (*homilêmata*) that every individual has to entertain throughout his life. What follows, from 5.730b5 to 734e2 (which marks the end of the preamble) concerns, by contrast, what a human being must "himself" be in order to "lead the most beautiful life."

The distinction at 730b3–4 between 'relationships' (*homilêmata*) and personal qualities and character (*poios autos ôn*) does not overlap with the distinction between one's behavior towards others and what we ourselves are, at least if 'others' and 'ourselves' are taken in their usual sense. For the relationships in question include prescriptions relative not only to gods, parents, the city, friends and family, foreigners, and fellow countrymen (the regular 'others,' in decreasing order of priority), but also and most remarkably to "oneself and what belongs to oneself" (*heauton kai ta heautou*, 730b1), which includes the features of one's own soul. The use of the term *homilêma* here is striking, even if the seeming duplication of the self is congruent with the idea of a "soul conversing with itself" (*Theaetetus*, 189e6–190a2; cf. *Sophist* 263e3–5), or for that matter, with the possibility that we might, each of us, provide some assistance to the golden string of the puppet we are.[6] It implies a construal of the 'self' according to which an individual can entertain a relationship to himself that amounts to a 'frequentation' (*homilêma*), of the same kind that we have with 'others.'

Relationships and personal character are connected. Virtues and other ethical dispositions manifest themselves in the way in which one behaves towards oneself as well as towards others; conversely, the very first 'relationship,' of obedience to the gods, is cashed out in a set of definite types of behavior. Man makes himself dear to the god by leading a temperate life, which is also (among other qualities) a just life (4.716d1–4).[7] In so doing, man likens himself to the true measure of all things (*pantôn khrêmatôn metron*, 716c4)—namely, god (and not man, as in the Protagorean phrase explicitly alluded to in 716c5–6). Religious rites such as sacrifices, prayers and offerings are "the finest and best of all things," as well as "the most conducive things for a happy life" only on the assumption that the performer is himself "good" (716d4–e2).

The life of a person who aspires to be "blessed and happy" (*makarios te kai eudaimôn*, 5.730c2–3) is defined by reference to a series of virtues and vices, as well as ways of behaving, which are listed in the second part of the preamble (on personal character). The latter is itself divided into two sections, the first of which considers the appropriate psychic dispositions and corresponding behaviors from a perspective that is called "divine" because the praise that is attached to them does not take pleasure or pain into consideration (730c1–732d7), whereas the second, which looks at things from a "human" perspective, does just this (732d8–734e2).

The soul lies at the intersection of the divine and the self: it is both "the most divine good after the gods themselves," whom we must obey as to our masters (*despotas*, 727a1, cf. *ta despozonta*, 726a5), and the good that is "most proper" to us (*oikeiotaton*, 726a3). The term 'proper,' here translating *oikeios*, refers to the proper self; i.e., the soul, and stands in a strict opposition to another 'proper' that corresponds to the term *idios*, which usually refers to the 'private' in a negative sense—to what has to do with misconceived personal interests, selfishness, and eventually the irrational drive that pursues pleasure and lust.[8] We treat our soul as we should when we "honor" it as its divine nature requires, by making it stronger (*auxein*, 727a5[9]). The parallel between the cult of the gods and the cult of the soul comes out clearly in 727a2–7: just as gods cannot be bought or swayed by simple ritual practices (the preamble of Book 10 will come back to this point), so should the soul be unmoved by "certain words, gifts, or favors."

There are seven ways in which one can inappropriately honor his soul and thus do it harm (727b3, cf. 727c1):

1. By an arbitrary exercise of the will, based on a presumption of being able to judge everything by oneself (727a7–b4)
2. By complacency leading to shifting responsibility onto someone else (727b4–c1)

3. By abandoning oneself to pleasure (727c1–4)
4. By avoiding toil (727c4–7)
5. By overvaluing life and fearing death (727c7–d5)
6. By neglecting virtue (the soul) in favor of beauty (the body) (727d6–e3)
7. By loving riches, which leads to injustice (727e3–728a5)

These seven headings encompass all possible violations of the legislative prescriptions, as well as all the different kinds of ignorance regarding the true, divine nature of the soul. The list is founded in turn on the systematic, tripartite classification of goods into goods of the soul (1–5), of the body (6), and external goods (7) that is recurrent in the *Laws*. Two overarching imperatives comprise the good of the soul as expressed by one's relationship to oneself (= 1 and 2). These imperatives are cashed out in terms of two requirements regarding the feelings of pleasure and pain encountered in the course of one's life (3 and 4) and one's death (5). The last two headings situate the good of the soul with respect to the two inferior kinds of goods (the 'slave goods' of 726a6), those of the body (6) and external riches (7). The fruitful use that can be made of the latter two categories of goods when they are correctly subordinated to the good of the soul, is dealt with briefly (728d6-e5 and 728e5–729a2). In both cases, subordination is cashed out in terms of a definite 'middle' or 'mean' that lies between two extremes (*en tôi mesoi*, 728e2), in agreement with what it means for human beings to take god as the measure of all things.[10]

The discussion of 'personal' qualities and behaviors, which is devoted their "divine" side, successively lists veracity and truthfulness (*alêtheia*, 730c1; *pistos*, c4), justice (730d2), and moderation (*sôphrosunê*, 730c1), and deals with anger and mildness, self-love, and some emotional reactions of lesser importance (*smikrotera*, 732b5) which must nevertheless be considered if one is to "remember himself" as well as others (732b6–7 and d6).

"Truthfulness" is the good that leads all the others, both among gods and men ("reliable"/*pistos* at 730c4 echoes 1.630b2, where it is said that one can't be reliable in civil wars without "the whole of virtue").[11] The praise consists in an *a contrario* evocation of the loneliness to which the untruthful person condemns herself (730c6–d2). What follows focuses, conversely (and positively) on the fame that virtues gain within the political community.

The "most beautiful life" (730b4) is characterized, beyond one's individual possession of virtue, by the wish to "spread" it throughout the city, since the latter cannot flourish or even sustain itself without everyone's being virtuous

(730d2–e3). This is why the just man receives more praise ("more than twice the praise") for preventing others from committing injustice and devoting himself to the propagation of justice than for practicing justice himself: the citizen who is proclaimed "winner" is the one who helps officeholders to punish injustice (730d2–7).[12] A "noble anger" is appropriate when fighting against injustice in cases where the latter is difficult or impossible to cure, but anger must yield to "pity" when injustice is curable, in accordance with the principle that all injustice is involuntary (731b4–d5).

The condemnation of "excessive self-love" (*tên sphodra heautou philian*, 731e4) that follows (731d6–732b4) is a counterpart to the praise of truthfulness. It harks back, in a kind of ring-composition, to the conception of the soul as man's most 'proper' good which was put forward in the first section of the preamble. Giving priority to oneself amounts to privileging a false self by turning upside down the true hierarchy (putting oneself before truth and justice, 732a1–4). As such, it is the expression of an ignorance (*amathia*) that claims to know everything (732a4–b2, cf. 727a7–b3).[13]

The second, distinctively "human" (732e2–3), second-best kind of praise argues that the virtuous (or "correct," 733a6) life is also the most pleasant. For what is by nature the most salient (*malista*, "above all," 732e4) characteristic of human beings (meaning what is distinctively human in human beings) are "pleasures, pains, and desires," on which they "hang" and from which they are "suspended" (732e6). The argument presents undeniable resemblances to that developed by Socrates in the *Protagoras* 353c1–354e2 (see especially 5.733a9–c1), to the point that it has sometimes been read as an endorsement of ethical hedonism. But it clearly carries a different and in fact opposed message.[14] Providing the decisive proof that "no one is intemperate (*akolastos*) voluntarily" (734b4, cf. 731c2–5), it aims at establishing the superiority of the *virtuous* life over its contrary for each of the four modes of life that are distinguished in the course of the argument—the temperate (*sôphrôn*), the wise (*phronimon*), the courageous (*andreion*), and the healthy (*hugieinon*) (733e3–5).[15] The contours of a properly human praise are sketched in relation to the first of these four modes. It asserts, rather than argues, that pleasure outweighs pain in a life characterized by 'moderation' (733a8-d6), keeping the *Philebus* and its analysis of pleasure in the background.[16]

Just as the praise of virtuous life from the point of view of pleasure presupposes a doctrine of pleasure which is not spelled out within the praise itself, so the ultimate justification for why one should subordinate self-love to civic duty is not provided in our passage. We are left with two references to the first part of the preamble and a condemnation of self-love as being mistaken about what is the true self—viz., the soul (731c5, cf. 727b1). Obviously, the preamble to the law is also a preamble to philosophy. The didactic preamble of Book 10 takes us one step further.

The Theological Foundation of the Law

Book 10 consists largely of one single preamble which far exceeds in length and complexity the general preamble of Books 4 and 5 (the term *prooimion*, 10.887a3 and c1, is taken up at 907d1 and d4, at the articulation between the preamble and the law).[17] Its prominent formal feature is a division into three sections of decreasing length, corresponding to three aspects of impiety (*asebeia*) listed at 885b6–9, in the general introduction to the whole development (cf. also 888c2–7): 1. Not believing in the existence of gods (888d7–899d3); 2. Believing in their existence, but thinking that they don't care about human beings (899d4–905d3); and 3. Thinking that they can be swayed by sacrifices and prayers (905d3–907b4).[18] Each of the first aspects gives rise to two preambles corresponding to two different levels of persuasion, one exhortative, the other argumentative.[19]

Beyond its immediate purpose as a preamble to the law on impiety, this triple (quintuple, with the duplicating of the first two) preamble provides justifications for a series of prescriptions featuring in the general preamble of Books 4 and 5 (to which it often implicitly refers) and elsewhere in the work. This is only to be expected, given that what is crucially at stake in this preamble is the theological foundation of the legislative enterprise itself, as reflected in the very first word of the dialogue and in the first sentence of the law-like exordium of the general preamble at 4.715a7–716a2. This foundational role makes the preamble of the law on impiety, in terms both of its contents and its form, the core of the entire text, by which the legislative project of *Laws* succeeds or fails. This is the reason why Clinias is quite right to observe that the first of the three preambles, which is also the crucial one, is

> our most beautiful and best preamble (*kalliston kai ariston prooimion*) on behalf of all the laws (*huper hapantôn tôn nomôn*). (887b8–c2)

This is also the justification for its exceptional length.

For the present purpose, it is not necessary to enter into a detailed analysis of the argument developed in this preamble. It will be enough to recall that the first argument (10.888d7–899d3) provides a demonstration of the existence of the gods based on the question of the origin of movement—the first instance in the history of philosophy of a proof that would enjoy a brilliant future, beginning with Aristotle, who arguably makes his own case for the necessary immobility of the first mover in *Physics* 8 and *Metaphysics Lambda* 6–7 by reference to and against the Platonic primacy of a self-moving soul.[20] Plato's proof for the existence of the gods coincides with the refutation of a doctrine that teaches the priority of the body over the soul, of which there are, according to Plato, two versions. The older and more primitive is presented in most general terms, and is easily recognized as a tweaked, materialistically oriented summary of archaic cosmo-theogonies, "ancient writings in verse and prose," says Plato, which allegedly begin by talking about "the first generation (*hê prôtê phusis*) of the sky and the rest" (886c2–3) to then speak in inappropriate terms about the birth of gods and their relationships.[21] The other more recent and much more elaborated version is an "extraordinary doctrine" (*thaumastos logos*), as the Athenian calls it at 888d8, which alone develops the implications of an anonymous materialist cosmology for the question of legislation proper and explicitly denies the existence of gods.

In its rejuvenated and radicalized form, the doctrine proceeds in two steps. First, the cosmic order is fully explained in terms of a cosmology that does without gods. The sun and the moon, the stars and the earth are not divine, but only mud and stones (889b3–c6, cf. 886d4–e2). Secondly, the belief in the gods is referred to a certain craft (*tekhnê*), namely the legislative craft, which is much less powerful than the two primordial forces, nature and chance, and lacks their seriousness (889c6–d6).[22] For, according to this view, all crafts (*tekhnai*) are chronologically derivative of and axiologically subordinate to these primordial causes, which are responsible for "the greatest [. . .] and the finest" things (889a4). These great and fine things, by contrast, are only conventional "impositions"/*theseis*. They can be ranked according to their degree of proximity to nature, which is the standard of "truth" (*alêtheia*, 889d1, cf. e1). At the bottom of the scale are imitative crafts and their products, such as painting and poetry, which are pure "entertainments" (*paidiai*, 889d1). At the top, we find a series of more "serious" crafts, among which medicine, agriculture, and gymnastics take pride of place, while politics and legislating are ranked at the lowest level. Proximity to nature is minimal for politics, and nonexistent for lawgiving, which is said to be in totality "not by nature, but by craft, the impositions (*theseis*) of which are not true (*alêtheis*)" (889d8–e1).

Legislation, which is of course the craft which is at the center of attention, bears on three kinds of items: (1) gods, whose existence and features, which are different in different places, are decided by laws and the result of an agreement between lawgivers (889e3–5); (2) what is fine/*ta kala,* which differs from what is fine by nature (889e5–6); and (3) what is just, which is completely severed from the truth of nature (889e6–890a2) and is imposed by force (890a2–5, with a clear allusion to the passage of Pindar alluded to at various junctures in the *Laws*[23]).

Is this extremely elaborate and coherent doctrine a Platonic construction that integrates, for the specific purpose of the demonstration, elements taken from different quarters, some of which are recognizable on the basis of the information at our disposal, or the report of an actual doctrine that was circulating in Athens at the end of the 5th century? Attempts at identification have been numerous, but it seems to me that the former is much more likely.[24] What the Athenian, a defender of crafts and of expert knowledge, wishes to attack, very much in the wake of Aristophanes' *Clouds,* is the objective complicity between Presocratic physics (insofar as it can be reduced to a materialist mechanism) and the most radical sophistic doctrines.[25]

The demonstration is bound to be long. "Won't it be too long?" asks the Athenian at 887a2–8 (cf. 890e1–3). The question is rhetorical. As Clinias is given the opportunity to observe once more, the principle according to which length is not a criterion to be taken in consideration when it comes to saying what is best, has been "quite often repeated in a short time" (887b1–2), so that any length will be appropriate if teaching requires it.[26] Putting off the moment of legislation is necessary in order to give the preamble its due place, and even welcome. The thought paradoxically echoes the ideal of a free discussion between the lawgiver and the citizens, which I call of the legislative utopia, an important point to which I shall return shortly.

The Athenian shows successively: 1. that elements (bodies) do not come first: priority belongs to the soul (891b8–896d4); this is the reason why, according to nature (*kata phusin*), the soul "rules" (*arkhein*) and body is ruled (*arkhomenon*) (896c2–3); and 2. that the organization of the universe by the soul was not carried out without *nous*/reason (896d5–899d4).

The first part of the Athenian's refutation turns on a blind spot in the atheist doctrine, which is the question of motion.[27] Fire, water, earth, and air are carried at random (889b5), joining and mixing. Without any contribution from any god or craft (889c5–6), they give birth to the whole cosmos, including animals, plants, and seasons. But: 1. Motion of any kind presupposes self-motion, which is consequently the 'oldest' and "most powerful" kind of change (895b5–6); and 2. Self-motion belongs to the soul only, whose name answers the definition of a "movement able to move oneself" (895e10–896a2). The

Athenian concludes that the soul is "prior" to the body (896b10–c3), which is enough to assert that soul, rather than the elements, is "by nature" (892c2–5, referring to 891c3). Aristotle will soon say, if he has not already said it, that nature is a principle of movement (and rest).

The materialist theory worked with three concepts: nature (*phusis*), chance (*tukhê*), and craft (*tekhnê*). As soul replaces body in the role of "nature," the antithesis between nature and craft loses its force. Far from being incompatible with the soul, craft is by essence "akin" to it (892a8), as are all faculties and dispositions—opinion, care, character, will, deliberation, memory, and feelings.[28] The latter are all "motions" of the soul (896c9–d3 and 897a1–3).

The first demonstration on the soul's motricity, is sufficient to refute the principles behind the atheist's position. But they are only fully refuted by the second, for priority of soul is not enough to ground a rational, i.e., theological legislation.

Psychic motions are not intrinsically good. There can be false opinions, bad characters, disastrous decisions. By itself, the soul is only a principle of motion, a source both of goods and of evils, of justice and injustice, and in general of "all [relevant] contraries" (896d7). This is why it will be able to escape "evil" only if it teams up with reason/*nous* to create the divine order of the world (897b1–4).

The final step of the argument (897b7–899d3) consists in showing that the soul did in fact organize the universe, and it did so guided by an intelligence (*nous*), i.e., rationally. The argument is based on the affinity (in the strict sense) between the motion of "heaven and everything it contains" (897c4–5) and the motion of reason, or rather of its visible image, circular movement.[29] The circularity of the celestial revolution forces one to recognize that

> the best soul takes care of the whole universe (*kosmos*) and drives it along
> that sort of path. (897c7–9; cf. the echoes in 898c2–5 and 899b3–9)

At that point, the whole argument of the atheist is reversed. True legislation is ultimately founded in a god, which god coincides with a soul endowed with divine *nous*. This is the more precise answer to the opening question of the dialogue.

A Structural Paradox

The didactic preambles of Book 10, especially the first of them sets out the ultimate and most detailed version of Plato's kinetics. Was this the kind of philosophical argument to which the ideal conversation between doctor and patient about the nature of bodies would be "close"? And is it, consequently, itself a sample of a utopian legislative conversation? Clinias, reacting to the Athenian warning that the argument he is about to engage in is "unusual" (*aêthesterôn* [. . .] *logôn*, 891d6, taken up at e3 by *ouk eiôtha*), remarks:

> I understand that you will think that we are going beyond legislation (*nomothesias ektos bainein*) if we engage in such arguments. But if there is no other way than this to reach agreement (*sumphônêsai*) that the gods whom we talk about according to the law are correctly conceived, then this is to be discussed as well, you admirable man! (891d7–e3)

Clinias' talk of "going outside legislation," i.e., exceeding its field of relevance, is understandable but no less misguided than the slave's reaction to the medical analogy in Book 9.[30] For there is a sense in which the demonstration of the priority of the soul over the body that follows does *not* exceed the limits of legislation, since it *is* a preamble to the law, and thus falls within the scope of the "twofold" legislation the Athenian has been advocating all along.

What we in fact have to do with here is one of Plato's most subtle constructions in the *Laws*.

At 885c8–d4, the atheists ironically defy the three interlocutors—as if they had been present at the discussion of the medical analogy in Book 4 and Book 9:

> We think fit, just as you thought fit with regard to the laws, that you attempt, before threatening us harshly, to persuade and teach us (*peithein kai didaskein*) that there are gods, presenting adequate evidence (*tekmêria*), and that they are too good to be beguiled and turned away from what is just by certain gifts.[31]

The situation thus created is two-sided.

On the one hand, there is little doubt that for the first and only time in the *Laws*, legislative persuasion takes the form of a teaching that goes back to fundamental questions about a physical doctrine that eventually supports the theological legislation the *Laws* advocates. In this sense, it represents the most advanced attempt, within the *Laws*, to 'reduce' the form of the law. There is also little doubt (even if this is more discreetly put), that Plato construes an analogical relationship between the content of the free doctor's conversation with his patient and that of the lawgiver with the atheist: both the doctor of Book 9 and the Athenian in Book 10 deal with the nature and properties of elementary bodies.[32] To be sure, we are not informed about the exact content of a medical conversation Plato is only adumbrating in Book 9, and the actual course of the latter might be difficult to fathom even after inspecting what the Hippocratic corpus has to say about elemental properties. But the fact is that in the preamble under consideration, the lawgiver "ascends to" questions concerning bodies no less than the free doctor is supposed to, although he does this from another standpoint, that of the origin of their motion, rather than of their properties. The possibility of an analogy between the two practices lies in this initial difference.

However, the relationship between the free doctor and his patient, on the one hand, and between the lawgiver and the atheists, on the other, shows a strong disanalogy, at least if we assume, as we have no reason not to, that the medical conversation depicted in Book 9 relies on a free cooperation between patient and doctor, in the spirit of the imperative famously formulated in the Hippocratic *Epidemics*:

> The doctor is the servant of the art. The patient must oppose (*hupenanthi-ousthai*) the disease with the doctor. (*Epidemics*, 1.11, trans. Jones modified)

The situation is quite different in the *Laws*, where the argument of the lawgiver, in the case of the atheists, is a response to a challenge which is the manifestation of their resistance to the cure: no collaboration is presupposed here, nor is it even in view. This explains why, symmetrically, the Athenian must first overcome an atypical and reproachable reaction of anger before engaging in a "gentle" demonstration of the gods' existence. From a certain point of view, which is that of the 'human wonder' as the spontaneous manifestation of rationality,[33] it would have been by far preferable if the atheists could be persuaded by some commonly accepted arguments, in this case the immediate evidence provided by the harmony of celestial movements (10.887c7–888a4). The atheists, however, differ from the rest of the citizens insofar as they believe doctrines which lead them to object to the legislation about gods, as long as the legislative program has not been fully implemented (i.e., as long as they have not been "persuaded and taught"). In this context, to appeal to the "ancient saying" which sees the god everywhere, as the lawgiver did at the opening of the general preamble, would be useless. Since the atheists argue, they require to be taught by way of proofs.[34] Whether the argument succeeds is quite another matter. For atheists represent an extreme case of illness: their "folly" (*manênai*, 888a3) is one of those which is likely to be incurable. The lawgiver must nevertheless give it a try (*peirateon* [. . .] *didaskein*, 888d3–4), and even persevere (*nun kai eis authis*, d4), so as to remain in agreement with his own principles. [35]

Does the disanalogy speak against the notion of a 'legislative utopia' that was applied to the didactic preamble of Book 10?[36] I don't think so, provided that we distinguish between the content of the argumentation and the context in which it is developed. The collaboration mentioned by the Hippocratic author of *Epidemics*, which I assume is taken for granted in the depiction of the medical conversation between the free doctor and the free patient in Book 9 has a normative dimension.[37] An ordinary view, reflected in various passages by Greek authors, is on the contrary that patients are *not* collaborators, not in the first place at least, because doctors harm in order to cure.[38] It is this ordinary situation that is reflected, in the legislative counterpart, by the provocative attitude of the atheists. But it in fact makes of them the lawgiver's best enemies, since they force him to engage, within the limits imposed by the objective difficulty of the topic and the particular circumstances of the address, in an argument that he could and would have spared in other, more regular situations.[39]

Whereas manifestations of the human wonder-puppet are available and to some extent encouraging, not the least in the case of the *consensus* (quasi-) *omnium*, the golden string of the puppet is always in need of strengthening. For demonstrations that address the golden cord will always be weaker than the uncontrolled drive towards pleasure, which affects atheists who are the prey, as Plato sees it, of "gluttony," an insatiable lust for pleasure (*laimargia hêdonês*, 888a3). This is the reason why the rational preamble is itself preceded by a "preliminary address" (*prorhrêsis*), which is the last attempt of the legislation to avoid engaging in a preamble that is, paradoxically, unwelcome in the present situation.[40] The fact is, however, that a lawgiver does not legislate for free men only, but also for psychological slaves who claim to "know" because they rely on a refined body of doctrines, whereas in reality they don't know (which is the proper definition of ignorance/*amathia*, cf. 5.732a4–b2, 9.863c1–6, and e.g., *Sophist* 229c1–10). In other circumstances, philosophical foundations would be reserved for philosophers, members of the Watch, or fellows of the Platonic Academy, none of whom need the form of the law to comply with its content. This is at least arguably the conclusion that was drawn by Xenocrates, Plato's second successor at the head of the Academy.[41]

10

Plato's Best Tragedy

All that is tragic relies upon an irresolvable contradiction; if a resolution is found or becomes possible, the tragic disappears.

GOETHE, LETTER TO THE CHANCELLOR MÜLLER,
JUNE 6, 1824[1]

IN A FAMOUS sentence in Book 7 of the *Laws* the Athenian declares that the political regime (*politeia*) he is advocating

> constitutes a representation (*mimêsis*) of the finest and best life, which is the very thing that we say tragedy really is, the truest sort. (817b3–5)

This makes of the lawgivers "poets too" (817b6), "who talk about the same practices" (c5–6) as tragic poets,

> [their] rivals and competitors for the finest play, which it is the nature of true law alone to complete (*apotelein*). (817b7–8)[2]

These provocative declarations, which provide the positive counterpart to the condemnation of Athenian theatrocracy in Book 3,[3] is a remarkable example of a pithy, self-referential extrapolation that transcends the immediate issue at stake.[4] It occurs in the final part of a section that discusses the physical education of children over age ten (7.813a7–817e4). The core of the program directed to these young human puppets is provided, in agreement with the conception of education to virtue as coupling pleasure with rational motions and statements, by various forms of dancing and training: war-dances, Bacchic dances, ritual dances, dances associated with peace, and wrestling; comedy and tragedy are introduced into this context in the first place because of comic and tragic choruses, which sing and dance.[5] The lawgiver, however, is now considering tragedy as a whole, plot included.

The thrust of the passage is identical, leaving aside the modifications due to the difference of settings and perspective, to the criticisms launched in the *Republic* Books 2–3 and 10 against tragedy in general and Homer, construed as the father of tragedy, in particular.[6] Poetic works are required to comply with the ethical standards formulated by the lawgiver and compliance will be overseen by officeholders charged with judging art in accordance with the law. It is not Homer, but the tragic authors, his progeny, who are now directly targeted and barred from entering the new colony—a scenario that would have hardly been applicable to Homer anyway. In both cases, what the city must be protected from is the 'tragic' side of Greek tragedies.[7]

The *Laws* here takes up the hubristic project, first broached in the *Republic*, of replacing the very foundations Greek culture as part of an education based on the philosophical principles articulated in the two dialogues. The *Laws*, however, go beyond the *Republic* in that the Athenian claims not only to have formulated the guidelines to be followed, among all poets, by tragic authors, but also to have himself produced "the finest and also the best tragedy" with the setting up his second-best constitution.[8]

The question that arises at this point concerns the sense in which the term 'tragedy' must be taken when applied to the constitution of the *Laws*.[9] It can't be the tragedy described and rejected both in the extended argument of *Republic* 2–3 and 10, nor for that matter in the passage of the *Laws* under consideration. A re-appropriation of tragedy by its fiercest opponent is at work here, in a move that is similar to the re-appropriation in the *Phaedrus* of the bad rhetoric condemned in the *Gorgias*, although here it is much more provocative.[10]

There are two presuppositions at work in this move. First, in order to be applied to a constitution, tragedy must be detached from the stage, in a kind of 'de-theatricalization' of the tragic. This extension in the notion of tragedy beyond tragic drama is already at work in the *Republic*, to the extent that the paragon of the tragic poets is not a tragedian, but Homer; but it is fully assumed in the *Philebus*, which provides the immediate background to the claim raised in the *Laws*. Starting at 47e1, Plato discusses feelings such as anger, fear, remorse, mourning and lamentation, love, jealousy and envy (*phthonos*), as specific mixtures of pleasure and pain, to conclude:

> The upshot of our discussion, then, is that in lamentations as well as in tragedies <and comedies>, not only on stage but also in all of life's tragedies and comedies, pleasures are mixed with pains [. . .]. (50b1–4, trans. D. Frede)[11]

Under the condition of the de-theatricalization implied by the interjected sentence ("not only on stage . . ."), what is common in the *Laws* to the play and the constitution, is that both of them there are representations of a certain life (*bios*).[12]

The proximity of this remarkable construal of the best constitution as "the truest tragedy" to the first part of Aristotle's definition of tragedy in *Poetics* 6 ("the representation of a serious and completed action [. . .]") is obvious.[13] There are two main points of contact: First, on the assumption that a 'life'/*bios* consists in a series of 'actions,' Aristotle's characterization of tragedy as "the representation of a serious action (*mimêsis praxeôs spoudaias*)" accords with the *Laws*' description of the best political regime as the "representation of the finest and best life (*politeia sunestêke mimêsis tou kallistou kai aristou biou*)." As a matter of fact, when in the course of the chapter he returns to the first component of his definition, Aristotle explains the first term by using the second: tragedy, he recalls at 6.1450a16–17, is "the representation not of human beings, but of an action *and of a life*."[14] The second correspondence between the two passages lies in the importance given to the *end point* of the action, its completion or perfection. The action represented, as Aristotle puts it, will be a complete one (*teleia*). Plato's use of the verb *apotelein* equally suggests that the constitutional drama considers a certain end. What is peculiar and distinctive about his formulation is that it states *what it is* that brings the constitutional drama to its completion, namely the law or, more exactly: true law (*alêthês nomos*, 817b8).[15]

How should we understand, then, the tragic character of the constitutional drama? Interpreters have opted for one of the two following strategies.

The first consists in taking the tragic character of Plato's "true tragedy" literally (linking it to the notion of misfortune), but relocating it, away from its immediate context, to somewhere else in the Platonic corpus, by appealing in particular to the philosophical life as illustrated by Socrates' fate in the *Apology* and the *Phaedo*.[16]

The second, symmetrical option assumes a non-tragic conception of tragedy or the tragic. This is the path followed by W. Kuhn who, with selected Aeschylean dramas in mind, defends the idea of a "self-transcending movement of tragic creation in the direction of philosophy itself":[17] the *Prometheus Bound* was followed by the *Prometheus Unbound*, where "both the dramatic and logical tensions" between Prometheus and Zeus were "finally solved"; the Persian disaster in the *Persians* is a just punishment; finally—and above all— the trilogy of the *Oresteia* culminates in a final reconciliation—as Kuhn sees it—with the integration of the Erinyes in the new political scheme devised by

Athena,[18] indicating that "the new order ushered in by the *Eumenides* leaves no more room for tragic conflict than does the Platonic cosmos."[19] Alternatively, one can strip the constitutional tragedy of its tragic character by weakening the scope of the metaphor to a minimum and assuming that the common feature of tragedy and a constitution is that both of them deal with "serious matters."[20]

But it seems to me that Plato's constitution, and by the same token the best life of which it is the representation, can be seen, apart from being related to serious matters (which it indubitably is) as a tragedy in the more usual sense of the term 'tragic,' which is attested in Plato himself, and this from two different perspectives.

The first will consider 'law,' taking it here to mean proceedings for the punishment of crimes. Although the Athenian does not detail in this passage how the tragedians' ideas are going, predictably, to contradict his own "in most cases" (7.817c6–7),[21] he describes the tragic poets ("you scions of soft Muses," 817d4) with an adjective that indicates most clearly what he has in mind. "Softness"/*malakia* is his target in the *Republic*, too, when tragedy is accused of putting on the stage characters who respond to the blows of fortune by yielding to despair (605c10–606e1). Such characters attribute to what has happened to them an importance that it does not have (604b12–c1) and thus arouse the pity of the audience when they should be provoking disgust.[22]

Bad tragedy, then, is a tragedy in which a reversal of fortune provokes an inappropriate response, whether in the tragic character or in the spectator. What will make a tragedy good will depend on the specifications of, or modifications to one or more of the following elements: the character of the person concerned, his reaction to the event, and the significance of the reversal in itself. It is quite possible that the tragic character might not be a good person, or that we should distinguish between different degrees of goodness.[23] The reaction to misfortune might be different (namely, "measured") from the one supposed to be typical of tragic heroes.[24] And finally, the modification might concern the manner in which one interprets the reversal: perhaps the latter is merely temporary and so no reversal really, all things considered, or else it results from an illusion, the supposed misfortune being actually no more than the appropriate punishment called for by previous offences.

This last perspective is essential in the context of the *Laws*. Consider, for example, the way in which tragic motifs are recruited in Book 8.838c4–7. The main idea of the passage is that when it comes to incest, the law finds support not just in religious prohibitions but also in common opinion and in the shared certainties that must be inculcated to children from their earliest years. Were not Thyestes, Oedipus, and Macareus punished for their fault (*hamartia*, 838c7)?[25] Tragedies of this sort, on the interpretation currently under consideration, are not 'soft' but properly constructed, insofar as they illustrate a virtuous sequence: transgression followed by the punishment for the transgression.[26] One can see easily enough how such stories (and their staging) might contribute to a life governed by a Platonic constitution; for the *Laws*, its commitment to persuasion aside, is also a penal code, and as such it relies on the principle that every transgression of the law brings punishment in its wake— even if this comes only after death, by virtue of a law named 'destiny' (*heimarmenê*).[27] In this eschatological sense, one can see how "true law alone brings to completion" a life governed by the constitution of the *Laws*, making of it the "truest tragedy."

There is another sense, however, no less 'political' in nature, in which the formula applies to the constitution of the *Laws*. Leaving behind the notion that punishment is unavoidable in the sense that it will necessarily follow disobedience and crime (at the cosmic level, if not at that of human justice), we look now at punishment as inevitable from the perspective of the lawgiver, who cannot avoid having to formulate and apply it. The distinction between law in terms of content, on the one hand, and law in terms of form on the other is once more operative here. For whereas the *content* of the law, insofar as its formulations are no more than the expression of reason (*nous*), says how things are and ought to be (this is the connection between law and reason, which is reflected in the 'etymology' of *nomos* as "the distribution [*dianomê*] of reason [*nous*]"[28]), the *form* of the law is irrational. And to the extent that it is irrational, it is violent: hence the lawgiver's attempt to reduce the share left to threats and imperatives in favor of preambles that will display various degrees of rationality. Legislative violence, however, cannot be avoided altogether. The conflict which plays out in the first place at the cosmic level between the good and the bad—a "fight"/*makhê* that is said to be "immortal"/*athanatos* and to require our utmost care at *Laws* 10.906a2–b3[29]—reflects in the *eventually* insuperable conflict, within the human puppet, wonderful as it is, between reason on the one hand and irrational feelings of pleasure and pain on the other. Howsoever virtuous a city may be, the Erinyes, too, will have their place in it.

In Retrospect

THE AIM OF THIS ESSAY has been to articulate the conceptual net that the *Laws* weaves around the term 'law.' Chapters 1 through 4 set the stage. The first chapter presents an overview of this bulky work foregrounding Plato's fundamental stance, which directs the internal dynamics of the treatise: namely, that true law has a theological underpinning that is integral to its content, but that laws in their traditional form falls short because they lack the critical component of persuasive force.

I turn in Chapter 2 to an intriguing feature of Socrates' answer, in the *Republic*, to the pressing question of the possibility (or: feasibility) of the just city. Socrates' argument leads, uniquely in Plato's work, to a definition of philosophy as the knowledge of the Forms and the Good and to a picture of the philosopher as initially reluctant to accept the political charge that, ironically, he alone is entitled to exercise. But prior to an extended discussion of this topic there is a short introduction that points to two ways of understanding 'possibility'—as a conceptual or logical possibility on the one hand, or as a real possibility on the other. The just city is declared possible if it can be approximated as far as possible. This surprising thought is not further explored in the *Republic*, which resolves the question by asserting that the just city is possible on the condition that either philosophers rule or rulers philosophize, which situation is declared to be possible. The occurrence of the phrase "as far as possible" to qualify feasibility at various junctures (albeit not in the conclusion) functions, however, as an insistent though also discreet reminder of a distinction that is crucial, because it opens the way to the *Laws*.

In Chapter 3 I argue that the *Laws* engages in a series of systematically related "retreats" from a paradigm that owes much, but not everything, to the *Republic*. This retreat is said to move away "from the sacred," for it is now the human condition that is fundamental in setting the limits of the possible. As a consequence, the constitution can no longer look to the rule of philosophers but must instead seek a middle point (or 'mean') between monarchic and democratic principles and, in the process, must resort to various kinds of 'mixtures.' Ruling is now the purview of the law itself; and the primacy of the divine, which is no less presupposed in the *Republic* than in the *Laws* (as indeed it always is in Plato) now takes the more substantial form of 'gods' or 'the god'—this though the relationship between the plural and the singular, or for that matter between the traditional gods and Plato's rational ensouled stars, is never clarified.

The human condition is the subject of my Chapter 4. Each of us is double. Humans host both divine reason (the internal paradigmatic model, one could venture to say) and a complementary pair of blind 'counselors': a drive towards excessive pleasure and a drive towards the avoidance of pain. The dynamic of these constitutive forces, one weak and the rest strong, are illustrated by a 'puppet.' The psychology at work in the *Laws*, I suggest, is not structurally different from that of the *Republic*, but there is a change in the balance of power within the soul, and as well the correlative inclusion of political power as a source of pleasure. Overall the picture is much closer to that advocated by Thrasymachus in the first book of the *Republic* than to Socrates' paradigmatic countermodel in this dialogue: human beings do crave, in the world as it is, for a power which, when it is excessive, and especially monarchic in the sense of undivided and unchecked, necessarily leads first to cognitive blindness and then to political disaster—to civil war instead of peace. Human reason, the divine side of human beings, cries out for reinforcement. The *Laws* ponders what the latter should, or for that matter can consist in. Whereas "education" is the key word, additional mechanisms must be put in play if political peace is to be preserved.

The second part of my essay explores the main issues that emerge, at the political level, from the coexistence of the possibility of the paradigm, on the one hand, and the conditions of its feasibility, on the other. 'Measure,' in the wake of an ontology of becoming that is not in the *Republic* but comes to the fore in the *Philebus* and in the *Statesman*, is here the leading notion. Grounded in divine reason, it defines the virtuous middle-point between shortcomings and excesses that is central to the paradigm of the second city. When a legislative scheme takes virtue (excellence) as the ultimate goal of the lawgiver, what happens to freedom and equality, two all-too-human democratic values that rank next to wisdom and friendship as legislative targets? Is there, for Plato, something like a true freedom, as there is a true equality and a true law, even if these can't be fully implemented under human conditions? What is, more generally, the relationship between historical 'mixed' constitutions and the 'middle' constitution advocated by Plato, which owes so much also to Athenian institutions? And what are we to make of the "voluntary enslavement" to the law of all the citizens, rulers and ruled alike? This cluster of knotty questions, which Rousseau's political works can illuminate (not solve) at various junctures, is dealt with in my Chapters 5 and 6.

In Chapters 7 through 9, I flesh out the tension between content and form that, as I have presupposed all along, is inherent to the law. The distant shadow of the *Crito* is perceptible here. If there is no law without obedience to the law, how is this obedience to be secured? At the core of this quandary are the nature and the limits of persuasion and its relation to constraint. Formally speaking, persuasion, which it is the function of legislative preambles to guarantee in order to secure political friendship, is situated between two extremes, command and threat, on the one hand, rational teaching and philosophizing, on the other. It is cashed out through a range of examples, the diversity of which vividly illustrates the principle of scalarity. The distinction between content and form also helps to fix the status of philosophy in the political landscape of the *Laws*. While an unambiguous ontology tacitly provides the doctrinal substructure of the work as a whole, philosophical practice functions as a remote paradigm for legislation. The lawgiver's mortal enemies, the atheists, serve as the best of all possible enemies, giving the lawgiver the opportunity to engage in philosophical discussion in a strictly political context. This *tour de force* is perhaps the most remarkable feature in the construction of the work, discreetly pointing to a political situation where the force of argument, embodied in a rational preamble, would render superfluous any additional enforcement of the law. The fact that this remains a legislative utopia is sufficient grounds, my last chapter suggests, for Plato to claim that his second-best constitution, the representation of a human life under the true law, is also "the best and truest tragedy," not only because it deals seriously with serious human matters, but also because the human situation that seems to please the gods is, seen from the lawgiver's point of view, far from fortunate.

In spite of the necessary riders and intricacies that bedevil almost every step of the reconstruction, the picture I attempt to defend here is a rather simple one: it shows that the obvious changes between the political programs of the *Republic* and the *Laws* are in fact the consequence of a fundamental consistency. This is not claiming that Plato's nomocratic "Second Republic" did not benefit from the acute gaze of old age that Clinias attributes to the Athenian in the passage that constitutes the first paragraph of my essay; nor is it denying that Plato's involvement with Syracusan politics raises interesting and persistent questions about the relationship between philosophy and political engagement both in Plato's case and more generally. The point is, rather, to do justice to the relevance of a crucial conceptual articulation that is inherent to Plato's paradigmatism.

On the Status of the *Statesman*

GUIDED BY THE PARADIGM of weaving, the *Statesman* combines, with an extreme virtuosity, a general epistemological argument about how to become a better dialectician with a specific political argument that takes the eponymous statesman as the topic of its particular inquiry. The fact that Plato emphatically foregrounds the general objective as the main concern, to the point of presenting the particular inquiry in an almost disparaging way (285c8–d8), requires interpretation—there is something evidently serious behind the no less evident irony. But what is certain is that the subordination of politics to dialectic must not restrict us from according to the latter its full weight.[1]

Considered from this partial angle, the *Statesman seems to* form, with the *Republic* and the *Laws*, a significant triad, even if there is no indication in any one of the three dialogues that Plato planned them as a triad, as he certainly did in the case of *Theaetetus-Sophist-Statesman* (or for that matter *Sophist-Statesman-Philosopher*) or of *Republic-Timaeus-Critias* (or for that matter *Timaeus-Critias-Hermocrates*).[2] What is the nature of the relationship between these three related dialogues, then?

Lane (1998) has convincingly shown that by contrast with the *Republic*, the *Statesman* focuses on the specifics of political expertise, putting the principles of ruling rather than philosophical knowledge at the center of attention. Its scope is thus a distinctive one. "In the *Republic*," she writes (p. 3), "the philosophers are to rule not in virtue of any peculiarly political knowledge they possess, but rather in virtue of their synoptic and pervasive understanding of the Good. If the question were to be pressed, however—what specifically counts as political knowledge in the *Republic*?—it is not clear what the answer would be. This is the question which *is* pressed in the *Statesman*."[3] If we now consider the *Laws* in addition to the pair *Republic-Statesman*, which it is natural to do given the many points of contact between the *Statesman* and the *Laws*, we find that what at first seemed a triptych, with three independent although related subjects, is instead a diptych, the second panel of which is subdivided, with the *Republic* on one side, the *Statesman* and the *Laws* on the other.

As a matter of fact, the *Statesman*, which broaches several crucial issues that are not subjects for discussion in the *Republic*, is opening the way to the *Laws*: the notion of law as an independent issue, to begin with, and more generally the notion of a political second-best; then the relation between legislative violence and legislative persuasion; the reference to the myth of Kronos; and last but not least the centrality of mixture and the notion of the mean as a political principle.

Of course, the presence of identical topics does not ensure that they are treated in the same way, as the case of the Kronos myth, for one, makes clear.[4] More generally, any interpretation of the relationship between the two dialogues will have to identify similarities and differences and decide whether the differences in question are context-related and thus functional, or signal a modification in the philosophical position.

On the latter view, which probably remains the majority view (best represented by Kahn [1995]), the *Statesman* occupies a "middle position" between the *Republic* and the *Laws* in the sense that it presents an "oscillation verging to contradiction" on the issue of the (possibility of) a philosopher-king:[5] Plato would, by this account, be in the process of abandoning the perfect ruler of the *Republic* without having yet reached the conclusion, drawn in the *Laws*, that power is ineludibly corruptible. What we know of Plato's involvement in Syracusan politics is often taken to support this view. The story, which is based on information provided by the *Seventh Letter* (the fact that it may be spurious is of no consequence here), is well known. It must be taken in consideration, if only because it raises in a paradigmatic way the recurrent question of the relationship between philosophy and politics, and more generally between an author's life and his work.[6] Briefly, the story goes like this:

In 388, Plato made his first visit to Syracuse, at that time a prosperous and powerful city ruled by a brilliant tyrant, Dionysius I. According to a likely dating, Plato wrote the *Republic*, culminating in the portrait of the philosopher-king, upon his return to Athens in 387 and the acquisition of a property in the grove named the Academy.[7] Plato made a second visit to the Syracusan court in 367, after the death of Dionysus I, at the request of Dion, Dionysus'

I brother-in-law whom Plato had befriended during his first stay. Dion's idea was that Plato might influence the successor of Dionysus I, Dionysius the Younger, who was then 30 years old. This attempt was a dramatic failure, vividly depicted in the *Seventh Letter*. Since the *Statesman* registers the actual unavailability of actual expert ruler, it is all too easy to assume a relationship between the disillusionment caused by this second trip and the writing of the *Statesman*, which one can situate sometime after 367. The *Laws*, according to this scheme, would represent a last step in Plato's growing pessimism about the possibility of a philosopher-king.[8] On this picture, resignation (the *Laws*) follow upon doubts (the *Statesman*) and hope (the *Republic*).

Can, or should, a reconstruction of Plato's psychological states of mind, plausible as it may be, guide, explicitly or otherwise, our understanding of the dialogues conceptual import? On the use I have thus far made of Plato's paradigmatism, Plato's second city is not the result of a disillusionment, but rather the all-things-considered consequence of an anthropological turn made possible by the logic of the paradigm itself. This does not preclude the possibility that it took the sharp eyes of an older Plato to unpack the consequences in question, and to decide, finally, to place the law above any human political power.

In what follows, I recapitulate briefly the main points that illustrate the deep solidarity between the *Statesman* and the *Laws*, which justify treating it as a 'transitional' dialogue. And by 'transitional' I do not mean to deny its crucial importance, quite the contrary, nor to refer to its place in the chronology of Plato's political thinking, since Plato may have been working simultaneously on both dialogues. The *Statesman* is transitional in the sense that it lays the conceptual ground for the *Laws*. The main issues, in order from the more simple to the more complex, are as follows:

1) Weaving. The end of the *Statesman* outlines what would be the two primary tasks of a political expertise conceived as an art of due measure: weaving together, after careful selection of the material, the two opposite virtues of "courage" and "moderation" (the "divine bonds") in individual souls, and male and female in view of procreation in "the human bonds" of marriage.[9] There can be no doubt that the whole legislative edifice of the *Laws* relies on an extensive application of this scheme to all the aspects of the life within a city, beyond the explicit reference to weaving at 5.734e6–735a4 (the issue being here the choice of officeholders, who present different degrees of education).

2) Ontology. In Chapter 6, I pointed to the centrality of the *Statesman* for the ontology that is presupposed by the *Laws'* notion of a 'middle.' One can add that this ontology of the mean, contrary to the ontology of pure Forms that is found in the *Republic,* is geared to generated and perishable entities in the world of becoming, to which the *Philebus* refers (27b8–9)as 'generated being' (*gegenêmenê ousia;* cf. *genesis eis ousian* 26d8). The fundamentals of this ontology are listed at *Philebus* at 23c4–d8: the non-limited (*to apeiron*), the limit (*to peras*),the mixture of both (*to summisgomenon*), and the cause (*hê aitia*) of the mixture. This ontology is clearly different from, but not incompatible with the ontology of Forms that features in the *Republic,* given that the senses in which "being" is used are different.[10] It is this ontology on which the *Laws* relies.

3) Law. The *Statesman* discusses and the *Laws* mentions the deficiencies of law (*nomos*) when compared to reason/*nous* and to direct, non-mediated noetic or 'royal' expertise (*basilikê*); and both dialogues grant it a second rank, whether in terms of a "second sailing" (*deuteros plous*) in the *Statesman* (300c2) or of a "second [choice]" at *Laws* 5.739a4–5 or 9.875d3. This agreement, however, is only part of the story, because the scope of the critique of the law is broader in the *Laws* than in the *Statesman.* At 9.875d4–5, the *Laws* endorses in passing (in a subordinate clause) the criticism of the law developed at length in the *Statesman* at 294a6–296a4: the law, which is by nature general, considers only "what happens for the most part" (*hôs epi to polu, Statesman* 295a5), without taking into account the totality of individual cases. The *Statesman* also insists that a law cannot adapt to changing circumstances (*Statesman* 294b2–6, 295c7–e2)—this second aspect is mentioned here because the discussion bears on the legitimacy of changing laws in general (cf. 300e11–301a4). The main focus of the *Laws,* on the other hand, is not on the impossibility for a law to adapt to particular cases and even less to new circumstances (its laws aspire on the contrary to final closure and stability, and its constitution is "closest to immortality"[11]), but on the tyrannical character or the legislative "order," which—in the wake of the criticism of writing in the *Phaedrus*—does not provide justifications of any sort.[12]

In this respect, the *Laws* clarifies an issue that is implicitly raised, but (quite strikingly) left open in the *Statesman.* On the one hand, the lesson of the central myth about the cosmic reign of Kronos and that of Zeus, which puts the diairetic course of the inquiry on the right track, is that a king differs from a tyrant in the manner (*tropos*, 275a4) by which he rules—the tyrant by force, the king by triggering voluntary action:[13]

[Eleatic Visitor]: I think we made a mistake [...] by behaving more simple-mindedly than we should have. We put king and tyrant into the same category, when both they themselves and the manner of their rule are very unlike one another. [...] But now should we set things to rights again, and, as I said, should we divide the expertise of the human carer into two, by using the categories of the enforced (*biaios*) and the voluntary (*hekousios*)? [...] And should we perhaps call tyrannical the expertise that relates to subjects who are forced, and the herd-keeping that is voluntary and relates to willing two-footed living things [i.e. human beings] that expertise which belongs to statesmanship, displaying, in his turn, the person who has this expertise and cares for his subjects in this way as being genuinely a king and statesman? (276e1–14, trans. Rowe)

On the other hand, the argument establishing the superiority of the expert, living king over the dead, tyrannical legislative command is that an expert ruler does not have to take into consideration criteria such as voluntariness or constraint, respect or disrespect for the law, or for that matter the ruler's wealth or lack thereof, given that he knows what is better:

[Eleatic Visitor]: [...] these people [i.e. the expert rulers], whether they rule over willing or unwilling subjects, whether according to written laws or without them, and whether they rule as rich men or poor, we must suppose—as is now our view—to be carrying out whatever sort of rule they do on the basis of expertise. This is no less what we believe about doctors, [293b] whether they cure us with our consent or without it, by cutting or burning or applying some other painful treatment:, or whether they do so according to written rules or apart from written rules; or as poor men or rich. In all these cases we are no less inclined at all to say they are doctors, so long as they are in charge of us on the basis of expertise, purging or otherwise reducing us, or else building us up—it is no matter, if only each and every one of those who care for our bodies acts for our bodies' good with the aim of making them better than they were, and thus preserves what is in their care. [293c] It's in this way, as I think, and in no other that we'll lay down the criterion of medicine and of any other sort of rule whatsoever; it is the only correct criterion. [...] It must then be the case, it seems, that of constitutions too the one that is correct in comparison with the rest, and alone a constitution, is the one in which the rulers would be found truly possessing expert knowledge, and not merely seeming to do so, whether they rule according to laws or without laws, over willing or [293d] unwilling subjects, and whether the rulers are poor or wealthy—there is no principle of correctness according to which any of these must be taken into any account at all. (293a6–d2 trans. Rowe slightly modified)

Is the king, then, as different from a tyrant as the conclusion of the myth suggests? "Yes and no" is the best answer that can be drawn from the *Laws*. The lawgiver can only hope for an appropriate tyrant, according to the famous passage in Book 4 which implies that the word 'tyrant' can be taken in more than one sense;[14] but the *Laws*, while resolutely embracing the lesson to be drawn from the Kronos myth in the *Statesman*—that under the present cosmic reign of Zeus, it is necessary to distinguish between a persuasive king and a tyrant—also explicitly registers the limits of the distinction. Recognizing that a tyrant can equally well use persuasion as constraint, the *Laws* has the lawgiver pair a persuasive preamble with a threatening law—a combination that is related to the familiar critique of the law that is central to the dialogue; namely that, to the extent that it makes tyrannical use of force, the law is a less than perfect instrument for the rule of a city. Consent, which in the *Statesman* was considered (for the sake of the argument, as in the *Gorgias*) as optional, inasmuch as constraint is a means to reach an end,[15] now appears (as it should) as a decisive legislative requirement, which it is the function of preambles to implement.

4) Constitution. The *Statesman* knows of seven types of constitutions: the one true constitution, under the rule of an expert statesman (the scheme most akin to the rule of the philosopher(s)-king(s) in the *Republic,* although the *Statesman* definitely tends towards a monarchic model), and six other so-called 'constitutions' (in reality "illegitimate constitutions" that are "non-constitutions"[16]). The number results from taking three basic types of regime—those with one ruler, those with a few, and those with many (the *dêmos*), and then dividing again according to whether the rulers stick to the laws or do not. This division gives rise to lawful kingship and lawless tyranny, lawful aristocracy and lawless oligarchy, lawful democracy and lawless democracy (291d1–292d1; 301a10–d6). All six constitutions are "imitations" (cf. *mimoumenas,* and kindred terms at 293e4 and 300d10–301c4) of the true constitution. Some are worse than others (293e3–6, 297c1–4), depending on their intrinsic nature and potentialities (knowledge is never going to belong to the multitude/*plêthos, Statesman,* 292e1–5), but also and above all on whether or not they abide by their specific laws.

Does this scheme make room for the second city of the *Laws*? Whereas this possibility is not usually taken into consideration (which introduces an important gap between the *Statesman* and the *Laws*), there is one crucial sentence that allows a positive answer to the question, at least if it is read in the way Christopher Rowe has suggested. The traditional understanding of 300c5–7 is represented by Skemp's translation (as revised by Ostwald):

> These laws (*tauta*) [referring in this interpretation backwards to the laws of the six constitutions under discussion] would seem to be written copies (*mimêmata*) of the scientific truth in various departments of life they cover,[17] copies based as far as possible on the instructions received from those who really possess the truth on these matters. (quoted by Rowe 2001, p. 69; see also 2005, p. 12)

Rowe is right, I think, to consider that the thought conveyed by this translation is inappropriate[18] and to adopt a construction of the sentence that makes it possible to apply the term "imitations" to the laws of the true constitution, or, as I would rather say, to those laws, too:

> Well, imitations of the truth of each particular issue would be these (*tauta*, looking forward)—the written [laws or prescriptions] stemming as far as possible from those who know? (300c5–7, trans. Rowe 1995 modified)[19]

One advantage of this reading (as briefly noted by Rowe[20]) is that the second-best constitution of the *Laws* gets its place virtually assigned in the constitutional scheme of the *Statesman* (no less than it had its place, at a higher degree of generality, in the paradigmatic just city of the *Republic*, as I read it[21]). When the Eleatic visitor adds, a few lines later:

> But as things are, when—as we say—a king does not come to be in cities as a king-bee is born in a hive, one individual immediately superior in body and mind, it is necessary—so it seems—for people to come together and write things down, chasing after the traces of the truest constitution (301d8–e4, trans. Rowe)

The general formula "people coming together" (*sunelthontas* at 301e3) would also be applicable to the setting of the *Laws*, even though it represents a rather special instance of such a gathering—the Athenian, his two interlocutors, with, on the horizon, the Knossian commission that will make the final decisions.[22]

5) Possibility. This one is, unsurprisingly, the most tricky issue. I have argued in Chapter 2 that the official thesis of the *Republic*, namely that the coincidence of philosophical knowledge with political power *is* possible, is potentially undermined by Plato's own qualifications limiting the meaning of the term 'possible' in Book 5; I have also argued that the *Laws*, relying on the distinction between divine and human as well as on the ordinary semantics of the term 'possible,' denies the possibility of an expert ruler exercising power through time, if humanity and its epoch are to be strictly distinguished from that of gods and heroes. (This is so because of the corrupting effect of excessive political power.) But at the same time, the *Laws* conjures a legendary epoch where the possibility in question would have been a real possibility, rather than a purely logical one. What the *Statesman* says on this issue is different, since the adoption of a second-best (which does not coincide in its content with the second-best of the *Laws*, but opens the way to it) is not immediately grounded on the principle of the corruptibility of power, but on the people's fear of tyrannical exactions, here illustrated by abusive doctors and shameless steersmen (ironically designated "the noble steersman and the doctor who is 'worth many others'"):

> Let's suppose that we all thought of them as doing the most terrible things to us. For the one as much as the other saves whichever of us he wishes to save; and whichever of us they wish to mutilate, they do it by cutting and burning us and directing us to pay them expenses as if they were taxes, of which they spend little or none on the patient, while they themselves and their household use the rest; and the final step is for them to take money from relatives or some enemies of the patient as pay for killing him. And steersmen, in their turn, bring about thousands of other things of a similar sort, leaving people stranded on voyages because of some conspiracy or other, causing shipwrecks on the seas and throwing people overboard, and doing other malicious things. Let's suppose then that we thought this, and came to a conclusion about them in a sort of council, no longer to allow either of these sorts of expertise to have autonomous control either of slaves or of free men, but to call together an assembly with ourselves as members, consisting either of the people all together or only of the rich [. . .]. (298a1–c3 trans. Rowe)

Plato's portrait of the political autocrat (*autokratôr*) in Book 9 of the *Laws*[23] is cast in a more general way and using less vivid words, but the substance is the same. The relevant difference is that what in the *Statesman* appears as an expression of the subjective opinion of the citizens, is given in the *Laws* as an objective state of affairs. Is this enough to conclude that there has been a significant shift in Plato's thinking between the *Statesman*, where hope would still be permitted, given that what people understandably think on the basis of what they see may not be necessary, and the *Laws*, where there is no human absolute power that will not in the end give blind tyranny the upper hand? Not necessarily. For the philosopher-king remains in the *Laws* a living force and an object of hope, in spite of the denial of his real possibility. Complementarily, we should not be surprised if, according to the *Statesman*, no one has ever seen the kind of king who rules in Plato's seventh constitution, since, by contrast with the visibility of the queen among the bees, he is in fact unavailable among actual human beings.

On a Supposed Evolution of Plato's Psychology

IN *PLATO'S UTOPIA RECAST*, Christopher Bobonich (2002) claimed that Plato's psychological theory in the *Laws* differs in one fundamental way from his thinking in the *Republic*. This thesis has been criticized by various authors with objections that I share;[1] but since it forms the basis of a construal of the relationship between Plato's just city in the *Republic* and the "second city" of the *Laws* which, though fundamentally different from the one I have been pursuing, also has some points of contacts with it (*Plato's Utopia Recast* is a title that I could have adopted), it is useful to come back to the issue. My own position is that whereas there is an important difference between the psychology of the *Republic* and that of the *Laws*, this difference, first, is not to be located in the abandonment, in the *Laws*, of the notion that the human soul has different parts and, second, is not to be construed in evolutionary terms as a philosophical 'improvement' on an earlier view (the model of the divided soul). If there are 'difficulties' in Plato's position (and there certainly are; this is the common lot of all philosophical theory), they are basically the same in the *Republic* and the *Laws*; interesting as they may be, they are not central, or even relevant to an understanding of the relationship between the two works.

Bobonich assumes that the human soul in the *Republic* not only has parts, but that each of these parts is endowed with a psychical apparatus that makes of them (quasi-)agents in their own right. This implies in particular that the inferior parts of the soul, besides having their own desires and pleasures (9.580d7–581e5), have opinions (4.442c10–d1), may be persuaded (8.554c11–d3), and can even reason (9.580d10–581a1).[2] To this extent, each part can be compared to an "homunculus,"[3] without there being any unifying 'I or 'ego' that stands as the person as a whole. To this conception, Bobonich opposes the psychology of the *Laws*, where different motivational forces coexist within the soul without being endowed each with its own psychological apparatus. Feelings and emotions are now properly irrational.[4] A psychology of this kind can be considered superior to that of the *Republic* for two reasons: first, negatively, because it avoids the difficulties to which a theory of the partition of the soul is exposed;[5] but also, positively, because it contains, at least in outline, the notion of a unified ego supposed to be lacking in the *Republic*. For, according to Bobonich, the *Laws* makes room, next to various motivational "states" (*pathê*) that may be either rational or irrational, for an ego that hosts these states ("each of us" at *Laws* 1.644c4 and d8) and is capable of acting in its own right and intervening in the internal fight between rational and irrational desires.[6]

First of all, it must be noted that Bobonich's description of Plato's psychology in the *Laws* sheds new light on important details of the text. That an 'ego,' construed as a responsible person, is presupposed in the *Laws* is beyond doubt. This is the case, in particular, in the passage comparing human beings to puppets (1.644b9–645c1), which opens with the premise that "each of us is one" (644c4) but then adds immediately that human motivation nonetheless derives from three sources that are "within" us and that "draw" and "pull" us in contrary directions (644e2–3): (a) pleasure and pain, (b) fear and firmness, and (c) reasoning, which can be correct or incorrect (644c6–d3). In the development that follows, the argument/*logos* (644e4) declares (*phêsin*) that "each one (*hekastos*) should always follow one of the cords [i.e., the golden cord of reason], never letting go of it and pulling with it against the others" (e4–6).[7] Along similar lines, one could add a fact that is particularly striking because of the lexical transgression it implies: we entertain an *homilêma*, i.e., a relationship, with ourselves, following a model that we might call 'reflexive' and which leaves behind both the idea that a soul is no more than the sum of its parts and also any notion that it is an homogeneous ego.[8]

So the question is not whether the picture that Bobonich gives of the psychology of the *Laws* is correct in this respect (it is), but whether what the *Republic* says is really something different from the relevant point of view.

In order to clarify the problem, it will be useful to distinguish two different issues:

(1) there is the general thesis that the soul (at least our human soul) is divided. This division is a division into parts (*merê*).[9] This thesis shows how one can "be superior [or inferior] to oneself": by either keeping control and ruling oneself, or being 'enkratic' or 'akratic.'

(2) there is the thesis, defended by Bobonich, of the homuncular
      character of the psychic parts, which asserts that each of the parts
      of the soul, and particularly the inferior parts, is endowed with an
      independent psychic apparatus. This particular version of psychic
      division is by no means implied in the general view about the soul
      partition.

Now it is important to realize that whereas the thesis of the division of the
soul is explicitly laid out in an elaborate argument that extends from 4.435c4
to 440c7, the notion of homuncular parts relies on (at most) three unrelated
sentences (quoted below) which can be interpreted in more plausible ways
than the way Bobonich interprets them.

I. I begin with the second point: homuncularity.

There exist good reasons to deny that the passages invoked are evidence for
Bobonich's evolutionary scheme (from an homuncular picture of the parts of
the soul, with inferior parts endowed with significant cognitive powers, to a
conception of a unitary soul hosting conflicting affections/states and motives), which have been voiced by, among others, two early reviewers of Bobonich's book—Kahn (2004) and Lorenz (2004).[10] Although Kahn and Lorenz converge in their result, which is that Bobonich has no real basis for
claiming that the *Republic* has a different take on the cognitive capacities of the
lower parts of the soul than the *Timaeus* or, for that matter, the *Laws* (which
explicitly declares them to be nonrational), they differ in their strategy. This
difference is interesting, because it involves the hermeneutical question (in
which neither of them engages) about whether and when it is legitimate to
interpret a given passage metaphorically.

To set up the scene, here is a sentence talking about "spirit" (*thumos*), a part
which, says Plato at 4.440e4–6, differs from "appetite" (*epithumia*), since

> in the civil war in the soul it places its arms on the side of the rational ele-
> ment (*to hopla tithestai pros to logistikon*). (= trans. Grube/Reeve modified)

It would obviously be a mistake to think that what Plato is saying here is
that the *thumos* shakes a spear and holds a shield.[11] What he says is that the
thumos "aligns itself far more with the rational part"; the rest is metaphorical.
One can even locate the rationale for the metaphor. To "take up arms" is a
characteristic of that part of the city which is the analogue of the spirit in the
soul, namely the military (the "auxiliary" guardians).

Here are the three passages that need to be taken into consideration.

1) Republic 4.442c10–d1:

[Socrates:] And isn't he moderate (*sôphrôn*) because of the friendly and harmonious relations between these same [sc. parts, *meros*, 442b11 and c5], namely, when the ruling one and the two that are ruled believe in common (*homodoxôsi*) that the rational part should rule and don't engage in civil war against it? (trans. Grube/Reeve modified)

Is Plato attributing opinions to spirit (*thumos*) and appetite (*epithumia*)? The term *homodoxein*/'share a belief' occurs elsewhere in Plato in a context that clearly forbids a literal interpretation of the compound, for example at *Phaedo* 83d7, where the body, which is by definition without a soul, speaks, and the soul is said to "share its beliefs (*homodoxein*) and delights" with it.[12] Moreover, as in the case of the spirit "taking up arms," the assumption that the soul is analogous to a city fosters the conceptual transfer. For both guardians and producers have opinions.

2) Republic 8.554c11–d3

[Socrates, talking of the oligarchic man:] And doesn't this make it clear that [. . .] he's forcibly holding his other evil appetites in check by means of some decent part of himself? He holds them in check, not by persuading them that it is better not to [sc. act in an appropriate way] or taming them with arguments, but by compulsion and fear, trembling for his other possessions. (trans. Grube/Reeve modified)

Kahn limits the implications of the sentence ". . . not by persuading them that it's better not to act on them or taming them with arguments . . ." on the grounds that it is negative and consequently does not allow for a positive conclusion.[13] This is true, but perhaps not sufficient, because the sentence does suggest that there is an (aristocratic) alternative to holding evil appetites in check by coercion as the oligarch does, namely by persuading them and even arguing with them. Lorenz tries to avoid this conclusion by suggesting that the alternative to compulsion could consist in "redirecting appetite's attention to some prospect it finds agreeable, so that it no longer feels, or is not so strongly inclined toward satisfying the objectionable desire in question."[14] I do not see, however, that this solves the problem: in order that appetite's attention be redirected, must it not be endowed with a capacity of being somehow persuaded and also of grasping arguments? I would again suggest that Plato talks in the way that he does about the soul of the oligarchic man because he is transferring to the parts of the soul notions that properly apply to the parts of the city, which is made of oligarchic individuals who do not undertake to persuade the citizens they rule in the same ways as philosophers would.[15]

3) *Republic* 9.580d10–581a1

The first, we say, is the part with which a person learns, and the second the part with which he gets angry. As for the third, we had no one special name for it, since it's multiform, so we named it after the biggest and strongest thing in it. Hence we called it the appetitive part, because of the intensity of its appetites for food, drink, sex, and all the things associated with them, but we also called it the money-loving part, because such appetites are most easily satisfied by means of money. (trans. Grube/Reeve)

A metaphorical license, as we could call it, would adequately explain why Plato calls the appetitive part "money-loving" without our having to assume that "it is because it calculates that money is an effective means to satisfying its desire that the appetitive part desires money."[16] The last claim relies on Bobonich's assumption that the passage is really attributing end-means reasoning to the appetitive part.[17] But this is not the case. For Plato is not only justifying two terminological choices, but also the licenses they imply: the third part is called 'desiring,' in spite of the fact that all three parts of the soul 'desire,' on the ground that its desires are particularly strong; the traditional term 'appetitive' is a way to distinguish the desire specific to this third part from the other desires. By the same token, it can be called "money-loving" because money is, objectively so to speak, one obvious way to satisfy the appetite's desires. One can add, if one wants to take into account the 'subjective' side of the question (i.e., looking at it from the point of view of the appetitive part itself), that the fixation of appetite on money in addition to its primary objects (which are food, drink, and sex) results from habituation.[18]

To sum up: the main reason why irrational parts are occasionally described in the *Republic* in terms that suggest they possess a higher cognitive apparatus is that they *represent* entities that are by definition endowed with these higher cognitive powers, namely the individuals that constitute the body of the city. There is of course no criterion permitting us to decide *a priori* whether a given expression is metaphorical or not. Bobonich denies that Plato speaks metaphorically, arguing that "Plato never suggests that such talk is intended as a metaphor or a convenient way of speaking." [19] But metaphors do not announce themselves as such. Aristotle would take this as a criterion to distinguish them from comparisons.[20]

II. I now turn to the first point, namely the supposed abandonment of the theory of the divided soul in favor of that of a unitary person in the *Laws*. That this is an erroneous view of the relationship between the *Republic* and the *Laws* is clear for two simple reasons. The *Republic* no less than the *Laws* knows of a unitary person beyond the three constitutive parts of the soul, and conversely the *Laws* no less than the *Republic* knows of a divided soul (whether into two or three is a separate question).

As far as the *Republic* is concerned, the very passage of Book 8 that is a prime basis for Bobonich's argument makes no mention of a rational part not engaging in the business of persuading the appetitive part, but of an individual, namely the oligarchic man. An agent entertaining a relation with (the different parts of) his soul is also presupposed by the depiction at 9.571d6–572b1 of "somebody" (*tis*, d6) who is capable of "quiet[ing] these two parts namely the *epithumia* and the *thumos*] and arous[ing] the third, in which wisdom [*to phronein*] resides" (572a5–6),[21] as well as at 4.443d1–7, where the just man

> does not allow any part of himself to do the work of another part or allow the various classes within him to meddle with each other. He regulates well what is really his own and rules himself. He puts himself in order, is his own friend, and harmonizes the three parts of himself like three limiting notes in a musical scale—high, low, and middle. (trans. Grube/Reeve)

Inversely, it is difficult to deny that the strings that pull at the puppet in the *Laws* are functionally equivalent to the parts of the soul, even if they are not called 'parts,' since what motivates the comparison of "each of us" with a puppet is the desire to explain (as in the *Republic*) what it is to be "superior to oneself." This presupposes the coexistence of at least two distinct psychological forces operating at the same time (cf. *hama* at 9.863e3) within the same subject. A few lines earlier (863b2–3), the Athenian left open the question whether 'anger' was a state (*pathos*) or a part (*meros*) of the soul. The manner in which the question was formulated does not in the least suggest a preference for the first option (*thumos* as a *pathos*).[22] One could even suppose, on the contrary, that since the first option is closer to the common view (anger is a 'passion'), the second evokes, by reference to the *Republic,* a more refined theory (*thumos* as a *meros*).

Last but not least, one should observe that the *Laws* occasionally uses language that, in Bobonich's view, suggests the homuncularity of the lower soul: pleasure and pain, which are feelings, are said to be "counselors" (1.644c6), and pleasure to do "through persuasion and forceful trickery [. . .] whatever she wishes [lit. what its wish/*boulêsis* desires]" (9.863b8–9). This of course does not speak in favor of a clear-cut distinction between the psychological models of the *Republic* and the *Laws.*[23]

To sum up: the most credible reading of the relevant passages in the *Republic* and the *Laws* is that, in both dialogues, a human being is both one and divided. Whether this must be considered a philosophical weakness is another question.

Trichotomy vs. Dichotomy

Finally, there is the classical question, of whether the *Laws* sticks to the tripartition advocated in the *Republic* or abandons it in favor of a bipartition.[24] The question requires probably less an answer than a reformulation.

The *Laws* doesn't mention any trichotomy that would reflect the one we find in the *Republic.* The two passages, 1.644c4–d3 and 9. 863b1–9, that have suggested the contrary can be interpreted in the framework of a bipartition. A presentation based on triads would look as follows:

Table 2

Republic	*Laws 1*	*Laws 9**
epithumêtikon/appetite	*hêdonê*/pleasure//*lupê*/pain	*hêdonê*/pleasure//*lupê*/pain
thumos/spirit	*phobos*/fear//*tharros*/firmness	*thumos*/anger//*phobos*/fear
logistikon/reasoning	*logismos*/reasoning	*hê tou aristou doxa*/belief about what is best

* Contrary to the two other columns, where the three terms in question are quoted in a row, this one puts together in a schematic way the substance of a passage dedicated to the analysis of the causes of delinquent conduct (*tôn hamartêmatôn aitia,* 863c1–2), which in the initial enumeration appear as: anger, pleasure, and ignorance (863b1–c2), to be further subdivided for legislative purposes. See 863e7 for 'pain' (and related effects) and 864a1 for the phrase "opinion about what is best."

But appearances are deceiving, because the relationship between the first two items and the third is not the same in the *Laws* and in the *Republic*. In the *Republic*, the *thumos* is the ally of the *logistikon*, which it helps in controlling the appetitive part; in the *Laws*, the *thumos* is clearly used in the sense of 'anger' (hence the question about whether it is a part or a passion associated with fear), and it is against this relatively homogeneous whole that reasoning and its upshot (the belief about what is best) must impose itself.[25] The passage in Book 9, where envies and desires are associated at 863e6–8 with anger, fear, pleasure, and pain as the factors that tyrannize the soul, is especially clear in this respect. The enumeration and classification of motivations, which matches almost exactly the list of affections/*pathêmata* of the mortal part of the soul in the *Timaeus* 69d1–4 (pleasure, pain, fear, anger, and expectation), is not only compatible with, but even points to a bipartite conception of the soul, with reasoning opposing alone all irrational factors.

Other passages in Plato's late dialogues, especially *Statesman* 309c1–3 and *Timaeus*, 69c5-d1 and 72d4, rely on a fundamentally dichotomic scheme (the soul includes an immortal and a mortal part) which is well attested in Aristotle and traceable to the Ancient Academy.[26] On the other hand, the *Timaeus* also knows of a tripartition that points to the limits of the alternative between trichotomy and dichotomy: the *logistikon* is localized in the head, the *epihumêtikon* under the diaphragm, the *thumos* in the chest (69d6–70a7). If, instead of starting from the *Republic*, one takes as the *Timaeus* as a guide, one can see how the mortal part of the soul, which is a species when it is opposed to the immortal part, is also a genus for the two species that it encompasses, the *thumos* and the *epithumêtikon*.[27]

Table 3

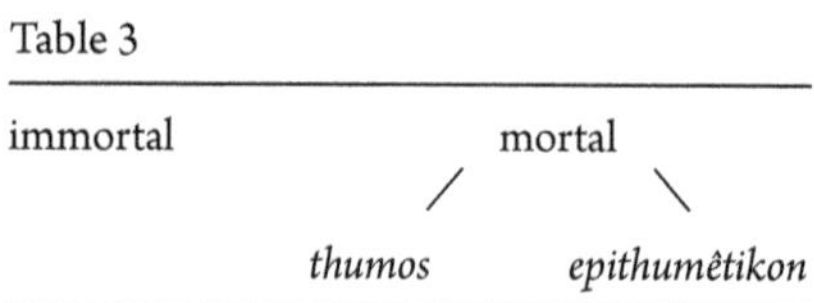

Is it not better, then, to reverse the terms and, instead of looking to see whether the late dialogues contain 'traces' of a tripartite psychology, ask whether the *Republic* does not ultimately rely, too, on a dichotomic scheme? After all, it is pretty clear that the city/soul analogy in the *Republic* exerts a strong pressure regarding what Plato must say about the nature of the soul at various points.

Aristotle and Posidonius on Plato's Preambles

IN HIS CRITICISMS OF Plato's *Laws* in the second book of the *Politics*, Aristotle does not mention (among other things that he also omits) the role Plato assigns to preambles. This can surely be counted as the consequence of a principle of selectivity: Aristotle tackles the *Laws*, as he does the *Republic*, only on topics that are not "exterior" to the subject of politics as he construes the discipline.[1] But in the *Nicomachean Ethics* 10.9 1180a5–14, Aristotle seems to approve of a lawgiver taking on a protreptic role, a view that most likely refers to Plato's conception of a preamble in the *Laws*:

> This is why some think that lawgivers ought to stimulate men to excellence and urge them forward by the motive of the noble, on the assumption that those who have been well advanced by the formation of habits will attend to such influences; and that punishments and penalties should be imposed on those who disobey and are of inferior nature, while the incurably bad should be completely banished. A good man (they think), since he lives with his mind fixed on what is noble, will submit to argument, while a bad man, whose desire is for pleasure, is corrected by pain like a beast of burden. This is, too, why they say the pains inflicted should be those that are most opposed to the pleasures such men love. (trans. Ross/Urmson)[2]

Although Plato's views on preambles may have indirectly influenced later legislative practice,[3] we have few ancient references to the doctrine, apart from Cicero's approval in his own *Laws* (*De legibus*, 2.14–16). But we do know of Posidonius' hostility to Plato's conception, thanks to Seneca's *Letter* 94, dedicated to criticizing Aristo of Chios' attack on the Stoic doctrine of precepts (*praecepta*).[4] Aristo had claimed that a knowledge of general principles, which he identified with philosophy, is required to induce ethical behavior, and that 'precepts,' which prescribe the way in which one should act in particular circumstances, are superfluous, not only because the knowledge of principles, which is primary, obviates the need for such instruction, but because recommendations that do not reach back to reasons are inefficacious. His argument was made *a fortiori* from the impotence of the laws, which he defined as "precepts mixed with threats":[5] how can one hope from a simple counsel to achieve something that even the threat of penalty, which characterizes legal dispositions, is unable to obtain?

" 'Still,' it is objected [i.e., by Aristo], 'laws do not always make us do what we ought to do; and what else are laws than precepts mingled with threats?'" Seneca objects to the objection:

> Now first of all, the laws do not persuade just because they threaten; precepts, however, instead of coercing, correct men by pleading. Again, laws frighten one out of committing crime, while precepts urge a man on to his duty. Besides, the laws also are of assistance towards good conduct, at any rate if they instruct as well as command [...].

The final qualification ("at any rate if...") induces Seneca to deviate a moment from his main argument and engage in a strategic defense of Plato's view of the educative function of the law against Posidonius' criticism:

> "[...] On this point," Seneca adds, "I disagree with Posidonius, who says: 'I disapprove of Plato's practice of adding preambles to his laws. A law should be brief, so that the unskilled may grasp it more easily. Let it be like a voice sent from heaven; let it order, not argue (*jubeat lex, non disputet*).[6] Nothing seems to me more pedantic (*frigidus*),[7] more pointless, than a law with a preamble. Advise me, tell me what you want me to do; I am not learning, I am obeying'" (trans. Kidd).[8]

Seneca opposes Aristo's view, which contradicts his own epistolary practice, and by the same token defends Plato's doctrine of preambles against Posidonius' criticism. Because counsels help us in resisting passions and finding out what each situation requires if we are to act appropriately—which rules (*decreta*) do not do—advice-giving belongs in its own right to a philosophical ethics.[9] Obviously, Seneca's defense of Plato against Posidonius (and Aristo) does not mean that he subscribes to the precise conception of preambles as developed in the *Laws*. What he accepts from it, in a very general way, is the notion that law must educate. Posidonius' objection bears on the way in which Plato conceives of the relationship between law and teaching, which leads to a dilution of what is proper to the *form* of the law, and relies, moreover, on a misunderstanding of its goal. By *adding* "preambles" (called here *principia*) to his laws, Plato forgets that the law is "a voice emitted by the divinity" (*vox divinitus emissa*) that must simply be obeyed, and that it is directed to the ignorant (*imperiti*), who can only memorize (if not understand) its terms if it is short. Only the wise person, who grasps the "right reason" (*orthos logos*) understands the meaning of the law.

Posidonius' objection to Plato's legislative preambles, which has sometimes been seen as reflecting a Roman conception of authority that was in fact incompatible with his own philosophical credo, has something intriguing about it, for it seems to neglect the problem that Plato meant to solve (which is also what attracts Seneca's attention). "I obey," says Posidonius' ignorant person; Plato asks about the conditions that make such an obedience possible. For it is precisely to the extent that law is reduced to an order that it incurs the risk of not being respected, as Aristo himself recognizes when he points to the inefficacy of laws. What is the source of the strange docility with which the ignorant person submits herself when she says "tell me what you want me to do" (*dic quid me velis fecisse*)? The problem of the law is not memorization, but assent. This is the point that makes of Plato's views on legislative persuasion an ally of Seneca's parainetic practice.

Indeed, Posidonius' criticism relies on a conception of the law that is not only compatible with Plato's analysis of the notion of "law," but presupposes it. For it is *because* law "orders and does not discuss" that Plato's lawgiver must take on himself the "discussion" which the law is unable to conduct.[10]

We have no evidence as to what Posidonius might have thought on this point. But a testimony about Aristo, to whom Posidonius is linked in Seneca's argumentation, is relevant here. Aristo's radicalism does not consist in rejecting *praecepta* in general, but in denying that they belong to philosophy, which alone is capable of reaching wisdom because it deals with general principles. He left parainetic to nurses and instructors.[11]

By distributing two kinds of discourse to two categories of persons or two stages in life, Aristo was drawing a dividing line analogous to the one that is presupposed by Posidonius' criticism: what Posidonius and Aristo's *decreta* have in common is that they see law as having nothing to do with pedagogy. The complexity of the position developed in the *Laws*, inversely, is due to the interlocking of philosophical communication, legislation, and education.

Introduction

1. Although 'feasibility' could in some cases advantageously replace 'possibility,' I will with a few exceptions stick to 'possibility,' as Plato uses one and the same term, *dunaton* (*dunata* in the plural), to refer to logical possibility and to real possibility (feasibility).

2. Cf. Schofield 2006, p. 75, who rightly observes: "we have no evidence of any prior history of theoretical writings going under that title [i.e., *Laws*] comparable with the *politeia* tradition to which the *Republic* belongs."

3. See e.g., Thucydides 2.37.3 or Lysias 2.19.

4. A general history of the reception of the *Laws* from Antiquity to Modern times is yet to be written. The account would include, in addition to the ancient authors mentioned above, chapters on Eusebius, Neoplatonic and Byzantine reception, al-Farabi and the Arabic tradition, Plethon, Georg of Trebizond, and Florentine Platonism (among others Ficino and Machiavelli), Jean Bodin, Jean de Serres, James Harington, Montesquieu, Rousseau, and the American Founding Fathers, to name just a few classical benchmarks. For some contributions bearing on these authors and the historical constellation, see e.g., Bradley 2017, Brown 1986, Des Places 1967, Dillon 2001, Fögen 2022, Gilbert 1968, Gregorio 2011, Hankins 2019, Neschke-Hentschke 1995/2003, Monfasani 2008, Nelson 2004, O'Meara 2002, de Nicolay (forthcoming), Ries 1983, Siniossoglou 2017, Vatter 2012 (among many other relevant contributions listed in the bibliography), and Webb 1989.

5. Cf. McIlwain 1947, an interesting and informative essay on ancient and modern 'constitutionalism,' although one that places the *Statesman*, rather than the *Laws*, in the foreground. On the relationship between the two dialogues, see below, Appendix A.

6. Schmitt's *Politische Theologie. Vier Kapitel zur Lehre von der Souveränität* was published in 1922 (English translation in Schmitt 1988). For a history of the qualification "theologico-political," see De Franceschi 2007, pp. 657–59, who provides an overview of the twentieth-century debate around the term (and more generally around 'political theology') in an ecclesiastical perspective. For a discussion of the stakes in the recent revival of the debate, see Vatter 2020.

7. See "On Abravanel's Philosophical Tendency and Political Teaching" (1937) in Strauss 1997, p. 198. For an orientation on Strauss' project, its complexities, and its evolution, see Strauss' preface to the English edition of his 1930 book on Spinoza's *Theologico-Political Treatise* (in Strauss 1965; German translation in Strauss 1996) and H. Meier's preface to Strauss 1997; further Vatter 2011 and 2021, Chap. 5.

8. The loss of semantic connotations in translation is an ailment of translations in general. It becomes critical when the terms at stake are foundational, as is the case with *nous*. Although 'reason,' which is also Menn's (1997) preferred rendering of the word, is a shorthand, the fact that it can be taken, like *nous*, in more than one sense, is an advantage of a sort. *Nous* implies 'grasping' and 'understanding,' 'intelligence' and 'wisdom,' all terms that may help to clarify what is at stake in different contexts.

9. Contrary to Bobonich's (2002) influential albeit much criticized take on the issue (see for example Lane 2010), I don't interpret the differences between Plato's two cities as reflecting a fundamental doctrinal change that would ultimately be motivated by philosophical difficulties affecting the psychology of the *Republic* (see below, Appendix B). On the contrary, one of the ideas that guides my essay is that Plato's 'anthropological turn,' which does imply a number of changes, is in keeping with the paradigmatic approach that is common to the two works.

10. Cf. Aristotle, *Politics* 2.4 1262b7–10.

11. See *Republic* 3.414b8–415c7 for the myth of the races and 5.459c8–460d8 for the eugenics.

12. It is characteristic that the term 'voluntary'/*hekôn* in the *Republic* refers mainly to the issue of the (non-)willingness of philosophers to rule and the necessity to persuade them to do so.

13. Aristotle, *Politics* 2.6 1265a1–2.

14. I used the passage as the epigraph of my Chap. 6.

15. On the political significance of Aeschylus' *Eumenides*, see Judet de La Combe 2010, pp. 141–47 and 2020, pp. 755–63.

16. "Plato's *Eumenides*: An Essay on His *Laws*" is the title I had come up with.

17. See Vatter 2012.

18. For a recent depiction of Plato's political agenda in terms of a 'cultural war,' see Allen 2010 (Gramsci could have been invoked). On the question of political ideology, see Schofield 2006, Chap. 6.

19. Which Saunders' 1991 analysis of Plato's penal code emphasizes.

20. The term "holism" comes from Dumont's 1966 analysis of the Indian caste system. For a problematization of the relationship between holism and totalitarianism, see Bensa 2008.

21. For an in-depth discussion of the issue, see the essay on which Vegetti was working before his death (Forcignano and Vegetti 2020).

22. Schleiermacher, Introduction to the *Republic*, trans. Dobson 1836, p. 380 (German text in Schleiermacher 1996, p. 360 = p. 35 of the original edition; cf. p. 278 Dobson: "The grounds upon which he [i.e., Plato] starts, as well as the consequences which he develops, are such that, from the standing point of Christianity, we must enter the most lively protestations against them" (Schleiermacher 1996, p. 359 = p. 33 of the original edition). The reaction is older. Leonardo Bruni, for one, wrote in the first half of the fifteenth century that "there are many things repugnant to our ways of life in the *Republic* that it is better for Plato's honor to keep silent about than to disclose" ("*multa sunt in iis libris abhorrentia moribus nostris quae pro honore Platonis tacere satius est, quam proferre*"; *Epistolarum Libri VIII*, ed. L. Mehus, Florence,1741, Pars secunda, p. 148). I owe the reference to Brown 1986, p. 389, n. 17.

23. See Laks 2019, p. 147, n. 4.

24. Cornford 1950, pp. 66–67. Cornford's conviction is "that Plato's prisoner, unlike the Inquisitor's would not have kept an unbroken silence." This is not certain even from Cornford's perspective, because, as Nietzsche observed, Socrates also knew how to keep silence (cf. Nietzsche, *The Gay Science*, §340). But the main point is that Socrates would arguably not have disagreed on the theological foundation of the law.

25. Popper 2013 (1945). An illuminating explanation of the reasons for modern attacks against Plato's political philosophy is provided by Goldschmidt 1970b, pp. 135–76. The author does not himself undertake a 'defense' of Plato, but indicates (p. 141, n. 5) that he fully embraces the massive response to Popper by Levinson (1953). His interpretation of Plato's theory of denunciation (Goldschmidt 1970a, pp. 173–201) is a good example of defense through historicization and transposition. For a more recent contribution to the genre 'defense,' see Neschke-Hentschke 2012.

26. For an explicit endorsement of this move (*Abkoppelung* is the German word), see Mai 2014, who dissociates the philosophical significance of the notion of preambles from the content of the laws they introduce (p. 71); see also, on the legislation on poetry, Mouze (2005, p. 419), who distinguishes Plato's justified presuppositions about the ethical import of art from the way in which he develops and applies them. Supiot's 2007 parallel between the way in which "even before arriving at the autonomy of the speaking subject through the heteronomy of language, the human being becomes a legal subject through the heteronomy of the law" (p. 21) would provide a good illustration of the productivity of the principle of dissociation, had he made reference to the *Laws* (his starting point is the *Cratylus*, 388d12–389a3).

27. Morrow 1993 (1960[1]); Schöpsdau 1994, 2003, and 2011 (citation under "Partial Editions, Translations, Commentaries" and henceforth referred to by volume number instead of date of publication).

28. Cases in point are my reading of *eggutata* ('very close') at *Republic* 5.472c1 and 473a8 and *Laws* 5.739e4 and of *eggus* ('close') at *Laws*, 9.857d2); *dunata* ('possible') at *Republic* 5.473b1 (and elsewhere); *thauma* ('puppet') at *Laws* 1.644d7; *sôphronein* at *Laws* 3.693c2; *didonai logon* and related notions at *Laws* 4.720c3–5, *kata brakhu* at *Laws* 9.875d3; and *tauta* at *Statesman* 300c5.

29. See Brisson 2000 and 2020; Lisi 2000, 2004, and 2010; Lane 2018. Lisi's 2010 article gives a summary of my reading (p. 158) and develops a refutation of assertions that bear some resemblance to what I have been trying to say, but in which I cannot recognize myself. What is clear is that we have different ways to "adhere to the text," to use his formula (*ibid.*).

Editorial Note

1. Schöpsdau's translation precedes his commentary in each of its three volumes. Lisi 1999, in Spanish, and Brisson and Pradeau 2006, in French, have also been useful, as well as the partial English translations by Meyer 2015 (Books 1–2) and Mayhew 2008 (Book 10).

Chapter 1. The Form of the *Laws*: An Overview

1. Adorno [1937] 2002 ("Late style [*Spätstil*] in Beethoven"), p. 565, pursuing a question that had already retained the attention of G. Simmel (see Thouard 2021, on Goethe's case).

2. Rowe 2007, p. 1, makes this point when he speaks about the "enormous *variety*" (his italics) of Plato's writing. For an approach based on the contrary assumption, see Goldschmidt's 1947 structural analysis of the "dialectical" dialogues (the *Laws* is not considered).

3. Schleiermacher, Introduction to the *Republic*, p. 352 Dobson (original text in Schleiermacher 1996, pp. 338–39 = pp. 5–6 of the 1828 edition).

4. Gould 1955, p. 71 is the one who praised "the involved and baroque prose style" of the *Laws*. Bury in his introduction to the Loeb edition (1926), vol. 1, p. vii, talked of its "uncouthness." On the growing tendency to hyperbaton, long periods, and assonances in late Plato and the characterization of the *Laws* as "a work in which a certain *presbeutikê paidia* [old-age game] not unfrequently appears," see Denniston 1960, pp. 54–55, 69–70, and p. 132. For an ancient appreciation of the style of the *Laws*, see Appendix C, n. 7.

5. On the relationship between the two dialogues, see Appendix A.

6. The main evidence comes from Diogenes Laertius 3.37: "Some say that Philip of Opus transcribed Plato's *Laws*, which was preserved in wax-tablets. They also maintain that Philip was the author of the *Epinomis*" (trans. Mensch). For a full discussion of the evidence on this question, see Tarán 1975, pp. 128–33 and Schöpsdau, vol. 1, pp. 138–42. Philip of Opus, if he was indeed the editor of Plato's *Laws*, might also be the author of the division into the twelve books as we know them. In any case, this division goes back to the fourth century BC, as the use of *sigma* (ς) for Book 6 indicates.

7. Schöpsdau, vol. 1, p. 98, is right to stress this.

8. For detailed tables of contents, see Schöpsdau vol. 1, pp. 95–98 (overview of the whole work); vol. 1, pp. 149–52 (Books 1–3); vol. 2, pp. 131–35 (Books 4–7); vol. 3, pp. 163–67 (Books 8–12). For a radical reduction, see the chart at the end of the present chapter. The two main subtleties I have in mind concern the relationship between the two medical analogies in Books 4 and 9 on the one hand, and the status of the prologue to the law against atheism in Book 10 on the other (see especially Chap. 7, pp. 113–18 and 120–23 and Chap. 9, pp. 142–44).

9. Two passages (8.848d2–3 and 11.919d3–4) show that the project consists in a refoundation rather than in a totally new settlement (cf. Clay 2000, p. 271, n. 20). Further mentions of Magnesia and the Magnesians: 9.860e6, 12.946b6, and 969a5–6 (which suggests that Magnesia stands for any city that might benefit from the discussion).

10. The Athenian stresses the affinity between Spartan and Cretan institutions at 3.683a2. The term 'Dorian'(which occurs at 682e3–4 has a heavy ideological history, which is linked with the enormous influence Sparta's political model has exercised from Antiquity to the twentieth century (see Rawson 1969). For the ominous history and a critique of the ethnicization and racialization of the opposition between Sparta and Athens, which was developed on the basis of the passage in Herodotus 1.56 that associates Athens with the Ionic, Sparta with the Dorian *genos*, see Will 1956 and Hall 1997. One can understand why Annas (2017) prefers to avoid the word (p. 40). I shall use it occasionally, as a way to refer to obvious commonalities between Spartan and Cretan institutions and modes. The cultural approach, as a matter of fact, stresses how exceptional the Spartan political culture was within the Greek context. Although this exceptionality nurtured what Ollier (1933) called the 'Spartan mirage' (see further Hodkinson 2005), it certainly reflects historical facts (in this sense, see Flower 2018, p. 448).

11. Herodotus (1.65) reports that "the Lacedaemonians themselves relate that it was from Crete that Lycurgus brought these changes [i.e., a new political and social system," trans.

Godley]; see also Flower 2009, pp. 215–16 with n.106 on Herodotus' rather implausible asser-tion. The ethical risks associated with the presence of the sea on an island like Crete are met by the location of Magnesia (cf. 4.704a1–705c6).

12. See below, Chap. 6. Schöpsdau, vol. 1, p. 106, talks of a "Doric-Attic synthesis." Morrow 1993, p. 533, says "mixture of Dorian and Ionian." The presence and function of Athenian and Spartan/Cretan institutions and spirit in Plato's integrative project is a recurring theme of Mor-row's 1993 analysis of "Plato's Cretan City." This is also an aspect that Saunders' (1991) specific analysis of penal law in the *Laws* emphasizes. From a strictly institutional point of view, however, Athens provides the model (see Piérart 1973, pp. 464–66; Annas 2017, pp. 36–38). This is the condition for its reinterpretation.

13. On Spartan *agôgê*, see Kennell 1995.

14. Approximatively twelve or thirteen hours in real time (see Schöpsdau, vol. 1, p. 103).

15. Morrow 1993, p. 27.

16. The story relies on an interpretation of *Odyssey*, 19.178–79, which says only that Minos visited Zeus when he was nine years old. Cf. also the pseudo-Platonic dialogue *Minos*, whose dating, philosophical profile, and relationship to the *Laws* is debated (see Lisi 2015), but which was surely conceived as an introduction to the *Laws* (Brisson, trans. 2014, p. 275).

17. 1.625b4–5, 3.685a6–8; 6.769a1–2. The thought is no doubt that political wisdom, which is a privilege of the elderly, is also the most valuable heritage they can bequeath to future genera-tions. "Since [. . .] we are in the crepuscule of life, and these are young compared to us [. . .]," says the Athenian at 6.770a5–7, before addressing in a fictive discourse the most important of-ficeholders of the projected city.

18. One may recall, with all due differences, Parmenides' travel to the mansion of the goddess (28B1 DK): we are in Crete, not at the edge of the world; three elderly men have replaced the gifted youth about to hear the goddess' revelation; Zeus, the anonymous female divinity, and politics, ontology.

19. On the faith of the ancient evidence that presents Zaleucus and Charondas, the more or less legendary Greek lawgivers of Western Greek cities, as having prefixed their laws with pre-ambles (cf. Cicero, *De legibus* 2.13; Diodorus of Sicily, 12.20–21, and Stobaeus, *Anthology* IV.2.19, pp. 123.12–127.19 Hense), a few commentators have defended the archaic origin of legislative preambles. Adcock (1927, p. 104) and Mühl (1929, pp. 444–46) adopt what I take to be the more plausible view, already defended by Bentley against Boyle (1781 [1699], pp. 342–51): Plato's in-novation, like many other elements of his doctrine, has been appropriated by the (neo-Pythagorean) tradition that ascribes to Pythagoras and Pythagoreans, such as Zaleucus and Charondas are thought to have been, doctrinal points originally made by Plato or his school. Delatte 1922, who admits that the notion of a preamble to the laws is foreign to early Pythago-reanism, thinks that ethical ideas that these alleged preambles convey are archaic (see pp. 181 and 202). For a recent *status quaestionis* with abundant bibliography, see the entry "Zaleucos" by Macris (2018), pp. 315–17. What is certain, on the other hand, is that Plato's legislative model is inspired by the succession prelude/'nome' in the musical sense of *nomos*, of which Plato makes use in the *Laws* (see below, p. 218, n. 45) and to which he refers in the *Republic* (7.531d7–8) as a well-known fact (cf. "don't we know that . . . ?" at d7). The extension to rhetoric is natural. Ac-cording to the *Phaedrus*, 266d7–8, a *prooimion* is "what has to be said first in the beginning of a speech."

On noon as a privileged moment of experience ("Zeit des Erlebnisses") in the poetic tradition, see Kambylis 1965, pp. 59–61.

20. See below, p. 26.

21. Compare *Laws* 1.625b1–c2 and 4.722c7–d2 with *Phaedrus* 229a1–b2 and 258e6–a4.

22. This does not mean that the *Laws* is itself a rhetorical, popular rather than a philosophical piece of work, which is the leading idea of Görgemanns' influential 1965 book.

23. According to some versions, Apollo inspired Lycurgus' institutions; others say that he approved of them (for the evidence, see Flower 2018, p. 447).

24. See in particular the preamble of the law against atheists in Book 10 (especially 890b3–891b4), on which see Chap. 9, pp. 142–44. On the identification of Plato's god with reason/*nous*, see Menn 1995, who takes reason to be a virtue of the soul; and Bordt 2013, for whom Plato's *nous* in an independent substance. Plato's circumlocutions (see below in the main text) take different routes, some more inclined to systematize than others. For a scholastic argument against Menn's and Bordt's positions, see Van Riel 2016, pp. 71–81 (who defends the idea that Plato's gods are souls, not *nous*). At *Laws* 10.897b1–2, *nous*, according to the text of the main manuscripts (adopted by the majority of interpreters), is said to be " a god (*theon*) for the gods." The phrase is weakened to "divine (*theion*) for the gods" according to an alternative reading attested in manuscript O and in the indirect tradition (Eusebius); see Schöpsdau, vol. 3, pp. 420–21.

25. Cf. Protagoras, 80 B1DK (= D9 LM).

26. The indefinite 'some' (*tis*) refers to an individual in as much as he is a representative of human kind (by contrast with the god); "they" refers to Protagoras. The reversal of the Protagorean motto quoted in *Theaetetus* 152a2–4 (cf. 89B1DK= D9 and R4LM) and criticized thereafter (cf. R5-R9 LM, and also *Cratylus* 385e4–386e4) lies at the centre of the *Laws*. The god 'measures' things in the sense that he is the standard by which they should be 'measured,' that is evaluated. On measure as an ontological determination, see Chap. 6, p. 96 and Appendix A, p. 162.

27. For the paradoxical formula ". . . completing his revolution in a straight line, according to nature," cf. Chap. 7, p. 111.

28. Cf. Goldschmidt 1970a ("Theologia," pp. 140–72,) who observes, rightly, that the word there does not mean more than stories concerning the gods, a subdivision of 'mythology' that also deals with different types of stories (pp. 147–51); see also Brisson 2005, p. 70, n.1, who is tempted to adopt the correction *muthologias*, which is found in one manuscript (reported in Diès' edition; not in Burnet), for *theologias*, which is an hapax in Plato.

29. This, and what follows, is highly illuminating on how Plato's political philosophy was read by the Jewish, and then the Christian tradition (see Morlet 2019, pp. 151–52).

30. *dianomê* evidently refers to *nomos*, but should not be translated with 'regulation' (cf. LSJ, which opens a special entry for this passage of the *Laws*). The word is chosen to capture the 'distributive' dimension of reason, which always has a mathematical aspect. The idea is echoed and specified in different contexts: the crucial distribution of lots and households at 5.737c1–738b1 (with five occurrences of the word and related terms) and the no less crucial discussion about true equality at 6.757b5 (*dianomas*) and c2 (*nemei*); the passage is translated in Chap. 6, p. 91; cf. also 3.697a2–3, 5.746d4–5, 6.756b8, 8.847e2 (cf. also *Republic* 7.535a3) and, at another level, the Egyptian game, based on distribution, which the Athenian recommends be adopted for educational purposes at 7.819b4.

31. Kronos' name is explained in the *Cratylus* by *to katharon* [. . .] *kai akêraton tou nou*, "the pure [. . .] and unmixed character of intelligence" (396b3–7). "Purity" in this passage alludes to Anaxagoras' *nous*, which is 'unmixed' (59B12 DK). The recognition of *nous* as a god does not imply its separability from the soul, against which Van Riel 2013 battles (see pp. 79 and 99–103), and which the weaker version is intended to avoid.

32. The passage adapts the myth of the alternating rule of the world by Kronos and Zeus as related in the *Statesman* (268d5–274e3). One difference between the two versions is that there are no cities under Kronos' reign in the *Statesman*'s version, whereas their existence is presupposed by the *Laws* (see Vidal-Naquet 1978). This is related to the specific function of the myth in the two dialogues: the *Statesman* aims at establishing a conceptual distinction between tyrant and king; the *Laws* sets up a model to be imitated.

33. The pairing of law with tyranny and violence goes back to the sophist Hippias, if we can trust Plato's parody in the *Protagoras* 337d2–3 (=86 C1 DK). In this latter passage, however, *nomos* has probably the broader sense of 'convention' (". . . whereas convention, which is a tyrant over men, commits violence upon many things against nature," D17LM).

34. Courage is said to be the 'less valuable' part of virtue (*to phaulotaton*, 1.630e2) and comes accordingly at the last place in the listing at 1.631c8–d1. This may be said by antiphrase, in view of the role it plays in the Spartan/Cretan model (contrast for example 2.659a1–b2, in the passage quoted below, Chap. 4, p. 70, as well as between two kinds of courage at 12.963e1–8, and the talk of a 'divine' kind of courage at 7.824a9). *Phronêsis*, here translated as 'wisdom,' and *nous*/reason are in quite a few cases interchangeable (see below, Chap. 5, p. 78 and p. 82, n. 25). *Sôphrosunê* I do not always translate with the same word; as appropriate, I use 'self-control,' which is close to the notion of 'being superior to oneself,' 'moderation' (Meyer's preferred translation), or 'temperance,' which I take to be closer to the resulting virtue. For the problems raised by the translation of the term, see Moore and Raymond's 2019 introduction to their translation of Plato's *Charmides*, esp. pp. xxxiv–xxxvi. Their proposal, as far as the *Charmides* is concerned, is "discipline" (pp. xxxvi–xxxvii). This word captures the spirit of several passages in the *Laws*, too, but I doubt it serves well as a translation.

35. Schöpdsau says that there is no transition to the question of the origin of constitutions as broached at the beginning of Book 3 (it comes "unvermittelt," vol. 1, p. 349). This is true in the sense that the only transition between the complex development on the appropriate usage of pleasure, education in general, choral education in particular and wine drinking started as early as 1.636d5 and concluded at 3.676a2 (*tauta men oun dê tautêi*), and the inquiry about the origin of constitutions that follows in Book 3 is the particle *de* (*politeias de arkhên tina de pote phômen gegonenai*). But the substantial continuity is clear enough, for this whole development is subordinated to the initial questioning about the source of some Cretan *laws* and practices. With Book 3, we turn to the question of the origin of *constitutions*, thus taking up the first term of the pair "constitution and laws," which was announced at 1.625a6 as the subject of the conversation.

36. Plato takes human history to be cyclical, like the history of the cosmos (cf. the mention of the 'perfect year,' *Timaeus* 39d4). Civilizations are periodically destroyed by cataclysms and other natural disasters such as diseases (3.677a4–6); survivors start each time from scratch to rediscover little by little, in the course of immense periods of time (3.676a8–b1, 682b7–8; cf. *Timaeus*, 22c7d3), skills and technology, including the skill of living in community and thus of devising constitutions and laws (3.678a3–9, 681c1–d10).

37. Cf. the back reference at 4.705d3–e1.

38. Although the defense and illustration of *symposia* and wine drinking serves, from a compositional point of view, as a frame for the complex development that extends from 1.638b7 to the end of Book 2, it is subordinated, as far as content is concerned, to the issue that constitutes the gist of this very development, namely, education. Plato's argument is not meant to be exhaustive. Self-control / *sôphrosunê* is chosen, rather than justice or wisdom, because it is the virtue that has most conspicuously to do with pleasure, that is the counterpart of pain on which courage focuses (see Schöpsdau 1986). For the intricate construction and the difficulties of the section on the benefits of *symposia* and drinking wine *more platonico*, see Schöpsdau, vol. 1, pp. 210–11.

39. The procedure is easy compared to the practices that are "now in use" (*ta nun*, 1.648c7). These allude to the harsh physical training of Cretan and Spatan institutions (see Meyer 2015, p. 199), which will be echoed in the war-training games in Book 8.829a8–832d8 (see Schöpsdau, vol. 1, p. 246). On the *symposium* as the occasion where truth comes to the fore thanks to wine in Greek culture, see Rössler 1995.

40. Recent studies often translate *khoreia* with "choral performance." I prefer the neutral "choral dance," which retains the explicit reference to dancing implied by the Greek *khoros/ khoreia*, but not by the modern sense of "choral." On the importance of choral dance for the education of the human puppet, see Chap. 4, pp. 169–171. Larivée (2003) has pointed out that the old men who form the chorus of Dionysus are in fact members of the most important organ of the constitution, the Watch (see below, n. 63). On the presence of Dionysus in the *Laws*, more generally, see Yu 2020.

41. What *phronêsis* and *noûs* are (the virtue of all virtues) is to be derived from the various contexts in which they are mentioned. For justice, see 6.757c1–d1 and Chap. 6, p. 94.

42. Chap. 5, pp. 75–80 and Chap. 6, pp. 96–99. The mention of wisdom and friendship is less of a surprise since wisdom was declared from the start to be the leading virtue and friendship was thematized as the counterpart of war in the initial argument of Book 1. The promotion of friendship as a legislative target in its own right is nevertheless significant, since it is tightly linked to freedom, as will become clear in the course of Book 3.

43. See Chap. 5, pp. 80–85.

44. Cf. also Megillus' willingness, in one of his rare interventions, to give up Spartan laconism at 4.721e4–722a5. Annas (2017) aptly talks about the Athenian succeeding in "enlarging the understanding" of his interlocutors "from within" (pp. 41–48, 51–54).

45. The section in between (cf. the announcement at 4.724a7–b5 and closure at 5.734e3–4) is devoted to characterizing and finding a name for the type of discourse that the lawgiver has been delivering (see Chap. 7, pp. 119–20).

46. See Chap. 9, p. 142.

47. On Magnesia as representative of other cities as well, see above, n. 9. In a complementary way, the general theoretical scheme admits of degrees, as implied by the famous evocation of a "third city" at 5.739a7, b3, and e5 (cf. also *allên* at 6.757d1), on which see below, Chap. 3, pp. 57–8.

48. On the reading of this passage as announcing the *Laws*, see Appendix A, pp. 165–66.

49. On this section, see Chap. 2, pp. 48–50.

50. Schöpsdau (vol. 2, p. 131) has a new heading corresponding to my point 6, which he names "Prologue to the legislation as a whole," and he collects my points 1 through 5 under the

heading "The conditions of the new foundation," which he subdivides into "External conditions" (= my points 1 and 2), "The most favorable presupposition for the realization of the best state" (=my points 3, 4, and 6) and "The best form of constitution is the rule of the law" (=my point 5). His suggestion (p. 138) is that the triad chance/craft/god as articulated in point 3 gives grounds to read the whole as a progression, from circumstances that depend from chance to normative considerations. Cf. also the discussion in Hentschke 1971, pp. 253–54.

51. 'Officeholder' is the term Lane uses in her fundamental forthcoming book. It is much better than the usual, less definite 'magistrate.' She argues for the centrality not only of offices but also of officeholders in Plato's political thought and emphasizes that *arkhai* often refers to the person of the officeholders rather than to the office itself. While this is true, the two can also be distinguished, as in the passage that picks up the present one at the beginning of Book 6 (*arkhôn kai arkhsantôn*, 751a5), so that one has to decide case by case.

52. On the process of selection as a crucial consequence of setting *aretê*/excellence as the aim of legislation, cf. Veyne 1982. The fact that the shepherd, who is rejected in the *Statesman* as inappropriate to characterize statesmanship under the reign of Zeus (275b1–7), appears as a positive figure in this passage of the *Laws* does not raise any real difficulty, because the aspect under which the shepherd is considered in the two texts is not the same. On the political shepherd in Plato, see Macé (2017), who criticizes with good reasons Foucault's (2004) view that the shepherd-king is an Oriental rather than a Greek figure.

53. The topic is interwoven, in the course of the extended discussion, with issues concerning the possession of goods and the use of money, which are limited and strictly regulated. For the subdivision of the passage, see Schöpsdau, vol. 2, pp. 132–33. On Plato's economic regulations, see Helmer 2010, 2017, and 2018.

54. "Immortality" evokes the divine condition, which is more than political absolute stability. It is the more striking since the just city of the *Republic* is not 'immortal.' It is doomed to decline in virtue of the principle stated at 8.546a2–3 that everything that is born is bound to perish (this would be true for the heavens itself were it not for the goodness of the Demiurge, *Timaeus*, 41b1–6).

55. See Helmer (2010, p. 201) for Plato's "politization of the economy."

56. See Schöpsdau, vol. 2, p. 288, *contra* Jaeger (1959[3], vol. 3, p. 450, n. 222), who took the postponement as a sign that Plato did not have the time to revise his text. Schöpsdau (vol. 2, p. 131) has a specific entry "Die Gesetze," from 6.769a1 (or rather 768d7) and through 12.960b5, that is subordinated to the general entry "Die Gesetzgebung," covering 5.734e3 down to 12.960b5.

57. The choice of marriage for initiating the formulation of laws is not accidental, see below, Chap. 8, p. 133.

58. See below, Chap. 8, p. 125.

59. Cf. 6.768d7–e3, 770a5, 771a5.

60. Cf. 8.842e3–5.

61. Cf. the classification at the beginning of Book 10 (884a1–885b4).

62. Cf. Chap. 7, p. 112.

63. The word "Watch," which is due to Luc Brisson's suggestion (*per.litt.*), captures the function of the body in question, which is to preserve the newly established laws (cf. *sullogos tôn peri nomous epopteuontôn*, 12.951d4–5, picking up the allusive 'guardians'/*phulakas* mentioned as early as 1.632c4, following Schöpsdau's suggestion, vol. 1, p. 188). It is much more revelatory than

the traditional denomination 'nocturnal council' (picking up Plato's expression *nukterinos sullogos* at 10.909a3–4, cf. 908a4; the council meets at dawn, before sunrise, cf. 12.951d6–7, 961b6). Brisson's (1999) original translation in French "Conseil de veille" is even more felicitous, given than the term 'veille' suggests both 'taking care' and 'being awake.' (During our paired seminars that took place at Princeton in the 2019 Spring, Melissa Lane suggested 'The invigilators,' which works too, but loses the collective singular.) On the relationship between the Watch and the Guardians of the laws whose function is described in Book 6, see Reid 2020b.

64. According to Tarán's convincing analysis, Philip of Opus, the probable editor of the *Laws*, thought that the education of the members of the Watch was missing in the *Laws* and so completed it by the *Epinomis*, which at 976e1–4 identifies the highest knowledge with the knowledge of number (see Tarán 1975, pp. 19–24). I don't touch on this issue in the present essay.

65. Bartels 2017 notes the fluidity of the distinction between law and preambles (pp. 136–37), which is certainly striking (cf. Laks 2000, p. 26, Brisson and Pradeau in their translation, vol. 2, p. 384, and below, Chap. 8, n. 3). This does not mean, however, that the *Laws* does not provide a legal code, too, a position that she rejects (against Saunders' 1991 book, *Plato's Penal Code*). One main point of the *Laws* is precisely the tension between the pole represented by the code, and the pole represented by the fluid preamble.

66. This is Görgemanns' 1965 interpretation of 7.811b6–c2 (pp. 7–17, esp. pp. 10–15), cf. also Schöpsdau, vol. 2, p. 571. Picht (1990, pp. 31–38) gives a detailed refutation of this reading, which hangs together with Görgemanns' view that the *Laws* is a rhetorical, and to this extent non-philosophical treatise. *Paradeigma*, at 7.811b8 and c6, surely means that the *Laws* must serve as a model for the *substance* to be transmitted by any educational handbook, not that it is itself an *example* of such a handbook, even if one might think of some passages appropriate for school purposes (see Mouze 2005, pp. 89–92, who aligns with Picht but notes [p. 91, n. 55] that the two options are not strictly exclusive of one another).

67. There is a jump in the traditional page numbering (from 747e11 to 751a1), but no gap between V and VI.

Chapter 2. Paradigms and Utopias

1. The verb *turannein*, 'to exercise tyranny,' names here the pure power that would enable a virtuous lawgiver to put his plan into practice in the best conditions, in agreement with the previous passage in the same book, which conjures the hypothetical encounter between a lawgiver and a temperate tyrant (see 4.709e6, and the use of *turannis* at 710e3 and 711a2). I deal with this episode below, pp. 48–50. As for the reason why an all-powerful virtuous tyrant would have to step back from the paradigm, it must be that his power, supreme as it is, remains limited by the constraint imposed on him by human nature. For the meaning of *kata dunamin* at 5.739e3, see Chap. 3, n. 4.

2. This does not mean, of course, that laws do not play a role in the discussion with Thrasymachus. Book 1 also evokes "a city of good men" where political power would not be relished, but on the contrary avoided (cf.1.347b9–d2, preparing the motif of the philosophers' return to the cave in Book 7.520e14–521a8).

3. On this requirement and its implications for the structure of the *Republic*, see Anderson 2019.

4. Cf. *pothen deuro exetrepometha*, 8.543c5. At 5.472e7, Socrates had already suggested that the long development that is about to begin is a digression from the main objective when he engaged in his argument "in order to please you [sc. Glaucon]."

5. Book 7 unambiguously concludes by saying, "Then isn't that enough about this city and the man who is like it?" (541b2–3, trans. Grube/Reeve).

6. On the difficult question of the status of Book 10 from a compositional point of view, see Else 1972 and Vegetti, in Vegetti 2007, ed., vol. 7.

7. The usual formula "community of women and children" translates more literally the word *koinônia* ("community") but does not strike the right note, it seems to me. Women and children belong to the community, but they are not to be held "in common."

8. This is the "female drama" completing the "male drama" (5.451c1–3). Plato is most probably alluding to the two categories of mimes that Sophron is said to have composed (references in Adam in his edition of the *Republic*, vol. 1, p. 279).

9. See below, p. 39.

10. Plato uses the word *trikumia*/'triple wave' at 472a3 to refer to the group formed by three distinct waves (cf. also 473c7–8). In other authors, it refers to one single, especially powerful wave.

11. *arist-* : 4.434e2; 5.450c9, 457a3, 462c7, 462d7, 6.497b7, 502c6, 520d3, and 521b8 ; *beltist-* : 5.456c4 and 10, 6.502c2; *ôphelima*: 5.457c2, d5–6, 457e3, 458e4; cf. *sumphorôtata*: 5.458b5; *dunat-* / *adunat-* : 5.450c8, 452e5; 456c4 and c8; 457a3, 457c2, d5, and d9; 457e4, 458a5, and b3; 466d1, 466d7, 471c6–7, 471e4, 472b1, 472d2 and d7; 472e4 and e8; 473b1and c4, 6.502c2, 7.521a1, and 540d3. Relevant occurrences of *gignesthai* or *genesthai*: 5.450c5; cf. 57c2 and d5; 457d9, 471c6–7; 472b1, d2, and d6; 473a6 and b1; and 7.521a1.; 473a6 and b1; and 7.521a1. For a related use of the pair 'possible'/'beneficial', see *Charmides*, 169a8–c1.

12. Cf. the general expression "this constitution" at 5.471c7 and e2.

13. For an overview, see Vegetti 2009.

14. Aristotle's leading question is, "Are things better (*beltion*) as they are now or according to the law written in the *Republic*?" (*Politics*, 2.1 1261a8–9), and his answer, that the latter is not the case. He is also skeptical about the possibility of implementing the project (cf. 1261a21–22 : "even if someone had the power to do it [*ei kai dunatos tis eiê touto dran*], it is not the thing to do"; see also the overall negative judgement at 2.3.1261b30–32 about all citizen "saying the same": "in one way it is fine, but not possible; in another way, it is not even producing unanimity"). On Aristotle's criticisms of Plato's *Republic* and the *Laws*, see Vegetti in Vegetti, ed., 2000, vol. 4; more specifically on the *Laws*, Morrow 1960.

15. See Introduction, p. 7.

16. Cf. Glaucon's urging at 5.471e4–5 to "forget about the rest," taken up at 472b2, "speak without wasting time."

17. *ôphelima*, 5.457c2 and d5–6, *arista*, 5.450c9, 6.502c6; *beltista*, 5.456c4, 6.502c2.

18. Not so much what 'ruling' is like, which is arguably the leading perspective in the *Statesman*, see Appendix A, p. 159.

19. *Paradeigmatos* [...] *heneka* [...] *all'ou toutou heneka, hin' apodeixômen hôs dunata tauta gignesthai*, 5.472c4–d1. Socrates is here summarizing the procedure described at 2.368e2–369a4 (where the word *paradeigma* does not occur). The infinitive complement of *dunata* (namely *gignesthai*, which picks up Glaucon's *pêi dunatê gignesthai* at 5.472b1) is not yet loaded, at this point, with the ontological import it will soon acquire (cf. also the final formula at 6.502c7).

20. This will be the line of defense of Plato adopted by Kant against Brucker (see the epigraph to the present chapter, and below, p. 51). Prof. Heiner Klemme (Halle) kindly confirmed for me (*per litt.*) that Kant is unlikely to have had any direct knowledge of Plato's *Republic* (one can ask, moreover, if this unique sentence would have detained his attention had he read the text).

21. Cf. Kant's formula according to which 100 real thalers differ from 100 possible thalers only in that the first exists, the other not (see below, n. 68).

22. Two instances of cities close in this sense are 9,000-year-old Athens depicted by an Egyptian priest at *Timaeus* 23e4–24d6 and in the *Critias* at 109a4–113b6, with which the Egyptian Sais is said at *Timaeus* 24a2–4 to share many common laws (cf. 21e4–6). Both cities fill out the picture of a trifunctional city (cf. *Critias* 110c3–d4) that Socrates presents at the beginning of the *Timaeus* (17c1–19b2) as a summary (*kephalaion*, cf. *en kephalaiois* 19a8) of a discussion held on the previous day (the '*Republic*' is meant), even if the substitution of priests for philosophers makes quite a difference.

23. See *Statesman* 300e11–301a4 and Chap. 3, p. 55.

24. As Barney did (in the conversation referred to above) in the introduction and the manuscript that she kindly showed me.

25. This is the only sense explored by Goldschmidt 1947.

26. The word 'example' in English displays the same range of meanings, from 'sample' to 'model to follow.'

27. Vegetti (in Vegetti, ed., vol. 6, 2005, pp. 156–62) has shown that *heauton katoikizein* at 592b3 does not mean that the philosopher, in actual cities, will retire from politics to dedicate himself to the exclusive cultivation of his "internal constitution" (9.591e1, cf. 590e3–4), but that he will "transport himself" to this internal city in order to use it as a paradigm for his actions, whether in relationship to himself (his internal constitution), the internal constitution of his co-citizens, or, if such time ever comes, to his city as a whole. Vegetti further argues (p. 160, n. 45) that the sky is a metaphor referring to Socrates' "city in words," against Burnyeat's (1992) suggestion that the sky in question is the sky of the visible stars, the orderliness of which is itself a model for a city. If so, 'sky' here is only the polar counterpart and equivalent of 'not on earth.' I am less sure about this.

28. See above, pp. 32–33, on *Laws* 5; and below, Chap. 3, pp. 58–60.

29. Starting at 5.476e3 to the end of the book and pervading the whole argument down to the definition of dialectic and the dialecticians in Book 7.531d7–535a2.

30. Cf. also *tôi ergôi*, 5.473a6. That Plato is not talking about the truth of a judgment is shown by the fact that both speech *and action* are said to be capable (speech more, action less) of "getting hold" of truth.

31. True philosophers are those who "love the spectacle of truth," Socrates will say a few pages later (5.475e4). The other occurrences of the expression "to get hold of the truth" (*tês alêtheias haptesthai*) in *Republic* 10 go in the same direction (9.572a78, 10.600e6, and 608a6–7); cf. also *Phaedo*, 65b9 and *Theaetetus*, 186e4.

32. The turn *eis to dunaton* is picked up in the conclusion of the argument by *mekhri tou dunatou* at 6.498e4. At 5.472b7–c2, Socrates had posited that, given that a just man is not the same as justice, "we should be satisfied if he comes *hoti eggutata*" (472c1), "as close as possible." On the linguistic level, note that the translation of the turn *hôs* or *hoti* + superlative is necessarily

ad sensum since the term 'possible' does not feature in the Greek expression; and that it is easy to be misled by the apparent parallelism between *hôs* and *hoti* before *eggutata* at 472c1 and 473a7. Assuming that the transmitted text is sound, the two are *not* parallel. The adverbial *hôs* before *eggutata* at 472c1 introduces a complementary clause after *heurein*, leaving *eggutata* to perform the same adverbial function as *eggutata tôn eirêmenôn* at 473a8.

33. Note that "the smallest" (*smikrotatou*, 5.473b6) cannot be said to be 'small' (*ou mentoi smikrou ge*, 473c3); by the same token, the strong interpretation of *eggutata* implies that the closest cannot be said to be simply 'close.'

34. See Chap. 3, pp. 56–58. The restrictive formula *kata* (or *eis*) *dunamin* is recurrent in the *Timaeus*, cf. e.g., 30a3, 37d2, 38c1, 42e2, 89d6. The parallel between the Demiurge shaping the world and the statesman shaping the city is less prominent in the *Republic* than in the *Laws*, since the dialogue does not engage in the question of realization beyond the issue of its first condition, the coincidence of power and philosophy. See, however, the most telling passage at 6.500d10–501c8, stating the conditions under which a philosopher-ruler and a painter would accept to undertake their respective work. The first requirement is a clean slate (*pinax*), which is not altogether easy to get, especially when it comes to 'a city and human characters' (501a2; cf. 7.540e5–541b1). "Then, don't you think that they'd next sketch the outline of the constitution?—Of course.—And I suppose that, as they work, they would look often in each direction, towards the nature of justice, beauty, moderation, and the like, on the one hand, and towards those they are trying to put into human beings, on the other. And in this way they'd mix and blend the various ways of life in the city until they produced a human image based on what Homer too called 'the divine form and image' when it occurred in human beings. [...] They'd erase one thing, I suppose, and draw in another until they'd made characters for human beings that the gods would love as much as possible (*eis hoson endekhetai*). [...] Then is it at all persuasive [...] that the person we were praising is a painter of constitutions (*politeiôn zôgraphos*)?" (6.501a9–c4, trans. Grube/Reeve). The plural 'constitutions,' in the last sentence, sounds like a prefiguration of the *Laws*, to which the rest of the paragraph would also apply.

35. At 6.498e3–499a2, Socrates says that people's distrust in his argument comes from the fact that "they have never seen a man rhymed in virtue (*parisômenon aretêi*) and assimilated (*homoiômenon*) to it perfectly as far as possible (*mekhri tou dunatou*) both in deed and in speech, ruling a city of the same type, neither one such man, nor many." The metaphor "being rhymed" alludes to a rhetorical figure, the *homoioteleuton* (an echo resulting from two words with similar endings) which the preceding lines wittingly exemplify (*ou gar pôpote eidon genomenon to nun legomenon*, 498d8). Isocrates is likely to be targeted (see Adam's edition of the *Republic*, Appendix 3 to Book 6, vol. 2, pp. 77–78). On the empirical argument about the origin of distrust ("they have never seen . . ."), see *Statesman*, 301c9–d6 (cf. below, Appendix A, pp. 166–67). Two further important passages go in the same direction, as René de Nicolay pointed out to me: 2.383c3–5, about the guardians who should not be raised with what Homer says about the gods, "if they are to be respectful of gods (*theosebeis*) and divine (*theioi*) to the fullest extent that is possible for a human being" (*kath' hoson anthrôpôi epi pleiston oion te*), and 6.500c9–d1, even more directly relevant for the question of the relationship between the *Republic* and the *Laws*, about the philosopher becoming "ordered (*kosmios*) and divine (*theios*) to the degree that it is possible for a human being (*eis to dunaton anthrôpôi*)."

36. The removal in 385 BC of the Mantineans to the villages by the Spartans (Xenophon, *Hellenica*, 5.2.5 and 7) is a case in point; see Lévystone (2022). Still, the specific notion of philosophers remaining within the walls of the city with young children is without parallel, and the situation considered in the *Laws* (a new settlement of colonist) is certainly closer to what is possible (there is a clear allusion to the problem at 5.736a3–5, see Chap. 3, p. 59). For the malleability of children's souls in a pedagogical context, see *Republic* 2.377a12–b3, which explains the first step towards the realization of the just city at the end of Book 7.

37. The only exception to this principle is the non-perishability of the world, which according to the *Timaeus* (41a7—b6) won't perish because the Demiurge does not want this to happen.

38. *tauta paralabein* is more, I think, than 'to appropriate this view' ("sich diese Ansicht einzueignen," Schöpsdau, vol. 3, p. 61; his commentary [p. 346] also uses 'principle'/ Grundsatz and 'insight'/Einsicht). Plato is not considering knowledge or belief alone, but their preservation through time. Schöpsdau's paraphrase at p. 346, which mentions "the moral and intellectual qualities of the rulers" is closer to the point. Apelt's translation, which Schöpsdau quotes approvingly, too ("die angegebenen Forderungen zu erfüllen"): to be able to "fill these conditions" boils down to being able "to assume such power" (Griffith's rendering in this translation). My translation keeps closer to the Greek expression.

39. The preverbs *en(m)*- and *dia*- underscore the point. What is at stake is 'persistance.'

40. One objection that Lisi (2004, p. 17) raises against my reading is that the optatives at 9.875c4–(*ei tis . . . dunatos eiê . . . ouden an deoito*) imply that the hypothetical clause considers a real possibility—the idea being, to flesh out Lisi's argument, that if Plato had wanted to deny the possibility of the condition expressed in the *ei* clause, he would have used imperfect indicatives, which is the regular way of expressing the unreality of a condition. Standard grammars are not that strict. According to Kühner-Gerth, vol. 2, §576, p. 477, "*ei* + opt. wird gebraucht, wenn die Bedingung als eine blosse Vorstellung, als etwas willkürlich Angenommenes (über Gegenwärtiges oder Zukünftiges) erscheinen soll, das ebenso wirklich wie nichtwirklich sein könne: *ei touto genoito*, wenn dies etwa geschehen sollte (vielleicht geschieht es, vielleicht auch nicht)." As Paul Demont signaled to me, Goodwin in his 1889 *The Moods and Tenses of the Greek Grammar* distinguishes the optative from the indicative imperfect in conditional sentences in the following way: "the latter implies that the supposition of the protasis is a false one [. . .], the former implies no opinion of the speaker as to the truth of the supposition" (§456, p. 168), and Bizos even writes, in the section dedicated to the "potential" in his *Syntaxe grecque* (1971, p. 158): "Fait considéré comme possible, même s'il est purement imaginaire et irréalisable." This neutrality sits well the complexity of Plato's argument.

41. Lisi (2004, p. 17) takes the adverb *nun* in the temporal sense ("now"). But *nun de* surely is here introducing the modal counterpart to the contrafactual clause at c3 (*ei pote . . .*): "but in reality . . ." (= "in fact, however . . ."), see Schöpsdau's analysis of the sentence, vol. 3, pp. 347–48, with the additional explanation of the placing of the particle *ou gar* as in *Protagoras* 347a2 (*nun de sphodra gar . . .*). Lisi is right, however, that Plato, in this passage "does not reject [the possibility of a philosophical government] for the whole eternity, only for the actuality." But this is enough, if the actuality in question defines what a human being (as opposed to a god or a hero) really is.

42. Cf. *Sophist* 240e4, *Protagoras* 329b3 and 338a2, *Gorgias* 449b8, *Hippias Major* 304a6, *Republic* 2.396d5, *Timaeus*, 27c2 y, as well as *Laws* 12.968b4.

43. "En pequeña medida," Lisi; "in geringem Masse," Schöpsdau. "petitement" (Diès) and "a hint of it here and there" (Saunders) reflect embarrassment.

44. Cf. Laks 2005, p. 109, n. 19 (and, with some unnecessary wavering, as I now think, Laks 2012, p. 32). My suggestion was made without being aware of Sharafat 1998, p. 122, nor of Brunschwig 1999, p. 131, n. 24, both of whom are mentioned by Schöpsdau, vol. 3, p. 348. I have not been able to access Scharafat 1998, but here is what Brunschwig writes: "When Plato says that the gift of kingly knowledge 'is not realized anywhere or in any way *all'ê kata brakhu'* (875d3), I think that a temporal sense must be given to *kata brakhu* ('except for a short time'), not a quantitative sense ('que petitement,' Diès). The general idea of the passage is that of the inevitable corruption, in time, of the kingly man who is given autocratic power and who need not account for his actions (see *emmeinai* and *diabiônai*, 875b4–5). There is an incompatibility in principle, not between human nature and possession of the kingly science, but between human nature and durable possession of that science." I would just add to the last sentence: "...under certain conditions, namely excessive power." For a similar temporal use of *kata brakhu* in an (also remarkable) restrictive clause, see *Republic* 3.396d4–5 (Plato is criticizing "imitation": "[the moderate man] will be unwilling to make himself seriously resemble that inferior character–except perhaps for a brief period in which he is doing something good," trans. Grube/Reeve). The reason why Schöpsdau does not really consider this reading in his commentary *ad loc.* may be that Plato uses the phrase *brakhu ti* at *Timaeus* 51e6 to refer to the small number of persons who share reason or understanding: "of true belief, it must be said, all men have a share, but of understanding (*nous*), only the gods and a small group of people do (*anthrôpôn de genos brakhu ti*)" (trans. Zeyl). The existence of a small number of human beings who possess *nous*, however, does not imply that they would be capable of keeping their sense if put in a position of autocratic power.

45. For an exceptionally sensitive commentary on this text, see Schofield 1997, pp. 230–41. As he notes rightly, "questions about the *Laws'* utopianism here dissolve in the self-reflexivity of Plato's writing" (p. 239), which is the point that is usually missed by interpreters.

46. This is the question, applied to the second city, that Plato raised at the end of Book 7 of the *Republic* in the case of the just city, but seen from the perspective of the ruler himself, not of the human material he is dealing with (in the case of the *Republic*, children under ten).

47. Oligarchy comes in last place because it is in fact there and not in democracy that the number of powers is the highest (4.710e6–7), cf. Schöpsdau, vol. 2, pp. 166–67 (*ad* 710d1–711a3).

48. On the tyrant as a positive figure, retaining something of his possibly primitive association with justice, see Luraghi 2013, pp. 138–39. At 709d9–710a1, the promising young tyrant is described, according to the transmitted text, as "a tyrannized soul." If we don't want to amend the text, the formula must be taken as a particularly audacious antiphrase (see the discussion in Schöpsdau, vol. 2, pp. 163–64).

49. 4.709e7–710a4. The parallel is at *Republic* 6.503c2–9.

50. See Appendix A, pp. 160–61. On "chance" and divine intervention in a closely related context, cf. *Republic* 6.499b3–6 and 9.592a8–9.

51. Cf. *Republic*, 5.473c11–d3. Cf. also "When a divine love for moderate and just practices arises in some great powers," *Laws* 4.711d6–7, which recalls *Republic* 6.499b3–c2.

52. Contrary to what many interpreters think, Nestor, the good orator, whose authority comes from words rather than from force, does not feature as a representative of the democratic

regime, at least on the right grammatical construal of the passage (correctly upheld by Schöpsdau, vol. 2, pp. 175–76). A perfect orator can live under any political regime, and tyrants, in the *Laws*, make use of persuasion also. To this extent, Hesiod gives a description of the eloquent king that clearly anticipates Plato's philosopher-king (cf. Laks 1996). For the quality of Nestor's voice and elocution, see *Iliad* 1.247–49; for the excellence of his reflection and counsel, *mêtis* and *boulê, Iliad* 7.324–26 = 9.93–5.

53. As it does in the *Statesman*, cf. Appendix A, p. 166.

54. Commenting on this passage, Lisi 2004 contrasts humans of this remote epoch to human beings of the present, whose nature is different (p. 14). But this amounts to saying that they are not just 'human beings,' but heroes. As for 7.818b9–d1, which Lisi invokes to support the idea that human beings can be called gods by Plato (which is of course true in a metaphorical sense), it seems to rely on the assumption that *tis* at 818b9 refers to a human being, of which *theos, daimon,* and *herôs,* 818c1–2, are attributes. But it is much more plausible that the group *theos, daimon* and *herôs* is in apposition to *tis,* with *hoios dunatos* [. . .] *poieisthai* as the attribute (which is how Diès, Saunders, and Schöpsdau construe it). What remains in this case is the regular distinction between a god, a hero, and a *daimon* on the one hand and a "divine man" on the other, and that is in fact the subject of the next sentence.

55. The word is opposed to the "possible" at 5.736d1–3 and associated to *muthos* at 8.841c6–7, in agreement with the meaning it has in the *Republic* (cf. below, n. 59).

56. See Rousseau's [1995] 2019 analysis of Zeus' plan in the *Iliad* (for example vol. 1, p. 388 and the index in vol. 2, *s.v.* Héros), cf. also Rousseau 2001. On the implications of the *Iliad*'s use of the formula *hoioi nun brotoi eisin* (*Iliad* 5.302–4;12.378–83 and 445–9; 20.285–7; and, in Nestor's mouth, 1. 271–2), see Rousseau 1995 [2019], pp. 23–110. It may (must) have been a source for the Platonic "we are human beings legislating now for the seeds of human beings." For the notion of a past 'age of heroes,' see further, among the most famous texts, Hesiod, *Work and Days,* 156–173.

57. One way to capture Plato's considered position about possibility and impossibility in the *Laws* would be to say that past or for that matter future examples of possible coincidence still fall under the understanding of the term 'possible' as specified in the *Republic* ('possible' as 'the closest possible'), as Melissa Lane pointed out to me as she was reading an earlier stage of my manuscript.

58. For an excellent presentation of the question, see Vegetti in Vegetti, ed., vol. 5, 2000. For more recent contributions, see Morrison 2007 (who distinguishes between 'utopia' in the sense of a perfect, presently unavailable but possible city, i.e., Kallipolis, and 'mere utopia,' meaning that the utopia is unrealizable) and Zuolo 2009 (who opposes 'efficiency' to 'utopia'). Along the same lines, see the resolute rejection of the term 'utopia' on the basis of assumptions that are totally opposed to mine, by Brisson (2020, in the wake of Wilamowitz's unabatable realism in his 1920 book, to which Brisson refers). The variety of positions is reflected in the collection of essays edited by Lisi 2012.

59. For 'wish' (*eukhê*), see 5.450d1 and 456b12; 6.499c4; 7.540d2; for 'dream' (*onar*), see 7.520c7.

60. (Scipio talks:) *optandam magis quam sperandam* (*De re publica* 2.52). At 2.3, *fingere* specifically applies to Plato's account of the origins of the city; one can argue that it also targets the just city that emerges at the very end of the process.

61. The name 'Kallipolis' occurs only once in the *Republic*: "Then as far as possible, we must order that those in our beautiful city (*en têi kallipolei*) don't give up geometry in any way, for even the by-products of this are not minor" (7.527c1–3). As Adam (1902) notes, after others, in his edition (vol.2, p. 119), the word expresses "tenderness and affection."

62. Brucker 1766–67, vol. 1, pp. 726–27.

63. See for example Trousson's 1975 restrictive definition: "we will speak of utopia when, within a narrative (which excludes political treatises) a community (which excludes Robinson Crusoe and his likes) is depicted, which is organized according to some political, economic, moral principles, in a way that does justice to the complexity of social life (which excludes the Golden Age and Arcadia), whether it is presented as an ideal to be implemented (constructive utopia) or as the projection of a hell (as in modern anti-utopia), in a real or fictitious space, or in time, after an imaginary voyage, whether it is credible or not" (p. 28; my trans.).

64. For a general presentation of ancient utopias, see Clay and Purvis 1999.

65. On *Nusquama*, see Prévost 1971, p. 162. For More's all-things-considered decision, cf. the poem that serves as an epigraph to the first edition: *"The ancients called me Utopia or Nowhere because of my isolation / At present however I am a rival of Plato's republic, / Perhaps even a victor over it. The reason is that what he has delineated in words/ I alone have exhibited in men and resources and laws of surpassing excellence. / Deservedly ought I to be called by the name of Eutopia or Happy Land"* (*Complete Works*, ed. Sturz and Hexter, vol. 4, p. 21).

66. Aristophanes, *Birds* 9; Plato, *Republic* 9.592a10–b1 (see above, n. 27). This is not Plato's only debt to Aristophanes in utopian matters. Book 5 of the *Republic* picks up in important ways on *Lysistrata* (see Capra 2018, pp. 120–23).

67. See the epigraph of the present chapter and above, n. 10. A little further on the same page, Kant calls Plato's city "an archetype."

68. Kant, *Critique of Pure Reason*, B627/A599.

Chapter 3. Paradigm and Retreats

1. The "third city" mentioned at 5.739a7 and e5 stays for all those implementations, see below, n. 19.

2. Cf. also "the move from the sacred," 5.739a1, on which see below, p. 58.

3. For more precisions about what the 'first city' stands for, see below, pp. 60–61.

4. Does *kata dunamin* qualify here the intensity of the effort in the search for the paradigm (". . . and seek *with all one's might* the regime which comes as close as possible to such a regime," Pangle; italics mine), or is it the restrictive, quasi-terminological formula ("as far as possible") that occurs in similar contexts (cf. Chap. 2, p. 42 with n. 34)? In spite of the word order, which could be invoked in support of Pangle's construal, I think that the traditional reading is to be preferred (cf. 5.746b8–c4 with *adunaton* at c1, quoted below, p. 54).

5. "[. . .] was aber von den verbleibenden Vorschlägen diesem am nächsten kommt und mit dem, was ausgeführt werden müsste, am engsten verwandt ist, für eben dessen Verwirklichung soll er sorgen," Schöpsdau, vol. 2, p. 51. In his 1991 article (p. 142, n. 16), he had adopted a different construction (cf. commentary *ad* 746c2–4, vol. 2, p. 344).

6. Cf. 5.742e1–4. If there is any place for 'pragmatism' in the *Laws*, it is at the last level (when things become arduous to put in practice) that it is to be found. Bartels 2017 thinks of Plato's overall project as being 'pragmatic' and thus "at odds with a number of core Platonic doctrines" (p. 23), because it is based on a norm that "contributes to social stability and the preservation of the group" and not "upon the recognition of a transcendent norm like the Idea of the Good" (p. 100, talking about the *symposium*). It will be clear that this is not how I see things. The transcendence of the norm need not to be thematized in order to serve as a basis for the discussion. It is a philosophical presupposition that goes beyond the perspective of the dialogue. Whether Forms are concerned or not or in what sense is a separate question, to be treated in a far-ranging discussion about Plato's late ontology.

7. Cf. Schöpsdau, vol. 2, p. 343, *ad* 745e7–746d2: "die zweibeste Regelung wird damit ihrerseits zu einem Muster (*paradeigma* 746b7 wie 739e1)."

8. For striking illustration of a kindred inversion (concerning 'imitation'), see *Statesman* 300e11–301a4 and Chap. 2, p. 39.

9. See Chap. 2, p. 43.

10. See Chap. 2, p. 49. The two "nows" are superposed in Megillus' remark at 4.722a2–5: "The laws presently (*nun*) established must also be satisfying to Kleinias here. After all, the city that is presently (*nun*) thinking of using such laws is his."

11. Plato suggests that even laws that are crucial in his just city, in particular the law on public ownership of women and children, could have in principle been left unformulated and entrusted to the future rulers, were it not for the pressure exercised by his interlocutors (see above, Chap. 2, p. 35).

12. At 6.770b4–8, the Athenian, addressing the guardians of the laws, explicitly says that he will be omitting many laws and will only provide a sketch of the major ones. See further 6.778b5–c1 (the plan of the second city and its architecture is a sketch (*tupos*, c1) in words (*logôi*, b5) to be later filled out when it comes to realization (*ergôi*, b6); 6.779c5–d2 (about a series of minor urban regulations); 8.828b3–5 (religious officials will organize what the lawgiver is putting to the side for now). This does not open the way to revisions of a more fundamental kind (on this point, see Reid 2021). Note that the question of the filling out of the sketch interferes with the question of the relationship between paradigm and realization (cf. Schöpsdau, vol. 2, p. 470, on the walls of the city).

13. Aristotle tends to assimilate the constitution of the *Laws* to that of the *Republic*, see *Politics* 2.6 1265a2–4. As for Cicero, the interpretation depends both on the scope of *res publica* and the antecedent of *eius* ('its laws') in the sentence: "Plato, who is the first to have written on the *res publica*, and also in a separate work about its laws . . ." (Cicero, *De legibus* 2.6.14: *Plato . . . qui princeps de republica conscripsit, idemque separatim de legibus eius*), see below, pp. 62–63 with n. 38.

14. Cf. also 9.877d5–e2. As noted by Pöhlmann 1893, pp. 502–3, tenure ("Nützungsrecht") is not private property (cf. also Brisson and Pradeau 2006, p. 100).

15. See below, Chap. 4.

16. The parallel, which was pointed out by Morrow (1954), has been the starting point for my reading of the *Laws* (Laks 1990); see now O'Meara 2017, pp. 50–51, 57, and Rashed 2018, pp. 128–37.

17. Persuasion of necessity by the Demiurge: *Timaeus* 47e5–48a5, 56c5–6; predisposition of the disordered *khôra* to be ordered: 53a2-b5; persuasion as the crucial legislative task and

challenge, cf. below Chap. 7; the lawgiver facing necessity, e.g., 6.757d5–6, 9.857e10–858a6, 9.880e4–6. Rashed (2018, pp. 128–37), has suggested the existence of a further structural analogy between the mathematical scheme at work in the *Timaeus* in the section devoted to the generation of the five geometrical solids from the elementary triangles and their distribution at the level of elemental and cosmic bodies (54d2–55c6), on the one hand, and the determination of the number of households in the *Laws* as 5040, on the other (cf. the chart, p. 137).

18. The story of the war between ancient Athens and Atlantis, which is said to have *truly* occurred in a remote past by its various narrators (cf. Pradeau 1997, pp. 23–24), is presented as a 'dynamic' complement of the paradigmatic just city set up in the *Republic* (cf. *Timaeus*, 19b3–c8). It is announced at the beginning of the *Timaeus* and was to be told in the *Critias*, but is not extant in the text that has reached us, for the dialogue breaks after the preliminaries of the war. On the coexistence of different temporalities in Plato, see Vegetti in Vegetti, ed. (1998–2007), vol. 6, 2005.

19. The status of this third city has always intrigued; see Schöpsdau; vol. 2, pp. 311–12. Rashed (2018, pp. 120–21) argues against the majority reading (also adopted in my previous publications) on the ground that it drives a wedge between the relation of the first city to the second, which is of a theoretical nature, and the relation of the second city to the third one, which is on the practical side. I don't think there is a difficulty there, once one assumes, as I suggested above (pp. 53–54), that 'practice' is a two-tier notion. The numerical series refers to a progressive addition of variables, all of which are practical until we reach a realization (*ergôi*) that by definition exceeds any verbal discussion. Whereas Rashed is right to insist that the third city is continuous with the first two, the consequences he draws from this are another matter: namely, that the city described from 739d8 onwards *is* the third city, coming after the mathematically oriented section 737c1–738a1 that would represent the second city (pp. 128–37). I take it that the third city refers to "another city that one might found sometime" as opposed to "the one that is now growing," mentioned at 6.757c8–d1 (quoted Chap. 6, p. 91). I shall come back elsewhere to the grammatical (and paleographical) arguments that Rashed puts forward in favor of his interpretation (see pp. 122–27), none of which seems to me to be decisive, but which are all interesting.

20. Axiom of corrupting power: 3.691c–d; 4.713c5–d2 and 714d1–3; 9.874e8–875d5, on which see Chap. 2, p. 45–50.

21. *Kinêsas ton ap' iras* [sc. *grammês*] *lithon* (Alcaeus, Frag. 351 Lobel-Page, quoted in the epigraph of the present chapter). The expression most probably refers to the central line of five that were drawn on a gameboard; our evidence is insufficient to reconstruct the specifics of the game (Lamer 1927, col. 1970–72, Schöpsdau, vol. 2, p. 312 *ad* 739a1, and Kidd 2017).

22. On the meanings that were given to the proverbial expression in Antiquity, see Kidd 2017, pp. 88–93. Rashed 2018, p. 118, translates *phora kathaper pettôn aph' hierou* with "comme quand au trictrac on joue son va-tout" ("as when a backgammon player risks all for all"), an interpretive translation that reflects an explanation found in Plutarch and Philo of Alexandria (cf. Lamer 1927, col. 1071; Kidd 2017, p. 90). Kidd argues that the game presented "an aggressive element which still exists in backgammon today: namely the hitting of [. . .] solitary pieces on the board" (p. 84); if true, it does not seem relevant for the *Laws* (Kidd's comments on the passage, pp. 86–88, miss the point).

23. One prominent example of a 'sacred' item is the golden cord of reasoning that is in us at 1.645a1, cf. Chap. 4, pp. 66–67.

24. 5.739a4, b3, e4; 9.875d3.

25. "For we are talking to human beings, not gods" (5.732e3); "gods or children of gods" (5.739d6); "but [. . .] we are not legislating, as the ancient lawgivers, for children of gods, the heroes, as the present account has it; they themselves sprang from gods and legislated for others who were born from those; we are human beings legislating now for the seeds of human beings" (9.853c3–7). "Ancient lawgivers" and "heroes" refer to an *epoch* fundamentally different from the present one which is identified at 4.711e4 with the 'time of Troy.' See Chap. 2, p. 50.

26. Allotment: 5.737c1–738b1 and 739e8–740b5. For the number 5040, see 5.738a1–b1, 746d3–e3 and 6.771a6–c7. Its virtue comes from its having fifty-nine dividers (prime factors), see Rashed 2018, pp. 129–32, with a summary of the mathematical demonstration by Marin Mersenne (who explicitly mentions Book 5 of the *Laws* in his letter to Torricello dated June 24, 1644).

27. The main passages concerning the rule of law are quoted in Chap. 6, pp. 98–100; for the relationship between a 'mixed' and a 'middle' constitution, see Chap. 6, pp. 86–88.

28. 5.732e7–733a4.

29. 4.710c6–711a3. See above, Chap. 2, pp. 45–50. See further 5.735d1–5 (relative to the best way to select the citizens for the new colony).

30. Cf. 5.737b5–9.

31. For this other, derivative kind of retreat, see 7.807b3–c1 (relative to the best way of life; the passage is quoted in Chap. 6, n. 57; 8.840e2–841c2 (relative to the best regulation concerning sexual relationships). Cf. further 5.735d 5–736b4 (on the question of how to select the colonists), and 6.778d3–779c4 (about the necessity for the city to build defensive walls).

32. Public ownership of women, children, and goods: *Republic* 5.449c2–450a2; shared feelings and speaking in a single voice: *Republic* 5.462a9–e3.

33. I shall follow this typographical rule only when the distinction between the two becomes relevant. Note that we find another such '*Republic*' at the beginning of the *Timaeus* (cf. Chap. 2, n. 22).

34. For more details about the status of the *Statesman*, see Appendix A.

35. See below, Chap. 7, pp. 120–22.

36. The relationship between a constitution and the character and behavior of the citizen, illustrated at a grand systematic scale by the analogy between city and soul in the *Republic*, is attested in a number of Greek sources, see e.g., Bordes 1982, pp. 375–78 (on democratic *politeia*).

37. *Laws* 5.735a5–6, cf. 1.625a6–7, 4.714b3–5, 6.751a4–b2. Cf. further, [Ps.-?]Plato, *7th Letter* 328c1, 332e4; Aristotle, *Politics*, 2.6 1265a1–4 (quoted below, n. 39), Isocrates, *To Philip* 12 (which has been taken, probably in too narrow a sense, to refer specifically to Plato's *Laws*). On the various ways in which Greek authors construe the relationship between *politeia* and *nomos*, see Bordes 1982, pp. 365–69.

38. Cicero, *De legibus* 2.14: *Plato . . . qui princeps de republica conscripsit, idemque separatim de legibus eius*. Ziegler in his edition wanted to delete *eius* because he construed 'its laws' as the laws of the paradigmatic city described in the *Republic*. Powell 2001, pp. 19–20, greatly lessens the problem by referring *res publica* not to the ideal constitution (or for that matter to the title of the work), but to the notion of a constitution in general, that is the topic of the *Republic* (see also Adkins 2013, pp. 20–21). A certain inconcinnity remains, since the *Laws* includes also a treatment of a constitution.

39. See Chap. 6. Aristotle found here a ground for critique: "In the *Laws* there is hardly anything but laws; not much is said about the constitution. This, which he had intended to make more of the ordinary type, he gradually brings round to the other form [i.e., that of the *Republic*]" (*Politics*, 2.6 1265a1–4, trans. Ross, in Barnes' *Revised Oxford Translation*).

40. See Chap. 1, p. 25.

41. See Chap. 7, pp. 107–110.

42. On the intriguing title *Politeai* (in the plural, referring to the injust constitutions as well), attested in the tradition, see Tarrant 2012.

Chapter 4. What Is Human?

1. Dörrie 1983 says rightly that the *Laws* are "much more than a second-best project" ("wesentlich mehr als ein zweibester Entwurf," p. 93); see also in this sense Helmer 2010, p. 209, except that I don't see this as an objection to using the language of 'concession' and 'retreat.'

2. We don't need the explicit affirmation of *Alcibiades I* (130c1–3), the authenticity of which is disputed, to accept the equivalence between an individual and his soul in the *Laws*. It is presupposed by the comparison between human beings and puppets, according to which "each of us" is our own motivations, and the word 'soul' appears, at 1.643d1, in the discussion of education that leads to the comparison. In the *Republic* Plato goes as far as saying that our rational soul is "the human being inside the human being" (*tou anthrôpou anthrôpos ho entos*, 9.589a7–b1).

3. The sentence, in Greek, is anacoluthic (lit.: "such a city, whether gods or children of gods inhabit it, they administer it etc.") The change of subject ("such a city" being taken up by "gods and children of gods") may reflect the enthusiasm provoked by the evocation. Moreover, the function of the phrase "more than one" (*pleious henos*) is uncertain. I follow Schöpsdau, vol. 2, p. 314 *ad* 739d7, in taking it with the second sentence, rather than with the first one; the usual construction sounds otiose ("by gods or children of gods (more than one) . . ." Pangle). The idea seems to be that gladness is collective, not to be restricted to a single individual (a god, in this case).

4. Human beings can be called 'wild' or 'tame' depending on the point of view or the circumstances: cf. *Sophist*, 222b7 (where the alternative remains open: *eiper ge . . .*) and *Laws* 7.808d4–5 (a child is "of all savage animals (*thêria*) the most difficult to handle"); further 4.718d3 and 9.870a2.

5. According to other sources, drinking wine was part of the Spartan *syssitia* ("common meals"), see Schöpsdau, vol. 1, p. 206, *ad* 637a2. Common meals are a central feature in the daily life of virtuous citizens, as is enthusiastically described in Book 7.806d7–807b (the rather terrible passage is quoted Chap. 6, n. 57). The fact that the *symposium* is a central feature of Athenian life explains the importance which Plato gives it at the beginning of the *Laws* (Morrow 1993, p. 316). Plato uses it to illustrate the necessity of a rule in collective gatherings (see Landauer, forthcoming). In her treatment of the recurrent worry, among commentators of the *Laws*, over why there does not appear to be any room in Plato's best human city as constructed in Books 6–12 for the *symposia* referred to in Books 1–2, Schmitt-Pantel (1992) suggests that Plato "hesitates" between the model of the *syssitia* and that of the *symposia* (see pp. 234–37). Is it not, rather, that the Athenian *symposium* serves in the course of the first two books as a dialectical reference that has in effect no place in the final picture?

6. Clinias takes the phrase as supporting his view about the universality of war, cf. 1.625e5–626a5; for the Athenian, in this context at least, it aims at making peace the supreme value. At another level, however, the fight between the good and the bad is eternal (see Chap. 7, n. 16).

7. For the quasi-official terminology (which makes room for contextual variations), see *Republic* 4.439d4–8 and 440e2–441a3. In the latter passage, the political counterparts are called "money-making"/*to khrêmatistikon*, auxiliary/*to epikouron*, and deliberative/*to bouleutikon*.

8. *Pathos*, which applies to rational reasoning as well as feelings and emotional expectations, does not overlap with *pathêmata* at *Timaeus* 69d1, which refers to the subset of irrational *pathê* that is also listed (with slight variations) in the *Laws* (cf. also *Republic*, 4.439d2). 'Affection' (a usual translation for *pathos*) too easily suggests that Plato is talking about this subset. 'State' is Bobonich's (2002) rendering of the term (see pp. 539–40, n. 77). The terminology remains troubling.

9. For confidence and fear being beliefs of a certain kind, cf. also e.g., *Philebus*, 32b9–c2. For a general treatment of the issue (but with no reference to the *Laws*), see Renaut 2020 (esp. pp. 117–18).

10. The reasoning in question bears on whether feelings and related psychic states, to which the pronoun *autôn* ("of them") must refer, are appropriate in any particular circumstance.

11. Not all reasoning is 'beautiful,' nor for that matter is every law a true law. Plato often uses a given term in a normative sense, one which (in his view) manifests the true concept or its referent.

12. The use by later authors of the verb *neurospasthênai* ("to be pulled by strings") and derivatives in psychologico-theological contexts is a clear echo of Plato's comparison; cf. Philo (*De opificio mundi* 117; *De fuga* 46; *De Abrahamo* 73; *Quaestiones in Genesin*, 1.24), Marcus Aurelius (2.2.4; 3.16.2; 6.16.1; 7.3.1, etc.), Clement of Alexandria, *Stromata*, 2.11.1; 4.79.1 (further references in Schöpsdau, vol. 1, p. 237 *ad* 644d7).

13. Wilburn (2012) insists, against a current reading of the passage (cf. p. 26, n. 2), that the comparison concerns the overall disposition, virtuous or otherwise, of a human soul. This is also how Schöpsdau construes the passage, vol. 1, p. 231. It is well taken as a complement to the traditional picture. But Wilburn's further claim is implausible, namely his contention that "nothing [Plato] says [in the *Laws*] commits him to acknowledging [the] possibility [of *akrasia*]" (p. 26, developed pp. 48–50), meaning that Plato actually denies the possibility of any akratic, conflictual episode. Conflicts are certainly implied in the initial analogy between states, families, and individuals (1.626e2–627b8), and they are said to occur "frequently" in one's soul at 9.863e2–3, in a sentence that clearly picks up the puppet analogy: "All these [sc. anger, pleasure, and ignorance], we say, impels each [sc. of us], as he is often dragged in contrary [sc. directions] at the same time (*eis tanantia pollakis hama*) towards his own willing." In the same sense, see Meyer 2015, pp. 181–82.

14. *Ho muthos aretês sesômenos an eiê*. Similar expressions are frequent in Plato, cf. *Republic* 3.395b8, 10.621b8, *Theaetetus* 164a1, 167d3–4, *Philebus* 14a3–4. To 'save' a story or an argument is to confirm it (Schöpsdau, vol. 1, p. 238 *ad loc.*) or vindicate it (Meyer 2015, p. 184), to "establish it in its full validity" (Pangle in the notes to his translation, pp. 517–18, n. 34). In the present passage, *muthos* refers in the first place to the story that has just been told about the puppet. An indirect reference to Prodicus' story of Heracles choosing virtue over vice (cf. 84B2DK= D21LM) is likely; but the word *muthos* might also refer to the principle that lies behind the story itself,

that is to the notion of virtue as the state of an individual who is "superior to himself" (for this usage of *muthos*, cf. *gamou muthos* at 6.773b4–5).

15. See especially below, Chap. 7 and 8.

16. Recent literature on Plato's puppets includes, apart from Wilburn 2012 (see above, n. 13), Sassi 2008, D. Frede 2010, and Schofield 2016.

17. Plato, *Theaetetus*, 155d2–4; Aristotle, *Metaphysics*, 2.983a12–15 (see below, n. 20).

18. For puppets, see Herodotus 2.48 (who calls them *agalmata neurospasta* / "figures pulled by strings") and Plato *Republic*, 7.514b6, where the puppets whose images the prisoners in the cave see are called *thaumata*. In *Laws* 2.658c1, *thaumata* is the last item in an enumeration of performances geared, in a hypothetic artistic festival, towards pleasure: rhapsody, citharoedy, tragedy, comedy, and the puppet show (cf. also c11, and Theophrastus, *Characters* 6.4). The sentence shows that the association between 'puppet' and 'wonder' was a matter of course: "it would not be surprising (*ou thaumaston*)," says the Athenian, "if someone thought he could best win by exhibiting puppets (*thaumata*)." Studies on the literary and archeological evidence on puppets and puppet-theater are mentioned in Schöpsdau, vol. 1, p. 237 at 644d7 and p. 282 at 658b7c1. On mechanical *automata*, which are not attested before Aristotle (cf. *On the movement of animals*, 6.701b17, *Generation of animals*, 2.1.734b10, and *Metaphysics Alpha* 2.983a14 [quoted below n. 19]), see Berryman 2003. The first two passages refer to *automata* as a term of comparison in the explanation of how living beings in general move. This is clearly an extension, in physical perspective, of Plato's use of the puppet analogy in the *Laws*.

19. See *Metaphysics*, Alpha 2.983a12–15: "For all men begin, as we said, by wondering that the matter is so as in the case of automatic marionettes or the solstices or the incommensurability of the diagonal of a square with the side . . . ," trans. Ross in Barnes' *Revised Oxford Translation*.

20. On the motif of the gods' entertainment in ancient traditions, see Burkert 2003 (on the *Laws*, pp. 105–7).

21. There is here both an implicit reference to, and a correction of Protagoras 80B4DK: what cannot be decided about them is not whether gods exist or not, but what their intention was in creating human beings.

22. *Laws* 10.906a7: *hêmeis* [. . .] *ktêma theôn kai daimoniôn, Phaedo*, 62b6–9 and d1–3 (Cebes is arguing against suicide).

23. See also Jouët-Pastré 2006 pp. 48–54. In the *Timaeus*, human beings are created by secondary gods, at the Demiurge's request, not as an entertainment, but so that the world might be complete: "Learn now, therefore, what I declare to you. There remain still three kinds of mortal beings that have not yet been begotten; and as long as they have not come to be, the universe will be incomplete, for it will still lack within it all the kinds of living things it must have if it is to be sufficiently complete. But if these creatures came to be and came to share in life by my hand, they would rival the gods. It is you, then, who must turn yourselves to the task of fashioning these living things, as your nature allows. This will assure their mortality, and this whole universe will really be a completed whole" (41b6-c5; trans. Zeyl). If one wished to systematize what escapes systematization, one could say that the god of the *Laws* is pleased with the way in which the secondary gods of the *Timaeus* have dealt with their task.

24. In his commentary to the *Laws*, Ficino renders '*thauma*' as 'miracle' and interprets it in conformity with his syncretic approach, in the light of the Hermetic tradition: "but since he

[i.e., Plato] said that man is an animal composed of such contradictory elements, he adds, not beyond the point, that man is among animals a divine miracle, thereby imitating Hermes who says that man is a great miracle. Why is man a 'miracle'? Both because, being divine, it is amazing that he is infected by mortality, and because, being mortal, it is amazing that he is drawn towards the divine. But why a 'divine miracle'? Because he has been made by divine providence" (Ficino 1576, t.2, 1491–92). Ficino here refers to the anthropogony of the Hermetic treatise *Poimandres*, §16 (cf. Laks 2007b).

25. For the etymological word play (*khoros* supposedly deriving from *khara*), cf. 2.654a4–5 (cf. 655b9–e1). Prauscello (2014, p. 128) stresses that both performers and spectators are "choreuts-citizens." On the political function of choral dance in Greek political life, see the introduction to Azoulay and Ismard 2020, pp. 18–22. Plato's *Laws*, referred to on p. 21, is one piece of evidence among others that "the Greeks themselves have resorted in a privileged way to the figure of the chorus to think about the functioning of the city" (p. 18; my trans.). The privilege is so great that the chorus is considered as representing in Athenian thought an "absolute metaphor," in the sense given by Blumenberg (2010) to the expression: a metaphor that cannot be reduced conceptually (pp. 18–19). Is the latter true of Plato's *Laws*, one might ask?

26. 2.653c7–654a7, with 7.813a5–817e3. For the relationship between Books 2 and 7, see Mouze 2005, pp. 80–98. On the educative and politically homogenizing function of choral performances, see Prauscello 2014, esp. Chap. 3.

27. For the idea that the puppet comparison leads to the centrality of music and dance in the educative process, see Kurke 2013 (cf. Laks 2005, pp. 41–42).

28. Hesiod, *Works and Days*, 287–90: "Misery (*Kakotês*) is there to be grabbed in abundance, easily, for smooth is the road, and she lives very nearby, but in front of Excellence (*Aretê*) the immortal gods have set sweat, and the path to her is long and steep" (trans. Most). Plato relies on an interpretation (cf. *hoi polloi* [. . .] *apophainousi*, 718e1) of moral virtue and wickedness, as represented by Hesiod's *Kakotês* and *Aretê*, that primarily reflects social criteria (cf. Schöpsdau, vol. 1, p. 230).

29. Cf. *pros tropou*, 2.655d7. The expression means both 'in agreement with one's character' and 'which pleases one.'

30. See below, Chap. 10. There is a formal continuity between choral dance and full-fledged drama, in which they are embedded.

31. Cf. below, Chap. 5, p. 83–84.

32. Most (2011) shows that the anonymous lines quoted by Plato in order to substantiate his talk of "an ancient quarrel between philosophy and poetry" (*palaia diaphora philosophiai kai poiêtikêi*, *Republic* 10.607b5–6) come almost certainly from the 5th century comic authors (pp. 7–12). The quarrel, however, may have been implicit rather than explicit at an earlier stage, and articulated in other terms. There is no doubt, on the other hand, that the terms in which Plato stages the quarrel in the *Republic*, as well as in the *Laws*, initiated a fight for millenia to come. Cf. Chap. 7, n. 49.

33. The language at 659b5–8 is difficult, because of uncertainty about the syntactical function of *kathaper* (b6). Most editors add a negation (*ou*) before the adverb of comparison, to get a contrast between the sound ancient Hellenic procedure and the degenerate Italic one (". . . not as the Sicilian usage; which . . ."); Schöpdsau, who notes that the contrast is not the expected one (vol. 1, p. 285), follows Des Places and has the comparison, without the negation, bear, not

on the preceding *gar* clause, but on the earlier one (expanding on ". . . not appropriate nor correct"). *Exên gar . . . nomoi* must then be put in parentheses. Another possibility is to assume a kind of semantic anacoluthon, which I have attempted to render by translating *kathaper* with "by the same token."

34. The shift is not marked as such. At 2.656c4–5, the term *rhêma* (word) is associated with rhythm (*rhuthmos*) and melody (*melos*), but by the same token clearly distinguished from both of them (contrast the pair *ta te skhêmata kai ta phthegmata* at 2.655a1–2). From 2.660e1 onwards, the content of what is said (*ta legomena*) comes to the fore and takes precedence.

35. The relationships (association and dissociation) between wordless music and words is the basis for the many metaphors in Plato's dialogues that make of philosophy an art of the Muse, and indeed the true or supreme music; cf. *Phaedo*, 60d8–61b8 (to be on the safe side, Socrates decides to take the dream enjoining him to practice the art of the Muse literally and to compose poems instead of taking philosophy as "the greatest music" (61a3–4); *Republic* 6.499d3–4 (the philosopher-king identified with the Muse), and 8.548b8-c1 (the "true Muse," goes with arguments and philosophy); *Cratylus* 406a3–6 (etymology of the name 'Muses' from *môsthai* "to desire eagerly," *scil.* "to investigate and to do philosophy"); *Philebus* 67b6 (evocation of "the philosophical Muse"). For the identification with philosophy of "the Muse" at *Laws* 12.967e2–3, see Cherniss 1953 (p. 377, n.1) and Schöpsdau, vol. 3, pp. 600–601. Cf. further *Statesman*, 309d2–3, where *mousikê* in *mousikê basilikê*, "royal music," stands for rhetoric.

36. Schöpsdau (1986, p. 107) points out the "functional correspondence" between *logismos* and *aidôs* in his detailed analysis of the relationship between courage and temperance (self-control) in Book 1 of the *Laws* and characterizes it, in his summary (Schöpsdau, vol. 1, pp. 242–44) as "das sittliche Wertgefühl" (p. 244) ("the moral feeling of value"). For recent discussions and further references about *aidôs*, see Pfefferkorn 2020 and de Nicolay 2021.

37. See Chap. 8, p. 127 and n. 6.

38. See Chap. 5, pp. 80–83.

39. On the parallelism between the construction of the world in the *Timaeus* and the *Laws*, see Chap. 3, pp. 56–58.

40. The phrase serves as an explanation, in the general preamble, of why the lawgiver must add, to a first series of arguments of "divine" character in favor of the beautiful life, a second series that will be more appealing to "human" nature. For the way in which his "mortal nature," which avoids pain and pursues pleasure, affects the human monarch endowed with absolute power, see 9.875b3–c6 (discussed in Chap. 2, pp. 45–48).

41. *Republic* 5.473 c11–e5 (cf. Chap. 2, p. 42).

Chapter 5. The Multiplication of Goals

1. Plato talks more often about the "parts of virtue" (1.630e1, 631a5) or of its "kinds" or "species" (*eidos*, 1.632e2 and 12.963c5) than about virtues in the plural. At 1.633a8–9, the Athenian leaves the alternative open: "whether we should call them parts or just that [i.e., virtues.]" But he also talks about the goal of the lawgiver as "one virtue, being four of them" (*mian aretên ousôn tettarôn*, 3.688a7), in a passage that refers back to the initial classification in Book 1 (3.688a3–b4); see also 12.963a6 (" that virtue is in a way (*pou*) four," says Clinias, and the Athenian assents).

2. Schöpsdau (vol. 1, p. 168), lists nineteen passages in the *Laws* that mention happiness as the goal or consequence of correct legislation. See e.g., 1.631b3–6; 5.742d7–e1, e4–6, and 743c5–6 (where friendship also features as a legislative goal); 7.816d1–2.

3. The reading *meta nou* is transmitted by Eusebius, *Evangelical Preparation* 12.16.4 and Theodoretus, *Therapy of Greek Diseases* 6.34 and in the Arabic philosophical compendium preserved in Bodleian ms. Or. Marsch 539 (see Moseley 2018, p. 173). Plato's manuscripts and Stobaeus, *Anthology*, II. 2.7 (p. 55.1 Wachsmuth) give *meta noun* "after reason" (with *nous* picking up *phronêsis* in the previous sentence), which is of course possible, but less interesting. The passages that speak in favor of the genitive rather than the accusative are listed by Schöpsdau, vol. 1, p. 184, cf. Meyer 2015, pp. 112–13 (see especially the distinction between temperance in the popular sense of the term and the one that is accompanied by *phronêsis* at 4.710a5–b2).

4. On the relationship between courage and temperance construed as self-control, see Schöpsdau 1986 and vol. 1, pp. 194–95. See also the distinction at 12.963e1–8 between two kinds of courage, the one that is natural and irrational, the other that is rational and belongs to a soul that is "wise and in possession of reason/*nous*" (963e6–7), cf. Meyer 2015, pp. 113–14.

5. For further precision on the relationship between the three terms, see Schöpsdau, vol. 1, p. 410, *ad* 1.688a6–b4. I side with those interpreters who refer the demonstrative *toutois* ("those") to the two last items, i.e., reason and opinion, rather than to all three items mentioned (which is Schöpsdau's preferred option).

6. Schöpsdau, vol. 1, p. 182, *ad* 1.631c5–d1. In the past, this irritation has led some to condemn the *Laws* as inauthentic (the last case seems to have been Müller 1951).

7. This is the way Schöpsdau takes it, vol. 3, p. 590.

8. As Schöpsdau himself notes, vol. 3, p. 591; cf. Tarán 1975, p. 29, n. 123.

9. See also the contrast between a life in peace and a life in war, both external and internal, at 8.829a6–b2.

10. Pangle has "in its entirety" modify "consonance," but see Schöpsdau (vol. 1, p. 257) and Meyer (2015, p. 210), both of whom also adopt the paleographically very easy addition of the article *tôi* after *logôi* (haplography based on the confusion of capital *gamma* and *tau*), from which the infinitive *eithisthai*, which cannot be construed with the transmitted text, can then depend.

11. On the centrality of "friendship" in Plato's and more generally in his political thought, see Schofield 2013, pp. 284–85, and Sheffield 2020.

12. About the settings, see Chap. 1, p. 8 with n. 35.

13. In a context which shows beyond doubt that he is alluding to Plato's *Laws*, Aristotle mentions in *Politics* 2.6.1265b33–35 "some people" (*enioi*) who say that "the best constitution must be mixed out of all the constitutions" (*dei tên aristên politeian ex hapasôn einai tôn politeiôn memeigmenên*); cf. *hoi pleious meignuntes*, "those who mix many [sc. constitutions]," 2.6 1266a4. Thucydides (8.97.2) speaks about the rule of the 5,000 (411 BC) as being, at the beginning, "the best government the Athenian enjoyed, at least in my time: for there was a moderate blending (*metria* [. . .] *sunkrasis*) of the few and the many" (trans. C. F. Smith). The passage is usually taken to be the first explicit formulation in Antiquity of this idea of a "mixed constitution," on which see von Fritz 1954 (with an emphasis on Polybius); Landauer (in preparation) focuses on Plato and Aristotle.

14. The ephors, five in number, were chosen yearly by acclamation (Plutarch, *Lycurgus* 26), a procedure that Aristotle qualifies as 'childish,' *Politics* 2.9 1270b28. Plato's presentation of the Spartan constitution matches what Herodotus' says of Lycurgus' reform (at 1.65).

15. See the chapter entitled "The Emergence of the Political Concept of Freedom" in Raaflaub 2004, pp. 58–127, esp. pp. 84–89. On Spartans' obedience to the laws, see von Fritz 1965 and Raaflaub 2004, pp. 233–34.

16. 'Freedom' at 3.687a7, which is the only occurrence of the term in this context apart from the passage under examination, concerns the war for the independence of Greece.

17. Another thematically marked surprise occurs at 5.739a1–3, on which see above, Chap. 2, pp. 32–33.

18. For the motif of indifference to words, cf. *Meno*, 87b8–c1, *Republic*, 7.533d7–e2, *Statesman*, 261e5–7. For the general problem that Plato's terminological flexibility raises for the translator, see Rowe 2019.

19. See 1.630b1 (first occurrence), 631c7 (*sophrôn hexis*), 632c7, 635e6.

20. Schöpsdau is wrong, I think, to minimize the importance of the substitution by taking "when we say" generally, and not as referring specifically to 693b3–4 (vol. 1, p. 450, following England's edition, *ad loc.*) For the promotion of 'temperance' at another juncture and with different implications, see 3.697b2–6.

21. See below, Chap. 6, pp. 102–3, cf. Retrospect, pp. 155–56.

22. There are strong similarities between Plato's description of the Persian regime under Cyrus and Xenophon's in his *Cyropaedia*, which Plato must have been using and assessing implicitly on various points (cf. Schöpsdau, vol. 1, pp. 458 and 469).

23. On the general and abstract character of Plato description, see Schöpsdau, vol. 1, p. 459–60.

24. Meyer (2021, section 3) came independently to a view of Ancient Persia that is very similar to the one proposed here. She calls the two aspects of Persian liberty 'epistemic' (for the counseling) and 'material' (for the absence of exploitation).

25. The triadic expression at 3.694b6 ("because of freedom and friendship and a common sharing in reason/*nous*") prepares the substitution of *phronêsis* by *nous* at end of the section (701d7–9), cf. above, p. 78. The "common sharing of reason" (*nou koinonia*) suggests the way "wisdom" is implemented, namely when a king admits of counselors. On *parrhêsia*, see Schöpsdau, vol. 1, p. 461.

26. I come back to the paradoxical formula "voluntarily enslaved, in a certain sense, to the laws" in the next chapter, pp. 99–102.

27. These two features—four classes of citizens and the servitude to the laws—will be taken up in Plato's own constitutional model. For the four classes (inherited from Solon's reform but imposed by circumstantial necessity), see 5.744a8–745b2.

28. Cf. Chap. 1, p. 19. *Nomos*/law is also the name of a musical genre, cf. Chap. 7, n. 45.

29. René de Nicolay suggested to me that *arkhontes* (here followed by the genitive to mark a beginning: poets "initiated" a certain process), also points to the illegitimate political rule that the poets are now *de facto* exercising, as if they were officeholders.

30. Cf. Chap. 4, p. 70.

31. On the role of shame in the *Laws*, see Chap. 4, p. 71 and n. 36. More specifically on the relationship between shame and freedom in the passage under consideration, see de Nicolay 2021.

32. Cf. 6.761e1 and 777e5 (756d1–2, 'to be free of penalty,' is irrelevant).

Chapter 6. Mixtures, Blends, and Other Metamorphoses

1. The Watch is the closest equivalent to a group of philosopher-kings in a constitution that does not allow that human beings rule. For the pyramidal structure of Plato's constitution, see the chart in Schöpsdau, vol. 2, p. 353. Detailed reconstructions and commentary are in Morrow 1993, Chapters 5 ("Government," pp. 157–240), 6 ("The Administration of Justice," pp. 241–96), and 9 ("The Nocturnal Council," pp. 500–514). The Assembly and Council are treated by Morrow in the first section of Chapter 5, pp. 157–78; on the Council, see also Schöpsdau, vol. 2, pp. 383–94. A useful synthetic description of the offices in Magnesia is provided by Reid 2020b.

2. This is firmly emphasized by Schöpsdau, vol. 2, p. 386 (at 756e9–758a2). One can also note that the scope of the phrase "a selection occurring in this way . . ." is somewhat indeterminate. Three selections have been described so far: (1) the 37 Guardians of the laws (*nomophulakes*) (752d7–755b6); (2) different military officers (755b6–756b6), among whom the most important are the three 'generals' (*stratêgoi*); and (3) the 360 members of the Council (756b7–e8). The selection of the members of the Council, which is the body that receives the greatest attention, is surely the best candidate for illustrating the general principle. But the other ones must by definition be considered as well.

3. At *Politics* 4.9 1294a35–b13, Aristotle, talking about democracy and oligarchy, distinguishes three ways of mixing: (a) combining laws that belong to each of the two regimes (*amphotera*, 1294a36); (b) taking a middle way (*to meson*, b2) between their respective political arrangements; and (c) combining features representative of the principle of the regimes in question. Senses (b) and, on a certain interpretation of what a 'feature' is, (c) go beyond the model of physical mixture, in which components keep their identity (*On generation and corruption* 1.10 328a5–18 and chapter 2.7). They are closer to the third type of mixture identified by the Stoics: not juxtaposition (to which they restrict the word *mixis*), nor fusion accompanied with destruction of the qualities of the components (*sunkusis*), but a blending (*krasis*) in which "certain substances and their qualities are mutually co-extended through and through, with their qualities being preserved in such a mixture" (Alexander of Aphrodisias, *De mixtione*, 3, 6.14–7.1 Groisard = *SVF* 2.473; 48C Long-Sedley, trans. in vol. 1, pp. 290–91). Groisard 2016 includes a detailed history of the notion of a (physical) mixture in Antiquity but does not discuss political mixtures.

4. For the application of the notion of 'middle' or 'mean' to politics, legislation, and the doctrine of virtue, Krämer's chapter "Mass und Mitte in der spätere Dialogen" in his 1959 book (pp. 146–243; pp. 159–62 on the *Statesman* specifically) is fundamental (cf. also Lisi 1985, pp. 106–50). One should add that the doctrine is the positive counterpart of Plato's rejection of Protagoras' sentence "man is the measure of all things." On the *Laws* as a whole considered as a large-scale theological anti-Protagorean treatise, see Chap. 1, p. 18. For a detailed analysis of the relevant passage in the *Statesman*, see Crivelli 2020.

5. The difference between 'mixture' and 'middle' is noted by von Fritz (1954, pp. 78–80) and Morrow (1993, p. 521), but not fully exploited. On the question whether Plato's mixed

constitution is legitimately called a mixed constitution, see Schöpsdau, vol. 1, pp. 432–34, and Ottmann 2008, pp. 38–40. What is surely true, and makes an important difference to Sparta's constitution, is that there is no conflict, and thus no real checks and balances in Plato's constitution. Pradeau (2004) is right to insist on the primacy of 'measure' over 'mixture' (pp. 111–19), but to speak of "an alleged mixed constitution in the *Laws*" surely goes too far.

6. Cf. Chap. 5, p. 80.

7. Cf. Chap. 5, p. 78.

8. A term covering all kinds of political-power-triggering obedience, including both legitimate, competent authority and arbitrary despotism, would be needed. Whereas 'authority' is too restricted, 'power' is too vague.

9. See Chap. 5, p. 81.

10. Reid 2020b, pp. 576–77 (cf. Morrow 1993, pp. 159–60 and Stalley 1983, p. 186).

11. *To metron*, the measure, refers here to a distribution that is proportionate to merits ('goodness,' 'wickedness'), whether those are construed as intellectual or moral.

12. This makes clear that monarchy in its pure form cannot be differentiated from despotism: the master reigns. By the same token, pure democracy is an extreme form of democracy.

13. See Schöpsdau, vol. 2, p. 387.

14. Cf. above, Chap. 5, pp. 80–82. The two interpretations go with a different way of taking the formula A *oude* B at 6.757a1–2: on the second reading, A and B represent two different notions (freedom and equality), both of which are conditions for friendship; according to the first reading, A and B are the two extremes of equality (extreme inequality: slave/master; extreme equality: arithmetical equality).

15. "Pythagorean, Philosopher, and Mathematician King," as Huffman (2005) describes him; on Archytas' leading political role in Tarentum, see pp. 8–18. Plato was personally acquainted with Archytas, and he is often presented as his friend. The ancient evidence is not as straightforward (pp. 32–42).

16. In Frag. B2 DK, Archytas distinguishes between three kinds of mathematical and musical proportions or 'means' (*mesē* in the original; later citators use *mesotēs*) which he calls 'arithmetic,' 'geometric,' and 'sub-contrary,' or 'harmonic' (see Huffman 2005, pp. 172–73 and 177–78). It is possible, but not at all certain, that Archytas himself gave a political application to his mathematical/musical distinction. Harvey (1965, pp. 105–6), argues that he did on the basis of B3DK, which praises *logismos* for guaranteeing peace between the rich and the poor. But as Huffman (2005, pp. 205–6) points out, *logismos* must not specifically refer to geometrical proportion. On the other hand, Socrates' exhortation to Callicles to study geometry, at *Gorgias* 507e6–508a8, in a context where 'community' (*koinōnia*) and 'friendship' (*philia*) are said to regulate the order of the world (with the implication that they should also regulate the order of the city) is likely to allude specifically to "geometric equality" (see however *contra* Huffman 2013, pp. 259–61 and 2005, p. 210).

17. The term *to metron*, 'measure,' is here on the side of the trivial kind of equality, even though virtue and education are also liable to measure (cf. Crivelli 2020, pp. 18–19, commenting on *Statesman* 284a5–b2 and *Philebus* 55d10–56a2). This is another instance of Plato's flexible terminology.

18. There are antecedents to this distinction. In his discussion of Phaleas' proposal to equalize citizens' possessions (*Politics* 2.7 1266a39–40), Aristotle refers to Achilles' complaint to

Ulysses, in the *Iliad*, about unjust distribution of the booty, and at 1267a1–2 quotes *Iliad* 9.319: "We are all held in a single honor, the brave with the weaklings" (trans. Lattimore). By the fifth century, it had become an anti-democratic leitmotif, which Plato takes up in the *Republic* when he characterizes the democratic regime at 8.558c5–6 as "distributing a sort of equality to both equals and unequals alike." Cf. also Aristotle, *Politics* 3.9 1280a7–31 and, for further references, Harvey 1965, p. 102 and Huffman 2005, pp. 211–14.

19. Partly quoted in Chap. 6, p. 104 [T6].

20. See Chap. 9, p. 139 (see especially below, entry 1).

21. The word *epieikes* is used by Plato in a negative sense (a kind of tweaking) that will not survive Aristotle's construal of 'equity' in *Nicomachean Ethics* 5.10 as a better kind of justice, on which see Brunschwig 1999. On the semantic evolution of *epieikes, epieikeia*, see Agostino 1973 and Saunders 2001. For *suggnômon* in Plato, cf. Griswold 2007, p. 279 ("Plato never sees it as a virtue or a commendable quality—certainly not one of any significance"); more generally, Christian 'forgiveness' is not yet on the map (see Konstan 2010, pp. 42–48). *Paratethraumenon* (lit. 'chipped') is said of small damage inflicted on an object that basically remains the same.

22. The "lot" is used marginally in a few cases, as in the selection of *euthunoi*/auditors at 12.946b1–3, which follows a pattern similar to that of the Councilors or of priests (6.759b7–c6) and of market-regulators / *agoranomoi* (6.763e2–3). The selection of judges at the level of tribes (see 6.768b1–c2) seems to be closest to a 'democratic' selection as practiced in Athens, and this gives rise to an interesting comment: "For someone who does not share in the power of collective judging (*sundikazein*) thinks that he is not at all a participant in the city." It is also put to work, interestingly, in the attribution of one of the twelve parts of the city (a tribe) to one of the twelve divinities (5.745d8–e2).

23. Schöpsdau, who clearly sees the difficulty of construing the middle course as resulting from the addition of some lot-equality to proportional equality, identifies the middle point to the "domination of the best people," which is the political expression of proportional equality (vol. 2, pp. 387–88); Morrow 1993, p. 171, suggests that the middle point in question consists in an equilibrium between the economic status of the voters (there are wealthier and poorer ones, depending on their property class): "for Plato it [sc. this equilibrium] would embody the supremacy of the mean, the 'middle way' characteristic of the mixed constitution." This is weaker and even less likely to be Plato's last word, although it is of course part of the overall picture.

24. From a grammatical point of view, the issue is linked to the function assigned to the two uses of the explicative *gar* / "for" at 757a1 and b1), which Schöpsdau considers "loose."

25. The Assembly is usually called *sullogos* (6.755e4 and 765a6) or *koinos sullogos* (6.764a3 and 9.871a4, cf. 11.935b7), but it is significant that it is also named *ekklêsia*, like its Athenian counter-model at 6.764a3, and *dêmos* at 6.768a5 (as noted by Morrow 1993, p. 157, n. 4; cf. pp. 206–8).

26. The extended powers of the Guardians of the laws, which amount to much more than the "moral authority" depicted by Morrow (1993, p. 198), is emphasized by Reid (2020b), who notes that they have "by far the most extensive responsibilities in Magnesia (p. 572). "Moral authority" is more appropriate for the Watch, which in a sense exceeds the constitutional scheme and whose function is primarily cognitive (its members must "know the aim" of legislation, 12.962b5–6). The prominence of the Guardians of the law is indicated by the fact that the review of offices and officeholders starts with them and is emphasized by Plato: "It is but a lesser

task for the other officeholders, whereas for the Guardians of the laws, it is absolutely necessary to choose them first with utmost seriousness" (6.752d7–e2).

27. The significance of the regulations regarding participation is open to two different interpretations, depending on whether one thinks that Plato is intentionally advocating an oligarchic, anti-democratic project (this is Aristotle's views, *Politics* 2.6 1266a14–22), or that he takes into account the constraints of all those who do not have time to participate in the assemblies (Morrow's preferred reading [1993, p. 171], to which I am also inclined).

28. Direct power (1) is the power exercised, generally speaking, by certain bodies, boards or individuals in their area of competence; indirect power (2), by contrast, is the power of empowering certain citizens, i.e., of selecting political bodies, boards, or individuals that will exercise direct (or for matter further indirect) power. Direct power may be further subdivided into (1a) the power to take political decisions (technically called *kratos* or more generally *dunamis* 'power'; see in particular 4.712a1–3, which speaks to "the greatest power" concurring in the same individual with wisdom and temperance; cf. further 6.751c6); and a specific power which is the power to educate (1b). For whereas education depends on a specific office (the officeholder responsible for education) and hence is a power in sense (1a), it is not reducible to the office in question, both because education is in the hands of many citizens (the mothers, to begin with), and because it is not in any case a matter of decision, but of formation (education is a capacity/ *dunamis* of a certain sort, cf. *Laws* 1.643a4–5 and 6.747b2–3).

29. Whether this indirect procedure should be described as non- or anti-democratic depends on one's conception of democracy. Second-level empowerment is certainly a fundamental trait of indirect, modern democracies, as opposed to democratic Athens (see Stalley 1983, p. 119).

30. A famous passage in the *Menexenus* is often quoted by commentators as encapsulating the spirit, if not the letter, of Plato's constitution in the *Laws* (see in this sense Morrow 1993, p. 229). The passage (238c5–239a4) praises an idealized Athenian constitution as a regime under which "the multitude (*plêthos*) grants offices and power [of decision: *kratos*] to those who are thought best by them in each case" (238d4–5), and as "an aristocracy (*aristocratia*) with the recognition [*eudoxia*, usually translated with 'approval,' a sense for which LSJ opens a separate entry] from the many (*plêthous*)" (238 d1–2, trans. Ryan modified). It should be added that Plato emphasizes that the regime in question is called by some a democracy, by others by some other name ("as he wishes," 238d1), and that it also involves kings (238d2), even if their political role is a minor one. The parallel with the *Laws* is the more difficult to assess in that the *Menexenus* is arguably a parodical praise of the Periclean regime, a parody which "condemns in praising and praises in condemning," according to Loraux's 1974 formula (1974, p. 230, my trans.). The *Menexenus* certainly goes further than the *Laws* by presenting the multitude as "having power on most affairs of the city" (*enkrates de tês poleôs ta polla to plêthos*); cf. Chap. 5, pp. 82–83. The confrontation between the two texts remains intriguing.

31. "Ce n'est point un ouvrage de politique, comme le pensent ceux qui ne jugent des livres que par leurs titres; c'est le plus beau traité d'éducation qu'on ait jamais fait" (p. 250 of the Édition de la Pléiade). In this tradition, see further Natorp 1922.

32. Plato gives two different versions of the selection in question. The procedure is summarized by Reid (2020b, pp. 572–73): the Guardians of the laws, who must be over 50, are "originally chosen by 100 people of Knossos and 100 of the new colonists (752e6–7, 754c6–7).

Once the city is established, those who are serving or have served in the cavalry or infantry 'in their prime' place tablets with their name and the candidate's name in the temple; for at least 30 days, anyone can remove a candidate's tablet; after this, up to 300 of the leading candidates' tablets are displayed; then, anybody can nominate a candidate; from this, the 100 leading candidates are displayed; the final 37 is elected from this group (753b4–d6)." Morrow's 1993 explanation (pp. 204–9), remains dependent (with some modifications) on Wilamowitz (1910, pp. 398–402), who considered that the two procedures described to represent two alternative versions, between which Plato would have chosen, had he had the possibility to revise his work. But Saunders (1970) has convincingly shown that the two selections of the 37 Guardians correspond to two different moments, before and after the constitution is in place (correcting Morrow, who considered that the second selection concerned only piecemeal replacements of the body originally selected; see p. 232).

33. Benveniste (1969, vol. 1, pp. 321–33) argues, against the commonly accepted view, that *eleutheros*/free originally means "belonging to an ethnic stock designated by a metaphor of vegetal growth," p. 324, my trans. This can come as a support for a reading of freedom as a positive concept in Plato (in this sense, see Muller 1997, pp. 49–57).

34. Whether this is also true of Plato's just city in the *Republic* is debated. Vlastos (1981) assumed that the reason why Plato mentions slavery in the relevant sense only incidentally (at 4.433d3) is that he takes its existence for granted; Cynthia Patterson defends the contrary view in a 2017 (unpublished) paper which she kindly communicated to me.

35. The idea is that human *nous* is not really free, since it has to fight against irrational psychic motivations.

36. See Chap. 1, p. 22.

37. Lane (2018, p. 710 and n. 34) construes the expression 'slavery to the law' as a synecdoche for 'rule of the law' ("[the] less comprehensive instance is used to indicate the broader whole"). This analysis is not objectionable at a linguistic level, but it seems to me that it neutralizes the force of the expression, since the broader term, which is supposed to be 'indicated' by the narrower one, does not imply what is specific to the latter, which is the important point. This is why I prefer to look at the formula as a metaphor, the transfer being from household to a certain political relationship. In both analyses, however, what is targeted is 'strict obedience.'

38. See Chap. 4, pp. 66–67.

39. Here is the full quote: "Well for these reasons a man must be confident about his own soul who in his life has bid farewell to the other pleasures, those of the body and its adornment, as being alien to him, thinking he'll accomplish more harm than good, and has eagerly pursued those pleasures of learning and has regulated his soul to no alien adornment, but to its own: with temperance, justice, courage, freedom, and truth; and thus he awaits the journey to Hades in order to proceed when the appointed hour calls" (*Phaedo* 114d8–115a3, trans. Emlyn-Jones and Preddy).

40. "Many attempts have been made to confuse independence and liberty. These two things are so different that they are even mutually exclusive. [...] Whoever is master cannot be free, and to rule is to obey [...]. Thus there is no liberty without laws, nor where someone is above the laws [...] A free people obeys, but [...] does not serve; it has leaders and not masters; it

obeys the laws, but it obeys only the laws, and it is from the force of the laws that he does not obey men [. . .]" (Rousseau, in the 8th of his *Letters written from the mountain*, 1764, trans. Vaughan). Rousseau is more interesting as a point of comparison than the Stoic conception of freedom as "the power of acting by oneself" (*exousia autopragias*, Diogenes Laertius 7.121; discussed in Burnyeat, forthcoming). Characteristically, Plato is only marginally mentioned in M. Frede's 2011 book on the concept of 'free will' in Antiquity. Lane's 2018 article, which emphasizes that Plato's conception of freedom is anchored in the traditional sense of 'independence,' considers that Plato here offers a corrective to Rousseau's construal of 'liberty,' rather than an anticipation of it; not so Muller 1997 (for example, pp. 19–20), which I am closer to, although my position is divided: "Rousseau and Kant redefined 'freedom' in terms of obedience to the law, and this is a conceptual move that Plato could certainly have entertained. He did not, however" (Laks 2007c, p. 143).

41. See Chap. 7, p. 22.

42. *Republic* 1.329c3–4. For further references to pre-Platonic authors and secondary literature on the issue, see Lane 2018, esp. p. 705 with n. 22.

43. See Chap. 5, p. 75.

44. I could not find any evidence that La Boétie, author of the famous pamphlet *On Voluntary Servitude or Against the One* (*De la servitude volontaire ou Contr'Un*, 1553) knew of Plato's use of the expression in the *Laws*. Günther's 1980 review of La Boétie's ancient sources (pp. 99–104) does not mention the work, but suggests that he may have been aware of the relevant passage in the *Symposium* quoted above. What is beyond doubt is that La Boétie uses the formula in a non-metaphorical sense; there is no virtue, for him, that can redeem servitude. La Boétie defends a kind of a liberty that Plato would hardly have recognized as legitimate, although tyranny is the target in both cases.

45. For a discussion of the semantic field of *hêkon* and a justification of its rendering with 'voluntary,' see Meyer 1993, pp. 9–14, who notes the 'elasticity' of the term (see also Meyer 2015, p. 90, at 627e2–3).

46. Muller (1997), however, dissociates rather than associates voluntariness (*hêkôn*) and freedom (pp. 94–100), while recognizing that "for an act to be free, it must be in the power of the person that accomplishes it, that it belongs to him in a certain way," he also notes that "the type of question that concerns [voluntariness] is less ambitious, less abstract, less radical than the other" (p. 97; my trans.).

47. Similar issues are raised the phrase *eph'hêmin*/in our power (cf. Horn 2014, p. 300 and M. Frede 2014, pp. 356–57).

48. See especially, in Book 9 (which deals with the greatest crimes), 866d5, 867c5, 868c2, 869d5–6, 872b4, 879a2–3, 882a2, and b3–4; see also 6.761e1 and 8.842 d2. The same legal use is the basis of inclusive formulas at 2.665c2–3, 8.838d7, 11.930d3–4 and 936b7, 12.949c6 and 954e5–6; see also 9.874c2, 881c2 and d7–8, 10. 909c2 and c5, 11.914a5–7 and c1, 927d6, 932d3–4, and 937a5.

49. A well-known example of tension between status on the one hand, norm and progressive re-semanticization on the other hand is provided by the pair good/bad (*agathos/kakos*), which referred to social status before it acquired a moral dimension that then became an independent criterion. The story of this differentiation has often been told through an evolutionary scheme that has led to misapprehensions of specific pieces of evidence (for instance in the case of

Simonides' *Ode to Scopas* quoted in Plato's *Protagoras,* on which see Most 2019, especially pp. 426–32). This is not to say that there was no semantic evolution. The only question is how to construe the evolution, which typically leads to accumulation rather than replacement, and consequently to tensions and conflicts.

50. This is what it is to be 'educated'/*pepaideumenos.* The notion is developed by Aristotle (cf. Aubenque 1963, pp. 282–89).

51. There are, however, principles that apply both to free persons, slaves, and children: punishment, should neither be dishonorable nor provoke anger (see 7.793e5–794a2).

52. Cf. 8.845c4–d3; 849c5–d5; cf. 9.919d2–e2.

53. Aristotle defines 'liberality' as the mean between meanness and prodigality (*Nicomachean Ethics,* 4.1, e.g., 1120b27–28).

54. One can see why Leo Strauss used in this context the aristocratic, old fashioned term *gentleman,* which has a specific philosophical function in Strauss' political thinking. Many thanks to Julia Annas, who pointed out to me (*per litt.*) that the term "ceased to pick out a clear social group some time between 1811 (Jane Austen, *Pride and Prejudice,* vol. 3, chap. 14) and 1879 (Anthony Trollope, *The Duke's Children,* chap. 8 (published 1879)." It is still used in Bury's (1926) rendering (in the Loeb collection) of the first sentence of [T10]: "What is becoming, what unbecoming for a gentleman (*to eleutherikon kai aneleutheron*) it is not easy to fix by law."

55. The relevant passages in the *Gorgias* are at 464b2–465e1 and 467c5–10 and in the *Statesman* at 293a6–c3; see Chap. 7, pp. 114–17.

56. See Chap. 7, p. 111.

57. The way in question, that of free persons who are free of any material work, has been described in a striking passage, at 7.806d7–807c1. The long passage is worth quoting for its violence and evaluation of one aspect of Plato's second-best constitution: "What then would be the way of life of human beings for whom the necessities were organized in due measure, for whom technical skills were handed over to others, whose farms were assigned to slaves [806e] who would deliver a portion of the products of the land sufficient to allow human beings to live in an orderly way, with common meals (*sussitia*) organized for the men, and nearby common meals for the members of their families, including female children and their mothers? At all of these common tables there would be male and female rulers assigned to dismiss each of them, having observed and watched over the conduct of the common meal each day; then, after the ruler and the others had poured [807a] a libation to whichever gods the particular night and day might happen to be consecrated, they would thus make their way home. To lives ordered in this way, is there no necessary and wholly appropriate activity left, but is each of them to live out his life getting fattened up, like a cow? We assert that this is not at all just, nor noble, nor is it possible for one who lives this way to avoid the appropriate fortune: for it's appropriate that an idle, soft-spirited, and fattened animal usually is ravaged by one of [807b] those other animals who have been worn very hard with courage and labors. Of course, these things we're now seeking probably wouldn't ever be realized with adequate precision so long as women and children and homes are private (*idiai*), and all such things are organized privately (*idiôs*) by each of us. But if the second-best arrangements after those would come into being for us as they've now been described, things would achieve a verty good measure" (trans. Pangle with modifications).

58. In Chap. 5, pp. 79–80.

59. In Chap. 7, pp. 120–23 and 9, p. 132.

Chapter 7. Construing the Preambles

1. Ostwald (1969, p. 1, n. 3) illustrates the variety of meanings taken by the term on the basis of its use in Plato: "In some examples taken at random from Plato *nomos* denotes (a) a conventional linguistic usage (*Crat.* 384d7, 388d12, *Tim.* 60e2); (b) a customary practice (*Symp.* 182a7, *Laws* 7.795a1); (c) a conventional belief (*Gorg.* 482e6, *Laws* 10.889e6, 890 d4, 6, 904 a 9); (d) a norm of individual behavior (*Rep.* 9.587c2, 10.604a10, b6, 607a7, *Polit.* 291e2, *Laws* 2.674 b7, 8.835e5, 836e4); (e) a religious practice (*Phaedo* 58b5, *Phaedrus* 256d7); (f) a condition of law-and-order (*Rep.* 9.587a10, *Laws* 6.780d5,10.904c9)." To which one should add the musical *nomos*, which Plato exploits (see below, n. 45). For the intellectual debates about the concept of *nomos* in the archaic and classical periods, see Heinimann 1945, Romilly 1971, and Gigante [1956] 1993; for an analysis of the historical evidence (especially epigraphical) that goes against philosophical rationalizations see Hölkeskamp 1992. On law in Plato's *Laws* and more generally in his political philosophy, see Lisi 1985 and 2000 (the latter partly against my previous work on the subject) and Kamtekar and Singpurwalla 2022.

2. See Chap. 1, p. 19, on the relationship between *nomos, nous* and *dianomê*.

3. Plato, *Protagoras* 337d2–3 (Hippias 86C1DK, D17 LM). On the likely displacement (from 'convention' to 'law') that the allusion implies, see Chap.1, n. 33. Antiphon, 87B44 DK=D38 LM, Frag. A, col. II.

4. The fragment in question (= Frag. 169a Maehler) is quoted by Callicles in the *Gorgias*, 484b1–c3: "I think Pindar, too, refers to what I'm saying in that song in which he says that *nomos, the king of all, / Of mortals and the immortal gods*—this, he says, *Brings on and renders just what is most violent / With towering hand. / I take as proof of this / The deeds of Heracles. For he . . . unbought. . . .* His words are something like that—I don't know the song well—he says that Heracles drove off Geryon's cattle, even though he hadn't paid for them and Geryon hadn't given them to him, on the grounds that this is what's just by nature, and that cattle and all the other possessions of those who are worse and inferior belong to the one who's better and superior." (trans. Zeyl, slightly modified). There are two other references to these lines (or more exactly to the interpretation Plato gives of them) in the *Laws*, at 4.715a1–2 and 10.890a4–5. On the history of their reception, which hangs in part on whether *nomos* is taken as 'custom' or 'law,' see Pini 1974 and Gigante [1956] 1993.

5. See Chap. 2, p. 32. and 5, p. 79.

6. On the correct way to punctuate the passage, see Schöpsdau vol.1, p. 422 *ad* 690b8-c3. The reference to Hesiod, whose name occurs at 3.690e2, is implicit, but transparent (cf. *Works and Days*, 275–89).

7. Cf. Chap. 4, p. 67.

8. See on the one hand, one Gortynian law: "If one copulates by force with a free man or a free woman, he shall pay one hundred staters; and if [. . .] a free man with a serf (*woikeus* or *woikea*), five drachmas; and if a serf with a serf, five staters" (72 II 2–10; quoted by Davies 2005, p. 314); and on the other, the definition of the law as "recommendations mixed with threats" in Seneca's *Letter* 94.37, cf. Appendix C. For a listing of Plato's most severe penalties–death, beatings, confiscation of property, or exile—cf. for example 10.890c3–5.

9. For the biographical pattern of Plato's legislation, see Chap. 1, p. 29 and Chap. 8, n. 4. In a sense, the law on marriage is itself preceded by legislative considerations about funerals in the discussion between the poet and the lawgiver (see below, p. 112. Human life is cyclical, after all.

10. The preverb *ep-* in the compound *epapeilêsas* could refer to this addition rather than simply mark direction ('address a threat *towards* someone').

11. This is because what is at stake is persuasion.

12. On the issue of the flexibility of the word 'voluntary'/*hêkôn*, see Chap. 6, p. 101 with n. 45.

13. An additional aspect of the violence exercised by the law, from Plato's perspective, comes from the fact that it is written, which makes it mute and thus irresponsive to questions (see *Statesman* 294b8–c4, in the wake of the criticism of writing in the *Phaedrus*, 275d5–9; cf. *graptôi nomôi biazomenon*, *Laws* 6.773e3–4). In the *Laws*, however, laws-with-preambles *are* written. This is, according to an argument that is put forward by Clinias but which the Athenian endorses, to the benefit of the citizens who can always return to them, study, and understand them (10.890e6–891a7).

14. See Chap. 1, p. 17 and below, the next section.

15. Brisson (2000, p. 236, n. 3) thinks this restrictive clause is "fatal" to any interpretation, such as the one I defend (agreeing on this point with Bobonich 2002, pp. 97–119), that allows persuasion (in this case, legislative persuasion) to go beyond exhortation and myth (to capture through those two terms whatever may belong to the sphere of non-rational discourse). The citizens of the *Laws*, however, are definitely not an indiscriminately uneducated crowd, although some of them will be more educated, some less; there is at least one preamble that is directed to highly educated persons, although these are atheists; and the other preambles reveal various degrees of rationality (see Chap. 8). The question is, rather, what work the sentence at stake is doing in the context in which it appears. Schöpsdau, vol. 2, p. 244, is on the right track, I think, when he notes that "the Athenian thinks of the new settlers, who have not yet received the education that is foreseen for the citizen of Magnesia" (my trans.); but one could go one step further and say that ancient legislators, to begin with, also had to do with an uneducated folk, arguably even more so.

16. The transmitted *makhên* was felt to be too strong in the context and to lack the expected symmetry with 'persuasion.' Various corrections have been proposed, such as *anagkên*/coercion, Ast; *tagên*/ order, Apelt; *arkhên*/command, Stallbaum and Badham. In Laks 1988 ("Note textuelle" *ad loc.*), I suggested that *makhê*/fight is not out of question (see also Lisi 1999, p. 386, note *ad loc.*, although he prints a crux in the text). Note that the fight between good and evil is an eternal one on earth (cf. *Theaetetus* 176a5–8) as well as in the universe as a whole (*Laws* 10.906a2–6). Cities are a place among others where this fight occurs.

17. See below Chap. 9, pp. 137–38.

18. As Schöpsdau notes, vol. 2, pp. 203–4.

19. Frag. 14 F Bernabé (II/1, pp. 25–26 with the numerous parallels and variants quoted in the critical apparatus). Cf. Frag. 21 Kern = 1B6DK and DERV. T12c LM.

20. Cf. 10.897c4–899a10, with the correspondence between "according to nature"/*kata phusin* and *phusin* at 10.897c6, and "completing its revolution" /*periporeuomenos* and *peripherei*, at 898e8 and e10.

21. Cf. Chap. 1, p. 18 and n. 26.

22. Plato is here tacitly applying the saying, already attested in the *Odyssey* (17.218), according to which "like is dear to like" (cf. *Lysis* 214a6).

23. The inclusive plural "we" (*hêmas*) replaces here the particularizing singular *ton emphrona* of 716b6–7, the man in his senses.

24. "Lack" and "excess" are what the *Statesman* calls "the extremes" (*ta eskhata*), 284e7–8, cf. *elleipseôn kai huperbolôn*, 285b7 (see Chap. 6, p. 88).

25. The mention of "two speeches" accentuates the Protagorean profile of the poet, but also stands for multiplicity in general. Note that the lawgiver would not deny that adaptation to circumstances is necessary in all cases, given that he defends proportional rather than arithmetic equality (see Chap. 6), provided that the norm itself remains unchanged.

26. The terminology regarding 'preamble' and its functions is shifting, in agreement with its flexible nature. 4.720a1 is the only occurrence in the *Laws* of the feminine substantive *paramuthia*. The neuter *paramuthion* occurs at 6.773e5, 9.880a7, and 11. 923c2; the verb *paramutheisthai* at 9.854a6, 10.899d6, and 11.928a1–2 (cf. Brisson 1998, pp. 120–21 and p. 152 for a list of the frequent occurrences of these terms in other dialogues).

27. The plural "laws" in the formula "the beginning of the laws" refers both to the laws as a whole and to each individual law (although not every law will need to be introduced by a preamble, cf. 4.723c1–d4).

28. Maslov (2002) argues—in a context that does not concern Plato—that the term *prooimion* originally referred to a prayer or an invocation addressed to the god before a journey; the word would derive from *oimos*, in the sense of 'route,' which he argues is in turn derived from the verb-root *ei-*, meaning 'to go,' rather than *oimê*, 'song,' pp. 198–203. On this hypotheis, a *prooimion* originally had the status of an independent piece. I wondered for a moment whether Plato's legislative utopia could be construed as a reactivation of this original meaning. Etymology, however, goes against Maslov's hypothesis, as Gregory Nagy told me (*per litt.*), since the Attic by-form of *prooimion, phroimion,* shows that the verb-root must be *sei-,* meaning 'to thread,' not *ei-* (see now Nagy 2021).

29. The term *prostagma,* which primarily refers to the law conceived as a command, can also apply to the preamble, cf. 10.891a1 with Schöpsdau's note *ad loc.* (vol. 3, p. 395) and above, Chap. 8, p. 119. Bertrand (1999, pp. 285–87) sees in this terminological interchange a sign of insincerity—preambles pretend to be persuasive, but in reality, they are no more than law pursued by other means. On the same line, see Fögen's (2022) virulent essay on laws, which takes Plato's preambules to be dissimulating devices, *Überredung,* not *Überzeugung* (pp. 10–11), cf. Popper 2013, p. 588, n. 10.

30. This is [T11] mentioned, but not quoted in the previous chapter, p. 105.

31. The literature on the subject is abundant (for a bibliographical orientation, see Schöpsdau, vol. 2, pp. 237–38).

32. "With all its discomfort" for *algein* in Zeyl's translation is probably too weak; cf. 521e8–522a3. The suffering is typically caused by "cutting" and "cauterizing," which Dodds in his edition of the dialogue calls "the twin horrors of pre-anaesthetic surgery" (*ad Gorgias* 465b4, pp. 210–11; cf. also 479a9–10). Cf. Heraclitus 22B58DK (even though the text is uncertain) and Hippocrates, *Aphorisms,* 7.87: "Those diseases that medicines do not cure are cured by the knife. Those that the knife does not cure are cured by fire. Those that fire does not cure must be considered incurable" (trans. Jones).

33. The description brilliantly fuses traits that refer to medical practice (cutting, burning) with others that belong to Socratic refutation, which can be harsh.

34. See Chap. 10, n. 10.

35. On this issue, see Appendix A, pp. 162–64.

36. Littré has collected the passages of the Hippocratic corpus that mention assistants (see the index in vol. 10 of his edition, s.v. 'aide'). They are one of the factors the surgeon must take into account in *The Surgery* (3.2, with the commentary of Galen *ad loc., CMG* 5, 10.2.2, pp. 257ff.; cf. 3.5). Elsewhere, their subordination is stressed (they keep silent and listen, 3.288.1). They often appear as 'another' (i.e., other than the doctor). Whether these assistants were considered doctors as described in the next lines (slave-doctors curing slave-patients) is a separate question, see next note.

37. Whether slave-doctors existed in the classical period and whether they exclusively cured slaves is an open question. It is uncertain to what extent Plato's construal of the analogy in the *Laws* relies on a sociological reality. Kudlien 1968 interprets the passage as an extended metaphorical construction (p. 35). Joly 1969 defends the realism of the description. He notes (pp. 6–10) that a significant number of slaves feature among the 450 cases or so that can be distinguished in the *Epidemics*. Between the two positions there is room for a middle ground: we might have to do here with a Platonic construction inspired by contemporary practices but not simply reflecting them. On the concept of 'freedom' that is put to use here, cf. above, Chap. 6, pp. 105–6.

38. Cf. for instance, the description of Socrates' practice in the *Laches* 187d2–3 (*didontes kai dekhomenoi logon par' allêlôn*, resulting in giving an account "of oneself," 187e10) or *Republic* 7.531e4–5 ("Did it ever seem to you that those who can neither give nor follow an account know anything at all of the things we say they must know?" trans. Grube/Reeve, cf. 6.510c6–7) and 534b3–6 ("Then, do you call someone who is able to give an account of the being of each thing dialectical?").

39. The parallels to Plato's description and terminology in the Hippocratic writings are collected by. Bourgey 1975, p. 215, and Jouanna 1978, p. 90.

40. See p. 109.

41. On the persuasiveness of which see below, Chap. 8, pp. 129–30.

42. The law in the simple version leaves undetermined the amount of the fine and the nature of the penalty. The dual version adds some specifics: unremitting bachelors will be deprived of the honors paid by the young to the elders (721d5–6), and they will be subject to an annual fine (d2–3).

43. Cf.10.890e4–6 (Clinias speaks:) "What, stranger? About drunkenness and music, we endured ourselves talking so long, but we are not going to bear it when it comes to gods and these kinds of issues?" On the appropriate length of speech, see *Theaetetus* 172d8–9 (cf. also *Protagoras*, 337e2–338b1 and *Statesman*, 283b1-c6). Cf. Lycurgus, *Against Leocrates*, 102–3; "Laws are too brief to give instruction; they merely state the things that must be done." (trans. Burtt). See further Appendix C.

44. See Chap. 6, pp. 87–89.

45. Cf. 3.700b5–6 with Schöpsdau's commentary (vol. 2, p. 510); further 4.722d6–e1 ("It is the case, I suppose, that of the songs sung to the kithara, the so-called *nomoi*, and music in general, are preceded by preludes composed with amazing seriousness," trans. Pangle) and 7.799e10–12, where the musical and legal meanings of *nomos* are put in parallel. The Peripatetic *Problems* (19.28) suggests an explanation: the laws were sung before being written (cf. Köller 1954, pp. 173ff.). For the transposition from citharoedic poetry to rhetoric, see Köller 1956 (in particular p. 188). See also Chantraine 1999 (s.v. νέμω, p. 743a), who derives the general sense of 'melody' for *nomos* (as in Alcman, Frag. 39 PMGF) and its specific application to the musical

form invented by Terpander (the 'nome') from the notion of 'appropriateness' ('convenance') and 'fit organization' ('bon arrangement').

46. Cf. also 722b4–c2 and, with reference to the present passage, 9.857c1–3. Plato's claim to innovation, as far as we can see, is legitimate, see Chap. 1, n. 19.

47. The importance of the reference to music in legislative rhetoric comes to the fore through the frequent association of preambles with *epôidê*, 'incantation' (see Chap. 8, n. 10), and through the exceptional identification of the Muse with philosophy (see Cherniss 1953, p. 377, n. 1, on 12.967e2).

48. This passage corresponds to text [T12], mentioned, but not quoted in the previous chapter (p. 93).

49. The other occurrence is found at 12.967c5–d2: "At that time, these things were the out-workings of many atheistic views and much loathing to engage with these sorts of things, and then railing even took over the poets, who were comparing those who philosophize to female dogs that vainly howl, as well as speaking other nonsense." Cf. Chap. 4, n. 32.

50. Laughs and mockeries are often a strong signal that a crucial issue is at stake: the sarcasm of the Thracian maid in the *Theaetetus* 174a4–8; the reaction Socrates expects to be triggered by his proposals in the *Republic* at 5.452a7–c2 that naked women exercise in common with men; at 5.473c7–8, on a different level, about philosopher-rulers. In the *Laws*, women laugh at 7.790a5–6 when it comes to legislation related to how to handle newborns (cf. Laks 2013b).

51. The model is distinct from, but reminiscent of a medicine that does not heal the body before healing the soul, as evoked at the beginning of the *Charmides*. There, the "incantations" (*epôidai*) recommended by the Thracian king Zalmoxis and his doctors (156d4–157c1) are con-strued by Plato as "beautiful speeches" (157a3–5, cf. 157c1–6).

52. In an extremely valuable article devoted essentially to discussion of Bobonich (1991 and 2002) and Schofield (2006), but which refers at various junctures to my previous work (partly approvingly, partly critically), Lane (2010) emphasizes the discontinuity between the situation evoked in the analogy, which would imply the necessity of 'legislating,' and the 'present' situa-tion of a free conversation between the interlocutors of the dialogue, who are under no obliga-tion to legislate (pp. 189–91). I insist, by contrast, on the continuity between the two moments. The free discussion between the three interlocutors represents the analogue of what a medical conversation would be between a free doctor and his free patient: both sides have the leisure to pursue it. I take it that the force of the Athenian's reply—"Perhaps he would, if (*takh'an, ei . . .*) he were to bear in mind this further point, that anyone who discusses the laws in a detailed way as we are now doing, is educating the citizens, not legislating" (9.857e3)—is that he is ready to recognize that what the slave doctor says is correct under a condition that in fact strips the objec-tion of its force: surely the Athenian is arguing in favor of a free, pedagogical conception of legislation, as far as possible. This is another instance of the recurring literary scheme whereby an opponent—here, the slave doctor—plays into the hands of the lawgiver. For the case of the poet in Book 4, see above, pp. 112–13. A further example would be the way in which the lawgiver makes use, in Book 7, of women's resistance to the idea of introducing laws about early child-hood in order to promote the notion of 'unwritten laws'; see Laks 2013b, pp. 180–84. (Many thanks to Melissa Lane who pressed me on this issue, on which we may still diverge, in our discussions at Princeton in the spring 2019 and afterwards.)

53. Laks 1991 (pp. 426–27) and 2005 (p. 107), cf. also by Lane 2010, pp. 190–91, cf. p. 174.

54. Cf. the expression *biazesthai tois logois* ("force by arguments") at 10.903a10 to refer to a refutation, as opposed to incantations through tales (b10–11).

55. Brisson (2000, p. 241), criticizing Bobonich's 1991 talk of 'rational persuasion,' considers that the expression is a contradiction in terms once the theory of Forms has been introduced (which would not yet be the case with the *Gorgias*, where *didakhê* / scientific teaching is presented at 454e3–4 as a species of *peithô* / persuasion): unchangeable scientific knowledge is the exclusive property of the Forms; of the changing world, there are only opinions that are themselves unstable and open to "persuasion" (the main passages quoted are *Theaetetus* 201a7–c7 and *Timaeus* 51d3–e6, pp. 240–41; cf. also *Phaedrus*, which states at 277c3–6 that a philosopher in possession of the truth can use the art of discourse either to teach or to persuade). But in the *Sophist*, Plato talks of "an argument accompanied by constraining persuasion" ([*logos*] *meta peithous anagkaias*, 265d7, which White is right to translate, it seems to me, as "cogent, persuasive argument." This is not the place to discuss issues of evolution in Plato's thought. The important point is that there is clearly a sense in which some preambles are more rational than others. This does not mean that I am embracing Bobonich's position (as will be clear in the next chapter). As Brisson himself recognizes, even though he tends to associate my position with Bobonich's, I consider teaching in the *Laws* as an *ideal* horizon of persuasion, and therefore distinct from ordinary forms of persuasion. On Brisson's two specific objections to my reading (one concerning 4.722b6–7, the other the status of the first didactic preamble of Book 10), see Chap. 7, n. 27 and Chap. 9, p. 142.

56. I introduced the idea of a utopia internal to the *Laws* in Laks 1991. There, I distinguished the legislative utopia of the *Laws* from the constitutional utopia of the *Republic*. I am now using the formula less restrictively.

Chapter 8. A Rhetoric in the Making

1. See Chap. 2, p. 32.

2. The debate was launched by Bobonich's (1991 and 2002) excessively rationalistic reading of the preambles. On the confused character of the debate, see Lisi 2000, pp. 58–59, who talks rightly of a "continuum" of persuasive means, ranging from philosophical persuasion to extreme forms of coercion (pp. 71–72); see further Laks 2007a (responding to Brisson 2000 and Lane 2010). Fossheim (2013) insists on the personal dimension of the preambles. This is certainly one aspect of their flexibility, although the 'you' to whom some preambles are explicitly addressed is evidently generic.

3. The count is approximate for a variety of reasons. On the one hand, not all the laws stated in the *Laws* are preceded by a preamble. Leaving aside the cases where this absence may be contingent (the work is unfinished), the Athenian explicitly declares that "even though there does exist by nature a preamble for all of them, it ought not to be employed in every case" (4.723c8–d2). This may be because some laws are more important than others (cf. 723c6–8) or else derivative; on the other hand, a number of considerations that could have been subjects of a preamble are not fleshed out in the form of a regular preamble (see for example 11.913c1–d3), or not followed by any law, or take the form of a meta-legislative development. This occurs for example at 8.837c2–842a2, which deals with sexual behavior, and 9.857b8–864e7, where the issue is homicide. See also the famous passage of Book 9.874e7–875d6 on the corrupting effect of

power (Chap. 2, pp. 45–47), which is introduced as a preamble of sorts to the law on assault. For a more extensive listing of preambles and preamble-like passages, see Brisson and Pradeau 2006, vol. 2, pp. 384–86.

4. For a clear formulation of the biographical pattern, see 12.958c7–d3, justifying the legislation's turn to wills: "After this, for a man who has been born and brought up, and has begotten and brought up children, and has mingled in business transactions with due measure—paying judicial penalties if he has done someone an injustice and receiving the same from another—or a man who has aged according to destiny in the company of the laws, the end would come, according to nature." The biographical pattern also explains why the discussion between the poet and the lawgiver (see Chap. 7, p. 112) deals with burials, which mark the end of a generation, before a new one begins.

5. Young citizens in the first place, but Plato also mentions more generally "domestic servants, as well as foreigners and the slaves of foreigners" (9.853d8–10). The prejudice is patent; in this case as elsewhere.

6. 'Honor' (*timê*), as distinguished by its specific object from "praise," is another term to consider in this context, see Chap. 9, p. 138. On *eumenês* and *eumathês* (forms of which appear jointly at 4.723a3–7, with the second subordinated to the first), see Schöpsdau, vol. 2, pp. 228–29 (cf. also Görgemanns 1960, pp. 40–42). Praise and blame are tightly associated with education, see e.g., 5.730b5–c1: "After this we must turn to all those things that not law, but praise as well as blame achieve by education (*paideuôn*): that each [citizen] may become easier to guide (*euênios*) and well-disposed (*eumenês*) to the laws that are going to be laid down."

7. Aristotle, *Rhetoric* 1.3.1358a1–b13.

8. On the narrowness of Aristotle's definition of epideictic rhetoric, as well as its surprisingly idiosyncratic traits, see Rapp in his translation of Aristotle's *Rhetoric*, vol. 2, p. 390 ("eng"). The choice of the term 'epideictic' to refer to a kind of discourse the exclusive aim of which is to praise virtue (cf. *Rhetoric* 1.9.1366a23–33 and 1367b26–28) strikes us as weird, because Plato and the rhetorical tradition after him links it with sophistic performances (cf. *Gorgias*, 447a5–c4); see Rapp's note *ad* 1.3,1358b8, vol. 2, pp. 257–58 and p. 390 ("vorführende Rede," his suggested translation for *epideiktikos logos*, seeks to capture the specificity of Aristotle's conception). It is most significant for the scholarly neglect of the *Laws* that Rapp's commentary does not mention it in his analysis of 1.9 (Rapp refers to Isocrates' *Evagoras* as a plausible background for Aristotle's characterization of an *epideiktikos logos*). On the post-Aristotelian, scholastic organization of the *genos epideiktikon* (*genus demonstrativum*), see Lausberg's 1973[2], §§239–254.

9. Most relevant to the *Laws* (and to the difference between Plato's and Aristotle's perspectives) is Aristotle's observation, at *Rhetoric* 1.9 1367b38–68a10, that praise (*epainos*) and advisories (*sumboulai*) have something (a 'form') in common (*koinon eidos*) that allows for "transpositions" (*metatithenai*, 1367b38 and 68a3). On the marginality of mixed forms, see Rapp (trans. 2002), vol. 2, *ad* 3.13 1414b3 and 3.17 1417b36.

10. References to *muthos* in Lausberg 1973 all relate to poetics, not to rhetoric, with one exception that concerns the composition of animal tales. There is no entry for *epôidê*. The occurrences of the word and the corresponding verb *epaidein* are frequent in the *Laws* (cf. e.g., 2.659e1; 664b4; 665c4, 666c6 and 671a1; 6.773d6; 7.812c6; 8.837e6; and 12.944b3), cf. Brisson 1998, pp. 77–80; Mouze 2005, Chap. 3; and Schöpsdau, vol. 1, p. 288–89. Gastaldi (1984, pp. 94–100) presents Plato as taking a middle position on the question of incantation, between its original

associations with thaumaturgy and its rationalization by Gorgias (see also Lain-Entralgo 1958 and 1970, pp. 120–27; Belfiore 1980). In the *Euthydemus*, 289e4–6, rhetoric is introduced as "a part of the craft of incantations"—a part, moreover, which is "slightly inferior to it," because its addressees are much more restricted (it concerns human beings, not animals). On the role of *epôidê in healing*, the classic passage is *Charmides*, 156d3–157c6 (cf. Chap. 7, n. 51). It is significant that Aristotle uses the word, disparagingly, on one single occasion (*History of animals* 9.24.605a4–6).

11. See Chap. 7, p. 113.

12. Contrast 4.721b1–3, quoted Chap. 7, p. 109.

13. Müller 1951 (p. 172) thought of these differences as a regression.

14. "[. . .] what was said before this, namely that one must adhere to ever-generative nature (*khrê tês aeigenous phuseôs antekhesthai*) by successively leaving behind children of children as servants of the gods to replace oneself" (6.773e6–774a1).

15. The Demiurge mentions explicitly in his discourse to the secondary divinities (41a7–d3) that the indestructibility of the world as a whole implies the indestructibility of the species of mortal living beings without which the world would not be complete. The desire for procreation, however, is mentioned only at the very end of the *Timaeus* as a consequence of the appearance of women as the reincarnations of ethically deficient males (90e6–91a1).

16. See Rowe 2010, p. 49, whose point is that the passage is directed, even more than to the two interlocutors, to the reader of Plato's other works (cf. also Rowe 2016, pp. 87–88). The contrast between the colonists, that "They'll just have to take it or leave it" and the reader who "can, and presumably, should, ask questions" (p. 49) is well taken. For a similar case, see Chap. 7, p. 111.

17. It is to this that the expression "a certain nature" at 721b7–8, which was athetized by Schanz, probably refers. Rowe (2010, p. 49) thinks of human *rational* nature.

18. Some aspects of the educative program, in particular concerning choral dance, are understandably anticipated in the course of Books 1 and 2, see Chap. 4, pp. 69–70. Book 7 provides the systematic picture (see Schöpsdau, vol. 2, pp. 499–504).

19. Not only or even primarily the body, as suggested by the chart in Schöpsdau, vol. 2, p. 502. The ethical ideal represented by hunting is well developed by Annas 2017, pp. 98–101. On hunting as a part of 'classical' education, see Schnapp 1997, Chap. 4.

20. Condemnation of sleeping: *Phaedrus*, 259a1–b2, cf. *Laws* 7.808b5–c2.

21. It is not hard to fathom why Plato sees this choice as persuasive: for him the only legitimate form of hunting is the one that is 'aristocratic' in nature and so consistent with his conception of a free life (see Chap. 6, p. 103 [T3]).

22. Not to marry is a crime against the species, just like committing suicide (cf. *Phaedo*, 62b6–c4). The *Laws* is more nuanced (see below, n. 33).

23. *Muthos* refers here to the content of the following sentence, introduced by *gar*, which states a principle. The term is best interpreted in the light of its primitive connotation, "authoritative statement" (cf. Martin 1989, p. 13, n. 42 and p. 68). Schöpsdau's translation captures this: "Überhaupt soll [. . .] nur ein Wort gelten" (cf. above, Chap. 4, n. 14).

24. Cf. Chap. 4, p. 70, on the issue of musical taste.

25. Another good illustration of Plato's handling of 'private' behaviors is provided by the legislation in Book 7.786c6–814c1 about how pregnant women and young mothers should behave (cf. Laks 2013b).

26. This divide does not necessarily imply the existence of a category of laws that would not be punitive in the sense of Book 4.722b4–c1. If laws tend towards advice in this case, it is because of the quality of the addressee. The use of the word 'teaching' is significant, even if the issue at stake is limited in scope. For a similar use of the verb *didaskein* in the first version of the medical analogy, see Chap. 7, p. 114 and the General Index under "teaching."

27. Cf. above, p. 221, n. 5.

28. Cf. 9.872e2 with 873a3–4. At 5.728c2–5, retaliation is distinguished from 'fair' *dikê*, which cures.

29. On the temporary success of injustice and ultimate inescapability of justice, see 10.905a1–c1. Whether punishment is immediate or not, it is said to be quick. What is inescapable is always, in a way, already accomplished, even if it is slow to come (cf. Solon, Frag.1.13–31 Gentili-Prato).

30. On the Athenian's flexible attitude toward names, see Chap. 5, n. 18.

31. The two verbs *humnein* and *epaidein* are associated at 7.812c5–6.

32. About this construal of voluntariness, see Chap. 6, p. 101 and 7, p. 109.

33. The condemnation of suicide in 9.873c2–d1 also makes room for this exception.

Chapter 9. Two Exceptional Preambles

1. See Chap. 7, esp. pp. 113–18.

2. See Chap. 1, p. 29.

3. See Chap. 1, p. 28; for a different, but analogous case, see Chap. 7, p. 123.

4. Hentschke (1971, pp. 266–73) is right to read the whole preamble as a Socratic ideal of life (see especially pp. 271–72); cf. also Gaiser 1959, pp. 215–16.

5. *Nicomachean Ethics* 1.12 1101b10–27. The division between *timia* and *epaineta* also features in (Ps.-?) Aristotle's *Magna Moralia*, 1.2 1183b20–27 and in the Aristotelian *Divisions* (Frag. 1 Ross = Alexander of Aphrodisias, *Commentary on the Topics*, p. 242, 3–9 Wallies). A series of overlaps makes it likely that this division belongs to an Academic theory of goods.

6. See Chap. 4, p. 67.

7. As Schöpsdau indicates (vol. 2, pp. 211–12), the article *hô* should not be added before *adikos* at 716d3, as is often done by the editors.

8. At *Laws* 9.875b7, Plato coins a wonderful word in order to refer to the principle of self-centered, egoistic action (in agreement with a certain conception of the 'self'): *idiopragia*, "action in one's own private interests." The term is coupled there with *pleonexia*, the drive towards acquiring more. *Oikeios*, which etymologically refers to the household (*oikos*), commonly applies not only to the individual himself, but to his family and relatives. In a kind of inverted extension of the 'household' terminology, Plato uses the term to refer to what 'truly' belongs to me—my 'innermost' self. The coining of *idiopragia* at this crucial juncture in the *Laws* echoes another of Plato's coinages, that of the term *oikeiopragia* at *Republic* 4.434c8, also *hapax* in the Platonic corpus (on the centrality of the term *oikeios* in the *Republic*, see Murgier 2017). Interestingly, later authors who use *idiopragia* (34 occurrences according to a TLG search, most of them belonging to the Platonic and Christian tradition) probably have the word from Plato, but they don't retain the negative connotation it has in the *Laws*. On the contrary, the word regularly refers to Plato's definition of justice in the *Republic*, when all the parts of the soul mind their

own business (cf. for example Origen, *Against Celsus*, 5.47: *tous apo Platônos idiopragian tôn merôn tês psukhês phaskontas einai tên dikaiosunên*, and more generally, Hesychius' entry *idiopragei: ta idia prassei, hesukhazei*, "he minds his own business").

9. Cf. LSJ, *s.v.*, 1.2.

10. The question whether it is legitimate to accumulate goods for the benefit of one's progeny (5.729a2–b2) is tied to the preceding treatment of external goods, but it also marks a return to the discussion of (external) relationships. In each case, the rules of conduct are dictated by one's relationship to the divinity and one's soul. Respecting strangers and honoring our kin are divine duties no less than complying with the laws of the city. In the case of services given to friends, what is decisive is not to overestimate the magnitude of the assistance one is providing to them.

11. Schöpsdau, vol. 2, p. 263, signals that the praise of truthfulness was one of the most quoted passages from Plato in Antiquity.

12. This is the passage that Goldschmidt (1970a, p. 200; and cf. p. 188) construes as an anticipation of the concept of 'public opinion,' rather than as a justification of denunciation (see above, Introduction, n. 25).

13. This section closes with a paragraph devoted to laughter and tears, which must be held in check if one is to maintain a decent composure (732c1–4).

14. The point is clearly made by Warren (2013, p. 324), who notes that the argument is "in outline [. . .] a cousin of the set of arguments in *Republic* 9 that conclude that the life of the just person will contain the greatest and best pleasures (581d–588b)." "Above all" (*malista*) makes all the difference from a hedonistic position, as Warren points out (p. 323). It can be added that the adverb picks up and amplifies the idea, in the initial comparison of human beings with puppets, that the rational string is soft and weak, in contrast to the multitude of the hardened ones (1.644e6–645a4). The images for expressing the inevitability of dependence, 'hanging' and 'suspension' at 5.732e4–7 (*exêrtêsthai te kai ekkremamenon einai*), 'being tied up' at 733d2–4 (*en toutois endedemenoi pephukasin*), are the strongest in the whole work, but of course perfectly compatible with the puppet passage in Book 1 and the picture of the soul at 9.863b6–9, which presents pleasure as "exercising domination (*dunasteuousa*) by persuading humans, through the use of forceful deceit, to do whatever she wishes." The fact that human beings are so by nature (*phusei*, 732d4; *pephukasin*, 733d2) does not mean that they cannot be educated so as to give virtue the upper hand.

15. "Healthy" obviously replaces "just." The substitution can be explained both by contextual and systematic reasons (see Schöpsdau, vol. 2, pp. 285–86, who does not quote *Republic* 4.444d3–e3, which is surely relevant; cf. above, Chap. 2, p. 22). It is also interesting as a further example of the pattern that is put to work in the case of temperance / *sôphrôsunê* (see Chap. 5, p. 80).

16. For a detailed discussion of the passage, see Schöpsdau, vol. 2, pp. 271–77 and Warren 2013.

17. The general conclusion of the triple preamble is stated at 10.907b5–d3 before the formulation of the law at 907d6. The law properly speaking is itself preceded by a last preliminary proclamation (*logos hermeneus* [. . .] *proagoreuôn*), inviting the atheist to abandon his views (907d4–6).

18. The argument is regressive: there are no gods; if they exist; they do not take care of humans; if they take care of them, they can be swayed (the structure is notoriously Gorgianic, cf. Görgemanns 1960, p. 86, n. 3).

19. The reason why two kinds of preambles are being used is that psychic origin of impiety is dual. The lawgiver deals first with the "lust for pleasure" (888a3) through a (rather desperate) warning: the young atheist will change his mind as he grows older; frequenting elderly people, in particular the lawgiver (888d2), will lead him to believe in the existence of the gods he currently denies; he should therefore anticipate what will necessarily come about. He must then deal with his argument, which he describes in 888d8 as an "extraordinary" one (*thaumastos logos*) and deliver a "teaching" (*didaskein*, 888d4, picking up 888a2), as promised. The complex, carefully differentiated structure clearly makes room for the notion of a didactic preamble that is neither exhortative nor mythical. I take it that *nouthêtôn hama didaskein*, 888a1–2 does not signal simultaneity, but complementarity; see however Schöpsdau, vol. 3, p. 383.

20. The relationship of Plato's cosmological argument in *Laws* 10 to Aristotle's *Metaphysics Lambda*, however, does not seem to have detained the attention of commentators.

21. Plato collects under a single heading Hesiod's *Theogony*, Orphic cosmo-theogonies and similar (prose) works by Pherecydes and Acusilaus, all of whom tell a different story. The synthesis is of a different kind, but no less striking, than the one that follows about the more recent writings.

22. This triad echoes and replaces that put forward by the Athenian in Book 4.709b7-c3: god, chance together with occasion / *kairos*, and craft.

23. Cf. above, Chap. 7, n. 4.

24. See in this sense Hentschke 1971, p. 311 n. 30; cf. also e.g., Solmsen 1942, p. 137, n. 16. There are two interesting defenses of the alternative view. Sedley (2013), who rightly insists, against the majority of the commentators (in particular De Mahieu 1964, p. 45), on the coherence of the doctrine, subtly suggests that the anonymity of the report is equivalent to its signature—to profess atheism was dangerous and atheists had to hide their identity (for example by having dramatic character express the view on stage, as in the case of the *Sisyphus* fragment attributed either to Critias or to Euripides, 88 B25DK= DRAM. T63 GM). In a different vein, Betegh (2016) puts forward valuable arguments in defense of Archelaus' doctrine, which in his view presents a series of essential features that make it "material to" the doctrine that Plato is attacking (see esp. p. 24–32). References to older literature that looks for specific authors or trends—a follower of Antiphon or Archelaus, Prodicus, etc.—are given in De Mahieu 1964, pp. 16–17 and Sedley 2013, p. 334, n. 19. Mayhew (2008, p. 76), dismisses the question of identification because of the massive presence of references and allusions in Plato's construct, some of which no doubt escape us.

25. Aristophanes and the *Laws*: see Laks in Laks and Saetta Cottone 2013 (a volume of essays dedicated to Aristophanes and the Presocratics), pp. 231–32.

26. Cf. 1.642a1–4; 4.722a7–b1; 6.781d9–e3 (9.858a–b, listed by Schöpsdau in his note *ad* 887b1–2, vol. 3, p. 379, does not specifically concern this point). On the reason why the reminder is put in the mouth of Clinias, cf. Chap. 7, n. 13 and 43.

27. This is the 'dangerous' step in the argument, which is compared to the crossing of the powerful stream of a river. It is dangerous not only for the Athenian's interlocutors, but also for anyone who engages with it, however experienced he may be (892d2–893a7). On the soul as the non-generated and indestructible self-mover and source of movement, the main passage is *Phaedrus*, 245c5–246a2.

28. The second list at 897a1–3 is slightly more extensive than the one at 896c9–d3.

29. On the meaning and consequences of the shift from the intellect's motion to its visible image, see Lee 1976.

30. Cf. Chap. 7, p. 122.

31. And again, a little further down: "Coming from lawgivers who are deemed to be not savage but gentle, we think that it is fitting they first use persuasion with us [...]" (10.885e1–3). Clearly, what the atheists want is to be persuaded by truth (*alêtheia*, 885e5), not by myths. It might even be that the *kai* they use to link *peithein* / persuade and *didaskein*/teach at 885d2 (quoted above in text) has an explanatory value: for them to be persuaded means to be taught (see also above, Chap. 7, n. 55).

32. See 9.857d3–4, quoted Chap. 7, p. 121.

33. See. Chap. 4, pp. 71–72.

34. One is reminded of the sophist who resembles the philosopher as a wolf resembles a dog in Plato's *Sophist*, 230e6–231a6.

35. The law (10.907d7–909d2) differentiates types and degrees of impiety. Attempts at persuading the atheist will continue in jail. But the unrepentant atheist eventually will be put to death (10.909a5–8).

36. This is Brisson's (2000, pp. 242–43) perceptive but I think resistible objection to the views that I put forward in Laks 1991 and elsewhere.

37. The infinitive *hupenantiousthai* in the sentence quoted above in text has an imperative valence.

38. Heraclitus 22B58DK, Plato, *Gorgias*, 456b1–5 (Chap. 7, n. 32).

39. For a similar pattern (the objection of the poet, in Book 4.719b4–7), see Chap. 7, p. 112.

40. Schöpsdau, vol. 3, p. 383, observes rightly that this preliminary address is not strictly speaking a preamble.

41. "Only the philosophers voluntarily do what the rest of humankind does against their will, because of law." Xenocrates, Frag. 3 Heinze, quoted by Plutarch, *On moral virtue*, 7.446d. (This is the epigraph of my Chapter 7.)

Chapter 10. Plato's Best Tragedy

1. "Alles Tragisches beruht auf einem unausgleichbaren Gegensatz. Sowie Ausgleichung eintritt, oder möglich wird, schwinden das Tragische" (in F. von Müller 1956, p. 118).

2. Here is the entire passage: "[817a] As for what people say are the serious poets, the ones we see occupying themselves with tragedy, let's suppose that some of them came to us and asked us the following sort of question: 'Do we have your permission, as hosts, to enter your city and country, or not, and may we bring our poetry with us? Or what policy have you decided on in these matters?' What would be the correct response to this to give to these divine men? I think our answer is: [b] 'Most respected of guests, it's we who are the tragic writers, of the finest and also the best tragedy that we have it in us to create: thus the whole political regime (*politeia*) that we are proposing constitutes a representation (*mimêsis*) of the finest and best life, which is the very thing that we say tragedy really is, the truest sort. So, you are poets, but we are poets too, working in the same genre, your rivals and competitors for the finest play, which—so the hope is, on our side—it is the nature of true law alone to complete. [c] So don't imagine that

we'll be too ready, ever, to give you permission to set up your stage in the agora, bringing on actors with fine voices carrying further than ours, and to give you license to harangue women and the crowd at large—talking about the same practices but not saying the same things about them as we do, indeed as a general rule saying exactly the opposite, in most cases. We'd be completely mad, surely, and so would the city as a whole, [d] if it gave you that kind of license to act, before the magistrates had established in the first place whether you'd written things that should be said and were suitable for public consumption or not. So now, you scions of soft Muses, start by showing the magistrates your songs for comparison with ours, and if it's clear that you're saying the same as we do, or indeed better, we'll give you a chorus; if it's not clear, friends, we would never be able to accommodate you'" (*Laws* 7.817a2–d8). The translation is by C. Rowe (Laks 2010). On the meaning of *mimêsis* and *apotelein*, see below, n. 15.

3. See Chap. 5, pp. 83–84.

4. Cf. Chap. 1, pp. 30–31.

5. On the context of the passage, see Schöpsdau, vol. 2, pp. 583–84 and Prauscello 2014, pp. 124–25. Prauscello insists on the performative dimension of Plato's *politeia* in the *Laws*. To be sure, one can say that the constitution of the *Laws* is *in part* the representation of a life performance (in the sense of the performance of a life), cf. Laks 2010, pp. 222–23. However, there remains an important difference between the *comparandum* and the *comparans*, which should not be erased, because it is the bearer of its meaning.

6. *Republic* 2.377b11–3.398b9. For Homer as a tragic poet, and the first of them, see 10. 595b10–c2; 598d7–8; 602b8–9, 605c11, and 607a2–3. Cf. also the general characterization of tragedy in *Gorgias* 502b1–c8 as uniquely geared to the pleasure of the viewer. For other passages in Plato concerning tragedy, see below, n. 20 and 26. I leave aside here the radical, ontological criticism of *mimêsis* as 'reproduction' or 'imitation' in *Republic* 10 and its relationship to *mimêsis* as "representation" in *Republic* 2–3 and the *Laws* (and *Republic* 2–3), on which see e.g., Halliwell 1997. The *mimêsis* of the *Laws*, which represents, is neither the (mimetic and ontologically inferior) *mimêsis* of *Republic* 10 nor, despite its proximity, the (performative) *mimêsis* of Book 3, where it features in contrast to *diegêsis* ('narration'). One suggestion to distinguish these different uses would be to render *mimêsis* of *Laws* 7 with *representation*, that of *Republic* 3 with *performance* or *enactment*, and for *Republic* 10 *reproduction*. But terminological consistency is not always possible.

7. In the *Republic*, Homer's (tragic) poetry is not admitted in the just city, only hymns to the gods and praises of good individuals (10.607a2–8). In the *Laws*, the tragedians are imagined as arriving from outside (we are in Crete, in the city of the Magnesians). The *Laws*, however, is potentially more generous than the *Republic*, for it allows the possibility of tragic plots that would be in conformity with legislative standards, cf. below, pp. 152–53).

8. In a sense, this is a reply to the political dimension of the Greek tragedies themselves, which were presented in the context of the Great Dionysia. How to appreciate the nature of this political dimension, is another matter.

9. The question, which has long been tackled in an inappropriate way, has now received much more focused attention (cf. Mouze 2005, pp. 343–50, Laks 2010 and 2011, Meyer 2011, Prauscello 2014, pp. 119–28).

10. The re-appropriation of rhetoric is in fact prepared, at the end of the *Gorgias*, by the evocation of "the expert and good orator" (504d5–6). It is also not often noticed that even

Republic 10 does not exclude a redefinition of the tragedy that is rejected under a different description. At 10.604e2–5, Plato says only that to imitate a "wise and unexcitable" character is "not easy," which implies that it possible (in the straightforward sense of the term); cf. also Book 3.398a8–b4 (a passage cited by Panno 2007, p. 61, as a parallel to the relevant lines of *Laws* 7).

11. The addition of "< and comedies >" at 50b2 is due to G. Hermann and has been widely accepted since Bury's edition of the dialogue (1932). It is motivated by the coupling of comedy with tragedy in the following line.

12. 'Constitution' also refers here to a mode of life under a constitution informed by its laws—which the *Laws* organizes, as we have seen, to function along the same lines as the cyclical development of an individual life between two generations (see Chap. 8, n. 4).

13. *Poetics* 6.1449b24–25. Who is echoing the other? It is generally agreed that it is Aristotle who knows the *Laws* rather than Plato who knows the *Poetics*. On the other hand, if one were to suppose that the *Poetics* in the form in which we have it "actually contains some material first drafted before 347" (Halliwell 1986, p. 330), it is not out of the question that the passage from the *Laws*' might already have been written with an eye on Aristotle's definition.

14. Manuscript (B) substitutes the plural *praxeôn* for the singular *praxeôs*, presumably simply because a life is consists of a series of actions. This must be a well-intentioned although unnecessary intervention: whereas it is true that a tragic action is typically a particular one, its bearing will also extend to an entire life—as is confirmed, in the immediately following sentence, by the reference to 'happiness' and 'misfortune,' since these are for Aristotle fundamentally holistic concepts (cf. *Nicomachean Ethics* 1.7 1098a18–20; 10.7 1177b24–5).

15. The force of *apotelein* is lost when the verb is reduced to an auxiliary (cf. Meyer 2011, p. 393, n. 20, referring to *teleitai* at *Statesman* 288c3 and *apoteleitai* at *Laws* 2.668b6–7; note, however, her translation at p. 401: "This explains why 'true law' alone is able to 'bring to perfection' (*apotelein*) the human drama [...].")

16. Cf. Halliwell 1984, p. 58: "The *Phaedo* gives vivid form to the idea later found in the *Laws* that 'the finest and best life is the best tragedy' (817b), in a passage that, in the boldest and most provocative of Plato's dramatic metaphors, sets up the philosophical life as an alternative to the life of the tragic hero." For the *Apology*, cf. Cameron 1978, pp. 32–33. Of course, Plato does not think in the relevant passage of the *Laws* about "philosophical life."

17. Kuhn 1941, p. 63 [= 1960, p. 296].

18. Kuhn 1941, p. 36–7 [= 1960, p. 267–68]. Kuhn borrows from Cornford (1937, pp. 361–64) the idea of a parallel between Aeschylean trilogies and the sequence *Timaeus-Critias-Hermocrates* (finally giving way to the *Laws*). Wise's (2008) claim that our 'tragic' (Aristotelian) conception of tragedy is dependent on the fragmentation of original, 'optimistic' tetralogies in the course of their transmission is rightly rejected by Prauscello (2014, p. 186, n. 108). For a more elaborate treatment of the question "Are Greek tragedies tragic?" see Judet de La Combe 2010.

19. Kuhn (1941, p. 39 [=1960, pp. 269–70]), and more generally (p. 63 [= 1960, p. 296]). Kuhn's position, based on the idea of theodicy, leaves room for the construal of tragedy as depicting misfortune and conflict (in the *Agamemnon* and the *Choephors*). By the same token, in the account that Er gives of his *post mortem* experience in Book 10 of the *Republic* (that is, in the very book that condemns the tragedy of the tragic poets), the tragic "manifests itself not in the contingencies of life, but in the ignorance and forgetfulness of the soul" (Kuhn 1941, p. 51 [= 1960, p. 285]. The mythical account shows an "interplay of true happiness and true misery

[which] is neither devoid of fear nor unfamiliar with the saying 'suffer to learn' (*ibid.* [= 1960, p. 284]. The allusion is of course to Aeschylus' *pathei mathos* (*Agamemnon*, v.176) taken as definitional of the tragic genre. For the idea that Plato leaves no room for a philosophical tragedy, see also Goldschmidt 1970a: "Le problème de la tragédie d'après Platon," pp. 136–37.

20. See Meyer 2011, pp. 392–93: "within the broader genus of choral drama, tragedy is the genre that depicts good and worthy people, while comedy represents low life." She herself recognizes, however (with Halliwell 1996, pp. 336–40), that Plato might well be considered the originator of the 'modern' sense of the word 'tragic,' not only in *Philebus* 50b1–4 (quoted above, p. 150), but also in the *Cratylus* 408c5–d2 (which associates 'tragic' and 'rough'). At *Phaedo* 115a5–6, 'tragic' refers to the grandiloquence of the word *heimarmenê*/('destiny').

21. For an example of contradiction applying to poets in general rather than to tragic authors in particular, cf. the criticisms levelled by the poet against the lawgiver on the subject of the latter's conception of funeral rites at *Laws* 4.719d1–e5, contrasted with 12.958c7–959a3 (see Chap. 7, p. 112).

22. Cf. also 3.387c9–d3 (with the examples that follow) and *Phaedrus* 268c5-d2 (in a descriptive passage related to Sophocles and Euripides). The thought is not elaborated in the passage of the *Laws* under consideration (cf. Schöpsdau, vol. 2, p. 596 *ad* 817a2–d9).

23. Aristotle requires that the tragic hero not be too perfect (perfectly virtuous) because an undeserved misfortune is something "repugnant"/*miaron* (*Poetics* 13.1452b36).

24. Cf. *Republic* 10.603e7–8.

25. This is Aristotle's *hamartia tis*, "some kind of error," *Poetics* 13.1453a10, on which he remains notably discreet (see Halliwell 1986, pp. 216–17); cf. Schöpsdau, vol. 3, pp. 200–201.

26. One may wonder whether the restriction implied by the phrase *en ... tragikêi legomenêi* (*"which is called tragic"*), according to the transmitted text at 8.838c4, might be intended to limit the extent of the parallel between the tragedies invoked there and "true tragedy." But the reverse may be more appropriate: Plato could be referring here to what is commonly called 'tragic' (false tragedy) in order to emphasize that, in this case, the tragedies mentioned precisely *do not* belong to that category. In any case, Orelli's correction *en ... tragikêi legomena* ("what is said in tragedy"), which is adopted by Schöpsdau (vol. 3, pp. 200–201), is unnecessary.

27. "According to the order and law of destiny" (*Laws* 10.904c8–9). For an analysis of this myth of *post mortem* mechanical punishment in the *Laws*, see Saunders 1991, pp. 202–7.

28. *Laws* 4.714a1–2 and above, Chap. 1, p. 19.

29. See Chap. 7, p. 110 with n. 16.

Appendix A. On the Status of the *Statesman*

1. On the relationship between the two levels in the *Statesman*, see Lane 1998, p. 2.

2. At *Sophist* 216d2/3–217a2, Socrates wishes to know what people in Elea think about the sophist, the statesman, and the philosopher; and at 218b6–c1, the Eleatic Stranger proposes to start with the sophist. The *Statesman* is explicitly presented at 258a3–b5 as a follow-up on this conversation held 'yesterday.' The virtual content of a dialogue that would have been entitled *The Philosopher* is not known and the potential announcement might be a red herring, because what would have been the ontological content of the *Philosopher* may well actually be included in the *Sophist*. A more tangible triad is formed by the *Theaetetus* (also supposed to have taken

place the day before the *Sophist,* cf. *Sophist* 216a1), the *Sophist* and the *Statesman* (on this issue, see M. Frede 1996, pp. 146 and 149–51). At *Critias* 108c5–6, Critias announces that his account of the war between primitive Athens and Atlantis, following upon Timaeus' preliminary account of the formation of the universe down to human beings (cf. *Timaeus* 27a3–b6), will be followed by yet another exposition by Hermocrates, of which we know nothing. More graspable and arguably more important is the triad made out of the *Republic,* the political gist of which is also supposed to have been the topic of a conversation held the day before the *Timaeus* ("yesterday" at 17a2) the *Timaeus* and the *Critias.*

3. See also Schofield (1997, p. 228), who presents the *Statesman* as "a fresh attempt to think about politics, in a mode wholly different from the *Republic.*" In the same vein, El Murr (2014, pp. 16–17) sees the *Statesman* as a 'complement' to the *Republic.*

4. See Chap. 1, n. 32.

5. Kahn 1995, pp. 52–53.

6. Plato's involvement in real politics has become proverbial; see, for example, Lilla 2001 on Heidegger's political engagement. The question does not of course concern only philosophy, but artistic production in general—literary, pictural, musical, cinematographic. Only specific answers, if any, are possible.

7. Dillon 2003, pp. 2–5, gives a vivid description of the physical settings and related intellectual business at the Academy, a place where philosophers had begun to meet one generation before Plato.

8. Cf. e.g., Stalley 1983, p. 92, talking about the encounter between the lawgiver and an appropriate tyrant at *Laws* 4.711d1–712a7 (see above, Chap. 2, p. 49): "The passage reeks of the Syracusan affair with Plato himself cast in the role of the wise legislator and Dionysius as the young tyrant."

9. *Statesman* 309c1–310a6 (immortal divine bonds, concerning the good and virtues); 310a7–311a2 (mortal human bonds, in marriage).

10. See on this point Delcomminette 2005 (on the relationship between the *Statesman* and the *Philebus*) and his 2006 reconstruction of Plato's 'agathology.' Cf. also Krämer 1959 and Lisi 1985 (cf. above Chap. 6, n. 4).

11. The striking expression is found at *Laws* 5.739e4 (cf. *eis ton aei khronon* at 740b2).

12. *Statesman* 294b8–c4, *Phaedrus,* 275d4–9, cf. Chap. 7, p. 109.

13. See Chap. 2, p. 48.

14. See Chap. 2, p. 48. The famous controversy between Strauss and Kojève following Strauss' essay on Xenophon's *Hiero* or *On Tyranny,* originally published in 1948, turns on the issue of the philosopher's 'temptation' to tyranny. The relevant texts are included in Strauss 2013. For a contextualization of Strauss' essay, see Vatter 2011.

15. See Chap. 7, pp. 115–17.

16. *ou gnêsias oud'ontôs ousas,* 293e2–3.

17. A somewhat inflated paraphrasis for *hekastôn* (lit. 'each matter').

18. "[H]ow? How did the advisers to the assemblies, or the assemblies themselves, ever get access to the 'original truth'"? (Rowe 2001, p. 70). See, however, the next note.

19. Rowe's translation of the second part of the sentence runs: ". . . the things issuing from those who know which have been written down so far as they can be." The main grammatical move consists in recognizing that the demonstrative *tauta* (300c5), announces the subject *ta para tôn eidotôn* [. . .] *gegrammena* in c6–7 and does not specifically refer back to the deficient

constitutions resulting from "long experience" mentioned in the previous lines (300b1–6); see Rowe 1995, pp. 230–31; cf. further Rowe 2001, p. 71 and p. 72, n. 39; and Rowe 2005. This being said, the important point is not that the question does not concern the laws of the pseudo-constitution (the presence of the restrictive "as far as possible," *eis dunamin einai*, allows for this possibility) but that it concerns *also*, and to be sure in a primary way, the laws of the true constitution. René de Nicolay pointed out to me that *Laws* 12.951b4–c4 says that observers will be sent abroad "on the track" (*kat'ikhnos* [. . .] *zêtein*, 951b7–8) of the very few "divine men" who are always to be found among the many—whether their city is well-governed or not—and profit from frequenting them (*suggignesthai*, b5–6) in order to consolidate or improve the institutions of Magnesia. The vocabulary resonates with *Statesman* 301e3–4.

20. Rowe 2001, p. 74: "The 'second-best of the *Laws* [. . .] is a city [. . .] which is much more like what the *Politicus* [= the *Statesman*] surely means by an 'imitation' of the truth.'" I would not support the thought, however, by pointing to the revisability of the laws in the *Laws*, which surely is restricted to a relatively short period of time and concerns minor adaptations. The laws of the *Laws* are meant eventually to be definitive (on this issue, see Reid 2021).

21. Cf. Chap. 2, e.g., p. 40.

22. Cf. 6.751d8–752a1 and Chap. 1, p. 16. This is, once more, Rousseau's problem (see the chapter "On the Lawgiver," in the *Social Contract*, 2.7).

23. Cf. Chap. 2, p. 46.

Appendix B. On a Supposed Evolution of Plato's Psychology

1. See in particular the reviews by Kahn (2004) and Lorenz (2004). Cf. Laks 2005, pp. 85–92 (written without knowledge of Lorenz's review), of which what follows is a revised version.

2. Cf. Bobonich 2002, pp. 219–20 with p. 526, n. 2.

3. The notion comes from Dennett 1981, cf. Bobonich 2002, pp. 221–22 with notes.

4. Bobonich 2002, p. 324 (referring to *Timaeus* 42a3–b1 and 69c7–d6).

5. Bobonich 2002, p. 280.

6. Bobonich 2002, p. 280.

7. On this reading, the *logos* ('reason') evoked here is distinct from and stronger than the *logismos* ('reasoning') at 644d2. Plato does not work out this difference (see the discussion in Schöpsdau, vol. 1, p. 233).

8. On Plato's striking use of *homilêma*, see Chap. 9, p. 138.

9. Plato uses *eidos*/kind in the initial formulation of the question at 4.435c5; *meros*/part is implied at the beginning of the argument, 4.436a8–b2, cf. 439d4–8 and occurs at 4.442b19 and c4 and at 9.581a6.

10. See also Laks 2005, pp. 85–92.

11. Adams has a note *ad loc.* on the grammar of the phrase and quotes other occurrences (in particular Aristotle, *Constitution of the Athenians*, 8.5) of what he rightly calls a metaphor. Other examples of the same kind are in Kahn 2004 (p. 355), who quotes in particular *Republic* 8.553b8 and d1.

12. "Because every pleasure or pain provides, as it were, another nail to rivet the soul to the body and to weld them together. It makes the soul corporeal, so that it believes that truth is what the body says it is. As it shares the beliefs and delights of the body, I think it inevitably comes to share its ways and manner of life . . . ," *Phaedo* 83d4–8 (trans. Grube).

13. Kahn 2004, p. 335.

14. Lorenz 2004, pp. 563–64.

15. Note that the license is productive in the sense that what is said about the individual soul teaches us something about the city that has not been explicitly said of it. (Another interesting instance of *husteron-proteron* in the *Republic* is the treatment of temperance, the analysis of which as a psychic virtue, at 4.430d6–431b5, precedes and guides that of self-control at the city level, contrary to the official procedure.) For a related, but more general explanation of why Plato introduces the reference to argument in this passage, see Wilburn 2014, pp. 202–3.

16. Bobonich 2002, p. 244.

17. See Bobonich 2002, pp. 534–35, n. 47.

18. See Lorenz 2004, p. 564, who refers to *Republic* 7.522a3–b1, 9.590b6–9 and *Laws* 2.653b1–c4.

19. Bobonich 2002, p. 221.

20. Aristotle draws the line at *Rhetoric* 3.10.1410b17–8. One should also keep in mind Plato's explicit reservations about the accuracy of the analogical account about the soul at 4.435c9–d5 (and 6.504c9–d3). Although the remark concerns the general question of the tripartite division of the soul (the *retractatio* comes in Book 10.608d2–612a6, where the soul in its disembodied state is shown to be an undivided, unitary entity), it surely applies also to features that are specific to each part of the soul (*contra* Bobonich 2002, p. 528, n. 11).

21. Cf. Robinson 1995, pp. 47–48: "the question is, *what* pacifies and moves the three parts of the soul?"

22. Bobonich supposes that the alternative at 863b3 is purely rhetorical, *thumos* having been classified as a *pathos* at 1.644e1, cf. 645d6–7. This is not what the formulation suggests.

23. Bobonich (2002) is obliged to get rid of the notion of counseling at 1. 644c6, which he says is "immediately rejected as unclear at 644d4–6" and which is replaced by the puppet image (p. 540, n. 78). However, the image in question is not meant to replace, but to clarify the preceding lines; as for the second passage, Bobonich quotes it (p. 261), but his comments do not bear on the point that is relevant here.

24. See among others Rees 1957; Saunders 1962, pp. 37–41; Sassi 2008; Wilburn 2013.

25. The treatment of *thumos* is quasi-Aristotelian (cf. v. Arnim 1927, p. 43). Lisi (2008, p. 96) observes that the two senses of *thumos* (anger, the affection, and the part of the soul) play a role in Plato's argumentation at 863b6–9, which, in the absence of any explicit statement, suggests that the tripartite scheme remains on the background (see also p. 93 on the tripartition of the causes of injustice: anger, pleasure, and ignorance). Schöpsdau, however, correctly limits the implications of the passage (vol. 3, p. 301). On *thumos* in the *Laws*, see further Sassi 2008, esp. pp. 133–38; Wilburn 2013; and Renaut 2014, pp. 306–13.

26. Cf. Aristotle, *Nicomachean Ethics* 1.13 1102a27–8; *Magna Moralia* 1.1 1182a23–24 straightforwardly attributes the dichotomic psychology to Plato; cf. Dirlmeier 1958, p. 164, and 1967, pp. 278–79 and 292.

27. This is the schema we get in Aetius' handbook (4.4.1), which is an appropriate rendering of the *Timaeus* rather than an attempt at harmonization. Saunders (1962, p. 37) observes rightly: "the bipartite analysis can never exclude the tripartite" (see also Renaut 2014, p. 311). "Tripartition always presupposes bipartition, and bipartition is always capable of expansion into tripartition" (this in Saunders serves as an argument to construe the *thumos* as an 'independent' part in the *Laws*; I rather take it the other way round).

Appendix C. Aristotle and Posidonius on Plato's Preambles

1. See Vegetti in Vegetti, ed., vol. 4, 2000, pp. 440–41 (cf. Aristotle "he [i.e., Plato in the *Republic*] has filled his argument with extraneous considerations," *tois exôthen logois peplêrôke ton logon*, 6.1264b39–40).

2. Cf. Hutchinson and Johnson 2014, pp. 184–85.

3. Although Plato's specific theory "had no influence on legislation in Greece" (Ries 1983, p. 113; my trans.), preambles flourished in the Roman Empire and the Byzantine period (see Ries 1983, pp. 127–223 and Fögen 2022, p. 12, cf. Fögen 1995).

4. Aristo the Stoic is named at the beginning of *Letter* 94.2. His views are reported up to 94.17. Then come Seneca's answers to each of Aristo's arguments against counting 'parainetics' (advice-giving) as a part of philosophy. *Letters* 94 and 95 constitute a whole devoted to the question of the relationship between *praecepta* and *decreta*, on which see Inwood 2005, defending the centrality of *praecepta* in Stoic ethics in the light of a definite conception of how morality functions. See also Schafer 2009, who relativizes the distinction between *decreta* and *praecepta* in Seneca's argument (pp. 105–6). For Aristo's position on the question of *praecepta*, see also Ioppolo 1980, p. 123.

5. This construal of laws as being *minis mixta praecepta* (*Letter* 94.37) supposes an unusual but interesting interpretation of law as telling us how to act *in a particular circumstance*, as precepts are supposed to do (by contrast with general principles, which are called *decreta*). On this construal, the main characteristic of law is not its generality, as opposed to particular circumstances (as it is prominently in Plato's *Statesman* but also in the *Laws*, see Appendix A, p. 162): rather, a law, provided that it is sufficiently detailed, indicates what is to be done in each circumstance, and what is common to precepts and laws lies in their *prescriptive* character.

6. The formula is quoted by François Duaren at the beginning of his commentary to the *Digest* published in 1560 (*Commentationes in Digestum* I, 3), cf. Jones 1956, p. 8, n. 6. H. E. Troje indicated me long ago (*per litt.*) that the issue is not tackled by other commentators.

7. *Frigidus* corresponds to the Greek *psukhros*, lit. 'cold.' The term is also used metaphorically in rhetoric (see Lausberg 1973, §§1074, 2 and 1076). Lucian plays on both levels (the literal and the rhetorical) by having Zeus complain in his *Icaromenippus* (24) that "his altars have become colder (*psukhroreterous*) than Plato's laws or Chrysippus' syllogisms." The parallel with Chrysippus is probably more pointed if Lucian has in mind the laws that feature in the *Laws* rather than the work as a whole, but both readings are possible. On the other hand, it is impossible to know whether Lucian is thinking of the law as opposed to its preamble or the law as preceded by a preamble, in which case his judgement would be closer to Posidonius.' In any case, the two references show that Plato's *Laws*, in one way or another, were associated with (rhetorical) "coldness."

8. *Letter* 94.37f.= Frag.178 Edelstein-Kidd (cf. 451 Theiler). From Plato's point of view, Posidonius is treating citizen as if they were slaves, cf. *Laws* 6.777e6–7 and above, Chap. 7, n. 43.

9. See *Letter* 94.32.

10. What Posidonius could have perhaps more legitimately reproached Plato for is having attributed to the law itself a pedagogical or didactic function that only concrete discussion can achieve.

11. Sextus Empiricus, *Against the Logicians* 1.2, cf. Seneca, *Letter* 89.3.

BIBLIOGRAPHY

Ancient Authors, Texts, and Translations

Plato

COMPLETE WORKS

Edition

Platonis Opera, ed. J. Burnet, 5 vols. *Oxford Classical Texts*, 1900–1907. Volume 1 (*Euthyphro, Apologia, Crito, Phaedo, Cratylus, Theaetetus, Sophista, Politicus*) was reedited by E. A. Duke, W. F. Hicken, W.S.M. Nicoll, D. B. Robinson, and J.C.G. Strachan in 1995; and the *Republic* separately by S.R. Slings in 2003.

Translations

Platon, *Werke, mit Einleitungen und Anm. von F. Schleiermacher*, 6 vols., Berlin, 1855³. The introductions have been translated by W. Dobson in: Schleiermacher, *Introductions to the Dialogues of Plato*, Cambridge 1836, repr. New York 1974.

Plato, *Complete Works*, ed. J. M. Cooper, Indianapolis/Cambridge: Hackett, 1997.

PARTIAL EDITIONS, TRANSLATIONS, COMMENTARIES

Laws

Brisson, L. and J.-L. Pradeau, Platon, *Les Lois* (introduction, translation and notes), Paris: GF Flammarion, 2006.

Bury, R. G., *Plato: Laws*, London and New York: Loeb Classical Library, 1926.

Diès, A., E. des Places, Platon, *Les Lois*, Collection des Universités de France, Paris 1951–1956 (many reimp.), in four volumes: Books I–II, ed. and trans. E. des Places, introduction by A. Diès and L. Gernet; Books III–VI, ed. and trans. E. des Places ; Books VII–X, ed. and trans. A. Diès; Books XI–XII, ed. and trans. A. Diès and E. des Places; *Epinomis*, ed. and trans. E. des Places.

England, E. B., *The Laws of Plato*, 2 vols., Manchester, 1921 (New York, 1976²).

Griffith, T., *Plato: Laws* (ed. M. Schofield), Cambridge University Press, 2016.

Lisi, F., *Platón, Diálogos. Leyes*, 2 vols., Madrid: Gredos, 1999.

Pangle, T. L. *The Laws of Plato*, Chicago: Chicago University Press, 1988.

Saunders, T. J. *Plato: The Laws* (Penguin), 1970; reprinted in J. M. Cooper, *Plato: Complete Works*, Indianapolis/Cambridge: Hackett, 1997.

Schöpsdau, K., *Platon: Nomoi (Gesetze)*, 3 vols. (vol. 1: Books I–III; vol. 2: Books IV–VII; vol. 3: Books VIII–XII), Göttingen: Vanderhoeck & Ruprecht, 1994/2003/2011. See also Mayhew 2008 and Meyer 2015 in the section "Secondary Literature" below.

Other Dialogues

Charmides, trans. C. Moore and C. C. Raymond, Indianapolis/Cambridge: Hackett, 2019.

Écrits attribués à Platon, translated by L. Brisson, Paris: Flammarion, 2014.

Euthyphro; Apology; Crito; Phaedo, trans. Ch. Emlyn-Jones, and W. Preddy, Loeb Classical Library, 2017.

Gorgias, A revised text with introduction and commentary by E. R. Dodds, Oxford: Clarendon Press, 1959.

Philebus, edited with introduction, notes and appendices by R. G. Bury, Cambridge, 1897.

The Republic of Plato, edited with critical notes, commentary, and appendices by J. Adam, 2 vols., Cambridge, 1902 (Reprint Cambridge University Press, 2009).

Symposium, edited and translated by R. G. Bury, Cambridge: W. Heffer, 1932.

Statesman, translated by J. B. Skemp, introduction by M. Ostwald, Indianapolis: Hackett, 1992.

Statesman, edited with an introduction, translation, and commentary by C. J. Rowe, Warminster, England: Aris & Phillips, 1995.

Other Authors

ANCIENT

Aeschylus, *Eumenides*, ed. and trans. A. H. Sommerstein, in Aeschylus, *Works*, vol. 2, Loeb Classical Library, 2008.

Alexander of Aphrodisias, *In Aristotelis Topicorum libros octo*, ed. M. Wallies, Berlin, 1891.

———, *De mixtione*, in Alexandre d'Aphrodise, *Sur la mixtion et la croissance*, ed. J. Groisard, Paris: Les Belles Lettres, 2013.

Aristotle, *The Complete Work of Aristotle, Revised Oxford Translation*, ed. J. Barnes, Princeton University Press, 1984.

———, *Fragmenta selecta*, ed. W. D. Ross, Oxford: Clarendon Press, 1955.

———, *Rhetorik*, translated and with commentary by C. Rapp, 2 vol., Berlin: Akademie Verlag, 2002.

Cicero, *The Republic; The Laws*, trans. N. Rudd; introduction and notes by J. Powell and N. Rudd, Oxford University Press, 1998.

———, *De legibus*, ed. K. Ziegler, rev. W. Görler, Freiburg: Ploetz, 1979.

Diogenes Laertius, *Lives of Eminent Philosophers*, trans. P. Mensch (ed. J. Miller), Oxford University Press, 2018.

Early Greek Philosophy, ed. and trans. A. Laks and G. W. Most, 9 vols., Loeb Classical Library, 2016.

Herodotus, *The Persian Wars*, ed. and trans. A. D. Godley, 4 vols., Loeb Classical Library, 1920–1924.

Hesiod, *Theogony, Works and Days, Testimonia*, ed. and trans. G. W. Most, in *Hesiod*, vol. 1, Loeb Classical Library, 2006.

Hippocrates, *Aphorisms*, in *Hippocrates*, vol. 4, ed. and trans. W.H.S. Jones, Loeb Classical Library, 1931.

Hippocrates, *In the Surgery*, in *Hippocrates*, vol. 3, ed. and trans. E. T. Withington, Loeb Classical Library, 1928.

Isocrates, *Speeches*, ed. and trans. G. Norlin, 3 vols., Loeb Classical Library, 1928–1945.

Josephus, *Against Apion*, vol. 1, ed. and trans. H.St.J. Thackerey, Loeb Classical Library, 1926.

Lycurgus, *Against Leocrates*, in *Minor Attic Orators*, vol. 2, ed. and trans. J. O. Burtt, Loeb Classical Library, 1954.

Orphicorum Fragmenta et Testimonia, in *Testimonia et Fragmenta* II, Fasc.1, ed. A. Bernabé, Munich and Leipzig: K.G. Saur, 2004.

Posidonius, vol. 1, *The Fragments* (ed. L. Edelstein and I .G. Kidd); vol. II. *The Commentary* (i. Testimonia and Fragments 1–149; ii. Fragments 150–293), Cambridge University Press, 1972/1988.

Sappho and Alcaeus, in *Greek Lyric*, vol. 1, ed. and trans. D. A. Campbell, Loeb Classical Library, 1982.

Seneca, *Epistles*, vol. II (Epistles 66–92), ed. and trans. R. M. Gummere, Loeb Classical Library, 1920.

Solon, in B. Gentili and C. Prato, *Testimonia et Fragmenta*, vol. 1, Leipzig: Teubner, 1988^2.

Thucydides, *History of the Peloponnesian War*, 4 vols., ed. and trans. C. F. Smith, Loeb Classical Library, 1919.

MODERNS

Kant
Critique of Pure Reason, trans. N. Kemp Smith, New York: St. Martin's Press, 1965.

Rousseau
Émile in *Œuvres completes*, vol. IV, Paris: Gallimard (Bibliothèque de la Pléiade), 1969.

Emile: or, On education, introduction, trans., and notes A. Bloom, Harmondsworth: Penguin, 1991.

Political Writings, ed. introduction and notes C. E. Vaughan, New York: Wiley, 1962.

The Social Contract and other later political writings, ed. and trans. V. Gourevitch, Cambridge University Press, 2019^2.

Spinoza
The Collected Works of Spinoza, ed. and trans. E.Curley, 2 vols., Princeton University Press, 1985/2016.

Secondary Literature

Adcock, F. E. 1927. "Literary Tradition and Early Greek Code-Makers," *Cambridge Historical Journal* 2, pp. 95–109.

Adorno, T. W. [1937] 2002. "Late Style in Beethoven," in *Essays on Music*, selected by R. Leppert, trans. S. H. Gillepsie, Berkeley: University of Calfornia Press, pp. 564–68.

Agostino, F. 1973. *Epieikeia. Il tema dell'equità nell Antiquità Greca,* Milano: Giuffrè Editore.

Allen, D. 2010. *Why Plato Wrote,* Hoboken, NJ: Wiley-Blackwell.

Anderson, M. 2019. "What Are the Wages of Justice? Rethinking the *Republic*'s Division of Goods," *Phronesis* 65, pp. 1–26.

Annas, J. 1955. Introduction to Plato's *Statesman,* Robin Waterfield, trans., Cambridge University Press.

Annas, J. 2017. *Virtue and Law in Plato and Beyond,* Oxford University Press.

Assmann, J. 1995². *Politische Theologie zwischen Ägypten und Israel.* Introductory essay by von H. Meier, Munich: Siemens Stiftung.

Atkins, J. W. 2013. "Cicero on the Relationship between Plato's *Republic* and *Laws,*" *Bulletin of the Institute of Classical Studies* 117, pp. 15–34.

Aubenque, P. 1963. *La Prudence chez Aristote.* Paris: Presses Universitaires de France.

Azoulay, V., and P. Ismard. 2020. *Athènes 403 : une histoire chorale,* Paris: Flammarion.

Barney, R. unpublished ms. "Utopia and Imagery in Plato's *Republic.*"

Bartels, M. L. 2017. *Plato's Pragmatic Project: A Reading of Plato's* Laws, Stuttgart: Franz Steiner.

Belfiore, E. 1980. "*Elenchus, Epode,* and Magic: Socrates as Silenus," *Phoenix* 34, pp. 128–37.

Bensa, A. 2008. "Louis Dumont et le totalitarisme," *Annales. Histoire, Sciences Sociales,* 63, pp. 377–81.

Bentley, R. 1781. *Responsio ad censuram Caroli Boyle* (1699), in *Opuscula philologica Dissertationem in Phalaridis epistolas et epistolam ad Ioannem Millium complectentia,* Leipzig, pp. 151–452.

Benveniste, É. 1969. *Le Vocabulaire des institutions Indo-européennes,* 2 vols., Paris: Éditions de Minuit.

Berryman, S. 2003. "Ancient Automata and Mechanical Explanation," *Phronesis* 48, pp. 344–69.

Bertrand, J.-M. 1999. *De l'écriture à l'oralité: lectures des* Lois *de Platon,* Paris: Publications de la Sorbonne.

Betegh, G. 2016. "Archelaus on Cosmogony and the Origins of Social Institutions," *Oxford Studies in Ancient Philosophy* 51, pp. 1–40.

Bizos, M. 1971⁶. *Syntaxe Greque,* Paris: Librairie Vuibert.

Blumenberg, H. 2010. *Paradigms for a Metaphorology,* trans. R. Savage, New York: Cornell University Press and Cornell University Library, 2010 (German original: *Paradigmen zu einer Metaphorologie,* Frankfurt am Main: Suhrkamp Verlag 1960).

Bobonich, C. 1991. "Persuasion, Compulsion and Freedom in Plato's *Laws,*" *Classical Quarterly* 41, pp. 365–88.

———. 2002. *Plato's Utopia Recast: His Later Ethics and Politics,* Oxford: Clarendon Press.

———, ed. 2010. *A Critical Guide to Plato's* Laws, Cambridge University Press.

Bordes, J. 1982. Politeia *dans la pensée grecque jusqu'à Aristote,* Paris: Les Belles-Lettres.

Bordt, M. 2013. "Die theologische Fundierung der Gesetze," in C. Horn, ed., *Platon. Gesetze—Nomoi,* Berlin: Akademie Verlag, pp. 209–26.

Bourgey, L. 1975. "La relation du médecin au malade dans les écrits de l'École de Cos," in *La Collection Hippocratique et son rôle dans l'histoire de la médecine,* Leiden: Brill, pp. 209–27.

Bradley, L. V. 2017. "Eusebius of Caesarea's Un-Platonic Platonic Political Theology," *Polis* 34, pp. 94–114.

Brisson, L. 1998. *Plato, the Myth Maker*, trans. G. Naddaf, Chicago: University of Chicago Press (French original: *Platon, Les mots et les mythes: comment et pourquoi Platon nomma le mythe?* Paris: Éditions de la Découverte, 1994).

———. 2001. "Le Collège de veille (*nukterinos sullogos*)," in F. L. Lisi, ed., pp. 161–77.

———.2000. "Les préambules dans les *Lois*," in L. Brisson, *Lectures de Platon*, Paris, pp. 235–62.

———.2005. "La critique de la tradition religieuse par Platon et son usage dans la *République* et dans les *Lois*," in E. Vegleris, ed., *Cosmos et psychè. Mélanges offerts à Jean Frère*, Zurich: Olms, pp. 67–82.

———.2020. "Plato's Political Writings: A Utopia?" *Polis* 37, pp. 399–420.

Brown, A. 1986. "Platonism in Fifteenth-Century Florence and Its Contribution to Early Modern Thought," *Journal of Modern History*, 58, pp. 383–413.

Brucker, J. J., [1742–44] 1766–67. *Historia critica philosophiae a mundi incunabilis ad nostram usque aetatem deducta*, 4 vols., Leipzig.

Brunschwig, J. 1999. "Rule and Exception: On the Aristotelian Theory of Equity," in M. Frede and G. Striker, eds., *Rationality in Greek Thought*, Oxford: Clarendon Press, pp. 115–55.

Burkert, W. [1982] 2003. "Götterspiel und Götterburleske in altorientalischen und griechischen Mythen," in *Kleine Schriften II: Orientalia*, L. Gemelli Marciano et al., eds., Göttingen: Vandenhoeck and Ruprecht, pp. 96–118.

Burnyeat, M. [1992] 1999. "Utopia and Fantasy: The Practicability of Plato's Ideally Just City," in G. Fine, ed., *Plato 2: Ethics, Politics, Religion and the Soul*, Oxford University Press, pp. 297–308.

———. Forthcoming. "Ancient Freedoms," 1996 Howison Lecture in Philosophy at the University of California, Berkeley, in M. B., *Explorations in Ancient and Modern Philosophy*, vol. 3, Cambridge University Press.

Buxton, R.G.A. 1982. *Persuasion in Greek Tragedy: A Study of peitho*, Cambridge University Press.

Cameron, A. 1978. *Plato's Affair with Tragedy*, Cincinnati: University of Cincinnati.

Chantraine, P. 1999². *Dictionnaire étymologique de la langue grecque*, Paris: Klincksieck.

Cherniss, H. 1953. Review of Müller 1951, *Gnomon* 25, pp. 367–79 (also in H. C., *Selected Papers*, L. Tarán, ed., Leiden: Brill, 1977, pp. 376–88).

Clay, D. 2000. "Magnesia: The *Laws*" = Chap. 8 (pp. 267–81) of *Platonic Questions: Dialogues with the Silent Philosopher*, University Park: Pennsylvania State University Press.

Clay, D., and A. Purvis. 1999. *Four Island Utopias: Being Plato's Atlantis, Euhemeros of Messene's Panchaia, Iamboulos' Island of the Sun, and Francis Bacon's New Atlantis*, Newburyport, MA: Focus Publishing.

Cornford, F. M. 1937. *Plato's Cosmology. The Timaeus of Plato translated with a running commentary*, London: Routledge & Kegan Paul.

———. [1935] 1950. "Plato's Commonwealth," in *The Unwritten Philosophy and Other Essays*, Cambridge University Press, pp. 46–67.

Crivelli, P. 2020. "Measurement in Plato's *Statesman*," in G. R. Giardina, ed., *To metron. Sur la notion de mesure dans la philosophie d'Aristote*, Paris and Bruxelles: Vrin, Éditions Ousia, pp. 9–29.

Davies, J. 2005. "The Gortyn Law," in M. Gagarin and D. Cohen, eds., *The Cambridge Companion to Early Greek Law*, Cambridge University Press, pp. 305–27.

De Franceschi, S. H. 2007. "Ambigüités historiographiques du théologico-politique. Genèse et fortune d'un concept," *Revue historique* 643, pp. 653–85.

Des Places, E. 1967. "La tradition patristique de Platon (spécialement d'après les citations des *Lois* et de l'*Epinomis* dans la *Préparation évangélique* d'Eusèbe de Césarée)," *Revue des Études Grecques*, 80, pp. 385–94.

Delatte, A. 1922. *Essai sur la politique pythagoricienne*, Liège-Paris: Champion (reprint Genève: Slatkine, 1974).

Delcomminette, S. 2005. "La juste mesure. Étude sur les rapports entre le *Politique* et le *Philèbe*," *Les Études philosophiques*, 74, pp. 347–66.

———. 2006. *Le* Philèbe *de Platon. Introduction à l'agathologie platonicienne*, Brill: Leiden-Boston.

Dennet, D. 1981. *Brainstorms*, Cambridge, MA: MIT Press.

Denniston, J. D. 1960. *Greek Prose Style*, Oxford: Clarendon Press.

Destrée, P., Salles, R., and Zingano, M., eds. 2014. *What Is Up to Us? Studies on Agency and Responsibility in Ancient Philosophy*, Sankt Augustin: Academia Verlag.

Dillon, J. 2001. "The Neoplatonic Reception of Plato's *Laws*," in F. L. Lisi, ed., pp. 243–54.

———. 2003. *The Heirs of Plato: A Study of the Old Academy, 347–274 B.C.*, Oxford: Clarendon Press.

Dirlmeier, F. 1958. Aristoteles, *Magna Moralia* (= Aristoteles Werke in deutscher Übersetzung, vol. 8), Berlin: Akademie Verlag.

———. 1967. Aristoteles, *Nikomachische Ethik* (= Aristoteles Werke in deutscher Übersetzung, vol. 6), Berlin: Akademie Verlag.

Dörrie, H. 1983. "Die *Gesetze* Platons im Rahmen seines Gesamtwerkes," *Boreas* 6, pp. 81–94.

Dumont, L. 1996. *Homo hierarchicus. Essai sur le système des castes*, Paris: Gallimard.

El Murr, D. 2014. *Savoir et gouverner: Essai sur la science politique platonicienne*, Paris: Vrin.

Else, G. F., 1972. *The Structure and Date of Book 10 of Plato's* Republic, Heidelberg: Carl Winter.

Ficino, Marsilio. *1576. In dialogum primum De legibus, Opera Omnia*, T. 2, Basel.

Flower, M. A. 2009. "Spartan Religion and Geek Religion," in S. Hodkinson, ed., *Sparta: Comparative Approaches*, Swansea: Classical Press of Wales, pp. 193–229.

———. 2018. "Spartan Religion," in A. Powell, ed., *A Companion to Sparta*, Hoboken, NJ: John Wiley & Sons, vol. 2, pp. 423–51.

Fögen, M. T. 1995. "The Legislator's Monologue—Notes on the History of Preambles," *Chicago-Kent Law Review* 70.4, pp. 1593–1622.

———. 2022. *Dos Lied vom Gesetz*, Munich: Siemens Stiftung.

Forcignano, F. and M. Vegetti. 2020. "Il Platone totalitario di Karl Popper," in M. Bonazzi and R. Colombo, eds., *Sotto il segno di Platone. Il conflitto delle interpretazioni nella Germania del Novecento*, Rome: Carroci editore, pp. 179–204.

Fossheim, H. J. 2013. "The *prooimia*, Types of Motivation, and Moral Psychology," in C. Horn, ed., *Platon. Gesetze—Nomoi*, Berlin: Akademie Verlag, pp. 87–104.

Foucault, M. 2004. *Sécurité, territoire, population*: cours au Collège de France, 1977–1978, Paris: Seuil, Gallimard.

Frede, D. 1997. *Platon. Philebos*, Göttingen: Vanderhoeck and Ruprecht.

———. 2010. "Puppets on Strings: Moral Psychology in *Laws* Books 1 and 2," in C. Bobonich, ed., *A Critical Guide to Plato's Laws*, Cambridge University Press, pp. 108–126.

Frede, M. 1996. "The Literary Form of the *Sophist*," in C. Gill and M. M. McCabe, eds., *Form and Argument in Late Plato*, Oxford: Clarendon Press, pp. 135–51.

———. 2011. *A Free Will: The Origins of the Notion in Ancient Thought*, Berkeley: University of Calfornia Press.

———. 2014. "*The eph' hêmin* in Ancient Philosophy," in P. Destrée, R. Salles, and M. Zingano, eds., *What Is Up to Us? Studies on Agency and Responsibility in Ancient Philosophy*, Sankt Augustin: Academia Verlag, pp. 351–63.

Gaiser, K. 1959. *Protreptik und Paränese bei Platon. Untersuchungen zur Form des platonischen Dialogs*, Stuttgart: W. Kohlhammer.

Gastaldi, S. 1984. "Legge e retorica. I proemi delle 'Leggi' di Platone," *Quaderni di Storia* 20, pp. 69–109.

Gigante, M. [1956] 1993. ΝΟΜΟΣ ΒΑΣΙΛΕΥΣ [*Nomos basileus*] (with an Appendix "Nuovi testi dell' ode pindarica"), Naples: Bibliopolis.

Gilbert, F. 1968. "The Venetian Constitution in Florentine Political Thought," in N. Rubinstein, ed., *Florentine Studies: Politics and Society in Renaissance Florence*, London: Faber, pp. 463–500.

Goldschmidt, V. 1947. *Les Dialogues de Platon. Structure et méthode dialectique*, Paris: Presses Universitaires de France.

———. *1949. La Religion de Platon*, Paris: Presses Universitaires de France.

———. *1970a. Questions platoniciennes*, Paris: Vrin.

———. *1970b. Platonisme et pensée contemporaine*, Paris: Aubier.

Goodwin, W.W. 1889. *Syntax of the Moods and Tenses of the Greek Verb*, London: Macmillan.

Görgemanns, H. 1960. *Beiträge zur Interpretation von Platons Nomoi*, Munich: C. H. Beck.

Gould, J. 1955. *The Development of Plato's Ethics*, Cambridge University Press.

Goulet, R., ed. 1994–2018. *Dictionnaire des philosophes antiques*, 7 vols. and a Supplement, Paris: Éditions du CNRS.

Gregorio, F. 2011. "La question du Platonisme de Rousseau," *Philosophie Antique* 11, pp. 43–71.

Griswold, C. 2007. "Plato and Forgiveness," *Ancient Philosophy* 27, pp. 269–87.

Groisard, J. 2016. *Mixis. Le Problème du mélange dans la philosophie grecque d'Aristote à Simplicius*, Paris: Les Belles-Lettres.

Günther, H., ed. 1980. É. de La Boétie, *Von der freiwilligen Knechtschaft* [*De la servitude volontaire*], Frankfurt am Main: Europäische Verlagsanstalt.

Hall, J. M. 1997. *Ethnic Identity in Greek Antiquity*, Cambridge University Press.

Halliwell, S. 1984. "Plato and Aristotle on the Denial of Tragedy," *Proceedings of the Cambridge Philological Society* 30, pp. 49–71.

———. 1986/1998². *Aristotle's Poetics*, London: Duckworth.

———. 1996. "Plato's Repudiation of the Tragic," in M. S. Silk, ed., *Tragedy and the Tragic*, Oxford University Press, pp. 332–49.

———. 1997. "The *Republic's* Two Critiques of Poetry," in O. Höffe, ed., *Platon. Politeia*, Akademie Verlag, pp. 313–32.

Hankins, J. 2019. *Virtue Politics: Soulcraft and Statecraft in Renaissance Italy*, Cambridge, MA: Harvard University Press.

Harvey, F. D. 1965. "Two Kinds of Equality," *Classica et Mediaevalia* 16, pp. 101–46.

Heinimann, F. 1945. *Nomos und Physis; Herkunft und Bedeutung einer Antithese im griechischen Denken des 5. Jahrhunderts*, Basel: F. Reinhardt.

Helmer, E. 2010. *La Part du bronze: Platon et l'économie*, Paris: Vrin.

———. 2017. "Le 'marché' chez Platon: un lieu de justice et de vérité," *Études platoniciennes*, 13, https://doi.org/10.400/etudesplatoniciennes.1164.

———. 2018. "Le commerce de la vérité: Économie et commerce dans les *Lois* de Platon," *Plato Journal: The Journal of the International Plato Society* 17, pp. 51–64.

Hentschke, A. B. 1971. *Politik und Philosophie bei Platon und Aristoteles. Die Stellung der 'Nomoi' im platonischen Gesamtwerk und die politische Theorie des Aristoteles*, Frankfurt am Main. See also under Neschke-Hentschke.

Hodkinson, S. 2005. "The Imaginary Spartan *politeia*," in M. H. Hansen, ed. *The Imaginary Polis* (Acts of the Copenhagen Polis Centre 7), Copenhagen: Det Kongelige Danske Videnskabernes Selskab, pp. 222–81.

Hölkeskamp, K.-J. 1992. "Written Law in Archaic Greece," *Proceedings of the Cambridge Philological Society* 38, pp. 87–117.

Horn, C., ed. 2013. *Platon. Gesetze—Nomoi*, Berlin: Akademie Verlag.

———. 2014. "How Close is Augustine's *liberum arbitrium* to the Concept of *to eph' hêmin*?" in Destrée, Salles, and Zingano, eds., pp. 295–310.

Huffman, C. A. 2005. *Archytas of Tarentum, Pythagorean, Philosopher and Mathematician King*, Cambridge University Press.

———. 2013. "Plato and the Pythagoreans," in G. Cornelli, R. McKirahan, and C. Macris, eds., *On Pythagoreanism*, Berlin: De Gruyter, pp. 237–70.

Hutchinson, D. S., and Johnson, M. R. 2014. "Protreptic Aspects of Aristotle's *Nicomachean Ethics*," in R. Polansky, ed., *The Cambridge Companion to Aristotle's* Nicomachean Ethics, Cambridge University Press, pp. 383–409.

Inwood, B. 2005. "Rules and Reasoning in Stoic Ethics," in B. Inwood, ed., *Reading Seneca: Stoic Philosophy at Rome*, Oxford: Clarendon Press, Oxford University Press, pp. 95–131.

Ioppolo, A. M. 1980. *Aristone di Chio e lo stoicismo antico*, Naples: Bibliopolis.

Jaeger, W. 1934/1959³. *Paideia. Die Formung des griechischen Menschen*, 3 vols., Berlin.

Joly, R. 1969. "Esclaves et médecins dans la Grèce Antique," *Sudhoffs Archiv* 53, pp. 1–23.

Jones, J. W. 1956. *The Law and Legal Theory of the Greeks*, Oxford: Clarendon Press.

Jouanna, J. 1978. "Le médecin modèle du législateur dans les *Lois* de Platon," *Ktèma* 3, 77–91.

Jouët-Pastré, E. 2006. *Le Jeu et le sérieux dans les* Lois de Platon, Sankt Augustin: Academia Verlag.

Judet de La Combe, P. 2010. *Les Tragédies grecques sont-elles tragiques? Théâtre et théorie*, Montrouge: Bayard Éditions.

———. 2020. "La critique du jugement dans l'*Orestie* d'Eschyle," *Les cahiers de la justice* 4, pp. 749–64.

Kahn, C. H. 1995. "The Place of the *Statesman* in Plato's Later Work," in C. J. Rowe, ed., *Reading the Statesman: Proceedings of the iii Symposium Platonicum*, Sankt Augustin: Academia Verlag, pp. 49–60.

———. 2004. "From *Republic* to *Laws*: A Discussion of Christopher Bobonich, *Plato's Utopia Recast*," *Oxford Studies in Ancient Philosophy* 26, pp. 337–62.

Kambylis, A. 1965. *Die Dichterweihe und ihre Symbolik. Untersuchungen zu Hesiodos, Kallimachos, Properz und Ennius*, Heidelberg: Carl Winter.

Kamtekar, R. and R. Singpurwalla. 2022. "Law in Plato's Late Politics," in R. Kraut and D. Ebrey, eds., *The Cambridge Companion to Plato*, Cambridge University Press.

Kennell, N. M. 1995. *The Gymnasium of Virtue: Education and Culture in Ancient Sparta*, Chapel Hill: University of North Carolina Press.

Kidd, S. 2017. "*Pente grammai* and the Holy Line," *Board Games Studies Journal* 11, pp. 83–99.

Kojève, A. See Strauss, L. 2013.

Köller, H. 1954. *Die Mimesis in der Antike; Nachahmung, Darstellung, Ausdruck,* Berne: A. Francke.

———. 1956. "Das kitharodisches Prooimion. Eine formgeschichtliche Untersuchung," *Philologus* 100, pp. 159–206.

Konstan, D. 2010. *Before Forgivness: The Origins of a Moral Idea,* Cambridge University Press.

Krämer, H. J. 1959. *Areté bei Platon und Aristoteles. Zum Wesen und zur Geschichte der platonischen Ontologie,* Heidelberg 1959 (= Abhandlungen d. Heidelberger Akad.d. Wiss., phil.-hist. Klasse, Amsterdam 1967).

Kudlien, F. 1968. *Die Sklaven in der griechischen Medizin der klassischen und hellenistischen Zeit,* Wiesbaden: F. Steiner.

Kuhn, H. 1941/1942/1960. "The True Tragedy. On the Relationship between Greek Tragedy and Plato," *Harvard Studies in Classical Philology* 52, 1941, pp. 1–140; and 53, 1942, pp. 37–88 [= "Die wahre Tragödie. Platon als Nachfolger der Tragiker," in K. Gaiser, ed., *Das Platonbild,* Hildesheim/Zürich/New York: Olms Verlag, 1960, pp. 231–323].

Kurke, L. 2020. "Imagining Chorality: Wonder, Plato's Puppets and Moving Statues," in A.-E. Peponi, ed., *Performance and Culture in Plato's Laws,* Cambridge University Press, pp. 123–70.

Lain-Entralgo, P. 1958. "Die platonische Rationalisierung der Besprechung (*épôidê*) und die Erfindung der Psychotherapie durch das Wort," *Hermes* 86, pp. 298–323.

———. 1970. *The Therapy of the Word in Classical Antiquity,* New Haven, CT: Yale University Press.

Laks, A. 1988. *Loi et persuasion. Sur la structure de la pensée politique de Platon,* typewritten thesis (Doctorat d'État), Université de Paris 4-Sorbonne.

———. 1990. "Legislation and Demiurgy: On the Relationship between Plato's *Republic* and *Laws*," *Classical Antiquity* 9, pp. 209–29.

———. 1991. "L'utopie législative de Platon," *Revue philosophique* 116, pp. 417–28.

———. 1996. "Le double du roi," in F. Blaise, P. Judet de La Combe, and P. Rousseau, eds., *Le Métier du mythe. Lectures d'Hésiode,* Villeneure d'Ascq: Presses Universitaires du Septentrion, pp. 83–91.

———. A. 2000. "The *Laws*," in C. Rowe and M. Schofield, eds., *The Cambridge History of Greek and Roman Political Thought,* Cambridge University Press, pp. 258–92.

———. 2005. *Médiation et coercition. Pour une lecture des 'Lois' de Platon,* Villeneuve d'Ascq: Presses Universitaires du Septentrion.

———. 2007a. "Préambule sur les préambules," *Rhetorica* 25/1 (special issue: "The interface between philosophy and rhetoric in classical Athens"), pp. 53–71.

———. 2007b. "Marionnette ou miracle ? Une note sur l'interprétation ficinienne d'un passage des *Lois* de Platon (I, 644c1—645c8)," in L. Boulègue and C. Lévy, eds., *Hédonismes. Penser et dire le plaisir dans l'Antiquité et à la Renaissance,* Villeneuve d'Ascq: Presses Universitaires du Septentrion, pp. 255–60.

———. 2007c. "Freedom, Liberality and Liberty in Plato's *Laws*," in D. Keyt and F. Miller, eds., *Freedom, Reason, and the Polis: Essays in Ancient Greek Political Philosophy,* Cambridge University Press, pp. 130–52 (also in *Social Philosophy and Policy* 24/2, 2007).

———. 2010. "Plato's 'truest tragedy' (*Laws*, 817a-b)," in C. Bobonich, ed., *A Critical Guide to Plato's* Laws, Cambridge University Press, pp. 217–31.

———. 2011. "Une insistance de Platon: à propos de la 'vraie tragédie' (*Lois* VII, 817a–d)," in C. König and H. Wismann, eds., *La Lecture insistante. Autour de Jean Bollack*, Paris: Albin Michel, pp. 35–52.

———. 2012. "Temporalité et utopie: remarques herméneutiques sur la question de la possibilité des cités platoniciennes," in F. Lisi, ed., pp. 19–37.

———. 2013a. "Encore une histoire primordiale de la théorie" (Postface to A. Laks and R. Saetta-Cottone, eds., pp. 227–34).

———. 2013b. "Private matters in Plato's *Laws*," in C. Horn, ed., *Platon. Gesetze—Nomoi*, Berlin: Akademie Verlag, pp. 165–88.

———. 2019. "Schleiermacher on Plato: From Form (*Introduction* to Plato's Works) to Content (*Outlines of a Critique of Previous Ethical Theory*)," in A. Kim, ed., *Brill's Companion to German Platonism*, pp. 146–64.

Laks, A., and R. Saetta-Cottone, eds. 2013. *Comédie et Philosophie. Socrate et les "Présocratiques" dans les* Nuées *d'Aristophane*, Paris: Éditions Rue d'Ulm.

Lamer, H. 1927. "Lusoria Tabula," in *Realencyclädie der classischen Altertumswissenschaft* XIII, cols. 1900–2029.

Landauer, M. Forthcoming. *From Democracy to the Mixed Regime: Plato and Aristotle on Constitutional Reform.*

———. Forthcoming. "Drinking Parties Correctly Ordered: Plato on Mass Participation and the Necessity of Rule," *Journal of Politics*. https://doi.org/10.1086/715998.

Lane, M. 1998. *Method and Politics in Plato's* Statesman, Cambridge University Press.

———. 2010. "Force et Persuasion dans la politique platonicienne," in Brancacci, A., D. El Murr, and D. P. Taormina, eds., *Aglaïa. Autour de Platon. Mélanges offerts à Monique Dixsaut*, Paris: Vrin, pp. 165–98.

———. 2018. "Placing Plato in the History of Liberty," *History of European Ideas* 44, pp. 702–18.

———. Forthcoming 2022. *Of Rule and Office: Plato's Ideas of the Political*, Princeton University Press.

Larivée, A. 2003. "Du vin pour le Collège de veille ? Mise en lumière d'un lien occulté entre le Chœur de Dionysos et le *nukterinos sullogos* dans les *Lois* de Platon," *Phronesis* 48, pp. 29–53.

Lausberg, H. 1973/1960[1]. *Handbuch der literarischen Rhetorik*, 2 vols., Stuttgart: Max Hueber.

Lee, E. N. 1976. "Reason and Rotation: Circular Movement as the Model of Mind (*Nous*) in Later Plato," in W. H. Werkmeister, ed., *Facets of Plato's Philosophy*, Assen-Amsterdam (=*Phronesis*, Supplement 2), pp. 70–102.

Levinson, R. D. 1953. *In Defense of Plato*, Cambridge, MA: Harvard University Press.

Lévystone, D. 2022. "Dioecismo y ciudad ideal; acerca de la *República* de Platón, VII 540e4–541a1," *Journal of Ancient Philosophy* 16/1, pp. 1–26 (https://doi.org/10.11606).

Lilla, M. 2001. "The Lure of Syracuse," *New York Review of Books*, September 20, 2001.

Lisi, F. L. 1985. *Einheit und Vielheit des platonischen Nomosbegriffes. Eine Untersuchung zur Beziehung von Philosophie und Politik bei Platon*, Königstein im Taunus: Anton Hain.

———. 2000. "Les fondements philosophiques du *nomos* dans les *Lois*," *Revue Philosophique*, 190, pp. 57–82.

———, ed. 2001. *Plato's Laws and Its Historical Significance: Selected Papers from the 1. International Congress on Ancient Thought (Salamanque 1998)*, Sankt Augustin: Academia Verlag.

———. 2004. "Héros, dieux et philosophes," *Revue d'Études Anciennes* 106, pp. 5–22.

———. 2008. "*Nemo sua sponte peccat*. Platons Begründung des Strafrechts in der *Nomoi* (IX 859d-864c)," *Politisches Denken. Jahrbuch* 2008, p. 87–108.

———. 2010. "Violence and Law in Plato's Second-Best Constitution," in A. Bosch-Veciana and J. Monserrat-Molas, eds., *Philosophy and Dialogue: Studies on Plato's Dialogues*, Barcelona: Barcelonesa d'Edicions, vol. 2, pp. 157–68.

———, ed. 2012. *Utopia, Ancient and Modern: Contributions to the History of a Political Dream*, Sankt Augustin: Academia Verlag.

———. 2015."Legge ed essere. Il Minosse e il pensiero politico platonico," in *Seconda navegazione. Ommaggio a Giovanni Reale*, Milano: Vita e pensiero, pp. 355–64.

Loraux, N. 1974. "Socrate contrepoison de l'oraison funèbre. Enjeu et signification du *Ménéxène*," *L'Antiquité classique*, 43, pp. 172–211.

Lorenz, H. 2004. Review of Bobonich 2002, *Philosophical Review* 113, pp. 560–66.

Luraghi, N. 2013. "One Man Government: The Greeks and Monarchy," in H. Beck, ed., *A Companion to Ancient Greek Government*, Oxford: Wiley-Blackwell, pp. 131–45.

Macé, A. 2017. "Purifications et distributions sociales: Platon et le pastorat politique," *Philosophie antique* 17, pp. 101–23.

Macris, C. 2018. "Zaleucos," in R. Goulet, ed., *Dictionnaire des philosophes antiques*, vol. 7, Paris: Éditions du CNRS, pp. 308–17.

Mahieu, W. de. 1963/1964. "La doctrine des athées au Xe livre des *Lois* de Platon," *Revue Belge de Philologie et d'Histoire* 41, 1963, pp. 5–24 (I. Essai d'analyse) and 42, 1964, pp. 16–47 (II. Étude des sources).

Mai, H. 2014. *Platons Nachlass. Zur philosophischen Dimension der Nomoi*, Freiburg/Munich: Karl Alber.

Martin, R. P., 1989. *The Language of Heroes. Speech and Performance in the* Iliad, Ithaca, NY: Cornell University Press.

Maslov, B. 2012. "The Real Life of the Genre of Prooimion," *Classical Philology* 107, pp. 191–205.

Mayhew, R. 2008. Plato, *Laws* 10, Oxford: Clarendon Press.

McIlwain, C. H. 1947. *Constitutionalism: Ancient and Modern*, Ithaca, NY: Cornell University Press.

Menn, S. 1995. *Plato on God as* Nous, Carbondale: Southern Illinois University Press (Journal of the History of Philosophy Monographs Series).

Meyer, S. S. 1993. *Aristotle on Moral Responsibility*, Oxford: Basil Blackwell.

———. 2011. "Legislation as a Tragedy: On Plato's *Laws* VII, 817B–D," in P. Destrée and F.-G. Herrmann, eds., *Plato and the Poets*, Leiden: Brill, pp. 387–402.

———. 2015. Plato, *Laws* 1 and 2, Oxford University Press.

———. 2021. "Civic Freedom in Plato's *Laws*," *Polis* 38, pp. 512–34.

Miller, F., 2018. "Platonic Freedom," *Oxford Handbook of Freedom*, D. Schmitdz and C. E. Pavel, eds., Oxford University Press, pp. 143–59.

Monfasani, J. 2008. "A Tale of Two Books: Bessarion's *In Calumniatoris Platonis* and George of Trebizond's *Comparatio philosophorum Platonis et Aristotelis*," *Renaissance Studies* 22, pp. 1–16.

Morlet, S. 2019. *Symphonia. La concorde des textes et des doctrines dans la littérature grecque jusqu'à Origène*, Paris: Les Belles-Lettres.

Morrison, D. R. 2007. "The Utopian Character of Plato's Ideal City," in G.R.F. Ferrari, ed., *The Cambridge Companion to Plato's* Republic, Cambridge University Press, pp. 231–55.

Morrow, G. R. 1954. "The Demiurge in Politics: The *Timaeus* and the *Laws*," *Proceedings and Addresses of the American Philosophical Association* 27, pp. 5–23.

———. 1960. "Aristotle's Comments on Plato's *Laws*," in I. Düring and G.E.L. Owen, eds., *Aristotle and Plato in the Mid-fourth Century*, Göteborg: Almquvist & Wiskell, pp. 145–62.

———. [1960] 1993. *Plato's Cretan City: A Historical Study of the Laws*, Princeton University Press.

Moseley, G. 2018. "Pl. *Leg.* 631c6–7: Textual Gleanings from an Arabic Fragment," *Mnemosyne* 71, pp. 173–76.

Most, G. W. 2011. "What Ancient Quarrel between Philosophy and Poetry?" in P. Destrée and F.-G. Herrmann, eds., *Plato and the Poets*, Leiden/Boston: Brill, pp. 1–20.

———. [1994] 2019. "Simonides' Ode to Scopas in Contexts," in I. Rutherford, ed., *Oxford Readings in Greek Lyric Poetry*, Oxford University Press, pp. 412–41.

Mouze, L. 2005. *Le Législateur et le poète. Une interprétation des Lois de Platon*, Villeneuve d'Ascq: Presses Universitaires du Septentrion.

Mühl, M. 1929. "Die Gesetze des Zaleukos und Charondas," *Klio* 22, pp. 105–24.

Müller, F. von. 1956. *Unterhaltungen mit Goethe*, E. Grumach, ed., Weimar: H. Böhlaus Nachfolger.

Müller, G. 1951[1968²]. *Studien zu den platonischen 'Nomoi,'* Munich: Beck.

Muller, R. 1997. *La Doctrine platonicienne de la liberté*, Paris: Vrin.

Murgier, C. 2017. "*Oikeion* and Justice in Plato's *Republic*," Π Η Γ Η / F O N S II, pp. 65–85.

Nagy, G. 2021. "On the etymology of προοίμιον (prooímion)," *Classical Continuum*, November 21. https://continuum.fas.harvard.edu/on-the-etymology-of-prooimion.

Natorp, P. [1875] 1922. "Platons Staat und die Idee der Sozialpädagogik," in *Gesammelte Abhandlungen zur Sozialpädagogik*, vol. 1., Stuttgart: F. Frommann, pp. 7–42.

Nelson, E. 2004. *The Greek Tradition in Republican Thought*, Cambridge University Press.

Neschke-Hentschke, A. 1995/2003. *Platonisme politique et théorie du droit naturel. Contributions à une archéologie de la culture politique européenne*, vol. 1: *Le Platonisme politique dans l'Antiquité*, vol. 2: *Platonisme politique et le jusnaturalisme chrétien. La tradition directe et indirecte d'Augustin d'Hippone à John Locke*, Louvain-la-Neuve: Peeters.

———. 2012. "Platon, penseur de la liberté effective. Les utopies modernes et le réalisme platonicien," in L. Brisson, ed., *Études Platoniciennes* 9 (*Plato Today*), pp. 83–104. See also under Hentschke.

de Nicolay, R. 2021. "The Birth of Lawless Freedom in Plato's *Laws* 3," *Polis* 38, pp. 494–511.

———. Forthcoming. "Philosopher-King on a Leash: Combining Plato's *Republic*, *Statesman* and *Laws* in the Justinianic Dialogue '*On Political Science.*'"

Ollier, F. 1933. *Le Mirage Spartiate. Étude sur l'idéalisation de Sparte dans l'Antiquité grecque de l'origine jusqu'aux Cyniques*, Paris: E. de Boccard.

O'Meara, D. 2002. "The Justinianic Dialogue 'On Political Science' and Its Neoplatonic Sources," in K. Ierodiakonou, ed., *Byzantine Philosophy and Its Ancient Sources*, Oxford University Press, pp. 49–62.

———. 2003. *Platonopolis: Platonic Political Thought in Late Antiquity*, Oxford University Press.

———. 2017. *Cosmology and Politics in Plato's Later Works*, Cambridge University Press.

Ostwald, M. 1969. *Nomos and the Beginnings of Athenian Democracy*, Oxford: Clarendon Press.

Ottmann, H. 2008. "Platons Mischverfassung," *Politisches Denken: Jahrbuch* 2008, pp. 33–42.

Panno, G. 2007. *Dionisaco e Alterità nelle 'Leggi' di Platone*, Milan: Vita e Piensero.

Patterson, C. 2017. "Slavery in Plato's *Republic*?" unpublished paper presented at the Celtic Classics Conference in Montreal in 2017.

Peponi, A.-E., ed. 2013. *Performance and Culture in Plato's* Laws, Cambridge University Press.

Pfefferkorn, J. 2020. "Shame and Virtue in Plato's *Laws*: Two Kinds of Fear and the Drunken Puppet," in L. Candiotto and O. Renaut, eds., *Emotions in Plato*, Leiden: Brill, pp. 252–60.

Picht, G. 1990. *Platons Dialoge 'Nomoi' und 'Symposium,'* with an introduction by W. Wieland, Stuttgart: Klett Cotta.

Piérart, M. 1974. *Platon et la cité grecque. Théorie et réalité dans la constitution des 'Lois,'"* Brussels: Académie royale de Belgique.

Pini, G. 1974. "Sul Νόμος ὁ πάντων βασιλεύς di Pindaro [fr.169 Sn.⁴]," *Studi Italiani di Filologia Classica* 46, pp. 185–210.

Pöhlmann, R. von. 1893–1901. *Geschichte des antiken Kommunismus und Sozialismus*, 2 vols., Munich: C.H. Beck.

Popper, K. R. [1945] 2013. *The Open Society and Its Enemies*, one-volume edition, introduction by A. Ryan, essay by E. H. Gombrich, Princeton University Press.

Powell, G .F. 2001. "Were Cicero's *Laws* the *Laws* of Cicero's *Republic*?" in G. F. Powell and J. A. North, eds., *Cicero's Republic: Bulletin of the Institute of Classical Studies Supplement* 76, pp. 17–39.

Pradeau, J.-F. 1997. *Le Monde de la politique. Sur le récit Atlante de Platon*, Timée (17–27) *et* Critias, Sankt-Augustin: Academia Verlag.

———.2004. "L'ébriété démocratique: la critique platonicienne de la démocratie dans les *Lois*," *Journal of Hellenic Studies* 124, pp. 108–24.

Prauscello, L. 2014. *Performing Citizenship in Plato's Laws*, Cambridge University Press.

Prévost, A. 1971. "L'Utopie: le genre littéraire," in G. Marc'hadour, ed., *Moreana* 31/32 (Festschrift on More's Utopia in Honour of Edward Surtz), pp. 161–68.

Raaflaub, K. A. 2004. *The Discovery of Freedom in Ancient Greece*, Chicago: University of Chicago Press.

Rashed, M. 2018. "Une analogie méconnue entre le *Timée* et les *Lois*," in *Les Études philosophiques* 124, pp. 115–38.

Rawson, E. 1969. *The Spartan Tradition in European Thought*, Oxford: Clarendon Press.

Rees, D. A. 1957. "Bipartition of the Soul in the Early Academy," *Journal of Hellenic Studies* 77, pp. 112–18.

Reid, J. 2020a. "The Mixed Constitution in Plato's *Laws*," *Australasian Journal of Philosophy* 98, pp. 1–18.

———. 2020b. "The Offices of Magnesia," *Polis* 37, pp. 567–89.

———. 2021. "Changing the Laws of the *Laws*," *Ancient Philosophy* 41, pp. 1–29.

Renaut, O. 2014. *Platon, La Médiation des émotions. L'éducation du* thymos *dans les dialogues*, Paris: Vrin.

———. 2020. "Emotions and Rationality in the *Timaeus* (*Ti.* 42a,–b, 69c–72e)," in L. Candiotto and O. Renaut, eds., *Emotions in Plato*, Leiden: Brill, pp. 103–22.

Ries, G. 1983. *Prolog und Epilog in Gesetzen des Altertums*, Munich: Beck.

Robinson, T. M. [1970] 1995. *Plato's Psychology*, Toronto: University of Toronto Press.

Rösler, W. 1995. "Wine and Truth in the Greek Symposium," in O. Murray and M. Tecusan, eds., *In Vino Veritas*, O. Murray and eds., Rome: British School at Rome, pp. 106–12.

Romilly, J. 1971. *La Loi dans la pensée grecque, des origines à Aristote*, Paris: Les Belles-Lettres.

Rousseau, P. 2001. "L'intrigue de Zeus," *Europe* 79, pp. 120–58; trans. "The Plot of Zeus," on the website of the Center for Hellenic Studies, Harvard University.

———. [1995] 2019. *Destin des héros et dessein de Zeus dans l'intrigue de l'Iliade*, Villeneuve d'Ascq, Atelier national des Thèses.

Rowe, C. J., ed. 1995. *Reading the Statesman: Proceedings of the III Symposium Platonicum*, Sankt Augustin: Academia Verlag.

———. 2001. "Killing Socrates: Plato's Later Thoughts on Democracy," *Journal of Hellenic Studies* 121, pp. 63–76.

———. 2006. "The Treatment of Non-ideal Constitutions in the *Politicus*," in G. Anagnostopoulos, ed., *Laws and Rights in Ancient Greek Tradition* (Philosophical Inquiry Supplementary vol.), pp. 106–21.

———. 2007. *Plato and the Art of Philosophical Writing*, Cambridge University Press.

———. 2010. "The Relationship to Other Dialogues: A Proposal," in C. Bobonich, ed., *A Critical Guide to Plato's Laws*, Cambridge University Press pp. 29–50.

———. 2013. "The Statesman and the Best City," in A. Havlíček, J. Jirsa, and K.Thein, eds., *Plato's Statesman—Proceedings of the Eighth Symposium Platonicum Pragense*, Prague: OIKOYMENH, pp. 40–50.

———. 2019. "Philosophy and Linguistic Authority: The Problem of Plato's Greek," in C. Stray, M. Clarke, and J. T. Katz, eds., *Liddell and Scott: The History, Methodology, and Languages of the World's Leading Lexicon of Ancient Greek*, Oxford University Press, pp. 124–40.

Sassi, M. M. 2008. "The Self, the Soul, and the Individual in the City of the *Laws*," *Oxford Studies in Ancient Philosophy* 35, pp. 125–48.

Saunders, T. J. 1962. "The Structure of the Soul and the State in Plato's *Laws*," *Eranos* 60, pp. 37–55.

———. 1970. "The Alleged Double Version in the Sixth Book of Plato's *Laws*," *Classical Quarterly* 20, pp. 230–36.

———. 1973. "Penology and Eschatology in Plato's *Timaeus* and *Laws*," *Classical Quarterly* 23, pp. 232–44.

———. 1991. *Plato's Penal Code: Tradition, Controversy and Reform in Greek Penology*, Oxford University Press.

———. 2001. "*Epieikeia*: Plato and the Controversial Virtue of the Greeks," in F. L. Lisi, ed., pp. 65–93.

Schafer, J. 2009. *Ars didactica: Seneca's 94th and 95th Letters*, Göttingen: Vandenhoeck and Ruprecht.

Schmitt, C. 1988. *Political Theology: Four Chapters on the Concept of Sovereignty*, Cambridge, MA: MIT Press.

Schmitt-Pantel, P. 1992. *La Cité au banquet. Histoire des repas publics dans les cités grecques*, Rome: Publications de l'École Française de Rome.

Schnapp, A. 1997. *Le Chasseur et la cité: chasse et érotique en Grèce ancienne*, Paris: Albin Michel.

Schofield, M. 1997. "The Disappearance of the Philosopher King," *Proceedings of the Boston Area Philosophy Colloquium in Ancient Philosophy* 13, pp. 213–41 = M. S., 1999, *Saving the City: Philosopher-Kings and Other Classical Paradigms*, London-New York, Chap. 8.

———. 2006. *Plato: Political Philosophy*, Oxford University Press.

———. 2013. "Friendship and Justice in the *Laws*," in G. Boys-Stone and D. El Murr, eds., *The Platonic Art of Philosophy*, Cambridge University Press, pp. 283–97.

———. 2016. "Plato's Marionette," *Rhizomata* 4, pp. 128–53.

Schöpsdau, K. 1986. "Tapferkeit, Aidos und Sophrosyne im ersten Buch der platonischen *Nomoi*," *Rheinisches Museum für klassische Philologie* 129, pp. 97–123.

———. 1991. "Der Staatsentwurf der *Nomoi* zwischen Ideal und Wirklichkeit. Zu Plato *Leg.* 739a1–27 und 745e7–746d2," *Rheinisches Museum für klassische Philologie* 139, pp. 136–52.

Sedley, D. 2013. "The Atheist Underground," in V. Harte and M. Lane, eds., *Politeia in Greek and Roman Philosophy*, Cambridge University Press, pp. 329–48.

Sharafat, S. 1998. *Elemente von Platons Anthropologie in den* Nomoi, Frankfurt am Main: P. Lang.

Sheffield, F. 2020. "Love in the City: Eros and Philia in Plato's *Laws*," in L. Candiotto and O. Renaut, eds., *Emotions in Plato*, Leiden: Brill, pp. 330–71.

Siniosssoglou, N. 2017. "Plethon, Scholarios, and the Byzantine State of Emergency," in *The Cambridge Intellectual History of Byzantium*, Cambridge University Press, pp. 633–52.

Solmsen, F., 1942. *Plato's Theology*, Ithaca, NY: Cornell University Press.

Stalley, R. F. 1983. *An Introduction to Plato's Laws*, Oxford: B. Blackwell.

———. 1998. "Plato's Doctrine of Freedom," *Proceedings of the Aristotelian Society* 98, pp. 145–58.

Strauss, L. 1965. "Preface to the English Translation," in L. Strauss, *Spinoza's Critique of Religion*, trans. by E. M. Sinclair, New York: Schocken Books, pp. 1–31.

———. 1996. *Die Religionskritik Spinozas als Grundlage seiner Bibelwissenschaft. Untersuchungen zu Spinozas Theologisch-politischem Traktat* (1930), in L. Srauss, *Gesammelte Schriften*, vol. 1, Stuttgart-Weimar: Metzler.

———.1997. *Philosophie und Gesetz. Frühe Schriften* = L.S., *Gesammelte Schriften*, vol. 2, Stuttgart-Weimar: Metzler.

———. 2013. *On Tyranny* (1948) in L. Stauss, *On Tyranny—Including the Strauss-Kojève correspondence*, V. Gourevitch and M. S. Roth, eds., Chicago: University of Chicago Press, 2013.

Supiot, A. 2007. *Homo juridicus: On the Anthropological Function of the Law*, trans. by S. Brown, London-New York: Verso 2007 (French original: *Homo juridicus. Essai sur la fonction anthropologique du droit*, Paris: Seuil, 2005).

Tarán, L. 1975. *Academica: Plato, Philip of Opus, and the Pseudo-Platonic 'Epinomis,'* Philadelphia: American Philosophical Society.

Tarrant, H. 2012. "Plato's *Republics*," *Plato: Electronic Journal of the Plato International Society*, 12, DOI: https://doi.org/10.14195/2183-4105_12_5.

Thouard, D. 2021. "Une poétique de la résignation. Réflexions sur le style tardif," in C. König and D. Thouard, eds., *Goethe, le second auteur*, Paris: Hermann.

Trousson, R. 1975. *Voyages au pays de nulle part. Histoire littéraire de la pensée utopique*, Brussels.

Van Riel, G. 2016. *Plato's Gods*, London: Routledge.

Vatter, M. 2011. "Natural Right and State of Exception in Strauss's Teaching on Tyranny," in M. Vatter, ed., *Crediting God: Sovereignty and Religion in the Age of Global Capitalism*, New York: Fordham University Press, pp. 190–206.

———. 2012. "The Quarrel between Populism and Republicanism: Machiavelli and the Antinomies of Plebeian Politics," *Contemporary Political Theory* 11, pp. 242–63.

———. 2020. *Divine Democracy: Political Theology after Carl Schmitt*, Oxford University Press.

———. 2021. *Living Law: Jewish Political Theology from Hermann Cohen to Hannah Arendt*, Oxford University Press.

Vegetti, M., ed. 1998–2007, Platone. *La Repubblica*, with Italian translation and commentary by various authors, Naples: Bibliopolis. Vol. I (1998): Libro I; Vol. II (1998): Libro II–III; Vol. III (1998): Libro IV; Vol. IV (2000): Libro V; Vol. V (2003): Libro VI–VII; Vol. VI (2005): Libro VIII–IX; Vol. VII (2007): Libro X.

———. 1999. "L'autocritica di Platone: il *Timaeo* e le *Leggi*," in M. Vegetti and M. Abbate, eds., *La Repubblica di Platone nella tradizione antica*, Naples: Bibliopolis, pp. 13–27.

———. 2000. "*Beltista eiper dunata*: lo statuto dell' utopia nella *Repubblica*," in M. Vegetti, ed., *La Repubblica*, 1998–2007, Vol. IV, pp. 107–47.

———. 2000. "La critica aristotelica alla *República* nel secondo libro della *Politica*, il *Timeo* e i *Leggi*," in M. Vegetti, ed., *La Repubblica*, 1998–2007, Vol. IV, pp. 439–52.

———. 2005. "Il tiempo, la storia, l'utopia," in M. Vegetti, ed., *La Repubblica*, 1998–2007, Vol. VI, pp. 137–68.

———. 2007 "Introduzione al libro X," in M. Vegetti, ed., *La Repubblica*, 1998–2007, Vol. VII, pp. 13–34.

———. 2009. '*Un paradigma in cielo*.' *Platone politico da Aristotele al Novecento*, Rome: Carocci.

———. 2018. *Il potere della verità, Saggi platonici*, Rome: Carocci.

———. 2020. See under Forcignano and Vegetti.

Veyne, P. 1982. "Critique d'une systématisation: Les *Lois* de Platon et la réalité," *Annales* 37, pp. 883–908.

Vidal-Naquet, P. 1978. "Plato's Myth of the Statesman: The Ambiguities of the Golden Age and of History," *Journal of Hellenic Studies* 98, pp. 132–41.

Vlastos, G. [1941] 1981. "Slavery in Plato's Thought", in G. V., *Platonic Studies*, Princeton University Press, pp. 147–63.

von Fritz, K. 1954. *The Theory of the Mixed Constitution in Antiquity: A Critical Analysis of Polybius' Political Theory*, New York: Columbia University Press.

———. 1965. "*Eleutheria* in Herodotus," *Wiener Studien* 78, pp. 5–31.

Warren, J. 2013. "Comparing Lives in Plato, *Laws* 5," *Phronesis* 58, pp. 319–46.

Webb, R. 1989. "The *Nomoi* of Gemistos Plethon in the Light of Plato's *Laws*," *Journal of the Warburg and Courtauld Institutes* 52, pp. 214–19.

Wilamowitz-Moellendorf, U. v. 1910. "Lesefrüchte," *Hermes* 45, pp. 387–417.

———. 1920. *Platon*, 2. vol., Berlin: Weidmann.

Wilburn, J. 2012. "Akrasia and Self-Rule in Plato's *Laws*," *Oxford Studies in Ancient Philosophy* 43, pp. 25–53.

———. 2013. "Tripartition and the Causes of Criminal Behavior in *Laws* ix," *Ancient Philosophy* 33, pp. 111–34.

————.2014. "Is appetite ever persuaded? An Alternative Reading of *Republic* 554c-d," *History of Philosophy Quarterly* 31, pp. 195–208.

Will, E. 1956. *Doriens et Ioniens. Essai sur la valeur du critère ethnique appliqué à l'étude de l'histoire et de la civilisation grecques,* Paris: Les Belles Lettres.

Wise, J. 2008. "Tragedy as 'An Augury of a Happy Life,'" *Arethusa* 41, 2008, pp. 381–410.

Yu, K.W. 2020. "The Politics of Dance: Eunomia and the Exception of Dionysus in Plato's *Laws*," *Classical Quarterly* 70, pp. 605–19.

Zuolo, F. 2009. *Platone e l'efficacià. Realizzabilità della teoria normativa,* Sankt Augustin: Academia Verlag.

Plato, *Laws* (*continued*)

1.644d7, 183n28, 203n18
1.644d8, 170
1.644d8–9, 68
1.644d–645c1, 107
1.644e1, 66, 232n22
1.644e2–3, 66, 170
1.644e4, 170
1.644e4–6, 170
1.644e6, 170
1.644e6–645a2, 66
1.644e6–645a4, 224n14
1.644e6–645e2, 67
1.645a1, 67, 199n23
1.645a5, 66
1.645a5–6, 108
1.645a7, 67, 76
1.645a7–8, 67
1.645b1–2, 67, 76
1.645b1–3, 67
1.645c1–6, 65
1.645d6–7, 232n22
1.648a9–b2, 21
1.648c7, 188n39
1.648c7–e5, 21
1.649a4–5, 21
1.649d4–650b10, 21
1.688a6–b4, 206n5
2.653a3, 21
2.653b1–c4, 65
2.653b2–6, 20, 77
2.653d7–654a7, 69
2.654a4–5, 204n25
2.655a1–2, 205n34
2.655b9–e1, 204n25
2.655c8–d2, 70
2.655d1, 71
2.655d5, 71
2.655d7, 204n29
2.655e2, 70
2.656c1–d2, 111
2.656c4–5, 205n34
2.658b7–c1, 203n18
2.658c1, 203n18

2.658e6–659c5, 71
2.659a1–b2, 187n34
2.659b5–8, 204n33
2.660a3–8, 111
2.660e1, 71, 205n34
2.665d9–666c6, 21
2.668b6–7, 228n15
2.669c3–8, 103
2.674b7, 215n1
3.676a2, 187n35
3.676a8–b1, 187n36
3.677a4–6, 187n36
3.678a3–9, 187n36
3.681c1–d10, 187n36
3.682b7–8, 187n36
3.682e3–4, 184n10
3.682e8–693c5, 22
3.683a2, 184n10
3.683a2–3, 14
3.685a6–8, 185n17
3.685a7, 16
3.687a7, 80, 207n16
3.688a3–b4, 205n1
3.688a6–b4, 74
3.688b1–3, 75
3.688b2–4, 101
3.688d6–9, 104
3.689a7–9, 77
3.689d6–7, 77
3.690c1–3, 100, 108
3.691d8–692b1, 81
3.691d8–e1, 22, 78
3.691e2, 78
3.691e3, 78
3.692a7–8, 78
3.693b2–3, 78
3.693b3–4, 207n20
3.693b3–5, 22, 78
3.693b5, 75
3.693b5–6, 79
3.693b5–c5, 79
3.693c2, 183n28
3.693c7–d1, 80
3.693d2–e3, 80, 88

Aeschylus, 2, 6, 86, 182n15, 219n29

aim, as distinguished from 'goal' and 'target,' 25, 26, 31, 54, 74, 75, 78, 79, 107, 116, 117, 130, 154, 189, 210n26

analogy: between body and soul, 114; between city-in-speech and Form, 41, 218; between human beings and puppets, 21, 59, 66, 69, 107, 108, 155, 170, 201n2, 202n13, 204n27; between medicine and politics, doctor and lawgiver, 28, 110, 113, 115–22, 133, 145–47, 163–64, 217n33, 223n26; between ruler and shepherd, 19, 26; between soul and city, 33, 34, 40, 84, 176, 200n36

Anaxagoras. See *nous*

anger, 140, 147, 150, 174–76, 202n13, 214n51, 232n25; noble, 141. *See also* pity

animal, 144, 222n10; political, 132; tame and wild, human and divine, 65, 69, 72, 201n4, 204n24

anthropology, 3, 65–67. *See also* human being; *Laws* (Plato), substantial features

Antiphon, 108

Apollo, 16, 17, 186n23

approximation, 9, 38–40, 42, 62. *See also* paradigm

Archelaus, 225n4

Archytas of Tarentum, 93, 209n15

Argos, 22, 97

argument: human vs. divine, 59; rational, philosophical, 62, 106, 121, 128, 130, 132

aristocracy, aristocratic, 6, 19, 44, 78, 84, 95, 164, 172, 211n30, 214n54, 222n21

Aristophanes, 51, 144, 197n66, 225n25

Aristo the Stoic, 178, 233n4

Aristotle: on equality, 209–10n18; on the first mover and on nature, 143, 145; on liberality, 105; on the mean, 88; on metaphor, 174; on mixed constitutions, 208n3; on Plato's *Laws*, 2, 5, 31, 36–37, 151, 176, 177, 191n14, 198n13, 201n39, 206n13, 211n27, 214n50, 233; on rhetorical terminology, 127–28, 130, 138, 221n8; on Sparta's constitution, 78, 228n13; on tragedy, 228nn13 and 14, 229nn23 and 25; on voluntariness, 101; on wonder (*thauma*), 67–68

Assembly, 83, 85–87, 87, 95, 167, 208n1, 210n25

Athens. *See* constitution; *Laws* (Plato); Persia

Atlantis, 199n18, 230n2

Augustin, 3

authority: and freedom, 15, 22, 81, 83, 90, 92; moral and political, 18, 27, 95, 98, 112, 132, 179, 195n52, 209n8, 210n26

autocrat, 47, 67, 195n44. *See also* despot; tyrant

belief, 46, 66, 130, 134, 143, 172, 175, 176, 194n38, 195n44, 202n15, 215n1, 231n12. *See also* law

best vs. second-best: city, 1, 4, 5, 7, 20, 26, 57–62, 64, 137, 141, 150, 156, 165–66, 201n5; constitution, 4, 7, 31, 49, 65, 86, 150, 156, 189, 206n13, 214n57; in the *Statesman*, 160. *See also* city, first and second city; constitution

board game, 32, 58, 199nn21 and 22

Bodin, Jean, 181n4

Brucker, Jacob, 32, 50, 51, 192n20, 197n22

degrees of, 56, 70, 91, 161, 214n50; Dorian, 15; early, 29, 69, 101,190; educational program, 93, 130, 149–50, 186n30; extending throughout life, 57, 72; in general, 84, 126, 155, 179, 188nn38 and 40, 201n2, 209n17; highest, 190n64; and hunting, 222n19; and leisure, 105; musical and choral, 71, 187n35; and praise, 221n6; in the *Republic*, 36–38; 149. *See also* music; virtue; wine

egoism, selfishness, and self-love, 58, 132, 139, 140–142

ephors, 78, 81, 86, 88, 89, 207n14

equality: 1, 7, 37, 75, 81–82, 89; arithmetic (democratic) vs. geometric (proportional), 91–94, 209, 217; as a fourth legislative target, 93; and freedom, 1, 7, 95–96, 186, 204n28; and friendship, 90, 98; true, 90–93, 99, 155

equity, 210n21; and indulgence, 91, 94

etymology. *See* name(s)

Eusebius of Caesarea, 3

excellence (*aretê*). *See* virtue

excess: of confidence, 21; of freedom, 83–84; and mean, 1, 88–89, 195n44, 217n24; of pleasure, 155; of power, 58, 82, 166; of self-love, 141

exhortation, 28, 62, 111; and incantation or blame, 133; and persuasion, 113; self-exhortation, 135

expertise: medical, 114–16; political and legislative, 5, 7, 24, 46, 48–49, 114, 118, 122, 159, 161–63, 166, 189n50. *See also* craft; knowledge

al-Farabi, 4

feasibility. *See* possibility

Ficino, Marsilio 181n4, 203–204n24

fight: cosmic, 153; legislative, 110, 119, 134, 216n16, 202n6; for national independence, 78–81; between rational and irrational desires, 170, 212n35

flexibility. *See* name(s); preamble

foreigners, 137, 138, 221n5

form: of government, 18; Plato's Forms, 40–41, 43, 57, 72, 76, 154, 162, 198n6, 220n55. *See also* law; *Laws* (Plato)

Founding Fathers, 181n4

freedom: conceptions of, 99, 102, 105, 106, 212, 213, 218; excessive, 83–34; free life, 83, 222; and friendship, 96, 117, 148n42; as independence (national or otherwise), 78–79, 81, 84, 99, 207n15–16, 212n40; as a legislative goal, 22–23, 75, 77–85, 88–89; and leisure, 19, 105; as liberality, 105, 214; the poet's claim to, 111; political, 79, 92; of speech, 81, 82, 102; statutory, 85, 97, 102–106; and temperance, 79,106; true, 99, 103, 155. *See also* democracy; equality; servitude; target; theater (theatrocracy); virtue

friendship: meaning of, 5; as a legislative goal, 6–7, 22, 63, 74–75, 77–82, 92, 93, 95, 132, 133, 155–56, 188n42, 206n2, 207n25, 209n14. *See also* equality; freedom

Georg of Trebizond, 181n4

goal, legislative, 20, 22, 23, 74–80 116, 127, 155, 179, 205n1, 206n2; of marriage, 119. *See also* aim; middle; target

god(s) (*theos*): existence of, 72, 142, 143, 147, 225n19; first word of the dialogue, 17; holds the beginning, the middle, and the end, 18, 111; law on impiety, 111, 126, 136, 137, 142, 226; Plato's gods, 186n24, 196n54; secondary gods, 203n23; servitude to, 83, 98, 99, 125, 131, 134, 139; traditional, 4, 155,186n28. *See also* chance; divinization; goods; human being; knowledge; justice; *nous*/reason; puppet; rationality; rule; sacred items; servitude; soul; theology; theo-noo-nomocracy

good(s): divine, 139; division of, 21, 29, 75, 138, 140; leading, 75–76; psychic, 75; worthy of honor vs. of praise, 138–39, 221n6. *See also* virtue

Gramsci, Antonio, 182n18

guardians: Guardians of the law in the *Laws*, 94, 96, 189n63, 190n63, 198n12, 208n2, 210–12n12, 212n33; in the *Republic*, 26, 33–36, 60–61, 172, 193n35

Gyges' ring, 33

GPSR Authorized Representative: Easy Access System Europe - Mustamäe tee 50, 10621 Tallinn, Estonia, gpsr.requests@easproject.com

www.ingramcontent.com/pod-product-compliance
Ingram Content Group UK Ltd.
Pitfield, Milton Keynes, MK11 3LW, UK
UKHW040206210625
459930UK00016B/82/J